W9-COT-592

NEW DOCUMENTS ILLUSTRATING EARLY CHRISTIANITY

A Review of the
Greek Inscriptions and Papyri
published in 1977

by

G. H. R. Horsley

The Ancient History Documentary Research Centre
Macquarie University
1982

The Ancient History Documentary Research Centre (Director: E. A. Judge, Professor of History) has been formed within the School of History, Philosophy & Politics at Macquarie University to focus staff effort in research and professional development and to coordinate it with the work of other organisations interested in the documentation of the ancient world.

Committee for *New Documents illustrating Early Christianity*

Chairman: P. W. Barnett, Master of Robert Menzies College, Macquarie University.
Secretary: P. T. O'Brien, Head, New Testament Department, Moore Theological College, Sydney.
Members: P. Geidans, D. M. Knox, J. Lawler.

Editorial Consultants

F. I. Andersen, Professor of Studies in Religion, University of Queensland.
G. W. Clarke, Deputy Director, Humanities Research Centre, Australian National University.
W. J. Dumbrell, Vice-Principal, Moore Theological College, Sydney.
J. A. L. Lee, Senior Lecturer in Greek, University of Sydney.
K. L. McKay, Reader in Classics, Australian National University.

This volume has been produced with the support of Agies Ltd., the Australian Institute of Archaeology (N.S.W. Branch), F. K. Barton Classical Foundation, the Friends of Macquarie University, the Greek Orthodox Archdiocese of Australia, National Panasonic (Aust.) Pty. Ltd., The Macquarie University Research Grant, the Sydney Diocesan Educational and Book Society, the Walter and Eliza Hall Trust, and the following individual donors: — P. Geidans, P. E. Hollingdale, M. E. B. Holmes, V. Horniman, M. A. B. Horsley, M. L. Horsley, H. W. Piper, P. S. Rea-Young and G. Sperling.

Editorial correspondence should be addressed to Mr G. H. R. Horsley, School of History, Philosophy & Politics, Macquarie University, North Ryde, N.S.W. 2113, Australia.

Business address: The Ancient History Documentary Research Centre, Macquarie University, North Ryde, N.S.W. 2113, Australia.

©Copyright: Macquarie University

SUGGESTED CATALOGUING DATA:

Horsley, G. H. R.
   New Documents illustrating early Christianity. A review of the Greek inscriptions and papyri published in 1977.

Bibliography.
Includes index.
ISBN 0 85837 508 7
ISBN 0 85837 509 5 (pbk)

The United Library
Garrett-Evangelioal/Seabury-Western Seminaries
Evanston, IL 60201

1. Bible. New Testament — Language, style. 2. Inscriptions, Greek. 3. Manuscripts (Papyri). 4. Greek language, Biblical. 5. Church History — Primitive and early church. I. Macquarie University. Ancient History Documentary Research Centre. II. Title.

PA 810   1982   487.4

Typeset by Essay Composition, 225 Miller Street, North Sydney, Australia
Printed by J. Bell and Company Pty. Ltd., 15 McCauley Street, Alexandria, Australia.

PA810
.H82
v.2
GESW

CONTENTS

LIST OF ENTRIES

A. New Testament Context

B. Minor Philological Notes

C. Biblical and Related Citations

D. Ecclesiastica

E. Varia

PREFACE

The character of this project, its history and objectives are explained in my preface to *New Docs 1976*, which was published in 1981. In the past year we have had the benefit of extensive discussion and correspondence in response to the first volume, and to the article on the project by C.J. Hemer, 'Towards a new Moulton and Milligan', *Novum Testamentum* 24 (1982) 97–123.

With the death of Dr Robert Maddox of the United Theological College, Enfield, N.S.W., 1982 took from us the one to whom New Testament and Classics students throughout this country had looked as the embodiment of the highest standards of scholarship, especially where these fields meet. We had hoped to bring this project under his active scrutiny, as a former teacher in our School, and an Honorary Associate of it. His illness prevented this. But he was able to see the completion of his own major work, *The Purpose of Luke-Acts* (*FRLANT* 126, Göttingen, 1982). Robert Maddox wrote on the New Testament verbs of seeing for the Greek Department of the University of Sydney, on 'Son of Man' research for the Harvard Divinity School, and on historical issues in New Testament research as an Alexander von Humboldt Fellow at Mainz and Munich. His deep personal commitment to interpreting the New Testament for the present day found succinct expression in the weekly exposition *With Love to the World* which circulates in churches throughout Australia.

For 1983 our project has received financial backing from the Australian Research Grants Scheme, and we have engaged Mr Horsley to prepare a third volume, based on the documents published in 1978. We cordially invite critical appraisal of what is being done; correspondence should be addressed to Mr G.H.R. Horsley, School of History, Philosophy & Politics, Macquarie University, North Ryde, N.S.W. 2113, Australia.

December 1982   **E.A. Judge**

INTRODUCTION

This Review is primarily a reporting service, designed to make more widely known especially to biblical scholars published texts of philological and historical interest. Those who follow up the bibliographies to particular items will therefore find that much in these pages is derivative, although independent suggestions and comments are also offered. Entries in MM and BAGD are supplemented/qualified considerably more often than in *New Docs 1976*.

The reader who has been mainly kept in mind during the writing of entries has been the NT researcher, teacher, or student. Readers should be clear that the Review does not aim to provide definitive statements about any text treated. Undoubtedly some of the suggestions put forward in these pages will need correction or supplementation, and so **short notes** in reply (following the format of this volume) will be considered for inclusion. At present, the offer of long articles cannot be entertained.

While the main focus is upon the NT and the first four centuries, texts of later date have been included if it is judged that they may be of interest to students of that era (e.g., liturgical and homiletical texts; biblical citations). Some texts (e.g. **20,21,108**) have been included simply because they are representative of the times in some way, and make a general contribution to understanding NT background. It is envisaged that, as the Review proceeds over a number of years, it will gradually form a *Chrestomathie* for those whose main focus of interest is the NT and Early Church History but who do not have ready access to the epigraphic and papyrological documents.

This volume treats texts published during 1977, either for the first time or as re-editions, in corpora and 'conspectus' volumes (such as *AE, SB, SEG*). Occasionally such a text will render necessary more-than-passing discussion of texts published at some earlier date, which were not re-published in 1977. Following the practice of *SEG*, we have not refrained from including occasional references to texts and discussions published after 1977, where they are relevant. The emphasis is heavily upon Greek texts, although Latin documents and occasionally ones including Semitic words are noticed. Corpora consisting entirely of, e.g., Latin inscriptions, or hieroglyphic, demotic or Coptic papyri have not been taken into account.

A particular focus which has emerged for this volume has been the textual discoveries of K. Treu (Berlin). His brief article in *MPL* 2 (1977) has provided the impulse to survey over a number of entries his earlier publications of new papyrus and parchment fragments of Christian texts. The significance of his contribution, in this area alone, has not been sufficiently noticed except by professional papyrologists and textual critics of the Greek Bible. *New Docs 1977* hopes to make some of his material more accessible to a wider range of students.

Listed below are all collections for the year 1977 which have been read, arranged according to the abbreviations used in this volume. Where the abbreviation is bracketed, the work was read, but no texts were selected for noting in this volume. Unless otherwise specified, all references to texts throughout this Review are to item numbers in the work whose abbreviation precedes it, not to page numbers. Volume number and date are provided throughout the Review for all texts from non-1977 corpora. Where no volume number and date are given, the reference is to a publication of 1977 as listed below. Occasional publications from 1976 which were missed have been included. It is our aim to keep to the five-year lag between the year whose publications are being culled and the appearance of this Review.

List of works read

AE	—	*L'Année épigraphique 1977* [1981]
Anc. Maced., II	—	*Ancient Macedonia* II. *Papers read at the Second International Symposium held in Thessaloniki, 19-24 August 1973* (Thessaloniki, 1977)
Apis, III	—	*Apis* III. *Inscriptions, Coins and Addenda*, by G. J. F. Kater-Sibbes and M.J. Vermaseren (*EPRO*, 48; Leiden, 1977) [vol. I, *Monuments of the Hellenistic-Roman Period from Egypt*, 1975; vol. II, *Monuments from outside Egypt*, 1975]
BCH Suppl. IV	—	*Études Delphiques* (*BCH* Suppl. vol. IV; Paris, 1977)
BE	—	*Bulletin épigraphique*, by J. and L. Robert, in *Revue des études grecques* 90 (1977) 314–448
Budischovsky, *Cultes isiaques*	—	*La diffusion des cultes isiaques autour de la mer adriatique* I. *Inscriptions et monuments*, by M.-C. Budischovsky (*EPRO* 61; Leiden, 1977)
Buresch, *Aus Lydien*	—	*Aus Lydien. Epigraphisch–geographische Reisefrüchte*, by K. Buresch (Leipzig, 1898; repr. in the series *Subsidia Epigraphica* 8; Hildesheim, 1977)
CIMAH	—	*Corpus Inscriptionum Medii Aevi Helvetiae. Die frühchristlichen und mittelalterlichen Inschriften der Schweiz* I. *Die Inschriften des Kantons Wallis bis 1300*, ed. C. Jörg (Freiburg, 1977)
Düll, *Götterkulte Nordmak.*	—	*Die Götterkulte Nordmakedoniens in römischer Zeit*, by Siegrid Düll (*Münchener archäologische Studien* 7; Munich, 1977)
F. Delphes III.4	—	*Fouilles de Delphes* III. *Épigraphie*, fasc. 4. *Les inscriptions de la terrasse du temple et de la région nord du sanctuaire* (*Nos. 351-516*), by J. Pouilloux (Paris, 1976)
[*F. Delphes* IV.6]	—	*Fouilles de Delphes* IV. *Monuments figurés: Sculpture*, fasc. 6. *Reliefs*, by M.-A. Zagdoun (Paris, 1977)
Fraser, *Rhodes*	—	P. M. Fraser, *Rhodian Funerary Monuments* (Oxford, 1977)
Hajjar, *Triade*	—	*La Triade d'Héliopolis-Baalbek. Son culte et sa diffusion à travers les textes littéraires et les documents iconographiques et épigraphiques*, by J. Hajjar (2 vols, *EPRO* 59; Leiden, 1977)
[*I.agon.Aeg.*]	—	*Eine agonistiche Inschrift aus Ägypten und frühptolemäische Königshefte*, by L. Koenen (*Beiträge zur klassischen Philologie* 56; Meisenheim am Glan, 1977)
I.Charles Univ.	—	*Greek and Latin Inscriptions on Stone in the Collections of Charles University*, ed. V. Marek (Prague, 1977)
[*I.Delphi rel.*]	—	*Corpus des inscriptions de Delphes* I. *Lois sacrées et règlements religieux*, ed. G. Rougement (Paris, 1977)
I. Medizin	—	*Inschriften der Griechen. Epigraphische Quellen zur Geschichte der antiken Medizin*, ed. G. Pfohl (Darmstadt, 1977)
I.Pamphyl.dial.	—	*Le dialecte grec de Pamphylie. Documents et grammaire*, by C. Brixhe (Paris, 1976) [cf. id., *Études d'archéologie classique* 5 (1976) 9–16, which publishes a supplement of texts, nos. 179–192]
I. Pan	—	*Pan du désert*, by A. Bernand (Leiden, 1977)
I. Tyre	—	*Inscriptions grecques et latines découvertes dans les fouilles de Tyr* (*1963-1974*) I. *Inscriptions de la nécropole*, by J.-P. Rey-Coquais (*Bull. du Musée de Beyrouth*, 29; Paris, 1977)
I.Wadi Haggag	—	*The Inscriptions of Wadi Haggag, Sinai*, ed. A. Negev (*Qedem* 6; Jerusalem, 1977)
Lang, *Agora*	—	*The Athenian Agora* XXI. *Graffiti and Dipinti*, by M. Lang (Princeton, 1976)
MPL	—	*Museum Philologum Londiniense* II. *Special Papyrological Number*, ed. G. Giangrande (1977)
MPR	—	*Les monuments paléochrétiens de Roumanie*, by I. Barnea (*Sussidi allo studio delle Antichità cristiane* 6; The Vatican, 1977)
Nachtergael, *Galates*	—	*Les Galates en Grèce et les Soteria de Delphes*, by G. Nachtergael (Brussels, 1977)
[*O.Brüss.-Berl.²*]	—	*Au temps où on lisait le grec en Égypte*, edd. J. Bingen et al. (Brussels, 1977)
O.Medînet Mâdi	—	*Missione di scavi in Egitto a Medinet Madi. Rapporto preliminare delle campagne di scavo 1968-1969*, by E. Bresciani. *Ostraka e papiri greci da Medinet Madi nelle campagne 1968-1969*, by D. Foraboschi (Milan, 1976)
Onomast. lat.	—	*L'Onomastique latine, Paris 13-15 Octobre 1975*, ed. N. Duval (*Colloques internationaux du CNRS*, no.564; Paris, 1977)

P.Berl.Leihg.	— *Berliner Leihgabe griechischer Papyri* II, ed. A. Tomsin (Uppsala, 1977)
[*P.Cair.Mich.* 359]	— *A Tax List from Karanis*, edd. H. Riad and J. C. Shelton (2 vols.; Bonn, 1975, 1977)
P.Laur.	— *Dai Papiri della biblioteca Medicea Laurenziana* II, ed. R. Pintaudi (Florence, 1977)
P.Mich.	— *The Aphrodite Papyri in the University of Michigan Papyrus Collection* (*P.Mich.* XIII), ed. P. J. Sijpesteijn (Zutphen, 1977)
P.Mil.Vogl.	— *Papiri della Università degli studi di Milano* VI, edd. C. Gallazzi and M. Vardoni (Milan, 1977)
P.Oxy.	— *The Oxyrhynchus Papyri* XLV, edd. A. K. Bowman, M. W. Haslam, S. A. Stephens, M. L. West (London, 1977)
[*P.Pestman Recueil*]	— *Recueil de textes démotiques et bilingues*, by P. W. Pestman with the collaboration of J. Quaegebeur and R. L. Vos (3 vols; Leiden, 1977)
[*PSI Corr.*]	— *Correzioni e riedizioni di papiri della Società Italiana*, ed. M. Manfredi (Florence, 1977)
P.Stras.	— *Papyrus grecs de la biliothèque nationale et Universitaire de Strasbourg* V, 3, edd. J. Schwartz et al. (Strasbourg, 1977)
P.Tebt.Tait	— *Papyri from Tebtunis in Egyptian and in Greek*, ed. W.J. Tait (London, 1977)
P.Vindob.Salomons	— *Einige Wiener Papyri*, ed. R.P. Salomons (Amsterdam, 1976)
P.Wiscon.	— *The Wisconsin Papyri* II, ed. P. J. Sijpesteijn (Zutphen, 1977)
Painter, *Mildenhall*	— *The Mildenhall Treasure. Roman Silver from East Anglia*, by K. S. Painter (London, 1977)
Painter, *Water Newton Silver*	— *The Water Newton Early Christian Silver*, by K. S. Painter (London, 1977)
Pfohl,*Studium*	— *Das Studium der griechischen Epigraphik. Eine Einfuhrung*, ed. G. Pfohl (Darmstadt, 1977)
Raffeiner, *Sklaven*	— *Sklaven und Freigelassene. Eine soziologische Studie auf der Grundlage des griechischen Grabepigrams*, by H. Raffeiner (*Commentationes Aenipontanae 23, Philologie und Epigraphik*, Bd. 2; Innsbruck, 1977)
SB	— *Sammelbuch griechischer Urkunden aus Ägypten* XII, 2, ed. H.-A. Rupprecht (Wiesbaden, 1977)
SEG	— *Supplementum Epigraphicum Graecum* 27 (1977) [1980]
Thorikos.Test.	— *Thorikos. Les Testimonia*, by J. Labarbe (Ghent, 1977)
[*Urk.dramat. Griechen.*]	— *Urkunden dramatischer Aufführungen in Griechenland*, by H. J. Mette (Berlin, 1977)

[E.Pfuhl/H.Möbius, *Die ostgriechischen Grabreliefs* (2 vols; 1977, 1979) has been held over until *New Docs 1979.* We have not yet been able to see certain volumes, e.g., L. Barkóczi/A. Mócsy, *Die römischen Inschriften Ungarns. 2. Lief.: Salla, Mogentiana, Mursella, Brigetio* (Budapest, 1976); G. Florescu/C.C. Petolescu, *Inscriptiones Daciae Romanae* II. (Bucharest, 1977); I.I. Russu, *Inscriptiones Daciae Romanae* III.1 (Bucharest, 1977); D. M. Pippidi/E. Popescu (edd.), *Epigraphica. Travaux dediés au VIIᵉ Congrès d'Épigraphie grecque et latine, Constanza; 9-15 Sept., 1977* (Bucharest, 1977).]

Abbreviations

Other abbreviations follow standard conventions, except where altered for clarity.

Journals — as in *L'Année philologique* (but note, e.g., *RAC = Reallexikon für Antike und Christentum*, not *Riv(ista) di Ant(ichità) Crist(iana)*).

Papyrological works — as in S. R. Pickering, *Papyrus Editions held in Australian Libraries* (North Ryde, N.S.W., 1974²), part 1, 'General List of Abbreviations'.

Epigraphical works (for which no standard guide exists) — according to generally used conventions (see LSJ), preceded where necessary by *I.* (e.g. *I. Charles Univ.*).

Ancient authors, biblical and patristic works — generally as in LSJ, BAGD, and Lampe (see below).

Some other abbreviations used, occasionally frequently, in this volume:

Aland, *Repertorium*	— K. Aland, *Repertorium der griechischen christlichen Papyri*, I. *Biblische Papyri* (Berlin, 1976)
BAGD	— Bauer/Arndt/Gingrich/Danker, *A Greek-English Lexicon of the New Testament and other Early Christian Literature* (Chicago, 1979²)
BDF	— Blass/Debrunner/Funk, *A Greek Grammar of the New Testament and other Early Christian Literature* (Chicago, 1961)
Bib.Pat.	— *Biblia Patristica. Index des citations et allusions bibliques dans la littérature patristique* (Centre d'analyse et de documentation patristiques; 3 vols; Paris, 1975-81)
CIJ	— J. B. Frey, *Corpus Inscriptionum Judaicarum* (2 vols; Rome, 1936, 1952); vol. 1 repr. with Prolegomenon by B. Lifshitz (New York, 1975)
CPJ	— V. A. Tcherikover, A. Fuks, et al., *Corpus Papyrorum Judaicarum* (3 vols; Cambridge [Mass.], 1957-64)
DACL	— Cabrol/Leclercq, et al., *Dictionnaire d'archéologie chrétienne et de liturgie* (15 vols; Paris, 1907-1953)
Deissmann, *Bible Studies*	— G. A. Deissmann, *Bible Studies* (ET: Edinburgh, 1923; repr. Winona Lake, 1979)
Deissmann, *LAE*	— G. A. Deissmann, *Light from the Ancient East* (Grand Rapids, 1980⁴)
ECL	— Early Christian Literature
Foraboschi	— D. Foraboschi, *Onomasticon Alterum Papyrologicum* (4 vols; Milan, 1966-71)
Gignac, I/II	— F. T. Gignac, *A Grammar of the Greek Papyri of the Roman and Byzantine periods* I, *Phonology;* II, *Morphology* (Milan, 1976, 1982)
Hatch and Redpath	— Hatch and Redpath, *A Concordance to the Septuagint and other Greek Versions of the Old Testament* (Oxford, 1897; 2 vols. repr. Graz, 1954)
Lampe	— Lampe, *A Patristic Greek Lexicon* (Oxford, 1961, repr.)
LSJ/LSJ Suppl.	— Liddell/Scott/Jones, *A Greek-English Lexicon* (Oxford, 1940⁹, repr. with supplement ed. E. A. Barber, 1968)
LXX	— Septuagint (Rahlfs' edition)
Migne, *PG/PL*	— Migne, *Patrologia Graeca/Patrologia Latina* (Paris, 1857-87/1844-64)
MM	— Moulton and Milligan, *The Vocabulary of the Greek Testament* (London, 1930; repr.)
Naldini	— M. Naldini, *Il Cristianesimo in Egitto. Lettere private nei papiri dei secoli II-IV* (Florence, 1968)
NB	— F. Preisigke, *Namenbuch ... enthaltend alle ... Menschennamen ... in griechischen Urkunden ... Ägyptens ...* (Heidelberg, 1922)
Peek, *GVI*	— W. Peek, *Griechische Vers-Inschriften* I (Berlin, 1955)
Spoglio	— S. Daris, *Spoglio lessicale papirologico* (3 vols; Milan, 1968)
Turner, *Typology*	— E. G. Turner, *The Typology of the Early Codex* (Pennsylvania, 1977)
van Haelst	— J. van Haelst, *Catalogue des papyrus littéraires juifs et chrétiens* (Paris, 1976)
WB	— F. Preisigke, et al., *Wörterbuch der griechischen Papyrusurkunden* (Heidelberg, et alibi, 1924-)

An asterisk (*) beside a reference in the bibliography for an entry signifies, where more than one edition exists, which has been reprinted; otherwise the *editio princeps* has been followed.

Dates are AD unless otherwise marked. IV¹ = 'first half IVth century', IV² = 'second half IVth century'; etc.

Textual sigla used are as follows:—

αβ	— letters not completely legible
. . . .	— 4 letters missing
[αβ]	— letters lost from document and restored by editor
[± 8]	— about 8 letters lost
⟨αβ⟩	— letters omitted by scribe and added by editor

(αβ)	— editor has resolved an abbreviation in the text
{αβ}	— letters wrongly added by scribe and cancelled by editor
[[αβ]]	— a (still legible) erasure made by scribe
ˋαβˊ	— letters written above the line
α´ or ᾱ	— letter stands for a numerical equivalent
v.,vv.,vac.	— one, two, several letter spaces left blank (*vacat*) on document
m.1, m.2	— first hand (*manus*), second hand
recto, verso	— the conventional front and back of a papyrus sheet.

The Format of most entries is as follows:—

Item no.   Short title
Provenance   date
editio princeps
Text
Brief descriptive comment
Bibliography (very selective, normally including only actual references to the text)
Translation
Comment

Where a text is not quoted in full or at all this format is somewhat modified, but should still be clear (e.g. Section B, *Minor Philological Notes*). Within the larger subdivisions of the Review items have usually been arranged chiefly by genre (e.g. letters, epitaphs), and within that, chronologically. This arrangement does not apply to Section B, where entries are alphabetical; nor, of course, to Section E (*Varia*). In Section C entries follow canonical book order with non-biblical books at the end. Where an entry deals with a diversity of texts, it is placed in the genre grouping to which the first, usually the main, text belongs. No *Judaica* section has been included this year, simply because insufficient texts worth reprinting relevant to such a grouping were thrown up in the process of culling 1977 publications.

The **indexes** are to be regarded as an integral element in the Review. They will usually provide the easiest means of discovering which biblical words and passages are discussed, what ideas and institutions, etc.

Item numbers are in bold type throughout the Review, for cross-referencing.

The following individuals have contributed separate entries to this volume: B. Croke **(117)**, A.M. Emmett **(92)**, E.A. Judge **(83, 84, 107)**, W.L. Leadbetter **(105)**, J.A.L. Lee **(89)**. All other entries are by the undersigned. Translations have been made by the author of the entry.

For those wishing to refer to this Review, the **abbreviation** *New Docs, 1977* is suggested.

Acknowledgements

Advice from colleagues on specific matters is acknowledged in the appropriate entry. Detailed responses to draft entries by E.A. Judge. J.A.L. Lee (Sydney) and K.L. McKay (A.N.U.) have been particularly valued. M. Harding, who compiled the index of Greek words, has me greatly in his debt. B. Winter has left the Committee for teaching and pastoral work in Singapore, but his continued interest in the progress of the volume has been an encouragement. Once more D. Surtees has gone a second mile in the painstaking accuracy with which he has attended to the technical problems of the typesetting. A major omission from last year's volume was acknowledgement of C. J. Hemer's contribution to *New Docs, 1976:* his input at draft stage is not fully apparent in the finished book, but I wish to place on record how valuable it was. None but I can know the extent of my wife's inordinate patience with me. Her encouragement and stabilizing influence at times of pressure during the preparation of both volumes have been no small factor in ensuring their appearance. *New Docs, 1977* is offered to her with deepest affection.

                                                                    G.H.R. HORSLEY

A. NEW TESTAMENT CONTEXT

1. Nursing contract

Ptolemais Euergetis (Arsinoe)   9/8BC
ed.pr. — S.M.E. van Lith, *ZPE* 14 (1974) 145-62 (pls. 7-9)

45 (*m. 5*)   ] *traces*
   [*ca. 10 letters* ᾧ ὄνομα] Ἐπαφρόδιτος ἄρσης ἐφ' ἔτη δύο ἀπὸ
   [Παῦνι τοῦ δευτέρου καὶ εἰκ]οστοῦ ἔτους Κα⟨ίσ⟩αρος καὶ ἀπεσχηκέναι
   αὐτὴν σὺν τῶι ἀνδρεὶ Ἀρμιύσι νεωτέρωι παρὰ τοῦ Ἐπιφα-
   νίωνος διὰ χειρὸς ἐξ οἴκου τὰς ἐσταμένας δοθῆναι
50 κατὰ μῆνα ἕκαστον ἀργυρίου δραχμὰς ὀκτὼι τῶν προ-
   κιμένων ἐτῶν δύο τὰς συναγομένας ἀργυρίου δραχμὰς
   ἑκατὸν ἐνήκοντα δύο τοῦ τε ἱματισμοῦ καὶ σιτομετρίας
   καὶ τἆλλα ὅσα καθήκι δίδοσθαι τροφῶι {ἀπέχειν}
   νῦν ἐκ πλήρους ἐπὶ τὰ αὐτὰ ἔτη δύο. Ἔγγυος δὲ
55 τῶν κατὰ {τα} τὸ τρόφιμον πάντων Ἁρπαήσιος Κελε-
   βίνιος εἰς ἔκτισιν. Καὶ οὐκ ἐξέσται τῇ Διοδώρα ἀνδροκοι-
   τεῖν οὐδὲ οὐδὲν δυσένθετον προσφέρειν ἐπεὶ τῇ τοῦ
   γάλακτος ἐγλείψει, ἀλλὰ καὶ μετὰ τὸν χρόνον παραδό-
   τωσαν τὸ θρεπτὸν ὑγειῆ καὶ ἀθάνατον καθότι συνκε-
60 χώρηκαν τῶι Ἐπιφανείωνει ἢ τὸ ἴσον ἐάνπερ διαφω-
   νήσῃ ἀνειρήσονται ἐπὶ τὰ αὐτὰ ἔτη δύο ἢ καὶ τὰ [ἀρ]γύρια,
   τῆς πράξεως [γινομέν]ης Ἐπει[φανί]ωνι ἔκ τ[ε αὐ]τῶν καὶ ἐκ τῶν
   ὑπαρχόντων αὐτοῖς πάντων. Ἡ γραφὴ κυρία.
                                          Συγγραφοφύλαξ

Printed above are the first 20 lines of col.2 of a much lengthier papyrus containing in col.1 (*ll.*1-44) a lease arrangement concerning sheep and goats (pl.7); col.2B (*ll.*65-83) is a copy of the contract registered by a certain Isidoros, which differs in only a few details from what is printed here (the first 8-14 lines of col.2 are lost), although the form is rendered into the first person ('I, Diodora . . . agree . . . '). Col.3 (*ll.*84-124) likewise contains objective and subjective texts of the receipt concerning the agreement in col.2A.
Bib. – *SB* 11248

45 (*m.5*) |(*traces only*) . . . whose name is] **Epaphroditos, a male, for two years from [the month Pauni of the twenty-second] year of Caesar, and that she has received along with her husband Harmiysis the younger from Epiphanion by**
50 **hand from his house the |eight silver drachmai per month which have been agreed to be given for the above-mentioned two years, totalling 192 silver drachmai for both clothing and food allowance and whatever else is appropriate to be given to a nurse, now in full for the same two years. And**

7

55 guarantor |for the full payment of everything relevant to the nursing is
Harpaesios son of Kelebinis. And Diodora will not be permitted to have
intercourse nor to take any additional child to cause her milk to fail. But
rather, after the time they are to hand over to Epiphanion the foundling in
60 good health and alive just as has been agreed |(or if it has died they shall take
up the equivalent (in age?) for the same two years), or also hand over the
money. The right of execution exists for Epiphanion against them and all
their possessions. The agreement is valid. Syngraphophlylax.

This papyrus provides a useful addition to the small corpus of nursing contracts
and related documents already known. Other contracts include a group in *BGU* 4
(1912): 1058, 1106, 1107, 1108, 1109, 1153(1) (all from Alexandria, various dates
during Augustus' principate), which share close verbal affinities. Others from
elsewhere in Egypt include *P. Rein.* 2 (1940) 103, 104 (both Oxyrhynchos, 26AD;
the former = *SB* 5 [1955] 7619), and two nursing receipts, *P. Grenf.* 2 (1897) 75
(Great Oasis, 305) and *PSI* 9 (1929) 1065. The new text (col.2 *ll*.47ff., 73ff.; col.3
ll.109ff.) and *BGU* 1058 are the only ones to provide payment in advance to the
nurse. It is also the earliest example wherein a man other than her husband goes
surety for the nurse (*ll*.54-56); and it is the first contract of its type not to include
penalty clauses for failure to render the agreed service of milk and nuture — cf.
van Lith, 160. For bibliography on nursing contracts see ibid., 154 n.l. These
agreements are not discussed in A.J. Malherbe, '''Gentle as a Nurse'': The Cynic
Background to 1 Thess. 2', *NovT* 12 (1970) 203-17, which draws out parallels
between the Pauline passage and Dio Chrysostom *Or.* 32 (*To Alexandria*). His
references (211 n.4) to the expectation that nurses should not be irascible are worth
noting in relation to the new text.

A number of philological points merit comment. The false aspiration of ἐφ' ἔτη
(46) may be noted. ἱματισμός (52; NT, several times) is a further example to add
to MM in view of the date of the text; cf. the spelling εἱματ- (76), for which see
MM, s.v., ad fin. Likewise in the case of σιτομετρία (52; the NT only has the neuter
noun, at Lk. 12.42), this reference should be included in a redrafted MM entry; a
couple of examples had earlier been noted by Deissmann, *Bible Studies*, 158 (there
is no compelling need to follow his suggestion at his n.1), and *LAE*, 104 n.l. ἡ
τροφός (53) is also a NT *hapax* at 1 Thes. 2.7. (The BAGD entry for this word
highlights a more general problem concerning what data are to be included under
each lemma. Statements like 'inscr., pap, LXX . . . ' are too general to be much
help. Some reference to the papyrus nursing contracts is surely desirable.
Futhermore, if bibliographical details of important studies of words or concepts are
to be included under BAGD lemmata, many much older references should be
replaced where more recent work has superseded them. No bibliography is provided
s.v. τροφός, but at the very least Malherbe's article should be listed. The frequent
addition of 'MM' at the end of BAGD entries is also unsatisfactory, for there are
clearly many which have taken over documentary attestations of NT words from
MM as though no more relevant examples have become known in the half-century
since MM appeared in complete form.) The related τὸ τρόφιμον (55; cf. col.3 *l*.118)
may be the technical term for a nursing contract (cf. van Lith, 161-62).

In the prohibition clause (56-58) the wording is similar to the Alexandrian
contracts, which read μὴ φθείρουσαν τὸ γάλα μηδ' ἀνδροκοιτοῦσαν μηδὲ ἐπικυοῦσαν

μηδ' ἕτερον παραθηλάζουσαν παιδίον (variations in orthography occur between the *BGU* texts). The thrust of this requirement is that there should be no more mouths to feed. In our text οὐδὲ . . . προσφέρειν (57) is to be taken as an equivalent phrase for μηδ' . . . παιδίον in the *BGU* texts just quoted (for discussion of δυσένθετος see van Lith, 159, although he does not account satisfactorily for the δυσ- prefix).

The *athanatos*-clause (59-61) appears to be taken over into such agreements from lease arrangements concerning animals: it occurs, for example, in the lease of sheep and goats which precedes our text, col.1 *l*.38 (restored at *l*.7). It signifies that handing over a dead child does not fulfil the contract. The nurse is required to suckle another infant for the remaining term of the contract should the one entrusted to her die. The verb διαφωνέω (60-61), 'perish' (used of people), occurs also at *P.Mich.* 5 (1944) 231.16 (Tebtunis, probably 47/48): cf. H.C. Youtie, *Scriptiunculae* 1 (Amsterdam, 1973) 438-39. They are both relevant examples to add to *P. Petrie* 2 (1893) 13.3-4 which MM cite; they refer to LXX usage but give no examples (Ex. 24.11; Num. 31.49; Josh. 23.14; 1 Kings 30.19; Judith 10.13). MM's final sentence in that entry is telling. J.A.L. Lee tells me that, at least in the case of the two Pentateuch examples, this meaning is not certain. See his forthcoming monograph, *A Lexical Study of the Septuagint Version of the Pentateuch* (*Septuagint and Cognate Studies*, 14; Chico, 1983) 82. The subjunctive mood of this verb in our text is governed by ἐάνπερ, a usage which occurs but rarely in the NT (Heb. 3.14; 6.3; cf. BDF 454(2); BAGD, s.v. ἐάν I, 3c).

For τὸ θρεπτόν (59) note the discussion of *threptoi* in Asia Minor in M.R. Flood, *Epigraphic Evidence for Family Structures and Customs in Asia Mnnor during the early Roman Empire* (Diss. Macquarie, 1978) 95-153. On the question of the exposure of infants (females more commonly) — raised here by ἀναιρέω (61; on the spelling ει for αι see Gignac I, 260); relevant, too, is κοπριαναίρετος used of the child at col.2 *l*.70, col.3 *ll*.87-88 (both partly restored), *ll*.114-115 — see discussion and references in van Lith, 154 n.2. The wording of Stephen's speech at Acts 7.21 draws upon Ex. 2.5-10; both the LXX and the NT passages reflect the terminology of these nursing contracts from Egypt. In the Acts speech Pharaoh's daughter ἀνείλατο (cf. Ex. 2.5,10) αὐτὸν (i.e., Moses) καὶ ἀνεθρέψατο αὐτὸν ('had him nursed') ἑαυτῇ εἰς υἱόν. In the two Exodus verses just referred to, LXX ἀναιρέομαι renders two different Hebrew verbs: לקח (2.5), and the very rare משה (2.10) for which the LXX provides no standard Greek equivalent in its few occurrences. The LXX rendering at Ex. 2.10 thus virtually certainly reflects the terminology of the Hellenistic nursing contracts. In the LXX passage note also particularly v.9, Διατήρησόν μοι τὸ παιδίον τοῦτο καὶ θήλασόν (cf. παραθηλάζουσαν in the *BGU* prohibition clauses, quoted above) μοι αὐτό, ἐγὼ δὲ δώσω σοι τὸν μισθόν. In the theory, at least, exposed free-born infants who were reared did not become slaves at this period, but under the later Empire they could become so (thus, W.W. Buckland, *The Roman Law of Slavery* [Cambridge, 1908] 402-03). But practice by no means always conformed to the legal provisions, and foundling children were usually considered as potential slaves, at least in Egypt. 'The Greek custom of picking up an exposed child in order to bring it up as a slave had been firmly established among the Egyptians soon after the onset of the Ptolemaic era' (R. Taubenschlag, *The Law of Greco-Roman Egypt in the Light of the Papyri, 332BC-640AD* [Warsaw, 1955²; repr. Milan, 1972] 21; cf. 74 n.30). Two closely-related papyri throw interesting light on this. *P. Oxy.* 1 (1898) 37 (49AD) and 38 (49/50) are respectively a report of a lawsuit and a petition for enforcement of the judgement. A woman, Saraeus, had acted as nurse to a male foundling taken up to be a slave (ἀρρενικὸν σωμάτιον) by a certain Pesouris (or Syros). The nurse claimed that the foundling had died, and that the child which Pesouris seized from her home to carry into slavery (εἰς δουλαγωγία[ν]) was her own. Pesouris' claim that it was the foundling was rejected on the grounds of the child's likeness to Saraeus.

Two final observations do not relate to the passage printed. At col.3 *ll*.98-99, μέχρει [οὗ]|ἀποδῶσιν — van Lith (161) mentions ἄν as an alternative restoration — is a construction paralleled in the NT only at Mk. 13.30 and Gal. 4.19; cf. BDF 383. On the back of each of the three columns of the text there survive traces of a red stamp: on the *verso* of col.3 the letters ΚΑΙΣΑΡΟΣ can be made out. For these seals see Deissmann's important though not universally accepted discussion, *Bible Studies*, 240-47.

2. Doctors in the Graeco-Roman World

G. Pfohl has brought together in *I. Medizin* a number of earlier studies by a range of scholars translated into German dealing with various aspects of the medical profession in Graeco-Roman antiquity. Pfohl's introduction (1-30) provides a useful bibliographical survey of this area of study. Making these essays a springboard, a number of matters relating to doctors and their profession, and to attestations of miraculous cures, are brought forward here.

a. *Archiatroi* — public doctors under the Roman Empire

J. and L. Robert (*I. Medizin*, pp.88-94 = *Hellenica* 9 [1950] 25-27, plus addendum) have published a brief inscription on an altar from Thyatira, dated II/III init. Above the epitaph is carved a figure of a seated man.

> Ηλεις ἀρχίατρος
> τοῦ σύμπαντο[ς]
> ξυστοῦ ἐνθάδε
> κεῖμαι. (*leaf*) Χαῖρε

Heleis (= Helios) *archiatros* of the whole athletic association, here I lie. Hail!

Heleis is a chief doctor attached to an athletic club. At Rome such an association had its social meeting place at Trajan's baths. The organization possessed its chief priests (ἀρχιερεῖς) and chief secretary (ἀρχιγραμματεύς; Robert, 90). Cf. Buresch, *Aus Lydien*, p.55, where a brief inscription on an altar(?) from Koloe in Lydia (early III) is reprinted (= *IGRR* 4.1383): Αὐρή[λιο]ς ᾿Αρτεμίδωρος |ὁ ἀρχίατρος καὶ ἱεροφάν|της εἰδρύσατο. Artemidoros is both the doctor and instructing priest of the cult.

V. Nutton, *PBSR* 45 (1977) 191-226 (cf. *AE* 803; *SEG* 1262), has provided a detailed survey of the *archiatroi*: his study includes (192-93; pl. 31-32) three new inscriptions from Aphrodisias in Karia which mention doctors with this title, and an appendix (218-26) listing all known documentary attestations of the term (nearly 100 in all. Note, however, that his no.54 — cf. p.194 and n.13 — should be deleted: an untenable restoration in the text, according to P. Hermann, *AAWW* 111 [1974]

439 n.2.). His third inscription is very brief and late (Byzantine): cf. *SEG* 718; but his first two warrant reprinting here. (Inscriptions found when the city's theatre was excavated are published in J. Reynolds, *Aphrodisias and Rome* [*JRS monograph* 1; London, 1982].)

Nutton, no.1.

[Τίτος Φλάβιος Στα]-
βερίανος τὸν Ἀσ-
κλήπιον καὶ τὴν
Ὑγεῖαν σὺν τοῖς
5 βώμοις ἐκ τῶν ἰ-
δίων ἀνέθηκε τῷ

δήμῳ καθὼς
Τίτος Φλάβιος
Σταβερίανος ἀρ-
10 χιατρὸς πόλε-
ως ὁ πατὴρ αὐτοῦ
ὑπέσχετο

Titus(?) Flavius Staberianus set up at his own expense the (statue of)
5 Asklepios and (that of) Hygieia, | together with the altars, for the *demos* just
10 as Titus Flavius Staberianus, ar| chiatros of the city, his father, promised.

Nutton suggests 150-200 as a date for this inscription (cf. *SEG* 716). The full title, ἀ. πόλεως, is present here. He provides (192) references to other examples of doctors making dedications to the patron god of their craft. Here the son has fulfilled his father's vow, presumably owing to the decease of the latter. While the son here is apparently not a doctor there are numerous cases where the practice of medicine was a family tradition, surviving for two or more generations. Nutton (200, n.61) gives five examples of this for *archiatroi*, nos. 11, 43, 47, 53, 57 in his Appendix 3: *P. Cairo Masp.* 2 (1913, repr. 1973) 67151, *ll*.6,21 (Antinoe, 15/11/570); *CIG* 2 (1843, repr. 1977) 3953h (Heraclea Ulpia in Karia, II?; see Nutton's comment on this text, p.221); *CIG* 2 (1843, repr. 1977) 2987 (Ephesos, 160-200), the man is ἀ. διὰ γένους; *SEG* 17 (1960) 527 (Philadelphia in Lydia, II/ III; cf. *BE* [1958] 437 no.7), the man is ἐκ προγόνων ἀ.; *IGRR* 4 (1927, repr. 1964) 1278 (Thyatira, 150-300; cf. R. Merkelbach, *ZPE* 9 [1972] 132, who restudies the man's stemma to suggest that he may have a father, a nephew and a cousin who are all *archiatroi*). The reason for such family continuity will be considered below.

Nutton, no.2.

Αὐρ(ηλία) Φλ(αβία) Ἀντ(ωνία) Ἐλπὶς Νεικίο[υ φύ-
σει δὲ Εἰταλίκου Μάρκο[ν Αὐρ(ήλιον)?
Ἀπολλώνιον γ΄ τοῦ Ἀνδρ[....
ἱππικὸν ἀρχιατρὸν τὸν ⟨ι⟩έ[αυτῆς
5 ἀνδρὰ μνείας χάριν

Aurelia Flavia Antonia Elpis daughter of Nikias, but by natural descent of
Italikos, set up (the epitaph for) Marcus Aurelius (?) Apollonius, third son
5 of Andr . . . eques, archiatros, her own | husband, as a memorial.

The terminology of the fourth line of this text (III[1], cf. *SEG* 717) indicates that the husband's social status was that of a Roman knight. Nutton refers to several other examples of doctors who are men of some wealth and standing in their city; his no.48 (Ephesos, c. 180-250) employs the same phrase as in the text above, ἱππ.

ἁ.; no.82 (Beneventum, 231) has the equivalent in Latin, *eques Romanus archiater.* He doubts that the phrase can signify a vet., and this is probably right; for note *O. Florida* (1976) 15 (Edfu, II) where a certain Quintus is called a ἱπποιατρός (cf. *New Docs 1976*, **17** ad fin.).

In the Hellenistic period, where the word is first attested, an *archiatros* is a personal physician to a ruler; this usage carries over into the Roman Empire. But far more commonly under the latter is the term employed of civic or public doctors (c.80 of the 90+ listed in Nutton, App.3). These public physicians are not to be regarded as the same institution under another name as the *demosioi iatroi* of the Greek world; although there are some similarities it should not be forgotten that institutions change with changes in society. The Greek *demosioi iatroi* were doctors 'elected (or sent out), or hired, or sent for by some agency of the state' (L. Cohn-Haft, *The Public Physicians of Ancient Greece* [Northampton, Mass., 1956] 5; this monograph deals with the Hellenistic period). In return for his professional service to a city he might be voted some honour (a statue, a gold crown, an inscribed decree recording his philanthropy) or privileges (*proxenia, proedria, ateleia,* etc.). J. Benedum, *ZPE* 27 (1977) 265–76, has published five honorific inscriptions for doctors from Kos, all of Hellenistic date (nos.4 and 5 are very fragmentary). In no.1 the *polis* of Iasos honours the doctor from Kos, while in no.2 the man is specified as one of the *demosioi iatroi.* (ἰατρὸς κατασ|ταθεὶς ὑπὸ τᾶς ἐκκλησίας, *ll.*3–4). Cities in both periods wanted to secure for their population the permanent residence of a competent physician. The Hellenistic world largely offered citizenship privileges, the Roman tax immunity.

For the Greek East in particular the edict of Antoninus Pius to the *koinon* of Asia probably in the early 140s had a major impact (*Digest* 27.1.6.2-4). Until then cities had been able to attract not only doctors but also rhetoricians (or sophists) and grammarians in unrestricted numbers by offering them immunity from taxation; this had been especially prevalent under Hadrian. Pius' edict placed a ceiling on the number of such concessions which a town could offer, depending on its size: in the case of doctors, three (small towns), seven (large towns), ten (*metropoleis*). The reason for this limitation was largely financial: for the burden of liturgies was falling increasingly on citizens less able to afford them. The effect of Pius' decision was to introduce a two-class medical system of doctors who possessed immunity and doctors who did not. Nutton suggests that the spread of the term *archiatros* in the Greek East after Antoninus — it permeated much less quickly in other areas such as the Western provinces and Africa — may indicate that the term came to be equated with these civically approved, tax-immune doctors. Although some instances occur under the Empire before 140, the great majority of attestations occur after this date. Yet the distinction was evidently not absolute, for Nutton (201-02) refers to two clear-cut examples of immune doctors who are simply titled *iatroi.* (We shall return to this point later.) It was up to the town council to select its doctors for this privileged category. Specialists such as dentists could be included, but not those who worked with incantations or who were exorcists (Nutton, 205. For itinerant Jewish exorcists at Ephesos cf. Acts 19.13). A doctor so chosen had no automatic tenure: his position could be subjected to review by the city. It should not be inferred from the title of public physician in the Greek world that this was some kind of free medical service provided by the state. It is here that the article by A.G. Woodhead, 'The State Health Service in Ancient Greece', *CHJ* 10 (1952) 235-53 (= *I. Medizin*, pp. 31-65) is misleadingly anachronistic. No doubt *archiatroi* and *demosioi iatroi* before them were under some moral pressure to treat those who could not afford to pay; but it may have been as much because of their Hippocratic oath as anything else. Besides, a doctor bent upon receiving remuneration for his services — charges of avarice against the profession were not uncommon — could easily so busy himself attending wealthier patients that there was no time left to serve the poor. See generally Cohn-Haft, 32-45. Nutton (206, n.103) refers to a restored inscription of Ephesos, *JÖAI* 30 (1937) B200, in which 'the doctors themselves seem to have regulated the level of fees'.

Nutton's article deals with other geographical areas: in the Western provinces and at Constantinople the term *archiatros* is very rarely attested. The situation at Rome cannot be treated as typical for the rest of the Empire. In the late Republic most doctors at Rome appear to have been of servile or freed rank, with low prestige (S. Treggiari, *Roman Freedmen during the Late Republic* [Oxford, 1969] 129-32); but Julius Caesar granted citizenship to such foreign doctors as were resident in Rome (Suet. *Jul.* 42). Augustus followed this up by providing them with permanent freedom from public taxes (Dio 53.30; Suet. *Aug.* 59); by seeking to increase their prestige he laid the foundation for the trend towards free rather than freed doctors at Rome under the Empire (Treggiari, ibid.). Yet few doctors can be shown to have come to Rome to qualify for citizenship since 'by registering themselves in order to obtain citizenship, peregrine doctors were submitting themselves to some degree of official control, for some assertion of medical competence would have to be made' (Nutton, 207, following A. Momigliano). His appendix lists six *archiatroi* from Rome (nos.85-90, all late IV-VI) whom he holds to be Christian (cf. his p.208), although no.85 appears to be Jewish (*CIJ* 1, p.535 no.5*).

Egypt, too stands apart because of the long indigenous medical tradition there. Wealthy doctors of Roman Egypt are known, but their organization and legal status may be distinctive to their location. They were immune from liturgies and some public taxes. Nutton refers to *P. Oxy.* 1 (1898) 40 (late II/early III) as a clear illustration of this. This memorandum of a decision made in court by the Prefect is interesting and brief enough to be worth reprinting here. For revision of the text and commentary see H.C. Youtie, *Scriptiunculae* II (Amsterdam, 1973) 878-88 (pl. 2). Similar abstracts of court proceedings preceded and probably followed this text. The *P. Oxy.* editors suggest that the copy was made 'a good deal later' than the court case itself. The memorandum is written on the *verso*; *recto* contains unrelated accounts (late II). Youtie's revised text of *ll.*8-10 is printed in place of the original in *P. Oxy.* 1.

.   .   .   .

Ἀντίγραφον ὑπομνηματισμοῦ Οὐα[λ]ερίου (?) Εὐδαί-
μονος τοῦ ἡγεμονεύσαντος (ἔτους) [
[Κα]ίσαρος τοῦ κυρίου Φαμενὼθ ι[.   ἐπε]ρχο-
μένου Ψάσνιος. προσελθ[ό]ντ[ος Ψάσνι]ος
5 καὶ εἰπόντος, "ἰατρὸς ὑπάρχων τὴ[ν τέ]χνην
τούτους αὐτοὺς οἴτινές με εἰς λειτο[υ]ρ[γ]ίαν
δεδώκασι ἐθεράπευσα," Εὐδαίμων εἶπεν, "τά-

χα κακῶς αὐτοὺς ἐθεράπευσας. δίδαξον τ[ὸν στρα-]
τηγόν, εἰ ἰατρὸς εἶ δημοσ[ιε]ύων ἐπιτη[δείως],
10 καὶ ἕξεις τὴν ἀλειτουργησίαν.''

Copy of a memorandum of Valerius(?) Eudaimon who was prefect in the . . . year of Caesar the lord, Phamenoth . . . Psasnis undertook legal proceedings.
5 **Psasnis came forward | and said, 'I am a doctor by profession and I attended these very men who have given me over to a liturgy.' Eudaimon said, 'Perhaps you treated them badly. Give notification to the *strategos* if you are**
10 **a public service doctor, suitably qualified, | and you will have immunity from the liturgy.'**

Psasnis petitions that a liturgy has been wrongly imposed on him. To regain his immunity he simply has to follow the normal procedure of seeking a judgment from the *strategos* of his nome. For another mention of exemption from liturgy see *SEG* 937, discussed almost at the end of this entry.

There were clearly gradations of doctors in Egypt, for some were called δεδοκιμασμένοι, 'approved'. N. Lewis has suggested (*BASP* 2 [1965] 87-89; cf. id., *Atti dell' XI Congresso internazionale de Papirologia, Milano, 2-8 Sett. 1965* [Milan, 1966] 513-18) that these are to be equated with the *demosioi iatroi* who are attested in the papyri from 173AD. These doctors are not necessarily to be equated with *archiatroi* from other parts of the Empire. The title *archiatros* (which was used in the Ptolemaic period of court physicians) occurs in IV (*P. Lips.* (1906) 97, Hermopolis; = Nutton, no.5), but by V *fin.* the term *demosios iatros* had fallen into disuse and Egypt like the rest of the Empire was calling its public doctors *archiatroi*. Nutton nos.6-13 lists a series of Christian texts from Egypt mentioning *archiatroi*, dated V/VI–VI/VII (note that his no.9 is from C. Wessely, *Studien zur Palaeographie und Papyruskunde* VIII, not vol. VII). Nutton no.7 (= *P. Oxy.* 1 [1898] 126) of 572AD is a notification by a woman that she will in future pay various taxes hitherto paid by her father, since he had gifted property to her as her dowry. At *l.*23 the woman's husband gives his consent: he is an *iatros* and he refers to his deceased father as an *archiatros*.

The *dedokimasmenoi* mentioned above are known mainly from death and injury certificates. The formality of these documents makes them distinctive to Egypt (cf. Nutton, 213-14). *P. Oxy.* 44 (1976) 3195, col.2 is the most recently published example (13-14(?) June 331).

(*m.3*) ὑπατείας Ἰουνίο[υ Β]άσ[σο]υ κ[αὶ Φλαουίου
25 Ἀβλαβίου τῶν λαμπ(ροτάτων) [
Φλαουίῳ Ἰουλιανῷ λογιστῇ καὶ
Κλαυδίῳ Ἑρμείᾳ ἐκδίκῳ Ὀξ(υρυγχίτου)
παρὰ Αὐρηλίων Θεωνίνου καὶ
Ἥρωνος καὶ Σιλβανοῦ καὶ Διδύμου
30 δημοσίων ἰατρῶν τη[ς] λαμπ[ρᾶς]
καὶ λαμπ(ροτάτης) Ὀξ(υρυγχιτῶν) πόλεως. ἐπεστάλημεν
ὑπ[ὸ] τῆς ὑμῶν ἐμμελείας ἐκ βι-

βλιδίων ἐπιδοθέντων ὑπ[ὸ]
Αὐρηλίου Παησίου Σενενοῦφις
35 ἀπὸ κώμης Πέλα ὥστε ἐφιδεῖ(ν)
τὴν περὶ αὐτὸν διάθεσιν καὶ
ἐνγράφως προσφωνῆσαι. ὅθ[εν
τοῦτον ἐφίδαμεν ἐπὶ γρ[αβά]του
ἐν τῷ δημοσίῳ λογιστηρί[ῳ
40 ἔχοντα ἐπὶ τοῦ δεξιοῦ μ[έρους
τῆς κορυφῆς τραύματ[α ..
ο .[.] τ[. .] .[.]ια . ι ... ὑμένος
κ[α]ὶ ἐπὶ τοῦ δεξιοῦ μέρο[υς τοῦ
μετώπου οἴδημα κ[αὶ] ἐ[π]ὶ [τοῦ
45 πήχοιος τῆς ἀριστερᾶς χιρὸ[ς
πελίωμα μετὰ ἀμοιχῆς καὶ ἐπ[ὶ
τοῦ πήχοιος τῆς δεξιᾶς χιρὸ[ς
πελιωμάτιον, ἅπερ προσφων[οῦ-
μεν.
50 ὑπατείας τῆς προκ(ειμένης) Παῦνι κ.
(*m.4*) [Αὐ]ρ(ήλιος) Θεωνῖνος προσεφώνησα ὡς πρόκιται.
(*m.5*) [Αὐρ(ήλιος)] Ἥρων προσεφώνησα ὡς πρόκει[ται.
(*m.6*) [Αὐρ(ήλιος)] Σιλβανὸς προσεφώνησα ὡς πρόκιτ[αι.

25 (*3rd hand*) **In the consulship of Junius Bassus and Flavius | Ablabius the most
illustrious ... To Flavius Julianus auditor and Claudius Hermias public
advocate of the Oxyrhynchite (nome), from Aurelii Theoninus and Heron and**
30 **Silvanus and Didymos, | public doctors of the illustrious and most illustrious
city of the Oxyrhynchites. We were notified by your Diligences as a result of**
35 **a petition submitted by Aurelius Paesius son of Senenuphis | from the village
of Pela to examine his condition and make a report in writing. Accordingly,**
40 **we examined this man on a mattress in the public office. | He had wounds on
the right side of his head ... of (the) membrane and a swelling on the right**
45 **side of his forehead and a contusion with a skin wound on the | left forearm**
50 **and a small contusion on the right forearm. This constitutes our report. | In
the consulship previously mentioned. Pauni 20.**
(*4th hand*) **I Aurelius Theoninus have submitted my report as aforesaid.**
(*5th hand*) **I Aurelius Heron have submitted my report as aforesaid.**
(*6th hand*) **I Aurelius Silvanus have submitted my report as aforesaid.**

There are a number of similar documents extant. The introductory remarks to
P. Oxy. 3195 has some references; see also the commentary on *P. Oslo* 3 (1936)
95-96 (the first of which dates to April, 96AD). A few brief philological comments
may be made on the text above. At *ll.*35, 38 the aspirates in ἐφιδεῖν/ἐφίδαμεν have
been carried over from the present tense of ὁράω (see Gignac I, pp.136-37). For
γράββατον = κράββατον see Gignac I, 77; the word occurs in the NT at Mk. 2.4;
6.55, *et al.*; for the phrase ἐπί + gen. cf. Acts 9.33. In the papyrus it fairly clearly
refers to a 'poor man's bed'. The use of προσφωνέω in the NT varies somewhat,

but at Lk. 23.20 and Acts 22.2 it may not be so far away from its meaning in this papyrus (*ll.*48-49, 51-53; and note especially ἐνγράφως π. at *l.*37 where the original notion of a verbal address has clearly gone. For μέρος, 'side' (*ll.*40, 43) note Jn. 21.6. J.A.L. Lee, *Antichthon* 6 (1972) 39-42, had drawn attention to this usage particularly in non-Biblical Koine and the LXX.

Death and injury certificates attested to by as many as four doctors as in the case above (no traces survive of the fourth signature) are not the end of it: for the bureaucracy in Egypt was such that a dead male over 14 might continue to be assessed for poll tax unless a specific request was received from a near relative that his name be removed from the tax lists and registered on the list of the dead. These death notices were submitted primarily for fiscal reasons, hence only the death of males is reported since they alone were subject to poll tax. Four such notifications were picked up in the 1977 culling, *SB* 11111 (Karanis, 184), 11112 (Karanis, 48), 11175 (provenance unknown, 227/8), 11176 (Fayum, II/III). The second of these (= *P. Mich. Michael* [1966] 10) is printed below by way of example (note the commentary there, pp.80-86).

Μάρωνι κωμογραμματεῖ Φι-
λαδελ(φείας)
παρὰ Στρατίππου τοῦ Τεί-
τανος τῶν ἀπὸ Φιλαδελ-
5 φείας. ὁ υἱός μου Νεμεσίων
λαογραφούμενος περὶ τὴν
κώμην, ἐτελεύτησεν τῇ ε̄
τοῦ Χοιὰχ τοῦ ἐνεστῶτος
ἐνάτου ἔτους Τιβερίου
10 Κλαυδίου Καίσαρος

Σεβαστοῦ Γερμανικοῦ
Αὐτοκράτορος. διὸ ἐπιδί-
δωμί σοι τὸ ὑπόμνημα ὅπως
προσανενέγκῃς οἷς καθή-
15 κει καὶ τὸ αὐτοῦ ὄνομα περι-
αιρέθ[ῃ] καὶ ἀνενεχθῇ
ἐν τῇ τῶν τετελευτηκ[ό-]
των τάξει ἵν' ᾧ ἀναίτιος
καθάπερ καί εἰμι.
20 εὐτύχει.

To Maron, village secretary of Philadelphia, from Stratippos son of Titan,
5 **from Philadelphia. |My son Nemesion, enrolled for the poll tax in the village,**
10 **died on the 5th of Choiak of the present ninth year of Tiberius |Claudius**
Caesar Augustus Germanicus Imperator. Accordingly I give you the
15 **memorandum so that you may refer it to the appropriate people |and his**
name be deleted (i.e., from the tax register) and recorded on the list of the
20 **dead, in order that I may not be responsible, as indeed I am not. |Farewell.**

Nutton's appendix of over 90 documentary references to *archiatroi* includes only one woman, *MAMA* 7 (1956) 566 (Çeşmeli Zebir, IV–VI in E. Phrygia); cf. L. Robert/N. Fıratlı, *Les stèles funéraires de Byzance gréco-romaine* (Paris, 1964) 177; Nutton, no.24. This Christian epitaph is set up by a man who calls himself ἀρχι|είατρος (*ll.*2-3) and who refers to his wife Auguste similarly, ἀρχι|ειάτρηνα (*ll.*5-6). Other female doctors are known, more particularly in the Greek East. H.W. Pleket, *Epigraphica II, texts on the Social History of the Greek World* (*Textus Minores* 41; Leiden, 1969), conveniently includes five examples:

1. Pleket no. 1 (= *IG* II/II².3[1940, repr. 1974] 6873) a three-line verse epitaph for Phanostrate; Acharnai in Attika, after 350BC.
2. Pleket no.12 (= *TAM* 2 (1944) 595; cf. A. Wilhelm, *JÖAI* 27 (1932) 73-96 at 83-84 = *I. Medizin*, pp.98-124 at 109-10); Tlos in Lykia, IAD.

> Ἀντιοχὶς Διοδότο[υ] | Τλωὶς μαρτυρηθεῖ-
> σα ὑπὸ τῆς Τλωέων | βουλῆς καὶ τοῦ δή-
> 5 μου ἐπὶ τῇ περὶ | τὴν ἰατρικὴν τέ-
> χνην ἐνπειρίᾳ|ἔστησεν τὸν ἀν-
> δριάντα ἑαυτῆς.

Antiochis daughter of Diodotos, citizen of Tlos, being attested to by the
5 council and citizen |body of the Tloans for her experience in the medical
profession, set up the statue of herself.

3. Pleket no.20 (= W. Peek, *Griechische Versinschriften*, I [Berlin, 1955] 2040; cf. Wilhelm in *I. Medizin*, pp. 109-11); Pergamon, II. A verse epitaph set up for Pantheia, a doctor, by her husband Glykon who was also a doctor.
4. Pleket no. 26 (= Peek, ibid. 1486; cf. Wilhelm in *I. Medizen*, pp.100-10); Neoclaudiopolis (Phazimonitis, in Asia Minor, II/III). A verse epitaph for Domnina.
5. Pleket no.27 (= G.E Bean/T.B. Mitford, *Journeys in Rough Cilicia in 1962 and 1963* [Vienna, 1965] 43 ; Cilicia Tracheia, II/III).

> Ὄβριμον ἰητῆρα καὶ Ἀμμειν τὴν σώτειραν
> Καδου παῖς Κοπραῖς σῆμα τόδε ἀμφέ⟨βαλ⟩εν

Kopraïs daughter of Kados set up this tomb for Obrimos, doctor, and Ammis
her preserver.

Among others one may add *CIG* 4 (1877; repr. 1977) 9164 and 9209, two very spare Christian epitaphs from Cilicia for women doctors.

There are three husband/wife doctor pairs even in this short list; may we infer that they work in partnership as a team? In quite another *techne* we may have a parallel at Acts 18.2-3 with Aquila and Priscilla's tentmaking. R.F. Hock, *The Social Context of Paul's Mission* (Philadelphia, 1980), 81 n.46, has recently expressed doubt whether Priscilla is to be included here. It is true that the passage is not unambiguous, but on balance the subject of ἦσαν γὰρ σκηνοποιοὶ τῇ τέχνη ought probably to be taken as the husband and wife. The run of the sentence suggests Paul is not included in the subject here. A freed couple are both involved in the purple trade: see **3**.

The term *archiatros* is taken over into Christian usage and applied meta-phorically to Christ. Nutton (197 n.40) refers to four passages in Origen:

a. Migne *PG* 12.1021 (second homily on the book of Kings): τί ἄτοπόν ἐστι τοὺς ἰατροὺς καταβαίνειν πρὸς τοὺς κακῶς ἔχοντας; τί δὲ ἄτοπόν ἐστιν ἵνα καὶ ὁ ἀρχιατρὸς καταβῇ πρὸς τοὺς κακῶς ἔχοντας; ἐκεῖνοι ἰατροὶ μὲν ἦσαν πολλοί, ὁ δὲ Κύριός μου καὶ Σωτὴρ ἀρχιατρός ἐστι.

b. Migne *PG* 12.1369 (first homily on Ps. 37): in Latin, full of medical metaphors.

c. Migne *PG* 13.472 (18th homily on Jer.): (ὁ Θεὸς) ἐμακροθύμησε ἀεὶ πέμπων τοὺς θεραπεύοντας, μέχρις οὗ ἔλθῃ ὁ ἀρχιατρός, ὁ διαφέρων προφητῶν προφήτης, ὁ διαφέρων ἰατρῶν ἰατρός.

d. Migne *PG* 13.1831 (13th homily on Lk.): Latin text.

This metaphor occurs also in *P. Berl.* 9794 (= Schmidt/Schubart, *BKT* 6 [1910] pp.110-17 = C. Wessely, *Les plus anciens monuments du Christianisme écrits sur papyrus*, II [Paris, 1924], pp. 429-33), a third-century liturgical papyrus. At col.2 *ll*.37-39 the text reads, '. . . wash away our sins through your only most |holy son Jesus Christ τοῦ κυρίου ἡμῶν καὶ ἀρχιϊα|τροῦ τῶν ψυχῶν [ἡ]μῶ[ν].' Set against the larger perspective of Origen's use this striking idea shows itself to belong to the theological terminology that was in vogue in that period (Nutton, 215 n.174; the text is no.4 in his appendix 3).

Before leaving *archiatroi* one more observation may be made. There is a noticeable tendency to compound words with ἀρχ- in the Koine. On this predilection see MM, s.v. ἀρχι-, where the examples are mainly papyrological; for epigraphical examples see *Index du bulletin épigraphique*, *1938-1965*, I (Paris, 1972) 28-30; ibid, *1966-1973* (Paris, 1979) 29-30. In the case of the present term Nutton himself gives (201–202) two examples of eminent doctors exempted from taxes by the cities which honoured them, each of whom is called simply *iatros*. Further, from mid-IV physicians who served the imperial family are referred to with increasingly long strings of phrases and epithets (ibid., 198). In the case of the Thyatira inscription with which we began, is Helios simply a doctor called by a more impressive-sounding title? Some other examples may be cited: ἀρχιγερουσιάρχης in a Jewish inscription from a catacomb at Rome (*New Docs 1976* 73; perhaps, too, ἀρχιπρεσβύτερος καὶ ἀρχιμανδρίτης (*New Docs 1976*, **94**). Düll, *Götterkulte*, 105.4-5 (Stobi in Yugoslavia, IAD) is an honorific inscription set up by a Dionysiac cult for Τίτῳ ἀρχι|μύστῃ; does this refer to a grade of initiate or is it merely a more fulsome title than μύστης? *I.Pan* 70 and 86 attest the word ἀρχισωματοφύλαξ (partly restored in the former): on this noun see Deissmann, *BS* 98, who notes that at LXX 1 Sam. 28.2 its force is equivalent to σωματοφύλαξ. *P. Wiscon.* 50 (provenance unknown, 165) consists of parts of different documents (manumissions, marriages, etc.) written in Latin, which *ed.pr.* suggests may have been used as a practice sheet by the scribe. The sole (partial) line of Greek (9) includes the word ἀρχιραβδοῦχος, 'chief of the lictors', not previously attested in the papyri. The feminine form occurs as a title for a woman in the cult of Kybele: *IGRR* 1 (1911) 614.13 (Tomis, 200-01 (?)), ἀρχιραβ⟨β⟩δουχῖσα. (This same inscription accords to two men the title ἀρχιδενδροφόρος, *ll*.17 and 18.) See Sijpesteijn, p.46, for attestations in the papyri of ῥαβδοῦχος and -χία, which occur mainly in IV. In the NT, the noun -χος occurs only at Acts 16.35, 38 — not surprisingly, in the Roman colony of Philippi (see A.N. Sherwin-White, *Roman Society and Roman Law in the New Testament* [Oxford, 1963; repr. Grand Rapids, 1978] 74, 98). J.A.L. Lee informs me that in a posthumous article to appear in *Antichthon* on the language of *vita Aesopi* G, G.P. Shipp notes the occurrence of ἀρχέμπορε used in flattering address to return the compliment ἀρχιγεωργέ. This point has relevance for two of the ἀρχ- compounds in the NT, ἀρχιποίμην used of Christ at 1 Pet. 5.4 (on this word see Deissmann, *LAE*, 99–101), and ἀρχιερεῖς (numerous examples — see BAGD, s.v., 1b). In the latter case the plural has usually been explained as a reference to ex-high priests and members of their families, although J. Jeremias, *Jerusalem in the Time of Jesus* (ET; London, 1969) 175-81, holds that the term refers to 'chief priests of higher rank than the majority [of priests]' (178), between whom and the ordinary priests there was a wide social gulf. Yet one may note that just as ἰατρός may occasionally stand for ἀρχιατρός, so too in the NT ἱερεύς clearly can stand for ἀρχιερεύς. At Acts 5.27 D has ἱερεύς for ἀρχιερεύς; *Gosp. Egyptians* 1 speaks of Aaron ὁ ἱερεύς. In Hebrews Christ is called ἀρχιερεύς at 2.17; 3.1; 5.5 by the writer but at 5.6; 7.17, 21 when Ps. 110.4 is quoted ἱερεύς is used.

b. Itinerant doctors

L. Robert, *I. Medizin*, pp.79-87 (= *Hellenica* 2 [1946] 103-08], has published a number of Greek metrical epitaphs for doctors, the first of which is reprinted below (in metrical lines; the bar strokes indicate new line-beginnings on the stone).

Πῦρ μὲν σάρκας ἔκαυσε, |τὰ δ'ὀστέα ἐνθάδ' ἔνεστιν, |
Ἡδύος ἰατροῦ πολλὴν |γαῖαν κατιδόντος |
Ὠκεανοῦ τε ῥοὰς |καὶ τέρματα ἠπειροῖο |
Εὐρώπης Λιβύης |ἠδ' Ἀσίας μεγάλης· |
5   καὶ τὰ μὲν οὕ(τ)ω πάντα |ταλαιπώρως τετέλεσται |
τέκνα δὲ οὐκ ἐγένονθ' |Ἡδύος [οὐδ]αμόθ[εν] .
Ἡδὺς πρεσ(βύτερος)
ἐτ(ῶν) (*leaf*) νε' (*leaf*)
Δικαιοσύνη
10   ἐτ(ῶν) (*leaf*) ν' (*leaf*)

Fire burned the flesh, but here are the bones of Hedys the doctor who saw
many a land and the currents of the ocean and the bounds of the continent
5 **of Europe and Libya and Great Asia. |And in this way everything has come**
to a wretched end, and Hedys had no children at all. Hedys the elder, 55
10 **years; Dikaiosyne |50 years.**

This epitaph from Nicaea is one of a number of pieces of epigraphic evidence for travelling physicians, a subject in which Robert has shown more than passing interest (cf. *R.Phil.* 13 [1939] 163-73, where three of the four inscriptions relate to doctors who serve a community although their citizenship/origins lies elsewhere [one of these, for Evandros of Nikomedia who died in Numidia, is re-evaluated by B. Helly/J. Marcillet-Jaubert, *ZPE* 14 (1974) 252-56]; *BE* [1951] 249; *BE* [1953] 257, p.201). Literary allusions can be provided as well. The Hippocratic treatise *Airs, Waters, Places* devotes its first eleven chapters to describing the effect of a town's physical situation (exposure to certain winds; is the water hard? etc.) on the health of its inhabitants. It is explicit that this discussion is set forth to guide doctors who arrive to practise at a town with which they are unfamiliar. (The text is in the Loeb *Hippocrates*; translated in G.E.R. Lloyd, *Hippocrates* [Harmondsworth, 1978] 148-67; cf. H. Diller, *Wanderarzt und Aitiologie. Studien zur Hippokratischen-Schrift* περὶ ἀερῶν ὑδάτων τόπων [*Philologus Suppl.bd* 26.3; Leipzig, 1934] 5-7.) This passage makes very clear just how much the itinerant doctor had to adjust to by way of local conditions from one region to another.

While we should certainly not doubt the existence of doctors who practised their skills in various localities during their career, it seems to me that we should distinguish them from doctors who are born or trained in one place and spend their working life in one other locale. 'Wandering doctors' ought to refer not to the people who have spent their career years in one place away from their home town, but to doctors who moved to a new location perhaps every few years. (Equally clearly we should not think of them as being on the move as frequently as tinkers and pedlers.) Of the four references to wandering doctors given by Nutton (206 n.104) two at least should thus be ruled out. Eusebius, *HE* 5.1.49 (speaking of the late-II persecution in Gaul), mentions Alexander Φρὺξ μὲν τὸ γένος, ἰατρὸς δὲ τὴν ἐπιστήμην, πολλοῖς ἔτεσιν ἐν ταῖς Γαλλίαις διατρίψας. Augustine, *Ep.* 159.3-4 refers to Gennadius *frater noster, . . . qui nunc apud Carthaginem degit et Romae suae artis exercitatione praepolluit*, 'who now lives in Carthage and was a leading figure in the practice of his profession at Rome'. On the other hand, note Peek, *GVI* I 766, where in *l*.5 περιπλανίη is the crucial word which aligns Dorotheos, the doctor commemorated in that epitaph, with Hedys (see beginning of this section of the entry), as truly itinerant. (At *l*.6 read πετροφ[ύ]ης with Robert, *Hellenica* 2 [1946] 105-06 = *I. Medizin*, pp. 83-84.)

[Δ]ωρόθεον, ξένε, τόνδε σαόφρονα γαῖα κέκε[υθεν],
ἰητρὸν βιοτὰν γήραϊ λειπόμενον,
ὄμ ποτ' Ἀλεξάνδρεια λοχεύσατο πατρὶς ἀγ[ητή]
νειλόρυτος, πάσης ἁψάμενον σοφίη[ς]·
5   ἄστεα [δ'] ἐλθὼν πολλὰ περιπλανίη Τιθόρει[α]
πετροφ[υ]εῖ [ψ]υχρῶι τῶιδε κέκευθε τάφω[ι],
ὥς ποτε μοιρίδιον τέλος ἤλυθε· καὶ γὰρ Ὅ[μηρον]
νῆσος ἔχει βαιὰ θεῖον ἀοιδὸν Ἴος.

It is prudent Dorotheos, stranger, whom the earth hides, a doctor who departed life in old age. Once Alexandria was his birthplace, that wonderful
5 **homeland washed by the Nile, (where) he grasped all his skill. | But after coming to many towns with much wandering rocky Tithoreia has concealed him in this cold grave, when once he came to his allotted end. For Homer too, the divine poet, lies buried on a small island, Ios.**

For further bibliography on the phenomenon see Cohn-Haft, op.cit., 21-22 (and the notes), 26, 46-47, 53; and Pfohl's introduction in *I. Medizin*, 15 n.39. Nowhere in any of these discussions by classicists is Luke included, so far as I am aware. The general disfavour with which Hobart's views on Luke's medical vocabulary are today viewed should not thereby lead us to discount the sole NT testimonium to his profession at Col. 4.14, ὁ ἰατρὸς ὁ ἀγαπητός. Is it conceivable that Luke should be recognised as belonging to this group of itinerant physicians? The 'we' passages in Acts are generally held to indicate that Luke was present with Paul on those sections of his travels (*contra*, R.E. Brown, *The Birth of the Messiah* [New York,

1979] 235-36); since Paul worked at his own *techne* to earn his living where he went, it is a most natural inference to draw that those who accompanied him did the same. On the basis of the 'we' distinction Luke was with Paul at Philippi (16.10-17); he was again with Paul by the time the latter got to Troas (Acts 20.5). It would be intriguing if Luke had in fact been with Paul during some or all of his two year stay at Ephesos (19.10), all the more so in view of the comment at 19.11-20 on miraculous healings done by Paul and attempts to imitate them by τινες ... τῶν περιερχομένων Ἰουδαίων ἐξορκιστῶν (19.13). W.M. Ramsay, *Luke the Physician and other Studies in the History of Religion* (London, 1908) 16, observes that in Acts 28.8-10 a healing was effected by Paul (and in vv. 3-6 he survives a snakebite without recourse to medical attention) while Luke was in his company. Ramsay's essay is largely a critique of A. Harnack, *Luke the Physician* (ET; London, 1907), and has nothing helpful to say on the possibility of Luke practising his profession while on the move. The most recent commentary of any substance on Luke, by I.H. Marshall (London, 1978) is silent on this matter; so too Marshall's *Luke, Historian and Theologian* (Exeter, 1970) which is more concerned with theology than history, despite its title. C.J. Hemer, *BJRL* 60 (1977) 28-51 concentrates on Luke *qua* historian and has nothing to say on him as a doctor. R. Maddox, *The Purpose of Luke-Acts* (Edinburgh, 1982) 6-7, discounts but does not eliminate the possibility of the author of those books being a doctor. On the name Λουκᾶς in the Roman imperial period inscription from Apollonia printed in MM, s.v., and referred to in BAGD, s.v., as *Sb* 224, see *SEG* 1156, where is quoted the comment of J. Reynolds that 'the names [Egloge and Loukas] suggest (that Egloge was) a Jewess.'

c. Miraculous healings

W. Peek, *I Medizin*, pp.66-78 (1 fig.) = *Abh. Sächsischen Ak. der Wiss. zu Leipzig ph.-hist. Kl. 56.3* (Berlin, 1963) 3-9, works over the first 33 lines of the fragmentary *IG* IV².1, 123 (IV²BC), one of four stelai set up at the Asklepieion at Epidauros to record miraculous healings which are attributed to or claimed by the god of medicine and Apollo (cf. *IG* IV² 1.121, *l*.2). *IG* IV².1, 121 and 122 are largely complete texts containing 126 and 134 *ll*. respectively; in contrast no single line survives complete of the 20 that can be traced on *IG* IV².1, 124. No.123 had 137 lines but nearly 100 of these from *l*.33 are lost except for the last word or letters of each line. The miracles recorded on nos.121-123 are conventionally given a sequence number (1-20 on 121, 21-43 on 122, 44-48 on 123 *li*.1-33 plus another 15 calculated for the rest of the stone). Text and translation of *IG* IV² 121, 122 and 127 (the latter dated 224AD, a much shorter inscription testifying to one healing) may be found in E.J. and L. Edelstein, *Asclepius. A Collection and Interpretation of the Testimonies* (Baltimore, 1945) I, 221-38 (Test. 423-424).

On the five incidents dealt with by Peek the first three and the last involve no particular changes to the text, but in no.47 he rewrites large sections, rejecting earlier attempts at restoration. L. Robert, *BE* (1964) 180 (pp.162-65) has taken issue with Peek's restoration of this fourth text, especially with *ll*.25 and 28, although he is uncertain what may be a better restoration. Despite Peek's response in an addendum (1975) in *I. Medizin*, pp.77-78, the *IG* text of F. Hiller von Gaertringen for no.47 is reprinted below along with Peek's versions of nos.44-46, 48.

(44) κόρα ἄφωνος. α[ὕτ]ᾳ [τ]ὸ ἱε[ρ]ὸν [εἰσελθοῦσα . . . . .] εἶ[δε δ]ράκο[ν]τα ἀπὸ
δενδρέου τινὸς τῶν κατὰ τὸ ἄ[λσ]ος ἕ[ρποντα· φ]ό[β]ο[υ πλέα] δ' εὐθὺς βο-
ῆι τὰμ ματέρα καὶ τὸμ πατέρα κα[ὶ] ε[. . . .] ἀ[πῆλ]θε. *vac.*
(45) Μέλισσα ὑπὸ ἔχιος φῦμα. αὗτα ἐν τᾶι δ[εξι]ᾶι φῦμα ἔχο[υ]σα ἀφίκετο·
5   τῶν δὲ θεραπόντων ἐκ τοῦ ὄρεος [. . . ὀ]ρεξάντων [. . .] λ[.]α τᾶι γυναι-
κὶ ἔχις ἐν τῶι φορτίωι ἐγκοιταθεὶς φ[. . . . τ]ῶν ε[ὐ]νᾶν τὰν ὕλαν, ὡς
εἰς αὐτὰν κατεκλίθη ἁ Μέλισσα, πα[ρ]ελ[θὼν] ἀνοίγει τὸ ἐν τᾶι χειρὶ
φῦμα, καὶ ἐκ τούτου ὑγιὴς ἐγένετο. *vac.*(46) Καλλικράτεια θησαυ-
ρόν. αὗτα τελευτάσαντός οἱ τοῦ ἀνδρός, αἰσθημένα δὲ ὅτι εἴ[η π]ει τῶι
10 ἀνδρὶ χρυσίον κατορωρυγμένον, ἐπεὶ οὐκ ἐδύνατο μαστεύου[σα] εὑ-
ρεῖν, ἀφίκετο εἰς τὸ ἱερὸν ὑπὲρ τοῦ θησαυροῦ καὶ [ἐγκαθ]εύ[δου]σα ὄ-
ψιν εἶδε· ἐδόκει αὐτᾶι ὁ θεὸς ἐπιστὰς εἰπεῖν, Θα[ργηλιῶν]ο[ς μην]ὸς
ἐμ μεσημβρίαι ἐν τῆι λέοντος κεῖ[σθ]αι τὸ χρυσί[ον. ἁμέρα]ς [δὲ γε]νο-
μένας ἐξῆλθε καὶ οἴκαδε ἀφικομένα τὸ μὲν πρᾶτ[ον ἐν τᾶι] κ[εφαλ]ᾶι
15 τοῦ λέοντος τοῦ λιθίνου ἐμάστευε· ἧς δὲ πλατίο[ν ἀρχαῖο]ν [τι μν]ᾶμα
ἐπίθεμα ἔχον λίθινον λέοντα. ἐπεὶ δ' οὐχ ηὕρισκε[ν, ἐξειπ]ό[ντος] αὐτᾶι μάντιος διότι οὐ λέγοι ὁ θεὸς ἐν τᾶι λιθίναι [κεφαλᾶ]ι [τὸν θ]η-
σαυρὸν εἶμεν, ἀλλ' ἐν τᾶι σκιᾶι τᾶι γινομέναι ἀπὸ [τοῦ λέ]οντ[ος] ἐν τῶ[ι]
Θαργηλιῶνι μηνὶ περὶ μέσσον ἀμέρας, μετὰ δὲ τοῦτ[ο πο]ιουμένα [ἔρευ]-
20 ναν ἄλλαν τοῦ χρυσίου τὸν τρόπον τοῦτον ἀνηῦρε τὸν θησαυρὸν καὶ
ἔθυσε τῶι θεῶι τὰ νομιζόμενα. *vac.* (47) ἰχθυοφό-
[ρος Ἀμφί]μν[ας]τος. οὗτο[ς ἰ]χθυοφορῶν εἰς Ἀρκαδίαν, εὐξάμενος τὰν
[δεκάταν δωσεῖ]ν τῶι Ἀσκλ[απ]ιῶι τᾶς ἐμπολᾶς τῶν ἰχθύων, οὐκ ἐπ[ετ]έ-
[λει τὰν εὐχάν· πωλέο]ντ[ι δὲ τὸν ἰχθῦν ἐν Τεγέαι ἐξαπίνας [κωνώπια]
25 [πάντοθεν ἐπιφα]νέντα [οἵ] ἐ[τίτρω]σκον τὸ {τὸ} σῶμα· ὄχλου δὲ πολλοῦ π[ε]ρι-
[στά]ντος ε[ἰς] τὰν θεωρίαν, ὁ Ἀμφίμναστος δηλοῖ τὰν ἐξαπάταν ἅπασα[ν]
[τὰν . . . .] πρό[σθε γενο]μέναν· ἐξικετεύσαντος δ' αὐτοῦ τὸν
[θεὸν οὗτος αὐτῶι πολλοὺς] ἰχθύ[α]ς ἔφανεν καὶ ὁ Ἀμφίμναστος ἀνέθηκε
[τὰν δεκάταν τῶι] Ἀσκλαπιῶι. *vac.* (48) Ἐρατοκλῆς Τροξάνιος ἔμπυ-
30 [ος. τούτωι] ἐν Τροξᾶνι μέλλοντι ὑπὸ τῶν ἰατρῶν καίεσθαι καθεύδον-
[τι ὁ θεὸς ἐπιστὰς τὰμ μὲν] καῦσιν ἐκέλετο μὴ πο⟨ε⟩ῖσθαι, [ἐγ]καθεύδειν
[δ' ἐν τῶι ἱαρῶι τῶν Ἐπιδαυρί]ων· τοῦ δὲ χρό[ν]ου π[α]ρελθόντος, ὅμ ποτε[τέ]-
[τακτο, ἐρράγη τὸ πύος, καὶ ὑγιὴς ἀπῆλθε].

(44) A dumb girl. She entered the temple . . . saw a snake crawling from one
of the trees in the grove; and full of fear immediately she shouted for her
mother and father and . . . she departed.
    (45) Melissa (cured of) a tumour by a snake. She arrived with a tumour in
5 her right hand. |When the attendants stretched out . . . from the donkey . . .
for the woman, a snake that had been sleeping among the load . . . the wood
of the bed; when Melissa lay down on it, coming beside her the snake opens
the tumour in her hand and after this she became healthy.

(46) Kallikrateia (finds) treasure. After her husband died she was aware that
10 some |gold had been buried by her husband. When she could not find it
although she searched for it she arrived at the temple for the sake of the
treasure and while sleeping in it she saw a vision. It seemed to her that the
god standing over her said, 'In the month Thargelion, at midday, the gold lies
in the (*something feminine*) of the lion.' When day came she departed and
15 after arriving home started searching first of all in the head |of the stone lion;
for there was an old little platform set up as a memorial which had a stone
lion. But when she could not discover (the treasure) a seer explained to her
that the god did not say that the treasure was in the stone head, but in the
shadow which fell from the lion about midday in the month of Thargelion.
20 After this, making another search |for the gold in this manner, she found the
treasure and sacrificed to the god the usual offering.

(47) Amphimnestos the fish carrier. This man, while carrying fish to Arkadia,
vowed to give the tenth of his sale of fish to Asklepios, but he did not fulfil
his vow. But while selling fish at Tegea, suddenly gnats |appearing from
25 everywhere started stinging him on the body. Since a large crowd stood
around at the spectacle, Amphimnestos reveals his deceit completely . . .
which had occurred previously. And when he entreated the god the latter
caused many fish to appear for him, and Amphimnestos dedicated the tenth
to Asklepios.

30 **(48) Eratokles of Troizen, an abcess.** |While this man was asleep at Troizen,
being about to be cauterized by the doctors, the god standing over him urged
him not to have the cautery done, but to sleep in the temple of the
Epidaurians. When the time had passed which the god had prescribed the
abscess was dissipated and he departed healthy.

These anecdotes provide a representative sample from the fifty-odd surviving.
Those who attended the shrine for a medical reason generally had a chronic
condition which doctors had been unable to cure; cf. O. and C.L. Temkin (edd.),
Ancient Medicine. Select Papers of Ludwig Edelstein (Baltimore, 1967) 245-46; on
temple medicine more fully, Edelstein, *Asclepius*, II, 139-80. But not all the
incidents record cures. Included in the selection above is one (no.47) akin to a
'confession' text (cf. *New Docs 1976*, **7**), while no.46 is not far removed from an
oracle consultation (on oracles see **8**). Some of the more frequent cures attested in
the list on the three stones (nos.121-123) are for eye and gynaecological problems.
The god may reveal himself in some animal guise (nos.44,45) or may appear in a
dream and offer instructions (nos.46,48; for the wording of *l*.12 [cf. *l*.31 where
restored], note Acts 12.7-10; 23.11, and cf. *New Docs 1976*, **6**).

On the cult of Asklepios generally see Edelstein, *Asclepius*, passim; Pfohl,
introduction to *I. Medizin*, pp.22-23 and nn.59-60, includes further bibliography on
temple medicine and the cures effected there. A.E. Hill, *JBL* 99 (1980) 437-39,
suggests that Paul may have gained his inspiration for the 'body' metaphor in 1
Cor. (especially 12.14-25) from the presence at Corinth of the Asklepieion at which
votive offerings in the form of parts of the body have been excavated.

d. Miscellaneous items

A few other texts may be noted here, first *I. Charles Univ*. 38 (pp.88-89; pl.19), a Latin epitaph set up for a doctor by a woman (Rome, I-III).

> *Phi]lologo*
> *m]edico*
> *. .]nthis amico*
> *suo] fecit*

[Chrys(?)]anthis made this for Philologus the doctor, her husband(?).

The doctor's name may seem striking but in fact is commonly enough found in inscriptions and papyri (cf. Philomusus). Marek (88, n.198) refers also to the use of names like Comicus, Medicus, Mathematicus. The appearance of the *Lexicon of Greek Personal Names* (the first volume to be published, in 1983, covers the Cycladic Islands) will facilitate accurate plotting of the geographical, time, and status spread of such names. Marek suggests that both people in this inscription were slaves, given the lack of *gentilicia*. The woman, only part of whose name is extant — alternatives to (*Chrys*-) are possible; see Marek, ad loc. — calls the doctor her *amicus*. This is very rare, according to Marek (who refers to four examples in *CIL* VI): 'in the ancient world the view was strictly held that friendship is only possible between men.' This presupposes that there is really only one use of *amicus* in Latin. The *Oxford Latin Dictionary* distinguishes five, including personal friend, lover (note the citation quoted there from the Comedian Sextus Turpilius [late IBC], *quae mulier volet sibi suum amicum esse indulgentem*), political supporter, client king, and follower or disciple. In fact *CIL* VI has quite a few more examples of *amicus* being used by a woman of a man, as the Jory/Moore index (*CIL* VI.7.1) makes clear. While the majority provide no fuller definition some clarify the meaning of *amicus*. Nos.24709 and 34872 are dedications to *amico patrono* and *amico bono et patrono* respectively. At no.37245 a marital relationship is presupposed because Vipsania calls herself *casta* in her dedication to her *amicus*; and this is explicit at 37827 *coniugi optimo . . . amico*. One of Marek's examples is no.16967 *amico karissimo* (for a man who died at the age of 23), and there are numerous instances of this phrase. But they cannot always be taken to refer to marriage or a lover relationship since there are several texts dedicated by males to males where the same terminology occurs, e.g., no.6487. The Greek equivalent φίλος can be used to refer to marriage (cf. *LSJ* s.v., Ib). Quite what the relationship was between the two people in the inscription above must therefore remain open.

As an indication of the high regard with which doctors could be held in their city note *TAM* 2 (1944) 910 (= *IGRR* 3 [1906, repr. 1964] 733; cf. *SEG* 937 which gives recent bibliography but does not reprint the text), an honorific inscription on a statue base from Rhodiapolis in Lykia [IAD; but J.H. Oliver, *Historia* 24 (1975) 125-28, suggests the reign of Trajan] in which Herakleitos received very full tribute from his fellow citizens. He was a priest of Asklepios and Hygieia, and a benefactor honoured by other cities. His own town honoured him ἰκόνι ἐπιχρύσῳ καὶ τῷ τῆς παιδείας ἀνδριάντι, 'with a gold portrait and the statue of Education' (7-8). A little later (12-17) he is spoken of as πρῶτον ἀπ' αἰ|ῶνος ἰατρὸν καὶ συνγραφέα καὶ ποιη|τὴν ἔργων ἰατρικῆς καὶ φιλοσοφίας, |ὃν ἀνέγραψαν ἰατρικῶν ποιημάτων |Ὅμηρον εἶναι, ἀλιτουργησία τιμηθέντα, |ἰατρεύσαντα προῖκα . . , 'he is the first from ages past who is both doctor and historian and poet of works on medicine and philosophy; they recorded that he is the Homer of medical verse, honoured with exemption from liturgies, having served as a doctor without charging fees . . . ' (the text proceeds to mention some of his financial benefactions). For the phrase ἀπ' αἰῶνος cf. Lk. 1.70; Acts 3.21; 15.18; the example is worth adding to those in MM's entry. Other latter-day 'Homers' are discussed by C.P. Jones, *Phoenix* 32 (1978) 222-23 and n.9.

Raffeiner, *Sklaven*, includes three epitaphs for slaves and ex-slaves who were doctors: nos.32 = *IG* XIV.1813 (Rome, II/III), 47 = Peek, *GVI* 1321 [Bithynia, II], 53 = *IG* XIV.809 (between Naples and Nola, II). For a Christian doctor note *I. Tyre* 1.217.

The most recent contribution to study of Greek medical papyri is M.-H. Marganne, *Inventaire analytique des papyrus grecs de médecine* (Geneva, 1981) —*non vidi*.

3. The purple trade, and the status of Lydia of Thyatira

J.-P. Rey-Coquais' publication of *I. Tyre* 1 draws attention to the importance for that city of the purple trade. Numerous epitaphs, both Christian ones and those which provide no indication of such adherence, mention that the deceased was associated with this work in some way. Tyre was particularly identified with the purple industry in antiquity, but was by no means the only place where dyeing was carried on. Epigraphical texts help us to be aware of the importance of purple in Lydia and Phrygia, as well as in Macedonian cities like Philippi and Thessalonike, and in Egypt. R.J. Forbes, *Studies in Ancient Technology* IV (Leiden, 1964²) 99-150, provides a thorough study of dyes and dyeing practices in antiquity, dealing with both natural and synthetic techniques. For ancient discussions note particularly Pliny, *HN* 21.45-46. The use of purple was not restricted to the wealthy, for the majority of purple dyes was manufactured and readily accessible, in different grades of quality and colour variation, as the papyri attest. But colour-fast purple extracted from the murex was still very expensive in IIAD when this colour was at its most popular. M. Reinhold, *History of Purple as a Status Symbol in Antiquity* (*Coll. Latomus* 116; Brussels, 1970), covers the Near Eastern, Greek, and Roman worlds in his brief monograph. He draws attention (52) to the way in which the NT 'casually reflects the contemporary valuation of purple as a status color'. See Mk. 15.17, 20 = Mt. 27.28; Lk. 16.19; Rev. 17.3(?), 4; 18.12, 16 (note that some of Reinhold's references, 52 n.6, are incorrect). The moralizing reaction against purple — or what it stood for — came from both Stoic and Cynic quarters as well as the Fathers, and was well under way by mid-II/early III (Reinhold, 56-57, with the references), although Apollonios of Tyana in the first century had already voiced his disapproval (Philostratos, *Vita Apoll.* 4.21, noted by Reinhold).

Turning to the Tyre epitaphs, the great majority of the people explicitly linked with the purple industry are called κογχυλεύς, 'murex fisherman' (8, 8 *bis*, 24B [a brother and sister], 25 [two brothers, but the wording is hard to read], 26, 68, 107B, 118A, 141, 182, 182 *bis*, 188; of these 26, 68, 141, 188 carry overt Christian indicators), or the near-equivalent κογχυλευτής (7,77B, 103, 197; the last three are Christian). Rey-Coquais (p.160) suggests that a distinction between these two words may be possible. No.125 includes the fragmentary κονχυλευ---. These people harvested the special shellfish which Pliny discusses at considerable length (*HN* 9.124-42; cf. Vitruvius 7.13.1-3, also quoted by Forbes). *MAMA* 3 (1931) 309 (Korykos) interprets κογχυλεύς as a purple-worker. Purple dyers are attested in the Tyre necropolis too, κογχυλοκόπος (72, 95; both Christian), and κογχυλοπλυτής (28, 198): neither word appears in LSJ or the Suppl. No.28 is worth a passing glance.

- - - - -

φῖσε
μνῆμα μαρμάρινον
Καθηκουμένων, δι-
5 αφέρον Θεοκτίστου
κογχυλοπλυτοῦ τοῦ είεροτά-
του βαφίου.

[Lord ? ---] spare (φῖσε = φεῖσαι) the marble tomb of the Catechumens,
5 reserved for |Theoktistos, purple-dyer of the imperial dye-works.

The mention of these dye-works reflects the fact that purple was an imperial monopoly (cf. Eusebius, *HE* 7.32.2-3, noted by Rey-Coquais, p.21 n.2). The works at Tyre were destroyed by the Arabs in the second quarter of the seventh century; centres of the industry then became Constantinople in the East and probably certain Italian cities in the West. We have referred to in this text an association of catechumens, apparently. Cf. no.65B (on a sarcophagus), Καλεωνί|στας | Καθικου-μένων, 'belonging to Kaleonista, one of the catechumens'. The link between the purple industry and catechumens is also in evidence at no.78, Φωτίον Σαραφθηνοῦ | κονχυ Καθηκουμένων. Rey-Coquais points out that the third word could have been an abbreviation for any one of the four words noted above in this entry.

One Christian involved in the purple industry is also a banker: no.137, † Σωρὸς διαφέρο(υσα) | ᾿Ιωάννου άλη|θεινοβάφου | (καὶ) τραπεζ(ίτου), 'sarcophagus reserved for John the purple-dyer and banker'. άληθεινόβαφος here indicates dealer in or maker of best quality purple (see Rey-Coquais, pp.77-78). For discussion of bankers at Tyre see Rey-Coquais, pp.154-55, who refers also to another Christian with this profession from Corinth (J.H. Kent, *Corinth* VIII.3 [1966] no.640), and a Jew from Palmyra buried at Beth Shearim (*CIJ* 2.1010).

Finally among the words alluding to the purple trade in the Tyre necropolis inscriptions note πορφυρᾶς, which appears on nos.118B, 119, 120, three sarcophagi belonging to the same man: ᾿Υπερεχίου πορφυρᾶ. It is uncertain whether we are to translate this word as 'trader in' or 'maker of purple': perhaps 'purple dealer'. The possibility has been raised at *BE* (1970) 625 that it may be an abbreviation of πορφυροπώλης. This brings us to the question of the NT's Lydia, described at Acts 16.14 as a πορφυρόπωλις from Thyatira who was σεβομένη τὸν θεόν. (E.A. Judge tells me that at the XIV Congress of the International Association for the History of Religions, Winnipeg, 1980, A.T. Kraabel argued that the historicity of the 'God-fearers' in Acts is very questionable. This argument will be presented in an article forthcoming in *Numen*. In *ANRW* II.19.1 [1979] 477-510 he examines the archaeological evidence for the Diaspora Synagogue — Sardis, Priene, Dura, Delos, Ostia, Stobi — and suggests that none provides a certain indication of the presence of gentile sumpathizers with Judaism. Cf. idem, *JJS* 33[1982] 452.) MM's sole reference s.v. πορφυρόπωλις is to an inscription from Kos, W.R. Paton/E.L. Hicks, *The Inscriptions of Cos* (Oxford, 1891) no.309 = *IGRR* 4 (1927, repr. 1964) 107 = *CIG* 2 (1843, repr. 1977) 2519, an epitaph for what is apparently a husband/ wife team of purple sellers, both being of freed status: Μάρ(κου) Σπεδίου Νάσωνος πορφυροπώλου. | Ἐλπίδος Σπεδίας πορφυροπώ[λιδος]. On this text cf. *BE* (1962) 324; S.M. Sherwin-White, *Ancient Cos* (Göttingen, 1978), refers to it several times. For husband/wife teams engaged in the same occupation see **2**. A number of examples of the masculine form of this noun are known. *BE* (1970) 625 mentions an epitaph from Tyre for a woman whose father was a π. At *BE* (1955) 305 [πορφ]υροπῶλα is suggested as a possible restoration in a text from Abaecaenum in Sicily (Roman epoch). *BE* (1971) 650 mentions that an inscription on a sarcophagus from Phrygian Hierapolis should be corrected to read [πο]ρφυροπώλης κεῖμε (= κεῖμαι). Another purple-seller, Euschemon, set up a statue and shrine to Agathe Tyche at his own expense at Miletopolis in Mysia (F.W. Hasluck, *JHS* 27 [1907] 61–62, no.2). From Egypt note *O. Tait.* 1 (1930) P421, a Byzantine text which mentions Menas πορφυρ(οπώλης). *P.Herm.Rees* (1964) 52 (53 is an even less legible copy of it) is a petition dated 399 from Aurelius Annas, son of Joses, Ἰουδαίου πορφυροπώλου (*l*.4; *l*.5 in no.53). This pair of texts was published too late for inclusion in *CPJ* III [1964]. Listed in a very long register, *P.Flor.* 1 (1906, repr. 1960) 71.641 (Hermopolis Magna, IV) is a Dioskoros with the same title (BAGD, s.v., implies that this reference is to a woman).

The Vulgate at Acts 16.14 calls Lydia a *purpuraria*, a less specific word which could mean 'purple-dyer' as well as 'purple-seller'; but there seems to have been no single Latin word as specific as πορφυρόπωλις. A number of Latin inscriptions from Rome mention people who pursued this business: *CIL* VI.2 (1888, repr. 1960) 9843 (*purp.*; freedman), 9844 (*purp.*), 9845 (*purpurarius*), 9846 (*purpura.*; freedwoman), 9847 (*purpura[rio]*), 9848 (*purpurari*). *CIL* VI.4.3 (1933, repr. 1967) is of special interest, for Veturia Fedra, a *purpuraria*, set up the inscription for herself, her *patronus conlibertus* who lived with her (*vixit mecum*) for twenty years, and a *libertus*. Note also *CIL* XIV (1887, repr. 1968) 2433, an epitaph from Latium for a *purpurarius*.

One feature of these texts is that several people involved in this business are explicitly designated as ex-slaves. This may well be the most appropriate category in which to locate Lydia; that she is of freed status would be consonant not only with her occupation, but also with her name. For 'Lydia' suggests a servile status, many slaves being accorded a name which reflected their geographical origin (e.g. Thratta, Phryx). The index to *CIL* VI attests only one Lydia, who appears from her son's name to have been a slave: *D.M.* | *Tucciae Lydiae* | *M. Tuccius* | *Eutychus matri b.m.f.* (*CIL* VI.4.1.27711; dated I/II in H. Solin, *Die griechischen Personennamen in Rom. Ein Namenbuch* (Berlin, 1982) I, 609). Further, closely related names, Lydius, Lydus, Lyde — Lydia and Lydius are latinized forms of Lyde and Lydios — are possessed (where status can be determined) by either slaves or *liberti/libertae* as Solin, I, 608–09 makes clear. The sole example of a Lydios known to me from papyri is *SB* 6.5 (1963) 9615, a bald list of names (provenance unknown, II/III); no feminines are attested in *WB* or Foraboschi. In Lydia of Thyatira's case Acts 16.15 rules out the possibility of servile status (ὁ οἶκος αὐτῆς; her invitation to Paul and his company to stay with her; cf. v.40). E.A. Judge suggests to me that the latinized form of her name may be a clue that her former master was a Roman; and while we must not build too much on it we may at least recall that Philippi where she was resident was a Roman *colonia*.

One further tantalizing question may be raised here. *AE* 800 reports a fragmentary inscription from Miletos: [. . . Τιβ]ερίου [Κ]λαυδίου Νέρω|[νος] Καίσαρος ἐπάνω τῶν πορφυ|ρῶν. The importance of this brief wording is that it shows that the imperial monopoly on purple goes back at least to Nero. The person whose name is lost must have been a slave or freedman, whose function is described in Greek by the equivalent of the Latin *a purpuris*. The implication flowing from this is that those involved in the purple trade — who appear to be of freed status, as noted above — are members of the *familia Caesaris*. If this imperial monopoly were initiated prior to Nero — by Claudius, perhaps, since he is often claimed to be the great innovator in centralized administration? — we might just be able to identify Lydia more exactly, as being a member of 'Caesar's household'. (Despite what is sometimes inferred from Phil. 4.22, οἱ ἐκ τῆς Καίσαρος οἰκίας does not have to refer to people domiciled at Rome; and therefore this verse provides no certain evidence for that city as the place of writing of Philippians.) It must be emphasized, however, that this particular suggestion about Lydia is no more than an intriguing possibility.

It is at least consistent with Lydia's name and occupation, then, that she should be of freed status. But what sort of woman could act with her apparent independence? (One must say 'apparent', for it cannot be ruled out that Luke has accorded to her rather than to her husband the initiative of inviting Paul et al. to 'her home' because she was the one who responded to Paul's message. Cf. the way that the names of Timothy's mother and grandmother have been preserved because they were believers, 2 Tim. 1.5, but not that of his father, Acts 16.1.) Certainly, women who could own property and who were involved in financial transactions are known commonly enough. Covering a variety of dealings, the following examples from 1976 and 1977 papyrus publications may be instanced:—

P. Vindob. Tandem (1976) 24 (Soknopaiu Nesos, 14/11/45), a bilingual (Greek/Demotic) text concerned with the purchase of a house in which the husband acts for his wife 'because she is illiterate' (col.1, *l*.5; cf. col.2 *ll*.14-16).

P. Wiscon. 2.54 (Arsinoe, 27/6/116), a declaration to the property registry office in which Isaros has given her slave to another woman as mortgage for security on a loan from the latter.

P. Oxy. 44 (1976) 3198 (Dec. 145/Jan. 146?), a loan of money arranged between two well-to-do (so *ed.pr.*) women, the lender being of freed status.

BGU 13 (1976) 2222 (Fayum, 23/6/161) a census return in which the man's daughter is stated to own four houses and four halls.

———————— 2343 (Arsinoite polis, 168) notification by a bank to a priestess that earnest money (*arrabon*), which she is to pay to a soldier for a property, has been transferred to his account. Her brother acts as her *kyrios* (*l*.7).

———————— 2224 (Arsinoite polis, 175), two census returns, one a joint declaration by a brother and sister, the other (col.2) a return by a freedman and a freedwoman who own jointly a house and a court.

———————— 2223 (Arsinoite nome, 24-29/8/175), a property return in which Harpokratiane (who is both a Roman citizen and an Alexandrian, ἀστή) acting through her *kyrios* (?) — τῇ φροντιζομένῃ ὑπ' ἐμοῦ, *ll*.2-3 — states her shared ownership of a house, land, etc.

P. Oxy. 45.3242 (185-87), a property declaration by a woman, of particular interest because it shows that the property has been retained in the family for over a century; see *ed.pr.*'s n. to *ll.*10-11 on p.105.

CPR V.2 (1976) 9 (Hermopolis, 339), a petition in which a man acts as *kyrios* for his mother: she had inherited property from her maternal uncle, being his only heir at law, and a tenant farmer has been refusing to pay the rent.

P. Coll. Youtie 2(1976) 83 (provenance unknown, 12/12/353), a document in which a widow makes provision for her two sons, to take effect after her death.

CPR V.2 (1976) *P. Vindob.* G.39847 (Hermopolite nome, IV), a lengthy tax-list from the village of Skar; the number of female property owners out of the total of nearly 550 people appears surprisingly small.

P. Oxy. 44 (1976) 3202 (June/July 400), two nuns lease part of a house to a Jew: see *New Docs 1976*, **82**.

CPR V.2 (1976) 16 (Hermopolite nome, 16/9/486), a man leases land from a woman.

P. Mich. 13.669 (Aphrodite, 12-13/9/529, or 514), a woman lends money at 12½% interest to three men.

——————— 664 (Aphrodite, 585 or 600), Aurelia Judith sells her share of a corn measure to a man; previously she had bought it from her son, Aurelios Kyriakos, who had inherited it from his father.

——————— 662 (Aphrodite, VII), with her husband's consent a woman sells part of a house.

Of rather more interest for the present discussion are those texts in which the woman is specified as acting without her guardian. Under the *lex Iulia de maritandis ordinibus* (18BC) and the *lex Papia Poppaea* (9AD) freeborn women with three children and freed women with four were accorded a range of privileges, including the right to undertake legal transactions without the necessity to obtain the consent of their *kyrios*. This was commonly called the *ius* (*trium*) *liberorum*. The standard recent discussion of this is P.J. Sijpesteijn, *Aeg.* 45 (1965) 171-89. He tabulates (180-87) a list of 83 women known to have this right from papyri of Roman and Byzantine date. The usual formula is χωρὶς κυρίου χρηματίζουσα κατὰ τὰ ῾Ρωμαίων ἔθη δικαίῳ τέκνων, 'negotiating without her lord in accordance with the customs of the Romans in virtue of the *ius liberorum*'. There are certainly instances where women act without their *kyrios* but do not mention this privilege, e.g., *P. Oxy.* 9 (1912) 1199, the registration of a deed (dated 266) in which the woman herself presents the memorandum; note also *P. Mich.* 663 (below). Furthermore, Sijpesteijn's point (174) must not be forgotten that the women we know of explicitly who are in this situation may well be merely the tip of the iceberg: undoubtedly many other women must have had this right but we never hear of them owing to the necessarily incomplete picture which haphazard finds of papyri provide. As well, there must have been women in this position who are referred to in surviving non-commercial/legal documents — such as letters — where to mention the *ius liberorum* would be irrelevant. By way of illustration printed below is *P. Oxy.* 12 (1916) 1467, a petition — probably dated 263 — in which a woman claims the right to act without a *kyrios* in virtue of having three children and her ability to write. The first few lines are lost.

·   ·   ·   ·   ·   ·   ·

[. .] . α̣[. . .] . . [.] . . . . [. . .,] δ[ιαση-
μότατε ἡγεμών, οἵτινες
ἐξουσίαν διδόασιν ταῖς γυναι-
ξὶν ταῖς τῶν τριῶν τέκνων
5 δικαίῳ κεκοσμημένα[ι]ς ἑαυτῶν κυριεύειν καὶ χωρ[ὶς] κυρίου χρηματίζειν ἐν αἷς ποι-
οῦν[τ]αι οἰκονομίαις, πο[λλ]ῷ
δὲ πλέον ταῖς γρά[μ]ματα
10 ἐπισταμέναις. καὶ αὐτὴ τοίνυν τῷ μὲν κόσμῳ τῆς εὐ-
παιδείας εὐτυχήσασα,
ἐγγράμματος δὲ κα[ὶ ἐ]ς τὰ
μάλιστα γράφειν εὐκόπως
15 δυναμένη, ὑπὸ περισσῆς

ἀσφαλείας διὰ τούτων μου
τῶ[ν] βιβλειδίων προσφω⟨νῶ⟩
τῷ σῷ μεγέθι πρὸς τὸ δύνα-
σθαι ἀνεμποδίστως ἃς ἐν-
20 τεῦθεν ποιοῦμαι οἰκ[ον]ομία[ς
διαπράσσεσθαι. ἀξιῶ ἔχε[ιν
αὐτὰ ἀπροκρίτως το[ῖς δι-
καίοις μ[ο]υ ἐν τῇ σῇ τοῦ [δια-
σημοτάτου τ[ά]ξι, ἵν' ὦ β[εβο-
25 ηθ[η]μένη κ[α]ὶ εἰ[σ]αεὶ ὁ[μοίας ?
χάριτας ὁμολογήσω. διευτ[ύ]χ[ει.
Αὐρηλία Θαϊσ[ο]ῦς ἡ καὶ Λολλ[ι-
ανὴ διεπεμψάμην πρὸς ἐ-
πίδοσιν. ἔτους ι Ἐπείφ κα̣.
30 ἔσται σο[ῦ] τὰ̣ βιβλία ἐν τῇ [τάξι.

--- (There exist laws), most eminent prefect, which give authority to women
5 who are endowed with the right of three children | to be independent and to
negotiate without a *kyrios* in transactions which they undertake, and
10 particularly to women who know how to write. | And I myself, then, being
fortunate by being endowed with plenty of children, and being literate and
15 able to write with especial fluency, | by my abundant security through this
application of mine, I address your highness to be able to perform without
20 hindrance | the transactions which I undertake from now on. I request you to
hold it (my application) without prejudice to my rights in the office of your
25 eminence, so that I may receive help | and acknowledge my eternal thanks.
Farewell. I Aurelia Thaisous, also called Lolliane, have sent it for
30 presentation. Year 10, Epeiph 21. | Your application will be (kept) in the
office.

To supplement Sijpesteijn's list of women with this right the following texts
culled from 1976 and 1977 publications may be noted:—

P. Mil. Vogl. 6.269 (Tebtynis, 124), a sub-lease of land which includes a house; the
text forms part of a family archive. Philotera, daughter of Ptolemaios, hands
over the concession χω]ρὶς κ[υ]ρίο(υ) (*l.*31; cf. *l.*1, χω(ρὶς) [κυρίου]).

SB 12.11233 (= C. Wehrli, *ZPE* 12[1973] 75-85, pl.3; Oxyhrynchos, 4/6/247), a
very long act of sale to another woman by the illiterate (cf. L.C. Youtie, *ZPE*
21[1976] 15) Aurelia Germania χωρὶς κυρίου χρη[ματ]ίζουσα κατὰ τὰ Ῥωμαίων ἔθη
τέκνων δικαίῳ (*ll.*2-3).

P. Wiscon. 2.58 (Ptolemais Euergetis, Philadelphia, 5/4/298), sale of a small
building to Aurelia Tapaesis [χωρὶς κυρίου χρηματιζούσῃ κατὰ τὰ Ῥωμαί]ων ἔθη
τέκνων δικαίῳ (*ll.*5-6). The first part of this restoration is clear in the copy of this
text, *P. Wiscon.* 2.59 (these two documents, still unpublished at the time of
Sijpesteijn's article, were included by him there as no.44a).

P. Coll. Youtie 2 (1976) 92 (Antinoopolis, 569), a loan of money; this document is of some interest for the history of slavery in the late Roman/early Byzantine period. Martha, a salt-fish seller, acts without her *kyrios* to redeem her sister Prokla from slavery to one man and to transfer her to a similarly servile position to another man, the advantage being that with the latter eventual redemption is envisaged. In passing one may note that in this Christian text Martha addresses the secretary of the ducal staff who has been moved to act τῇ εἰς θ(εὸ)ν ἀγάπῃ (*l.*23).

P. Mich. 13.663 (Aphrodite, VI), sale of parts of a house to several people by Aurelia Maria, acting apparently without a *kyrios* in view of *ll.*36-40 where she speaks in the first person of having executed the sale and agreed to the terms.

Probably related to this group are those women designated as ματρῶναι στολᾶται. The rank of such women and the legal significance of the term is not clear. It is a latinism which appears a few times in the papyri. S. Daris, *Il Lessico latino nel greco d'Egitto* (Barcelona, 1971) 109, lists 15 examples, all dated III except one (IAD). This provides some indication of how relatively frequent the term became after the *Constitutio Antoniniana* of 212 (on the date see Sijpesteijn, 177 n.1, with his references there). This parallels the frequency with which the χωρὶς κυρίου clause occurs: of the 83 examples in Sijpesteijn's table (180-87) all but 10 are to be dated after 212. *P. Coll. Youtie* 2 (1976) 68 (Oxyrhynchos, Sept. 266) is a lease of flax land by Aurelia Herakleidiaine to other people. She is described as a ματρῶνα στολᾶτα (*l.*1), which J.R. Rea (who edits this papyrus) takes to mean (p.461) that she has the right to act χωρὶς κυρίου, but that a link with the *ius liberorum* should not necessarily be accepted. The phrase appears also at *P. Laur.* 1 (1976) 11, *recto l.*2, in a report concerning a silver account made to Aurelia Demetria, a woman well known from other texts (Arsinoite nome, 248 or 250). Among earlier texts note particularly *P. Ryl.* 2 (1915) 165.9-10 (partly restored), where a woman appears to be described as both ματρῶνα στολᾶτα and χωρὶς κυρίου χρηματίζουσα τέκνων δικαίῳ (Hermopolite nome, 266; this text is no.32 in Sijpesteijn's list).

Meriting discussion here, too, are several papyrus texts which should be considered in a slightly different category. In *BGU* 13 (1976) 2225 (Arsinoite polis, 189) a woman registers her ownership of a house and court via her *kyrios*, Heron. But at *l.*6 she registers ἐματ[ὴν καὶ τοὺς ἐμούς, κτλ], 'myself and my family'. If this restoration in *ed.pr.* is reasonable the papyrus should be related to a series of others recently reconsidered by H.C. Youtie, *ZPE* 14 (1974) 261-62. *P. Mil. Vogl.* 3 (1965) 193a, 193b, 194a, 194b are census returns all submitted by women who are heads of households. Youtie points out that each acts with a *kyrios* (e.g., 194b.5-6), but declares herself and her children (*ll.*13-15); he suggests that these are her children by a now-divorced husband (the participle ἀποπεπλεγμένος is to be taken in this sense in nos.193b, 194a, 194b — the last largely restored). Youtie believes that 'what we have in Nos.193 and 194 are fragments of a roll composed of declarations made by women with children who had been married and were now divorced, or had never married, and so were in charge of their own households. The roll may also have included declarations from women who were in this position because their husbands had died' (260-61).

Note also the concluding greeting in a letter, *P. Wiscon.* 72 (provenance unknown; II), from Caecilius Gemellus, a soldier, to Didymarion, τῇ ἀδελφῇ | καὶ κυρίᾳ (*ll.*2-3). After a final request to buy some olives he says (*ll.*23-29):

> ἐροτῶ δέ σε, ἀδελφή, γρά-
> ψον μοι ἐν τάχι περὶ τῆς
> 25 σοτερίας σου καὶ τῶν τέ-
> κνον σου. ἄσ⟨πασ⟩αι πάντες
> τοὺς σοὺς κα[ὶ τ]οὺς ἐν τῷ
> οἴκῳ σου πάντας. ἐρρῶ⟨σ⟩θαί
> σε εὔχομ[αι] .

25 **I ask you sister, write to me quickly about | your health and that of your children. Greet all your people and all those in your family. I pray that you fare well.**

Here apparently is another *oikos* controlled by a woman. While *ed.pr.* mentions that Didymarion is probably Gemellus' wife, he also raises a doubt about this by noting the repeated use of the second person singular, e.g., the health of *your* (rather than *our*) children.

All this brings us back to Lydia again. Unless Luke in focussing upon her accords to her an initiative and independence which is misleading we should consider whether she is a widow or a divorcee; the possibility should not be ruled out that she may be a freedwoman with the requisite number of children to entitle her to certain rights under the *ius liberorum*. A particular caution is in order, however. Under Roman law what may be relevant for well-to-do female Roman citizens in Egypt may not apply to a freedwoman in Macedonia. In earlier periods Roman law did not have universal and consistent application to those who lived in different areas of the Empire. The competition between legal systems is a problem still awaiting definitive resolution by modern scholars, but note most recently H.J. Wolff, *Das Problem der Konkurrenz von Rechtsordnungen in der Antike* (Heidelberg, 1979).

On the influence of Tyre on upper Galilee note R.S. Hanson, *Tyrian influence in the Upper Galilee* (*Meiron Excavation Project* no.2; Cambridge, Mass., 1980), where it is suggested that from the Hellenistic to the end of the Roman period Upper Galilee was oriented towards Tyre, at least economically.

4. 'The Prefect says . . .'

Oxyrhynchos or Fayum   120
ed.pr. — G.M. Parássoglou, *ZPE* 13 (1974) 21-37 (pl.2)

> Ἀντίγραφον προστάγματος.   Τίτος Ἀτέριος Νέπως
> ἔπαρχος Αἰγύπτου λέγει·   ὁ κύριος ἡμῶν καὶ θεὸ[ς]
> ἐνφανέστατος αὐτοκράτωρ Καῖσαρ Τραϊανὸς Ἀδριανὸς
> Σεβαστὸς καταστήσας, ὥσπερ ἴστε, τῶν θεῶν Σεβαστῶν
> 5 καὶ τοῦ μεγάλου Σαρά[πιδος ἀ]ρχιϊερέα καὶ ἐπὶ τ[ῶ]ν
> [κατὰ Ἀλεξάνδ]ρε[ιαν καὶ κατὰ Αἴγυ]πτον ἱερῶν .[

Fragment A, the best preserved of seven fragments of a Yale papyrus in poor condition. It belongs to the first of three columns of text. Parássoglou suggests that *P. Fouad* 1 (1939) 10 is part of the same edict. The *recto* of A contains an unrelated tax document.

Bib. — *SB* 11236.

> **Copy of an edict. Titus Haterius Nepos, prefect of Egypt says: our lord and god most manifest imperator Caesar Trajan Hadrian Augustus having**
> 5 **appointed, as you know [NN] as high priest of the gods Augusti | and of great Sarapis and in charge of the cults in Alexandria and in Egypt . . .**

The style of edicts like this affords a parallel to the form of the 'letters' to the Churches in the early chapters of Revelation (*New Docs 1976*, **9**, pp.39-40). This new papyrus provides us with more than just another example of the same in view of the way Hadrian is spoken of: ὁ κύριος ἡμῶν καὶ θεὸ[ς] |ἐνφανέστατος αὐτο-κράτωρ. The spread of the nouns κύριος and θεός (linked in various combinations) across the NT books is noteworthy: in the synoptics almost always quoting verses from Deut. 6 (Mt. 4.7 = Deut. 6.16; Mt. 4.10 = Lk. 4.8, 12 = Deut. 6.13; Mt. 22.37 = Mk. 12.30 = Lk. 10.27 = Deut. 6.5; Mk. 12.29 = Deut. 6.4), or alluding to the OT (Lk. 1.32; 20.32), or in a psalm (Lk. 1.68); note also Lk. 1.16. The pair occurs twice in Acts at 2.39 (where there is allusion to several OT passages) and 3.22 (= Deut. 18.15). The combination is not found in any of the epistles or Jn. But in Rev. the pair occurs in 11 of the 21 places where κύριος is used, mostly in addresses (e.g., 4.11). Note, further, Rev. 11.17; 15.3; 16.7; 19.6; 21.22 where παντοκράτωρ is added (cf. αὐτοκράτωρ in the papyrus above). None of the combinations occurs in the Letters to the Churches in ch. 2 and 3. G. Mussies, *The Morphology of Koine Greek as used in the Apocalypse of St. John* (*NovT Suppl.* 27; Leiden, 1971), does not discuss such vocabulary matters, but his general conclusion (352) that Jn. and Rev. have different authors receives support from this item of usage. Despite H.B. Swete, *The Apocalypse of John* (London, 1922³) 11 (*ad* 1.8), the combination of the two nouns need not be seen as derived exclusively from the OT. For κύριος used of a god see **6** below.

Parássoglou (27) mentions the problem of speaking of the living Hadrian as θεός here, although he does provide instances where it is used of Augustus, and two examples dated II one of which refers to Hadrian: *BGU* 1 (1895) 19.21 (135AD), προσφυγεῖν τῇ χάριτι τοῦ θεοῦ ἐπιφανεστάτου αὐτοκράτορος (for the phrase, ἡ χάρις τοῦ θεοῦ, see discussion in **116**). Parássoglou suggests that, given that our new text is a copy (*l*.1), θεός was added by the scribe writing after the death of Hadrian. Is it not simpler to assume that Hadrian is being thought of as the Pharaoh (and therefore divine) in a document for public consumption? Titles accorded to the Emperor varied not only with time but also with geographical locality. Inhabitants of the province of Asia had no trouble in calling its ruler θεός either. For epigraphic evidence of the first Caesars being called θεός see V. Ehrenberg/A.H.M. Jones, *Documents Illustrating the Reigns of Augustus and Tiberius* (Oxford, 1955²), e.g., nos.72, 88, 128. On divine honours attributed to Constantine — after his death — see **107**. The adjective ἐμφανής used of God occurs at Rom. 10.20 (quoting Is. 65.1); and note particularly Acts 10.40 where Peter speaks of the resurrected Christ as having revealed himself, clearly an attribution of divinity.

In *ll*.4-6 the subject of the edict is given, namely the appointment of the high-priest in Egypt, which leads on in the later fragments (not reprinted here) to regulations governing various temple activities. For this part and discussion of the high-priests of Egypt in general see Parássoglou, 32-37 (includes bibliography and a list of known high-priests and their deputies).

5. Politarchs

There have been three important studies by classicists of this term in the last quarter-cntury. (1) C. Schuler, *CP* (1960) 90-100 (cf. J.H. Oliver, *CP* 58 [1963] 164–65), provides a list (96-98) of all inscriptions known which refer to politarchs of Macedonia (the majority, 18 plus one doubtful out of a list of 32, come from Thessalonike). He is able to establish from his investigation a number of features of this office (90-91): the politarchate was widespread in Macedonian cities including Beroia as well as Thessalonike, but is not found at Roman colonies like Philippi in the province; the number of such magistrates — who came from wealthier families — varied from city to city; the office was of annual tenure, could be held more than once and contemporaneously with other offices. The incident in Acts 17.1-9 suggests that the Thessalonian politarchs were invested with judicial authority of some kind, and although we cannot define its nature more closely, E.A. Judge has offered some suggestions in *RTR* 30 (1971) 1-7. By mid-III the title had become largely honorific. Schuler believed that the politarchate was not instituted in Macedonia before the Roman period: either they introduced it or it was 'at least basically altered by them' (96). Our earliest definitely datable inscription providing evidence for the institution comes from 119/8BC. However, a very long (216 lines) gymnasiarchal law from Beroia refers twice to politarchs; but there is no agreement about its date beyond that it belongs to the second century BC (Schuler, 94, thinks 167-50 and not later than 150; J.M.R. Cormack, in *Ancient Macedonia*, II — see below — 140-41, opts for the 20 years before 148BC, when Macedonia became a Roman province; most recently B. Helly, 544 n.32 — see below — suggests c.140–120BC). (2) F. Gschnitzner, *PW Suppl.* 13 (1973) 483-500, provides a very useful survey of the evidence and includes discussion of the term found outside Macedonia. Both he and Schuler differentiated the πολίταρχοι of Thessaly from the Macedonian πολιτάρχαι. (3) But B. Helly, *Ancient Macedonia* II, 531-44 (3 pl.) — cf. *SEG* 243 — shows by a careful study of these and related terms (πολίαρχος/πολίταρχος, πολιάρχης/πολιτάρχης, πολι-φύλαξ/πολιτοφύλαξ) that Thessaly's poliarchs and Macedonia's politarchs are essentially the same. This means that we can no longer hold to the previous claim that the Macedonian politarchate was created by the Romans in 167BC. Furthermore, contrary to the commonly-held belief that Acts 17.6, 8 provides our only literary attestation of the word, Helly (533) points to Aeneas Tacticus 26.12 (IVBC) where πολίταρχος occurs: the difference in the suffix -αρχος/-αρχης is simply one of dialect. K. Lake and H.J. Cadbury had noted in their commentary on Acts (*Beginnings of Christianity* I.4 [London, 1933] *ad* 17.6) that 'the word is also found in the form πολίταρχος'.

Obsolete discussions dating back to the end of last century have remained the reference points in some works for the biblical field. Schuler's article was known to A.N. Sherwin-White, *Roman Society and Roman Law in the New Testament* (Oxford, 1963) 96, n.1, but Haenchen's commentary on Acts (14th German edition = ET, 1971) refers to nothing more recent than the 1890s (p.508, n.1). MM added a notice of a *P.Oxy.* text from Egypt which mentions a politarch; but BAGD, s.v., has not gone beyond the 1890s and MM in its references to secondary literature. The MM and BAGD entries both need a complete overhaul, in view of the recent philological discussion and epigraphical documentation: nearly four times as many politarch inscriptions from Thessalonike alone are now known as are mentioned in works like Haenchen, and H.J. Cadbury, *The Book of Acts in History* (London, 1955) 41.

The final line of the gymnasiarchal law from Beroia, published by J.M.R. Cormack in *Ancient Macedonia*, II, 139-50 (3 pl.) — see **82**, where other items of vocabulary are noted — reads: παρὰ τῶν πολιταρχῶν οὐ εἰς *vac.*, 'one of the politarchs voted "no" on the decree' (the word occurs also at side A, *l.*42, but is not very clear; Cormack lacks it in his *ed.pr.*, but *SEG* 261 prints it, drawing upon *BE* [1978] 274). The only other Beroian inscription mentioning these officials is dated IAD and refers to five of them (Cormack, 140). The account of the Beroia incident (Acts 17.10-14) is briefer than the immediately prior narrative of what happened at Thessalonike (17.1-9), but since in both places the Jews 'stirred up the mob' (vv.8, 13) and the politarchs at Thessalonike had to handle the situation, it is not unlikely that it also fell to the politarchs at Beroia to deal with the problem in their city.

For Roman officials of Macedonia from Augustus to Diocletian (27BC-284AD) note T.C. Sarikakis, Ῥωμαῖοι ἄρχοντες τῆς ἐπαρχείας Μακεδονίας, II (Thessaloniki, 1977). This volume (*non vidi*; cf. *SEG* 242) provides a prosopography covering the provinces of Macedonia, Achaia (cf. Gallio ἀνθύπατος of Achaia, Acts 18.12), and Moesia. Sarikakis, vol. I, covers the period 148-27BC.

6. An acclamation to 'the Lord, forever'

S. Mitchell, *AS* 27 (1977) 64-65, no.1 (= *SEG* 853) is an acclamation, possibly to Caracalla, which reads Ἀγαθῆι Τύχηι | εἰς αἰῶνα | τὸν ἀνεί|κητον, 'For good fortune. (Extol) forever the unconquered one' (Ankara, III). Mitchell refers to another inscription which carries related wording, εἰς αἰῶνα τὸν Κύριον, where the last word refers to an Emperor. For κύριος of an emperor in the NT note Acts 25.26. While not wishing to deny Semitic associations with the phraseology of the NT, one may at least compare with these acclamations the way in which God/ Christ *qua* βασιλεύς is sometimes spoken of. Note Lk. 1.33, βασιλεύσει εἰς τοὺς αἰῶνας; Rev. 11.15; 15.3; cf. 22.5 (of God's servants). Blessing and glory are also offered to God with the phrase εἰς τοὺς αἰῶνας at passages like Rom. 1.25; 9.5; 11.36; 2 Cor. 11.31.

For κύριος used of a god note, among 1977 publications, *SEG* 727, Θεό|φιλ|ος παρὰ τῷ κυρί|ῳ (Benler, near Teos in Ionia, n.d., *ed.pr.*). G. Petzl in M. Baran/ G. Petzl, *MDAI* 27/28 (1977/78) 306-07 no.4 (ph.) thinks that κύριος here may refer to Apollo or some other god, or that the inscription (found in a cave) may be Christian. *AE* 759 (Noviodunum in Moesia, II²) is a dedication made by two men θεῷ(ι) κ[υ]ρίῳ(ι) Ἡρακλ|εῖ. *I. Tyre* 1.1 (28/29) is a fragmentary dedication whose first line reads --- Ἀπόλλωνι κυρίω. Hajjar, *Triade* I.18 (pp.35-37) is a dedication from Baalbek-Heliopolis (Syria) of a statue in accordance with an oracle (κατὰ χ[ρη]|[ματισ]μόν, 7-8) to Διὶ μεγ[ίσ]τω Ἡλιοπολείτη | κυρίω (3-4); see Hajjar, 36 n.1, for further discussion and references. Cf. *Triade* I.169 for another example. See also **4** above.

7. A sacrificial calendar

An inscription (IV¹ BC) from the Attic deme Thorikos containing a sacrificial calendar, first published in 1975, has provided an intriguing epigraphical example of 'a murder without the corpse'. E. Vanderpool in *Thorikos and the Laurion in Archaic and Classical Times*, edd. H. Mussche et al. (Ghent, 1975), 33-42, published a transcription of a text made some time before by a man who was not himself able to see the stone. G. Dunst, *ZPE* 27 (1977) 243-64, published another, much fuller, version of what is clearly the same inscription, but again without direct access to the stone itself. J. Labarbe, *Thorikos Test.*, no.50, pp.56-64, has re-edited the text again. Mentions of the calendar have appeared in *SEG* 26 (1976/7) 136; *BE* (1976) 235, (1977) 186, (1979) 187. Most recently G. Daux, *CRAI* (1980) 463-70, has announced that the stele has now come to light and that he will publish it fully in the near future. A definitive text is lacking, therefore, but a few observations may be made on what appears secure.

The Dunst/Labarbe version extends for over 60 lines on one column and a few fragmentary ones on a second. The date is agreed to on the basis of letter forms, the use of the stoichedon ('grid' pattern) style of incising letters on the stone, and certain orthographical features. The text provides us with a list by Attic months of sacrifices, to be performed by the people of Thorikos, designated for particular deities and local heroes. Dunst's analysis sets forth this information clearly (250-60). Several different festivals are mentioned, and the variety of animals to be used in sacrifice is considerable (sheep, goat, ox, etc., but differing ages and quality are specified for particular occasions). It is occasionally stated (*Thorikos Test.* no.50, *ll.*9-10, 11-12, 23, 26, 27) that following the sacrifice of the animal its flesh is to be available for sale. The bald nature of the text encapsulates this in the single word πρατός following the name of the animal, e.g., *l.*23, Ἀθηνᾶι οἶν πρατόν, '(sacrifice) for Athena a sheep which may be sold'. Carcases or portions thereof which could be removed from the temple and sold provided a source of income for the cult in question (Dunst, 262). That this practice was entirely normal in the Graeco-Roman world is reflected, in the case of the NT, in the specific Jewish-Christian concern expressed in the communique circulated after the first Jerusalem Council, ἀπέχεσθαι εἰδωλοθύτων (Acts 15.29; cf. v.20, τοῦ ἀπέχεσθαι τῶν ἀλισγημάτων τῶν εἰδώλων), but which Paul subsequently felt was not a black-and-white issue (1 Cor. 8.1-13; 10.23-33). Again, at the second Jerusalem Council James uses the same phraseology (Acts 21.25). The conjunction of τὸ εἰδωλόθυτον with warnings against sexual sins found in the Acts passages appears again at Rev. 2.14, 20, and serves as one small indicator of the Jewish-Christian background of the writer of Rev. That this author is alert to the Hellenic milieu is not in doubt, however: see briefly *New Docs 1976*, **22**. τὸ εἰδωλόθυτον with its related forms came across into Christian usage from Judaism and appears always to have a derogatory connotation. It need not always refer to meat sacrifice, for all sorts of foodstuffs were offered to the gods, including meal, honey, cheese, liquids, etc.; see the following paragraph. But an animal would constitute the only offering of sufficient size that a saleable portion would be left over following the sacrifice. On Christian butchers see briefly *New Docs 1976*, **86**. *MPR* 28 mentions a butchers' guild in an inscription which contains a cross (Tomis, VI).

One other word in the calendar merits attention here. In place of the offering of a sheep or a pig to a deity, occasionally a τράπεζα is specified (*Thorikos Test*. no.50, *ll*.17, 19, 30, 44-45, 49, 51), e.g., Ἡρωΐνησι Θορίκο | τράπεζαν, 'for the Heroines of Thorikos, a *trapeza*' (18-19). In such a context the word refers to 'une collection de θύματα, probablement non sanglants, tels que fruits, gâteaux, fromages' (Labarbe, p.60). Dunst observes (261) that in all six cases in the inscription the *trapeza* is provided for female deities. This is merely an idiosyncrasy of that particular calendar, however; *IG* II² (1913, repr. 1974) 1363. 11-12 (Eleusis, IIIBC init.(?)) specifies a *trapeza* for Poseidon in another sacrificial calendar. A table of offerings for a god is mentioned in inscriptions from Iasos (cf. *BE* [1971] 624), Labraunda (cf. *BE* [1973] 413) and elsewhere. A Christian inscription from Macedonia (cf. *BE* [1970] 360) speaks of τὸ βῆμα τῆς τραπέζης. See Dunst n.37 for further references, but note in particular S. Dow/D.M. Gill, *AJA* 69 (1965) 103-14. In the NT and elsewhere τράπεζα may be used in an extended sense of the thing which rests on a table, such as a meal (e.g. Acts 16.34; probably also 6.2) or a bank (Lk. 19.23). The allusions to the messianic heavenly banquet (Lk. 22.30; Rom. 11.9(?), quoting Ps. 68.23) begin to move us into the area of a cultic meal; and certainly οὐ δύνασθε τραπέζης κυρίου μετέχειν καὶ τραπέζης δαιμονίων (1 Cor. 10.21) has the reader thinking in those terms. Numerous other examples are referred to in BAGD, s.v., 2; MM's entry for τράπεζα lacks any discussion of this usage. On papyrus invitations to cult meals and the relevance of their terminology for several passages in 1 Cor., see *New Docs 1976*, **1.** In the Fathers the notion of a Christian cult meal expressed by τράπεζα is abundantly attested in Lampe, s.v., B.6, especially B.6.b of the Last Supper, with phrases like μετέχειν τῆς ἱερᾶς τραπέζης and ὁ τραπέζης κοινωνήσας μυστικῆς (both Chrysostom).

8. Answer from an oracle

Provenance unknown   I fin.
ed.pr. — *P. Vindob.Salomons* 1, pp.1-7 (pl.1)

> Ὑπὲρ ὧν ἠξίωσας· ὑγιαίνεις.
> Ὃ ἐνθυμεῖς διὰ νυκτὸς καὶ ἡμέρας
> ἔστε σοί· εἰς ὃ θέλεις οἱ θεοί σε ὁδαγήσου-
> σιν καὶ ὁ βίος σου ἐπὶ τὸ βέλτιον ἔστε
> 5 καὶ εὐσχημόνως τὸ ζῆν ἕξεις.

A complete papyrus, *verso* blank.

> **Concerning the things about which you asked. You are well. What you desire night and day will be yours. As for what you want the gods will guide you**
> 5 **and your livelihood will be for the better | and your life will be distinguished.**

Literary essays like Plutarch's *de defectu oraculorum* (*Moralia* 409E–438E) have been formative in conveying the general impression that oracles in the early Roman Empire no longer possessed the great prestige and influence which they held in the classical Greek and Hellenistic periods. Anecdotes help to reinforce this view, such as that concerning Oribasius' visit to Delphi on behalf of the emperor Julian in the fourth century, where he was told that this was the last oracle that Apollo would give (preserved by Cedrenus, quoted in Loeb *Julian* III, intro. p.lvii). Yet this picture needs to be treated with some care, for papyrus finds have yielded a considerable number of texts of Roman date — so too have inscriptions though in smaller quantity — which fall into the general category of oracular material. If the decline of the classical oracle centres is a largely accurate perception of what was occurring, the popularity of this form of consultation about the future had not waned at least in Egypt. For the Egyptians' own oracular tradition extended back considerably further than did the Greeks'. Some of the oracle material survives in Demotic, not only Greek; and in Roman Egypt we should probably see the ready consultation of a wide range of deities as a survival of the indigenous tradition. Greek settlement in Egypt had no doubt caused some interpenetration of the two traditions, but the basic form appears to have remained Egyptian, even if Greek was the language used. For some bibliography on this see *ed.pr.*, pp.2, 3; and A. Henrichs, *ZPE* 11 (1973) 115 n.1.

The survival of questions put to an oracle are far more common than answers such as the text above. This ought not to occasion surprise. For one of the ways of seeking divine guidance was for the seeker to write his request — or deliver it orally before the god's statue — in a standard form: address (sometimes in a prayer-style), the question, request for an answer. This format shares some affinities with letters and petitions (*ed.pr.*, p.3). What is so unusual about the text above is that it appears to be an answer, not a question: the only other answer from an oracle known to Salomons is *P.Aberd.* (1939) 14 (III?; this two-line, partly metrical text is regarded by *ed.pr.* as 'possibly' an oracle answer for someone considering going on a journey); for a Christian example, see below. We can readily understand the survival in written form of questions if we think of them being left at the temple after presentation to the god by the petitioner. But a problem not raised explicitly by Salomons is why an oracle's answer would be written down. For a suggestion about this, see below.

On the wording of this text, the opening clause may remind us of 1 Cor. 7.1, περὶ ὧν ἐγράψατε. It is unclear whether βίος should mean 'life' or 'livelihood', but the latter has been preferred here in view of τὸ ζῆν in the following line. For εὐσχημόνως see **50**.

Commentators not infrequently draw attention to the triviality of the questions put to the god in these contexts. It is important not to confuse what is common in human experience with the banale. Questions about marriage, going on a journey, and advancing in one's career, figure large in the surviving examples; but each was of importance for the particular individual who importuned the god. For all their lack of context these brief documents illustrate common concerns of the time. Personal and domestic matters are to the fore, as was the case in the great Greek centres; but matters of wider importance, such as international politics, were also raised at the latter, but are scarcely in evidence in the papyri. (This may be a reflection, in part, of the medium of survival. Thus, Diocletian consulted an oracle whether he should presecute the Christians, an incident of the kind likely to be preserved in a literary tradition: in this case Lactantius, *de mort. pers.* 11.7.)

Some other oracles noted among 1977 publications include: *SB* 11226, 11227 (= A. Henrichs, *ZPE* 11 [1973] 114-19; respectively: Arsinoite nome, II/III, to Isis; and Soknopaiu Nesos, II, to lord Soknopaios and invincible Ammon). From beyond Egypt note *BE* 334 which mentions a restoration to an oracle found at Kos (IIIBC), noted previously at *BE* (1959) 229; and *BE* 398 which mentions supplements to an oracle from Smyrna (time of Alexander the Great), noted earlier at BE (1962) 281. A particularly intriguing inscription is *SEG* 933, which incorporates an oracle of Klarian Apollo and was set up at Oinoanda in Lykia (late III):

[α]ὐτοφυὴς ἀδίδακτος ἀμήτωρ ἀστυφέλικτος,
οὔνομα μὴ χωρῶν, πολυώνυμος, ἐν πυρὶ ναίων·
τοῦτο θεός, μεικρὰ δὲ θεοῦ μερὶς ἄγγελοι ἡμεῖς.
τοῦτο πευθομένοισι θεοῦ πέρι, ὅστις ὑπάρχει,
5 Αἰ[θ]έ[ρ]α πανδερκ[ῆ θε]ὸν ἔννεπεν, εἰς ὃν ὁρῶντας
εὔχεσθ' ἠῷους πρὸς ἀντολίην ἐσορῶ[ν]τα[ς].

Self-existent, untaught, without a mother, undisturbed, of many names although not spreading abroad his name, dwelling in fire: this is God, and we messengers are a small portion of God. To those enquiring about God, who
5 **he is, this is | what it (i.e., the oracle) said: that Aither is the all-seeing God, looking to whom pray at dawn as you look towards the east.**

Since its new publication in 1971 — G.E. Bean, *Journeys in Northern Lycia (Denkschr. Öst. Ak. Wiss. ph.-hist. Kl.*, 104; Vienna) no.37, pp.20-22 — this inscription has attracted several important discussions: L. Robert, *CRAI* (1971) 597-619, who showed that it includes an oracular response from Klarian Apollo, delivered probably to a citizen of Oinoanda; M. Guarducci, *RAL* 27 (1973) 335-47 (*non vidi*); C. Gallavotti, *Philologus* 121 (1977) 95-105, who argues that it is a religious manifesto rather than an oracle (but note *l*.4, and cf. *BE* [1978] 464); A.S. Hall, *ZPE* 32 (1978) 263-68 (pls. 11-13a; cf. *BE* [1978] 506). Hall emphasized the position of the inscription in a wall which received the day's first sunlight. A closely-adjacent dedication of a lamp (τὸν λύχνον) to *Theos Hypsistos* by a freed-woman (*CIG* 4380n[2], reprinted by Hall, p.265), suggests further the link with light. Hall argues that Helios is an appropriate deity to be thought of in this oracular inscription. As Robert noted (*CRAI*, p.610) the text offers a remarkable indicator of the trend towards monotheism. A number of philosophical and theological perspectives appear to be merged together at a popular level in this text. Note the negative theology of the first line. The ἄγγελοι of *l*.3 probably do not refer to the citizens of the town who belong to a private association, as Gallavotti argues, but to the gods (so *BE* [1978] 464) who as messengers form a portion in the one God: 'we gods are each an aspect of God'. This would fit with an oracular utterance from Apollo about what God is like.

Returning to the oracles of the style which began this discussion, they have counterparts in the Christian period which provide a very clear illustration of the assimilation of non-Christian forms to Christian use. K. Treu has published one such at *APF* 24/25 (1976) 120 (= *MPL* 2 [1977] 254). *P. Berl.* 13232 is of Byzantine date (provenance unknown):

$$+ \text{Μὴ βλάψης τὴν}$$
$$\text{ψυχήν σου ἐκ } \overline{\text{θυ}}$$
$$\text{γὰρ τὸ γενάμενον.}$$

Do not harm your soul. For what has happened is from God.

The cross and the *nomen sacrum* are the indicators of Christianity here. We may note that we have an answer from, not a question to, an oracle. Why would it have been written down? Generalized as the wording is, and commonplace as the situation to which it may have been addressed, nevertheless the response may have been felt sufficiently helpful that the recipient wanted to keep it — perhaps even wear it on his person as an amulet. Thinking back to *P. Vindob. Salomons* 1, with which this entry began, perhaps it was preserved by the petitioner of the god as a real and valued divine answer to his question. The wearing of magical charms was commonplace, and the preservation of this oracle answer because it was used as an amulet might be worth consideration. However, it should be pointed out that no mention is made by Salomons or Treu of the presence on either papyrus of folds which might indicate an amulet function (cf. *New Docs 1976*, **57**; for two amulets see **22** and **64** in that same volume).

Van Haelst lists four Christian oracles, to which the new example from Treu should be added:

1. *P.Oxy.* 6 (1908) 925 (V/VI), enquiry to God about a journey; van Haelst 954.
2. *P.Oxy.* 8 (1911) 1150 (VI), prayer to 'the God of St. Philoxenos' whether Anoup should be taken to hospital; van Haelst 958.
3. *P.Harr.* (1936) 54 (Oxyrhynchos, VI); van Haelst 915.

> † δέσποτά μου $\overline{\text{θεὲ}}$ παντοκράτωρ καὶ ἅγιε
> Φιλόξενε πρόστατά μου, παρακαλῶ ὑμᾶς
> διὰ τὸ μέγα ὄνομα τοῦ δεσπότου θεοῦ, ἐὰν θέλημα
> ὑμῶν ἐστιν καὶ συνέρχεσθέ μοι λαβεῖν τὴν τραπεζιτί῾αν
> 5   παρακαλῶ κελεῦσαί μοι μαθεῖν καὶ λαλῆσαι †
> (*verso*) † χμγ   † χμγ   † χμγ

My master God almighty and St. Philoxenos my patron, I request you, because of the great name of the master God, if it is your will and you go
5 **with me to get the bank, | I request you bid me learn this and speak (i.e., make an offer for it).**

4. *P.Oxy.* 16 (1924) 1926 (VI); van Haelst 963.

> † δέσποτά μου θεὲ παντοκράτωρ καὶ ἅγι(ε)
> Φιλόξενε πρόστατά μου, παρακαλῶ ὑμᾶς
> διὰ τὸ μέγα ὄνομ(α) τοῦ δεσπότου θεοῦ, ἐὰν οὐκ ἔστιν
> θέλημα ὑμῶν μὴ λαλῆσαί με μηδὲ περὶ τραπεζ(ιτίας) μηδὲ
> 5   περὶ ζυγοστασείας, παρακελεῦσαί με μαθεῖν ἵνα μὴ λαλήσω †
> (*verso*) † χμγ   † χμγ   † χμγ †

. . . (As for no. 3) . . . if it is not your will that I speak either about the bank
5 **or | about the weighing office, bid me learn so that I do not speak.**

H.C. Youtie, *ZPE* 18 (1975) 253-57 (pl.8) has revised these last two texts and his readings are incorporated above. He showed (with the help of R. Coles) that they are not merely similarly worded, but that they are twin texts, cut from the same papyrus sheet. They provide the positive and the negative formulations of the same request to 'God and St. Philoxenos'. Youtie mentions (254 n.3) the existence of a church of St. Philoxenos at Oxyrhynchos. On χμγ see **104**.

Moving from documentary to sub-literary texts we may note briefly L.L. Gunderson's discussion of the Judaeo-Christian Sibylline Oracles and their comments on Alexander the Great, in *Ancient Macedonia*, II, 55–66. Gunderson suggests that books 3 and 11 reveal their author to be an Alexandrian Jew, for parts of these sections read like Jewish Apocalyptic literature. There appears to be a strong allusion to Dan. 7.7 at bk. 3.397-400 where Alexander is spoken of as a beast with ten horns. In the case of bk. 11 he suggests a date of composition between 30BC–late 60s AD.

Returning again to the subject of the domestic level of the questions put to oracles, it is in this context that Salomons mentions (pp.4-5) the *Sortes Astrampsychi*, another sub-literary text. This oracle book acquired great popularity when it circulated in Roman antiquity under the name of Astrampsychos. An unsatisfactory edition exists, based on some MSS, but in recent years G.M. Browne has done most to revive interest in this material, of which some papyrus fragments are known. They are:

1. *P.Oxy.* 12 (1916) 1477 (late III/early IV), written on the back of a register of payments; first identified by G. Björck, *SO* 19 (1939) 94-98.
2. *P.Oxy.* 38 (1971) 2832 (late III/IV); the *verso* contains a letter written soon afterwards.
3. *P.Oxy.* 38 (1971) 2833 (late III/IV).
4. *P.Oxy.* 47 (1980) 3330 (late III/early IV) from the same roll as 2832.
5. *P.Oxy.* ined. (IV^2) part of a codex containing three sheets and fragments; discussed (but not yet published) by Browne in G.W. Bowersock, et al., *Arktouros. Hellenic Studies Presented to B.M.W. Knox* (Berlin 1979) 434-39.

Browne has re-edited nos.1-3 in *The Papyri of the Sortes Astrampsychi* (*Beitr. zur kl. Phil.* 58; Meisenheim am Glan, 1974). Two important articles have elucidated the mechanics of how the book was devised with its list of questions, and its answers grouped in decades (*BICS* 17 [1970] 95-100), and demonstrated that the *Sortes* originated in Egypt during III (*ICS* 1 [1976] 53-58). Apart from the fact that the mediaeval MS tradition betrays considerable Christian interference, Browne has shown that there were two editions of the *Sortes*: the first (represented by *P.Oxy.* 2832 + 3330, 2833, and one MS [XIIIAD]) has brief, succinct answers to the questions; the second has expanded (though still short) answers. *P.Oxy.* 1477 may be inferred to belong to this group for, although it contains no answers, its questions cohere with the numerous late MSS which have the longer answers. *P.Oxy.* ined. also represents the second edition, although it is a significant deviant because this codex contained many extra decades of answers. Browne suggests (1974: 8, 14) that the second edition was written not long after the first, and possibly by the same person.

Unlike the oracle questions proper, the enquirer who had recourse to the *Sortes* did not approach the god but an individual who possessed a set of the questions and answers and knew how to work the system. But the sorts of questions and answers attested for both contexts were very similar, and show very plainly that it was the ordinary individual who made these enquiries in a private capacity. From the *Sortes* we can infer that males and females, free people and slaves, businessmen and soldiers, the well-to-do and those who could not pay their taxes were among the anticipated clients of the oracle-monger. Purely by way of example some questions are:

οβ· εἰ λήμψομαι τὸ ὀψώνιον
ογ· εἰ μένω ὅπου ὑπάγω
οδ· εἰ πωλοῦμαι
οε· εἰ ἔχω ὠφέλιαν ἀπὸ τοῦ φίλου
5　οϛ· εἰ δέδοταί μοι ἑτέρῳ συναλλάξαι
οζ· εἰ καταλλάσσομαι εἰς τὸν τόπον [μου]
οη· εἰ λαμβάνω κομιᾶτον
οθ· εἰ λήμψομαι τὸ ἀργύριον
π· εἰ ζῇ ὁ ἀπόδημος
10　πα· εἰ κερδαίνω ἀπὸ τοῦ πράγματ[ος]
πβ· εἰ προγράφεται τὰ ἐμά

πγ· εἰ εὑρήσω πωλῆσαι
πδ· εἰ δύναμαι ὃ ἐνθυμοῦμαι ἀγο[ράσαι]
πε· εἰ γίνομαι βιόπρατος
15　πϛ· εἰ φυγαδεύσομαι
πζ· εἰ πρεσβεύσω
πη· εἰ γίνομαι βουλευτής
πθ· εἰ λύεταί (read λήσεται) μου ὁ δρασμός
ϟ· εἰ ἀπαλλάσσομαι τῆς γυναικό[ς]
20　ϟα· εἰ πεφαρμάκωμαι
ϟβ· εἰ λαμβάνω ληγᾶ[το]ν

72　**Shall I get the allowance?**
73　**Am I to remain where I am going?**
74　**Am I to be sold?**
75　**Am I to obtain profit from my friend?**
76　**Is it permitted me to make a contract with another?**
77　**Am I to be restored to my position?**
78　**Am I to get leave?**
79　**Shall I get the money?**
80　**Is the person who is away alive?**
81　**Am I to profit from the affair?**
82　**Is my property to be sold at auction?**
83　**Shall I find the means to sell?**
84　**Am I able to buy what I want?**
85　**Am I to become successful?**
86　**Shall I be a fugitive?**
87　**Shall I be an ambassador?**
88　**Am I to become a senator?**
89　**Will my flight be undetected?**
90　**Am I to be separated from my wife?**
91　**Have I been poisoned?**
92　**Am I to get a legacy?**

(*P.Oxy.* 1477 rev. Browne [1974], *col.*2, questions 72-92; his translation)

A representative passage of answers (decades 77 and 78) is *P.Oxy.* 2833 rev.
Browne (1974), *col.*2, *ll.*5-26 (his translation):

5   οζ   οη

οὐ παραμένι σοι ἡ πρώτη γυνή   ὄψι θάνατον ⟨ὄν⟩ οὐ θέλις
γίνη δεκάπρωτος   οὐ νικᾷς. καρτέρι
ἔχις τὴ⟨ν⟩ πατρίδα θεωρῆσαι   οὐ κληρονομῖς. σιώπα
ἀπαρτίζις ὃ ἐπιβάλλη   20 εἰὰν μισθῶσι, κερδένις
10 οὐ λαμβάνις ληγᾶτον   οὐκ οἰκονομῖς ἄρτι
οὐ πεφαρμάκωσαι. μὴ ἀγωνία   ἐκτιτρώσκι καὶ κινδυνεύει
οὐ καταλλάσσῃ τῇ γυνεκί   δάνισον ἐπὶ ὑποθήκῃ
οὐ λανθάνι σου ὁ δρασμός   οὐ πωλῖς ἄρτι τὸ φορτίον
γίνη βουλευτής   25 ἀπολύῃ τῆς συνοχῆς
15 πρεσβεύσις, οὐ μόνος   οὐ λαμβάνις ἣν θέλις γυνε͂κα

77

5   **Your first wife is not to remain with you.**
You are to become a dekaprotos.
You will see your country.
You are to finish what you undertake.
10 **You are not to get a legacy.**
You have not been poisoned. Do not worry.
You are not to be reconciled with your wife.
Your flight is not to be undetected.
You are to become a senator.
15 **You will be an ambassador, but not alone.**

78

You will see a death which you do not wish.
You are not to win. Persevere.
You are not to inherit. Silence.
20 **If you lease, you are to profit.**
You are not to be an oikonomos just yet.
She is to miscarry and she is to be in danger.
Lend with a mortgage.
You are not to sell the load just yet.
25 **You are to be released from prison.**
You are not to get the woman you want.

Browne notes (1974: 4 n.6) that the present tenses in answers is a mark of the first
edition (the second alters many to a future), and he compares the use of the present
tense in NT prophecies (cf. BDF 323). While they originated and had a vogue in
Egypt, the number of mediaeval MSS of the *Sortes* suggests that their popularity
spread well beyond there.

In their own small way the oracular texts of different types mentioned in this
rapid survey can help us to document some aspects of social history of the first few
centuries of the era. Concern for the future is reflected in their mere occurrence but
the concerns expressed are very markedly those that affect the individual personally.

That the form of the oracle question and answer was assimilated to a Christian context is simply one indicator of how important it was to have links with long-lived traditions. But unlike the apologetics of the Fathers, whose synthesis is self-conscious, documents such as the Christian oracles reveal how unconscious was the process of assimilation for the common man. It will be of great interest should Christian examples of, say, IVAD, ever be found, for documents of such earlier date may enable us to see the assimilation process as it was occurring, rather than in completed form as the extant VI examples do.

The *Corpus Papyrorum Graecarum* project, announced in *Aeg.* 57 (1977) 276–77, includes as its planned vol.2 *Le domande di responso oracolare*, to be edited by M. Vandoni.

9. The hand of God

A votive left hand represented on a bronze tablet from Palmyra (I/early II (?)), which also contains a short Palmyrene inscription beneath it, is published by H.W.J. Drijvers, *Semitica* 27 (1977) 105-16 (pl.13) = *SEG* 1278. The text reads, *mwd' | 'b' | b'šmn*, 'Abba gives thanks to Ba'ashamên'. *Ed.pr.* discusses examples of the depiction of a right hand — left hand depictions are rare — from Palmyra, elsewhere in Syria, Doura Europos, Carthage, etc. Most commonly it represents the salvific power of God. Cults with which it is associated include Theos Hypsistos, Jupiter Dolichenus, Sabazios. But there are also portrayals on altars of (usually) two hands in ex-voto thank-offerings where the hands symbolize the *orans* who now makes the dedication. The new Palmyrene example is to be categorized with that group (*ed.pr.*). This Near Eastern notion of the hand of God and hands upraised as an attitude of prayer finds parallels in the Bible and ECL. Note, for example, Lk. 1.66, χ. κυρίου. See also BAGD, s.v. χείρ, 2a; cf. s.v. αἴρω, 1a.

S.R. Pickering has drawn to my attention a Manichaean example of this symbolism: H.-J. Klimkeit, *Manichaean Art and Calligraphy* (*Iconography of Religions*, 20; Leiden, 1982), pl.17, fig.28 with commentary on pp.39-40. This illuminated leaf from a Manichaean book (Kočo in central Asia, VIII?) depicts two men kneeling before two tall figures who are probably to be interpreted as *Electi*. Klimkeit (39) thinks that it portrays a penitential scene. Consonant with this interpretation is 'the great (divine?) hand reaching into the picture from the upper leaf margin, holding over the kneeling men a cross-like object, evidently in blessing' (ibid.).

10. The battle between Good and Evil

A mosaic from a basilica at Aquileia, at the northern end of the Adriatic, portrays in strikingly concrete form the contest between the forces of Good and Evil, symbolized by a cock and a tortoise. An amphora stands above them, as the prize for the victor. This mosaic (Budischovsky, *Cultes isiaques* p.158, no.4c; pl.79) is dated to III fin. Budischovsky refers to other examples of this theme, and includes bibliography. R.J. Mortley suggests to me that the dualism so tangibly symbolized here makes one think of Zoroastrianism or perhaps Manichaeism.

11. Love charm
Provenance unknown   n.d.
ed.pr. — P.J. Sijpesteijn, *ZPE* 24 (1977) 89-90 (pl. 12A)

σιτ ᾿κουμ
αιεουω ιηαη
ιηω υο ιεω
αιηου ευ ιαη ια
5   ω αευια ιωα ιηω
ηα ιαω ωαι ἀξιῶ καὶ
παρακαλῶ τὴν δοίνα-
μήν σου καὶ τὴν ἐξουσίαν
σου ᾿κ ιαεου ασωρ ασκατανθιρι
10   σετωνεκου ἄξον Τερμοῦτιν τη᾿
ἔτεκεν Σοφία Ζοῆλ τω ἔτεκεν
Δρόσερ ἔρωτι μανικῷ καὶ ἀκατα-
[πα]ύστῳ ἀφθίρτῳ, ἤδη ταχύ.

A triangular-shaped lead tablet inscribed on one side only. Read τόν (*l*.11).
Bib. — *BE* 23; *SEG* 1243.

(*l*.6) I ask for and request your power and your authority (*nomina barbara*).
10 |**Bring Termoutis whom Sophia bore, to Zoel whom Droser bore, with crazed and unceasing, everlasting love, now quickly!**

The presence of *nomina barbara*, various permutations of vowels, and names for God are common in magical texts like this. A rather longer example, also on lead, was discussed in *New Docs 1976*, **8**. In *ll*.2-6, as *ed.pr.* notes, the writer of this spell provides a series of variations — including a palindrome at *l*.6 — of the vowel sequence ιαω, one of the divine names frequently used in magical texts. Two other common elements not commented on in *New Docs 1976*, **8** are the use of verbal doublets, ἀξιῶ καὶ παρακαλῶ (6-7), τὴν δοίναμήν σου καὶ τὴν ἐξουσίαν σου (7-9); and the practice of identifying a person by naming his/her mother — paternity may be in doubt but maternity cannot be. The writer's insistence that his charm be effective immediately (*l*.13) is common too. J.A.L. Lee draws my attention to *CIL* VIII, Suppl. 1.12511 (repr. with commentary in R. Wünsch, *Antike Fluchtafeln* [*Kleine Texte* 20; Bonn, 1912], no.4; Carthage, III?), which concludes (*ll*.32-33) with ἤδη ἤδη | ταχὺ τα[χύ]. That lead charm is designed to secure for the user victory in a chariot race. In it one may note the adoption of Jewish material partly as *nomina* *barbara*, e.g., ιακουβ (2), partly as incantation/quotation, e.g. ἔτι ἐ|ξορκίζω ὑμᾶς κατὰ τοῦ ἀπάνου (= ἀπάνω) τοῦ οὐρανοῦ θεοῦ, | τοῦ καθημένου ἐπὶ τῶν χερουβι, ὁ διορίσας τὴν γῆν | καὶ χωρίσας τὴν θάλασσαν, Ιαω αβριαω αρβαθιαω | αδωναι ˙σαβαω˙, κτλ (23-27); the passage draws on Gen. 1.7 and Is. 45.18. This phenomenon is also observable in *PGM*.

The adjective ἀκατάπαυστος (12-13) should also be noted. This fairly rare word is a Hellenistic coining, used by historians of civil and political strife (Polyb. 4.17.4; D.S. 11.67.7; Jos. *BJ* 7.421). Plut. *Mor.* 114F (*Cons. Apoll.*) couples it with the noun σύμφορα. A few further instances (scholiasts, grammarians) are provided in Stephanus' *Thesaurus Linguae Graecae* I, 1619. Papyrus usage appears to be confined to contexts similar to the new love charm. Sijpesteijn refers (n. ad loc.) to D. Wortmann, *Bonn. Jahrb.* 168 (1968) 90, no.4 *l.*49, ἔρωτα ἀκατάπαυστον καὶ φιλίαν μανικήν (Upper Egypt, V). M.M., s.v. ἀκατάπαστος, quote a similar phrase from *PSI* 1(1912) 28.52 (III/IV). The MM entry should have ἀκατάπαυστος as its lemma, not the variant reading found at 2 Pet. 2.14. Commentators on this verse offer no useful note on the word (e.g. C. Bigg, *ICC* series). The phrase ὀφθαλμοὺς ἔχοντες μεστοὺς μοιχαλίδος καὶ ἀκαταπαύστους ἁμαρτίας is one element in the long denunciation of false prophets which comprises this chapter; here the writer focuses upon their sexual vice. Given the presence of the adjective in the love charms, the use of it in the clause at 2 Pet. 2.14 may be especially appropriate, even though the construction with a dependent genitive is not the same as the papyrus formula.

12. Bilingual curse tablet

Dierna (Dacia)   Late imperial

ed.pr. — N. Vlassa, *AMN* 14 (1977) 205-19 (pl.) — *non vidi*

ὦἰ(-)	θεοὶ	*Demon im(m)unditi(a)e*
ὐύύύ	ὕψ(ιστοι)	*te agite(t) Aeli Fir(-)*
ἰύ ᾿Αδ(ω)να(ι)	≫	*me (.) Ste(t) supra caput*
θεός		*Iuliae Surillae*
≫		≫

Rectangular gold tablet, with inscription in three sections. In *l.*2 of the Latin the letter F has been pierced with a needle; in *l.*4 a small cross stands beside S.
Bib. — *SEG* 415

> **Lord God.**
> **Highest gods.**
> **May the demon of impurity pursue you, Aelius Firmus. May it stand over the head of Iulia Surilla.**

This magical text provides an opportunity to reiterate — cf. *New Docs 1976*, **5** — that the phrase θεὸς ὕψιστος is not a certain indicator of Judaism. The plural form here is enough to show that. From the same site the wording ᾿Ιαω ᾿Αθωναι was found on another gold plaque (III-IV): *SEG* 416. But this item is Jewish since the tablet carries a Semitic text as well.

13. Invocation of a dead man

Saqqara (possibly)   IV¹(?)

ed.pr. — B. Boyaval, *ZPE* 14 (1974) 71-73 (pl. 3a, b)

Side 1	Side 2

Side 1

Σαορ αυινι ενουτιὸ.
ἐξορκίζω σε τοὺς
θεοὺς τοὺς ἐνδα-
αθί, καὶ τοὺς σαρα-
5 φάκους, καὶ τοὺς΄
θούς σου [[π]] τοὺς
κατ᾽ Ἅδου περὶ
Σενβλυγπνῶτος΄,
κράξον εἰς τὸν
10 Ἅδην, μὴ ἀφῆς
τοὺς ἐν Ἅδω {τοὺ
ς} θεοὺς καθεύδι
ν, τὴν ταφήν
σου ἀπεστέ
15 ρηκε τὸ λοιπόν,

Side 2

μὴ ἀφῆς τοὺς
θεοὺς καθεύδιν
εἰσακούσι σε
ὁ Οὔσιρις ὅτι ⟨εἶ⟩
20 ἄωορος καὶ
ἄτεκνος καὶ
ἀγύναις καὶ
αχαβισσος
κϛ

Wooden tablet, side 1 containing *ll.*1-15, side 2 with *ll.*16-24. Boyaval prints a diplomatic text and his edition of it. Printed above is the diplomatic text incorporating some of his editorial interpretation.

Bib. — *SB* 11247

Saor avini enoutio. I adjure you by the gods here, and the (gods of the?)
5 **coffins, | and your gods in Hades, concerning Senblynpnos: scream to Hades,**
do not let the gods in Hades sleep! It is your tomb she has deprived you of
for the future! Do not let the gods sleep! Osiris will hear you because you are
untimely (dead), and childless and without a wife and (?). 26.

Here is a magical text in which an anonymous writer invokes an unnamed deceased person, summoning him to appeal against the theft of his grave, perhaps by a woman. The first of the three *nomina barbara* with which the text begins means 'son of Horus' (Boyaval, 72).

Boyaval adds καί after σε in *l.*2 of his edition of the text, but that is unnecessary. While the NT has ἐξορκίζω only at Mt. 26.63 (ἐ. σε κατὰ τοῦ θεοῦ) in a different construction from that of the present text, note Acts 19.13 where ὁρκίζω with two accusatives is used in a semi-magical context (here and in the following verse the compound ἐξ- occurs as a *v.1.*). Another compound, ἐνορκίζω, occurs with two accusatives at 1 Thes. 5.27 (here, the simple verb is a variant reading). MM, s.v. ἐξορκίζω, cite examples where the construction parallels the Mt. passage mentioned above. In a love charm from Egypt dated III/IV (*New Docs 1976*, **8**, *ll.*11-12, 14-15), both ἐξορκίζω and ὁρκίζω are used with accusative + κατά + genitive.

Again, Boyaval omits καί at *l*.4, making τοὺς σαρκοφάγους adjectival agreeing with
τοὺς θεούς. But could it be a separate noun, 'coffins'? While the noun form of this
word is much less common than the adjective (*LSJ*, s.v., cites only one example,
and it is feminine), since λίθος σ. refers to the special limestone which consumed
the flesh of a cadaver placed in it the occurrence of the noun with the masculine
gender ought not to be surprising. E.A. Judge suggests to me, however, that appeal
is being made to three classes of gods: those here, those (who preside over) coffins,
and those in Hades.

Other philological features to note are the use of the Attic deictic suffix particle
on ἐνδα|αθί (= ἐνθαδί): cf. Boyaval, 72. The use of κράζω εἰς (9) is not a NT idiom,
but for NT passages where the verb has a strong force — not simply 'cry out' —
see BAGD, s.v., 1. Hermas III. 9.9 is the only instance provided by BAGD of
ἀποστερέω τι τινος; the NT construction is ἀ. τινα τινος. The active form of the
future tense of εἰσακούω (18) is not classical: in the case of the simple verb Mt. and
Jn employ the active, Acts has the middle (references in BAGD, s.v. ἀκούω, *init*.).
It is unclear what word is intended at *l*.23, while the final line may provide the age
of the deceased.

14. Funerary practice in Hellenistic and Roman Rhodes

The very detailed monograph (more pages of notes and indexes than of actual
text) by P.M. Fraser, *Rhodian Funerary Monuments* (Oxford, 1977) — cf. *SEG* 457
— consists of two parts: a typology of the monuments, and an examination of
certain features of the epitaphs. The study is consciously limited in scope to the city
of Rhodes: founded in 408/7, the great bulk of its inscriptions are Hellenistic or
later in date. Sepulchral inscriptions on monuments such as altars and tombstones
constitute a large group of texts from the city. Fraser makes numerous comparisons
with other Dorian settlements, both nearby islands like Kos and cities in Asia
Minor: in the former case there is a striking difference in funerary styles from mid-
IIBC when Kos began receiving many Roman citizens as settlers (74). A number
of comments in Fraser's Part II are taken up here and considered for their
suggestive, *analogous* relevance to the NT. Care must be observed with what can
justly be extrapolated, for there are elements of Rhodian practice which are atypical
from what is attested elsewhere. Fraser's discussion is most restrained: for example,
he chooses not to discuss ideas about the after-life which may be implied by
terminology found on the epitaphs (46). He publishes 6 altars (from Rhodes, Kos,
and the Kyklades), three of which have brief inscriptions (43-45); none requires
comment here.

1. Family graves and monuments (Fraser, 52-58).

Numerous examples exist of a monument set up for the deceased by kinsmen,
but unlike Athens, for example, where one close relative erects it, at Rhodes a
whole series of relatives is named. This feature is found elsewhere in the Hellenistic
period (e.g., on Kos). 'Those group graves which contain the remains both of
related family groups of citizens and of persons of humbler status side by side, may

in addition indicate that the Rhodians of the later hellenistic age, like the Romans, associated slaves, and freedmen, with the members of the family in burial' (58). An example from 1977 publications is Raffeiner, *Sklaven*, no.49 (Sidon (?), II/III; = Peek, *GVI* I, 737 = *SEG* 7 [1934] 267), an eight-line metrical epitaph for four brothers, their aunt, and Eutychos a θεράπων (see also Raffeiner's n.1 to no.30). This epitaph is further discussed at **80**. Family graves like these are common in Roman Asia Minor (cf. 148-49 n.327). Such instances of 'household graves extending beyond recognized kinship groups' (58) may add a further dimension to consideration of the relationship between slaves and free in the NT.

2. Common burial for members of an association (Fraser, 58-70).

The custom of providing for a common resting place for members of a religious, professional, or social club, regardless of familial ties, goes well back into the classical Greek period. The practice may have originated with Dionysiac *koina*, the earliest example of which (Kyme in Campania, V¹BC) relates to a cult of chthonic Dionysos: οὐ θέμις ἐν|τοῦθα κεῖσθ|αι ἰ μὲ τὸν βεβαχχευμένον, 'it is not permitted for anyone to lie here except the bacchic initiate' (59, and n.328). Several other examples from various cities, Hellenistic and Roman, are given by Fraser (59, and nn.329-334). The custom was imitated widely by other types of association. (It is not to be identified with that of the Roman burial clubs, *collegia funeraticia*, which were established specifically to ensure a decent burial for their members. A few Greek examples of this Roman institution are known, from Rough Cilicia in Asia Minor: 150 n.340.) Provision for common burial was one way of giving tangible expression of the members' association together. Pre-Roman Rhodes provides particularly good evidence about this practice, for numerous *koina* existed there and were an important social focus for resident foreigners. In fact these associations had 'a highly developed system of benefits for their members; with their grandiloquent titles, their own magistrates, priesthoods, assemblies, cults, and social services, they provided foreign residents in Rhodes and Rhodian territory with the same opportunities for lavish benefactions as were provided by the civic organization for Rhodian demesmen, who themselves rarely, if ever, belonged to them. They were, so to speak, a microcosm of the state, and the loyalty that they evoked in their members was rewarded with honours similar to those awarded by the state' (60). Common burial and banqueting were elements which helped shape these associations as communal in focus and provided their members with a sense of belonging to a society (ibid.). Fraser (74) discusses a tombstone from Rhodes, Ἀναξίδος Κωΐας καὶ Τίμωνος | Αἰγίν[ατα] | ἀδελφῶν ἡρώων: to describe them as *adelphoi* may indicate that they are man and wife (an Egyptian usage, found also in the LXX; the couple are foreigners); but Fraser thinks it more likely that they are '"brothers" in the sense of fellow members of a koinon,' a usage attested elsewhere (74, and nn.430-435). Without drawing the implications out in detail, some features of the NT communities may be considered in the light of these suggestive ideas. As one example, the notion of possessing what is virtually a separate citizenship via these *koina* may be relevant for Phil. 3.20 and possibly Heb. 13.14 (although the latter is one of several places in that letter where the influence of Platonic Forms could perhaps be detected). In these two passages citizenship is located outside the existing order: this insider's view of Christians matches in embryonic form the later outsiders' perception of them as an alternative nation, a 'third race'. *I.Tyre* 1.24A and B are two inscriptions on a sarcophagus which mention two pairs of 'brothers', and a 'brother' and 'sister' respectively. The pair in 24B are involved with the purple dye industry (cf. **3** above), and Rey-Coquais wonders whether ἀδελφός in these texts may have the sense of members of an association, or whether perhaps they may even be monastics. For ἀδελφοί in Christian inscriptions to designate members of an association see Rey-Coquais' references, p.18 n.5. Adelphios occurs as a name on a sarcophagus carrying Christian crosses (*I.Tyre* 1.133).

3. The posthumous award of a crown (Fraser, 68).

Whereas elsewhere such an honour may be voted to a citizen after his death in recognition of some particular contribution, at Rhodes only the *koina* — not citizens — made use of the custom. It was thus placed within a cultic context. Fraser interprets the projecting conical bosses on a group of rectangular funerary altars as collars on which to hang wreaths (cf. pp.15-16, 19-24). One example (fig. 49d) actually has the garland carved on it. This practice may be of some relevance to certain NT passages. While 1 Cor. 9.25 and 2 Tim. 2.5 use στέφανος or its related verb to pick up an image from athletic contests, 2 Tim. 4.8 does this as well but suggests that ὁ τῆς δικαιοσύνης στέφανος is awarded by the Lord 'on that day'. (Note *MAMA* 8 [1962] 408.13-14, from Aphrodisias, where it is decreed about the deceased that ἐστεφανῶσθαι δὲ αὐτὸν κατὰ ἀξίαν τῷ τῆς ἀρετῆς στεφάνῳ; cf. L. Robert, *Hellenica* 13 [1965] 42 n.3.) At Jas. 1.12 τὸν στέφανον τῆς ζωῆς is spoken of as a reward for the person who endures trials; but the same phrase at Rev. 2.10 clearly refers to a reward for martyrdom of the faithful (γίνου πιστὸς ἄχρι θανάτου). The bestowal of a garland as a mark of martyrdom appears at Heb. 2.9 of Christ, Ἰησοῦν διὰ τὸ πάθημα τοῦ θανάτου δόξῃ καὶ τιμῇ ἐστεφανωμένον; and in ECL of the martyr Polycarp, ἐστεφανωμένος τὸν τῆς ἀφθαρσίας στέφανον (*MPol.* 17.1). With the 'crown of life' phrase in Jas. 1.12 (mentioned just above) compare the epitaph for a comedian (κωμῳδός) from Paphos in Cyprus who dies at Messana (*IG* XIV [1890] 441) and says of himself λιφθεὶς τὸν βιότου στέφανον; L. Robert, *Hellenica* 11-12 (1960) 330-342 argues that it is an agonistic allusion, and interprets it to mean 'I was defeated for the crown of life'. (Raffeiner, *Sklaven*, no.44 is another epigram for an actor who ἀσκήσας ⟨πάσης⟩ εἶδος ὑποκρίσεως [*l*.2].) Thus the NT usage employs a wider range of imagery than simply the athletic contest or straightforward honorifics. Do the NT passages where a crown is awarded after death reflect the notion attested on tombs at Rhodes and elsewhere? On the image generally note K. Baus, *Der Kranz in Antike und Christentum* (Bonn, 1940; repr. 1965). On gold crowns (worn by the elders and others in Rev.) see M. Guarducci, *Epigraphica* 35 (1973) 7-23; 39 (1977) 140-42; cf. *SEG* 1260. I have not seen M. Blech, *Studien zum Kranz bei den Griechen* (Berlin, 1982).

4. The epithet ἐλεήμων (Fraser, 72).

Fraser (162 n.409) cites an epitaph from Rhodes (IIBC?): Ἡράκλειτε | Ἀρτέμ-[ω]νος | ἐλεήμων | χαῖρε. The epithet is rare except as applied to a god: Fraser (72) instances its use of Aphrodite; BAGD, s.v., mentions Leto, Isis and Amenophis. The LXX uses it mostly of God, only four times of people (in Ps. and Prov.). It is in this latter way that should be based our understanding of Heb. 2.17, ὅθεν ὤφειλεν κατὰ πάντα τοῖς ἀδελφοῖς ὁμοιωθῆναι, ἵνα ἐλεήμων γένηται καὶ πιστὸς ἀρχιερεὺς τὰ πρὸς τὸν θεόν, κτλ. The beatitude at Mt. 5.7 uses ἐλεήμων of people. Fraser's cautionary note (72) must be mentioned, however: 'The notion of compassion or mercy probably refers less to the human compassion of the deceased when alive than to the compassion exercised by him as a kindly spirit, but it is not possible to be certain of such a delicate nuance when the use of the word, and even the concept of 'mercy' as an acclamation on a tombstone, is so rare'. The epitaph should be included in any reworking of MM's brief entry, where only one example is given.

Returning to Heb. 2.17, ὁμοίωσις is there said to be necessary in order that Christ can be merciful: is the writer here consciously turning on its head the Platonic notion of ὁμοίωσις θεῷ [*Theaitetos* 176B]? This notion has a long posterity in Greek and Christian Platonism, and that Heb. forms part of the latter is not in particular doubt; whether the author indulges in other similar reversals of ideas is 'a long shot, but not impossible' (R.J. Mortley, in a note to me). Basic to the study of the phrase is H. Merki, ΟΜΟΙΩΣΙΣ ΘΕΩ *von der platonischen Angleichung an Gott zur Gottähnlichkeit bei Gregor von Nyssa* (Freiburg, 1952; *non vidi*); cf. Mortley, *Connaissance religieuse et herméneutique chez Clément d'Alexandrie* (Leiden, 1973) 155-57. Reference to Merki should be included at BAGD, s.v. ὁμοίωσις. At Jas. 3.9, where men are made καθ' ὁμοίωσιν θεοῦ, the reference is straightforwardly to Gen. 1.27.

5. ἀγαθὸς δαίμων/ἥρως (Fraser, 73-74, 76-81).

Fraser (73) quotes two tombstones (IIBC) which make mention of two couples described as δαιμόνων ἀγαθῶν. The usage is attested in other places (ibid.; cf. *New Docs 1976*, 2, p.17), and is surely associated with the cult of *Agathos Daimon*. The term ἥρως, 'deceased', is very frequent on hellenistic and Roman epitaphs in some parts of the Greek world, rare in others. There are clear-cut examples where the term implies that the deceased was Heroized, i.e., accorded quasi-divine status; but the frequency with which the word occurs meant that 'already by the fifth century the religious content was no doubt much diluted by familiarity' (74). Numerous examples are known for some places where ἥρως is used simply after a name (77). Examples of ἥρως noted in the 1977 culling include *BE* 258, 289, 440, 469, 489 (p.419); *SEG* 195, 205, 217, 221, 223, 274, 276, 278, 284, 285, 289, 317, 343, 781, 803(b), 870, 905, 906, 907 (= **80** elsewhere in this volume), 908 ([τὸ ἡρ]ῷον), 911, 912.

From this list we may pick out just one text. *BE* 440 reports a metrical epitaph from Ephesos for a six-year old girl (*ed.pr.* — D. Knibbe/R. Merkelbach, *ZPE* 21[1976] 191-92 [pl.5b]):

τύμβος ὧδε κατέχει καλὸν
δέμας αἲ βιόμοι⟨ρ⟩ον.
ἡλικίην γὰρ ἔχουσαν ἐτ[ῶ]ν
ἒξ· ἢ ἔ{ι}τι πλῖον σε Κούρη [Π]λο[υ-]
5 τῆος ἤγαγεν εἰς ᾿Αίδην. ἀ[λλ]ὰ
θεοὶ μάκα[ρε]ς οἰκτείραντες
ψυχὴν οὐ πρόλιπαν δῦν[αι]

δόμον ῎Αϊδος ἴσω· ἠέρι δ' ἐμ[πεπό-]
τηται κατ' οὐρανόν· ἐν δὲ [θεοῖ-]
10 σιν εἴσην μοῖραν ἔχει ἡρ[ώϊσι δὴ]
Στρατονείκη. εἰ δέ τις ἦ[ν κ]ατέ-
χει τύμβος ζῶσάν ποτ' ἔ[βλεψεν,]
οὐκ ἂν ἀδακρυτεῖ τόν[δε]
διῆλθε τόπον.

This tomb encloses a beautiful body which — alas! — (suffered) a violent fate
(*read* βιαιόμοιρον). For Kore, wife of Ploutos, led you to Hades when you
5   **were six years old or a little more. |But the blessed gods taking pity did not**
abandon your soul to sink into Hades' dwelling, and in the air it is in flight
10 **in the sky; and among the gods |Stratonike has a portion equal to the**
heroines. But if anyone ever saw the one whom the tomb (now) encloses when
she was alive, he would not pass by this place without tears.

No date is offered by *ed. pr.* for the inscription, but we should think of the
Roman period at least. The stone carries a carved relief of a woman holding a
casket, seated in front of a burning altar. *BE* 440 notes that the image of a child
likened to the ἡρωΐδες as her privileged lot is not a common-place one. Of most
interest, however, is the view (reflected here at a popular level) that a child — the
'innocent' in general? — can escape Hades and have her abode in the sky in the
presence of the gods.

15. Brief notes on some epitaphs for slaves

Raffeiner, *Sklaven*, collects 56 metrical epitaphs for slaves and freedmen, a few
of which are discussed elsewhere in the present volume (**2** *ad fin.*, **14**, **80**). Some
comments are offered below on certain words and phrases which appear in these
inscriptions; a few other slave epitaphs appearing in 1977 publications are also
noted. But first a more general observation is made about master/slave relations,
which owes much to H.W. Pleket's brief review of Raffeiner, in *CR* 29 (1979)
175-76. The modern literature on Graeco-Roman slavery is enormous, but among
many one may single out the contributions of J. Vogt and W.L. Westermann.

Raffeiner's monograph is deliberately limited in scope: for example, only verse
epitaphs are included in the study. Not a few of the texts — mostly I-III, a few
earlier and a couple later — were erected by the owner or patron of the deceased,
and when the sentiments they contain are scrutinized they indicate that the masters
treated their slaves as people not things. But the inscriptions selected by Raffeiner
must not be taken as sufficient evidence for thinking that humane dealings between
owner and owned were normal. For while we do have these testimonies that such
attitudes really did exist, it must nevertheless be appreciated that the slaves so
documented constituted a tiny fraction of the entire servile population. Those who
were provided with a verse memorial tended to have had an important post in the
oikos (e.g. stewards), particular skills to offer (doctors), or been on close terms via
the master's children (nurses, *paidagogoi*). The great bulk of Graeco-Roman
antiquity's slaves did not receive so much as a headstone with their name carved
on it. Pleket speaks of the far more typical 'cynical paternalism' of masters who
'either despised or were indifferent to slaves *as a social group* and (who) bought the
loyalty of some slaves by paying lip-service to an ideal of cordial relations' (176;
his italics).

1. The slave/master relationship extends beyond death.

Raffeiner nos.7 and 8 are epitaphs set up for slaves by their respective masters: the first is dated IIIBC and both originate from Asia Minor, although they survived via a literary tradition as *Anth. Pal.* 7.178, 179 (= Peek, *GVI* I.1193, 1194; for the former see also Gow/Page, *The Greek Anthology. Hellenistic Epigrams* [Cambridge, 1965] II, 268-69). The last half-line of no.7 reads, σὸς ἐγώ, δέσποτα, κἢν Ἀίδην, 'I am yours (sc. δοῦλος), master, even in Hades'. No.8, *ll*.2-3, has σοὶ καὶ νῦν ὑπὸ γῆν, ναὶ δέσποτα, πιστὸς ὑπάρχω | ὡς παρός, 'to you even now under the earth, yes master, I remain faithful as before', since he does not forget the master's εὐνοίη (the text uses the Ionic form) shown towards him. It is not being over-cynical to remark that the erection by a master of a gravestone with such wording for his slaves is at least as much an exercise in cultivating an image of himself as a humane man who has deservedly earned the eternal loyalty of his underling. For the idea of the faithful slave in the NT, both literally, and metaphorically of the follower's relationship with Christ, note Mt. 24.45; 25.21a, 23a; Eph. 6.21 and Col. 4.7 (of Tychikos); Col. 1.7 (of Epaphras); Col. 4.9 (of Onesimos). MM, s.v., mention that πιστός occurs as a servile name. On this word, see **68**. Cf. *I.Tyre* 1.23*bis*, the sarcophagus of blessed Amene, τῆς μακαρίτες | Ἀμενης; *ed.pr.* says that the masculine form of this Semitic name, Ἀμινος, known from Doura-Europos, corresponds in meaning to the Greek πιστός.

2. *Sophron* used of slaves.

Raffeiner no.11 (= Peek, *GVI* 1729; Kos, II/I) is a ten-line verse inscription for an enslaved married couple. The man is praised for his σαόφρονα μῆτιν, 'prudent skill', even in Hades (*l*.3); and an implied comparison is drawn between him and the φιλ[οδέσπο]τον ἦθος of Eumaios (1-2), the ideal slave-figure of the Homeric *Odyssey*. On φιλοδέσποτος see Raffeiner, 30-31 and n.11 on p.32; in ECL it appears at *MPol.* 2.2. Cf. the use of φιλοκύριοι in an epitaph for a scribe (λιβράριος) and a barber, Raffeiner no.35, *l*.3 (= Peek *GVI* 1527; Heliopolis-Baalbek, II/III); see also Raffeiner, 61 n.2. The Kos epitaph is unique, for *sophrosyne* is not usually viewed as a slave's virtue (Raffeiner, 30). On *sophrosyne* see *MAMA* 8 (1962) 394 (quoted at **80**, with brief comment).

3. Death brings freedom.

Raffeiner no.16 (= *SEG* 7 [1934] 121; Syria, 538) reads:—

[Ζω]σίμη ἡ πρὶν ἐ|οῦσα μόνωι τῶι σῶ|ματι δούλη
καὶ τῶι σώματι νῦν ηὗρον | ἐλευθερίην.

I am Zosime who was formerly a slave only with my body; now I have found freedom for my body as well.

This couplet is spread over five lines on the stone; Raffeiner omits the sixth which contains the date since it is not part of the verse. He cites some very appropriate parallels from the Greek tragedians a millennium before (e.g. Soph., frag. 940 Pearson, εἰ σῶμα δοῦλον, ἀλλ' ὁ νοῦς ἐλεύθερος), thus attesting the long continuity of this motif. Raffeiner no.41 (noted below) provides another example. The notion of death as the ultimate bestower of freedom may be simply expressed in epitaphs, but we should not be oblivious to the yearning to cast off the servile state which lies beneath the sentiment. For discussion of death *qua* liberator see A. Brelich, *Aspetti della morte nelle iscrizione sepolcrali dell' impero romano* (Budapest, 1937) 59-60 (*non vidi*). Cf. Raffeiner no.18, *l.*5 (= Peek, *GVI* 696; Rome, III/IV) where a woman, originally from Tralleis in Karia, indicates that she is a freedwoman in the *familia Caesaris*: φῶς ἔλαβεν δὲ βλέπειν τόδ' ἐλεύθερον ἐκ βασιλήων, 'she received from kings the chance to look upon this free light'. That freedom is a prize to win is suggested at Raffeiner no.17, *l.*8 (= *IG* XIV.1839; Rome, II/III), where the freedwoman greets those who are left and says of herself that when a slave she gained στέφανον τὸν ἐλεύθερον (cf. **14**). Note other parallels at Raffeiner, p.39 n.1. That particular epigram is very probably Jewish: note *ll.*6-7: ἦν ἀγαθή, νομίμοις δὲ θεοῦ παρεγείνετο πᾶσιν· | οὐδὲν ὅλως παρέβαινε, 'she was good, and adhered to all God's laws; she transgressed absolutely none'. (As another view of death one may note here the — non-servile — epitaph for a daughter in which her parents have her say: *ab matre ad matrem deferor exanimis* (*I. Charles Univ.* 11.3 [I¹AD, Rome]. 'The journey from the real mother to mother earth is a euphemism: death is a "return home"' [Marek, 44; see his discussion of this conceit, 44-45 and nn. 47–48]. On other figurative uses of 'mother' cf. **60**.)

4. Fellow-slaves.

Düll, *Götterkulte*, 402-03, no.255 (III¹, near Stobi) is a dedication which a slave Diadoumenos, *oikonomos* of the polis of Stobi, and οἱ σύνδουλοι make to the Nymphs. A six-line metrical epitaph for a mule-driver from Singidunum, Upper Moesia (I/II?), is followed by the statement that Hierax the σύνδουλος set it up (Raffeiner no.41 = Peek, *GVI* 651 = M.Mirković/S. Dušanić, *Inscriptions de la Mésie supérieure*, I [Belgrade, 1976] 70, where slightly revised text and plate is provided; these editors think Peek's date of I/II for this inscription may be too early). Raffeiner, 68 n.2, notes some other examples: *IG* XIV.1812, 1910 (feminine), 2057. We may note also Raffeiner no.15 *l.*1 (= Peek, *GVI* 1948; Smyrna, III or later), a metrical epitaph for a young slave girl described as τὴν ὁμόδουλον | παρθένον . . . On ὁμόδουλος = σύνδουλος see MM, s.v. σύνδουλος, ad fin. At one level at least these terms imply a certain solidarity, the recognition of a common lot. It is from this that the metaphorical use of σύνδουλος in the NT has been developed (Col. 1.7; 4.7; Rev. 6.11). For the literal use in the NT note Mt. 24.49.

5. 'Slave of God . . . friend of all.'

S. Mitchell, *AS* 27 (1977) 97-103, nos. 39-55 (= *SEG* 873-88) is a series of brief Christian epitaphs from Ankara (undated by *ed.pr.*, but Byzantine), written on stone and tiles. The formula ὁ δοῦλος τοῦ θεοῦ which occurs in most of them adopts the NT metaphor. The phrase ὁ πάντων φίλος is also common to several (Mitchell nos. 39, 40, 45, 47, 54 = *SEG* 873, 874, 878, 880, 887 respectively). Mitchell no.39 is for a man who was both a goldsmith (χρυσοκ(όπος)) and a camel owner or driver (καμιλάρις). In the 'slave of God' phrase the abbreviated ΘV carries a small cross above it (Mitchell's pl. 14a shows this clearly). For another Christian goldsmith note *I.Tyre* 1.80. Mitchell no.42 (= *SEG* 875) mentions that the deceased died νεοφούτιστος. For this epithet referring to baptism see *New Docs 1976*, **88**. (In passing, note that *SEG* omits Mitchell no.33, a very fragmentary text.)

16. 'Charity motivated by piety' in an epitaph

Tomis   II/III
ed. — *SEG* 24 (1969) 1081

Χαῖρε, παροδεῖτα. — Καὶ σ[ύ].—
Ἔστηκες ἐπ' ἐννοίᾳ λέγων
"ἆρα τίς ἢ πόθεν ἥδε;" ἄκου-
ε δή, ξεῖνε, πάτραν καὶ οὔ-
5 νομα τοὐμόν· ἦν μέν μοι
χθὼν τὸ πρὶν Ἑλλάς· ἐκ μητρὸς Ἀθηναίας ἐφύην, πα-
τρός τε Ἑρμιονέος· Ἐπιφα-
νία δέ μοι οὔνομα. Πολλὴν
10 μὲν ἐσεῖδον ἐγὼ γαῖαν, πᾶσάν
τε ἔπλευσα θάλατταν·
ἦν γὰρ ἐμοὶ γενέτης καὶ γαμέτης
ναύκληροι, οὓς ἐθέμην

παλαμέσιν ἁγναῖς ὑπὸ τύνβῳ
15 θανόντας. Ὄλβιος δέ μοι βίος
τὸ πρὶν ἦν· ἐν Μούσες ἐφύην, σαφί-
ης τε μετέσχον. Φίλες τε λειπο-
μένες ὡς γυνὴ γυνηξὶ πολλὰ πα-
ρέσχον, εἰς εὐσεβίην ἀφορῶσα . . .
20 — Καὶ δὴ κλεινηρηκάματον πολὺν ἐ-
νενκαμένη, ἔγνω σαφῶς· οὐ κατ' εὐ-
σεβίαν εἰσὶν αἱ θνητῶν τύχαι.
Ἑρμογένης Ἀνκυρανὸς καὶ Τομίτης
φυλῆς Οἰνώπων τῇ ἑαυτοῦ συνβίῳ
25 εὐχαριστῶν μνείας χάριν ἀνέθηκα.

A well carved stone monument, though the lettering in the final lines becomes
crowded — a later addition, perhaps.
Bib. — *A. Slabotsky, *Stud. Clas.* 17(1977) 117-38 (2 figs.); *SEG* 404

'Greetings, wayfarer'. — 'You also'. — 'You stand in thought saying "Who
5 was she or where from?" Hear then, stranger, my country and name. |My
land formerly was Hellas: my mother was Athenian, my father from
10 Hermione, and my name was Epiphania. I have seen many |a land, and sailed
every sea: for my father and husband were ship-owners, (both of) whom I
15 buried with pure hands in a tomb |when they died. But previously my life was
happy: I was born among the Muses, and shared in wisdom. And to friends
20 abandoned as woman to women I provided much, with a view to piety.' |And
certainly, for one who endured much as an invalid she had clear knowledge
(that) mortals' fortunes are not in proportion to their piety. Hermogenes of
25 Ankyra and Tomis, of the tribe Oinopes, giving thanks to his own wife, |I
set this up as a memorial.

While this epitaph contains several standard elements in its phraseology and
content, as Slabotsky shows there are also some features which are distinctive: see
her article in general and particularly the notes which provide many references to
parallel and contrasting wording and ideas. In drawing this inscription to attention
here two features only are noted briefly.

First, Epiphania may be presumed to be a woman of some wealth: this may be
inferred not merely from the occupations of her father and first husband, but also
from her claim to be a source of support to other women who may like her have
been widowed (*ll*.17-19). It would be not unreasonable to call this charitable
activity, and we should note her explicit motivation — piety is what impels her to

this action for others. εὐσέβεια usually — though not always — refers to reverence towards the gods: see, e.g., Soph. *El*.245-50, where it is contrasted with αἰδώς (regard for other mortals). Slabotsky notes (134 n.178) three other inscriptions which testify to charitable activity by non-Christian/Jews. But it was not in fact such a rare commodity in the ancient world, if the term is used to embrace a wide range of types of activity. It could be performed not only on a one-to-one basis, but by an individual for a group, and the reverse. In general on this subject see A.R. Hands, *Charities and Social Aid in Greece and Rome* (Ithaca, 1968), which includes some discussion of early Christianity.

Second, the epitaph gives some emphasis in a non-specific way to the cultural education which the deceased had gained (*ll*.16-17). This attainment further supports the suggestion above that her background was not one of straitened means. For epigraphical testimony to education see Slabotsky, 153 nn.185-88. For illustrations from Greek vases portraying aspects of the education of girls see F.A.G. Beck, *Album of Greek Education* (Sydney, 1975) 55-62 (pls.69-88).

17. A soldier's epitaph

A twelve-line Latin epitaph from Nakolea in N. Phrygia for Flavius Aemilianus, set up by his sons, provides a surprising amount of detail (*ed. pr.* — T. Drew-Bear, *HSCP* 81 [1977] 257-74, pl.; cf. *AE* 806). Specifically dated to 356 (*ll*.11-12), the man's birthplace — Singidunum (Belgrade) in Moesia — is given, along with his age (47), years of service in the army (27), rank (*ducenarius*) and infantry regiment — or cavalry unit? (Drew-Bear, 272 n.64) — (*Cornuti seniores*). After an exegesis of the text, Drew-Bear shows (267-74) that this inscription, in revealing the presence of a unit of *seniores* in the East in 356, invalidates a recent hypothesis — growing into a consensus — that the *Seniores-Iuniores* division of units in the late Roman army first occurred in 364 (in the division of troops between Valentinian and Valens). But it is the general sentiments in the inscription that are worth a glance here.

The text begins, *in perpetuo sequolo sequritatis post omnia*, 'in the everlasting age of security, after all (mortal trials)' (*ed.pr*). No exact parallel is known for this first line, but Drew-Bear refers to Christian and pagan use of *perpetuae securitati*, *aeternae securitati* and the Christian *pacata in saecula*; in particular he notes Diehl, *ICLV* 3493, *optima femina manet aeterno s[ae]culo fruitur perpetuam securitatem* (Drew-Bear, 259-60, nn.7-8). Drew-Bear suggests (260) that the phrase in the newly-discovered inscription was 'perhaps influenced by the Christian expression *in seculo* meaning "in this life": awareness of this common Christian formula in a text which is certainly pagan would not be surprising for this period.' Could the phrase, *in perpetuo seculo*, range in sense from 'this (sinful) life' to 'the everlasting (next) life' (P.M. Brennan, in a note to me)? Note the use of *qu* for *c*.

At *ll*.4-7 we have: ... *Donicum vixit | delequit qu[o]s [o]portet amicus nec inimico[s] cre|avit, cui vi[d]u[us in] sepulchrum iacet dulci|tudine et luce*, 'while he lived he loved as a friend those whom he ought, nor did he make personal enemies, he who lies in this tomb deprived of the sweet light.' Friendship is a *topos* in both Christian and pagan epitaphs. So, too, the idea of avoiding giving offence to others is elsewhere attested (Drew-Bear, 263 and n.28). The hendiadys of the last two nouns is one indicator that the composer of this epitaph had some level of literary pretension (note, too, that the second half of *l*.7 and the beginning of *l*.8 form an iambic senarius). *Delequit* (5) is a morphological variant for *dilexit* (Drew-Bear, 262); note also *cui* = *qui* (*l*.6), and the breaking down of the accusative/ablative distinction at *in sepulchrum* (*l*.6).

Further on in the epitaph, at *ll*.10-11 we have : ... *vivate valete superi felices*, |*ego autem in sedes eternas*, 'live happily and farewell you who are alive (lit., above); I, however, am in my eternal home'. Drew-Bear comments (266-67), 'the author of this epitaph, written when Christianity was the state religion of the Roman Empire, was certainly a pagan in view of the attitudes revealed by the expressions *viduus ... luce* and *vivate ... felices*'. The final phrase quoted above — note again the accusative for ablative — does not refer to Hades but to the man's grave: the metaphor is common on both Christian and pagan tombstones (see Drew-Bear, 267 and n.49); but perhaps we cannot be so sure that Hades is ruled out. P.M. Brennan tells me that he doubts whether we can be confident of Aemilianus' religious adherence: 'since he is neither clearly pagan nor clearly Christian he might be technically either while actually/socially a hybrid'.

This epitaph illustrates well the way in which certain phrases and motifs occurring in non-Christian texts and taken over into Christian usage were still able to be used by non-Christians despite their having acquired a Christian colouring. The dividing line between Christian and non-Christian use of such clichés (not all, of course) must have been slight in the first century or so after the official Christianisation of the Empire.

The use of *securitas* in the epitaph above makes mention of *AE* 264 appropriate here. This is also an epitaph for a soldier (Faventia, in Italy, I¹) which concludes with the words *hic securus requiescit*: *AE* (n. ad loc.) speaks of this formula as having an 'allure chrétienne.' If its date is right a link with Christianity is virtually certainly ruled out, in which case the text illustrates well the way in which phraseology in non-Christian texts could in a later period be so thoroughly adopted for Christian use that it becomes thought of as a Christian formula.

With the Phrygian epitaph we may compare another in Latin from the same century, from Tomis (Constanța). *MPR* 3 is a largely complete stele which exhibits phraseology which could make it Christian or pagan.

> *Aur(elia) Ianuaria Ian[uarii] an(norum) ..., iu-*
> *ncta pari Fla(vio) Mart[i]no*
> *et amplius vixi m(enses) V, d(ies) ... pr-*
> *o comoda fuit spir[it]um D-*
> 5 *eo rede[re. Et] Aur(elia) Domna, so-*
> *ror Ian[uarii] a[n(norum) ...] III iuncta pa-*
> *ri vixit m(enses) X, d(ies) ... Fatum co-*
> *nplevit durus pro carita-*
> *te coniugi et sorori. Ip[si]*
> 10 *vivite parentes et nestr-*
> *is provid[et fil]is. Estote*
> *memores iterum [El]ysiis co-*
> *[ven]turi. Ave vale, viator.*

(I was) Aurelia Ianuaria, daughter of Ianuarius, aged ..., married to Flavius Martinus, and I lived a further 5 months, ... days. It was appropriate that
5 **she gave her spirit |back to God. And Aurelia Domna, her sister, daughter of Ianuarius, aged ...3, after her marriage she lived 10 months, ... days. Hard fate filled up (her time) in place of her love for her husband and sister.**
10 **You yourselves, |my parents, live and take care of our children. Be mindful that we will meet again in the Elysian fields. Hail and farewell, traveller.**

For the wording in *ll*.4-5 Barnea provides a few parallels; and it appears to be largely on the strength of this phrase that the text is included in *MPR* and earlier collections of Christian texts (such as Diehl, *ICLV* 2 [1927, repr. 1970] 3314). But, as Barnea notes, this phrase contrasts sharply with such standard non-Christian notions as *fatum . . . durus* (read *durum*) and the Elysian fields. If it is held to be Christian — and I think the question should remain open; cf. **110** for some other texts which are similarly problematical — then it should be compared with Christian texts dealt with at **111**, in which there are Homeric quotations.

18. Posthumous honours for civic and domestic virtues

Iulia Gordos (Lydia)   75/6
ed.pr. — P. Herrmann, *AAWW* 111 (1974) 439-44 (pl.2)

Ἔτους ρ´ καὶ ξ´, μη(νὸς) Ὑπερβερταίου τριακάδι.
    (*Crown*)
Εἰσαγγειλάντων τῶν στρατηγῶν Ἀθη-
νοδώρου τ[ο]ῦ Ἀ[θ]ηνοδώρου νεωτέρου
καὶ Μενάν[δ]ρου τοῦ Μενάνδρου Που-
5   πλίου καὶ Θυνείτου τοῦ Διονυσίου· γνώ-
μη γραμματέος (*sic*) τοῦ δήμου Μενάνδρου τοῦ Δημητρίου. Ἔδοξεν τῇ βουλῇ
καὶ τῷ δήμῳ τῷ Ἰουλιέων Γορδηνῶν καὶ τοῖς
παρ᾽ ἡμῖν πραγματευομένοις Ῥωμαίοις.
10 Ἐπεὶ Θεό[φιλ]ος Θοινείτου (?) εὐγενέστατος ἀπὸ
προγόνων πᾶσαν εὔνοιαν εἰσενηνεγμέ-
νος εἰς τὴν πατρίδα, οἰκοδεσπότην ζήσα[ς]
βίον, πολλὰ παρασχόμενος τῇ πατρίδι διά τε
στρατηγίας καὶ ἀγορανομίας καὶ πρεσβειῶ[ν]
15 ἄχρι Ῥώμης καὶ Γερμανίας καὶ Καίσαρος,
προσαινῆ (?) γενόμενον πρὸς τοὺς πολείτας
καὶ συνπαθῆ πρὸς τὴν γυναῖκα Ἀπφίαν, τὰ νῦν
δεδόχθαι τὸν Θεόφιλον τειμηθῆναι
εἰκόνι γραπτῇ καὶ εἰκόν{κον}ι χρυσῇ καὶ ἀγάλ-
20 ματι μαρμαρίνῳ. Ὁμοίως δεδόχθαι

Θεόφιλον προπενφθῆναι ἄχρι τοῦ τά[φου]
ἀναγνωσθῆναί τε τοῦτο τὸ ψήφισμ[α]
ἵνα πάντες εἰδῶσιν ὅτι οἱ τοιαῦτον (*sic*) ἀσκήσαντες βίον ὑπὲρ τῆς πατρίδος τοιαύ-
25 της τυνχάνουσι μαρτυρίας.

White marble stele used as grave lid. A large *stephanos* separates the first line
from the rest of the inscription.
Bib. — *AE* 808

Year 160, month Hyperbertaios, thirtieth day. (*Crown*) **The generals made
their report, Athenodoros son of Athenodoros the younger, and Menandros
5 son of Publius Menandros |and Thynites son of Dionysios; motion of the
people's secretary, Menandros son of Demetrios. The council and the people
of Iulia Gordos, and the Romans who are engaged in business among us,
10 resolved: |since Theophilos son of Thynites is of very noble ancestral stock,
having contributed all good-will towards his country, having lived his life as
master of his family, providing many things for his country through his
15 generalship and tenure as agoranomos and his embassies |as far as Rome and
Germany and Caesar, being amicable to the citizens and in concord with his
wife Apphia, now it is resolved that Theophilos be honoured with a painted
20 portrait and a gold bust and a |marble statue. Similarly it is resolved that
Theophilos be escorted to his tomb and that this decree be read aloud
(published ?) so that all may know that such people who exercise their life on
25 behalf of their country| meet with such a testimony.**

Sulla's settlement in Asia at the end of the First Mithridatic War (85BC) resulted
in a new calendar for cities like Iulia Gordos: year 160 of the Sullan era equates
to 75/6. This inscription reflects as perfectly normal the presence of resident
Romans engaged in commerce who have voting rights along with the town's
citizenry; for πραγματεύομαι (9) in the NT cf. Lk. 19.13.

It is clear from *l.*21 that the honorand has died and that the recognition of his
past services and merits is now (τὰ νῦν, 17) taking effect. Posthumous honorific
inscriptions are not altogether unknown (see Herrmann, 442 n.11, with reference),
but certainly less frequent than an inscription praising a still-living person.
Herrmann points out (441) that in the latter, a rider is not uncommonly included
that the honours should not begin until after the death of the individual. In the case
of Theophilos he is accorded a painted portrait, a gold bust and a marble statue,
along with an official escort to his grave ånd the publication of the decree which
has voted him these things. For εἰκόνι γραπτῇ (19) in the sense of 'painted portrait'
cf. *OGIS* 571.4-5 (Cadyanda in Lykia, Roman Imperial) — noted by MM, s.v.
γραπτός ad fin. — where a man is honoured with a gold crown, a bronze statue,
and εἰκόνι γραπτῇ ἐπιχρύ|σῳ. Dittenberger's n.4 to that text includes other
examples. In the NT γραπτός — only at Rom. 2.15, τὸ ἔργον τοῦ νόμου γραπτὸν ἐν
ταῖς καρδίαις — means 'written'.

Both Theophilos' personal qualities and his civic contribution are enumerated.
The sentiments at *ll.*10-12 are commonplace: for εὐγενής in this more common sense

in the NT cf. Lk. 19.12, 1 Cor. 1.26; at Acts 17.11 the meaning is metaphorical. The word οἰκοδεσπότης (12) occurs at Lk. 22.11, τῷ οἰκοδεσπότῃ τῆς οἰκίας; Mark's parallel context has simply τῷ οἰκοδεσπότῃ (14.14), suggesting that Lk's phrase may be a pleonasm. With the Lukan wording cf. *SIG³* 985.51 (Philadelphia in Lydia, late II/early I) where, in a private cult association the goddess Agdistis is described as οἰκοδέσποιναν τοῦδε τοῦ οῖκου. See further on the word S.C. Barton/G.H.R. Horsley, *JbAC* 24 (1981) 13 n.24. Theophilos served his city in various magisterial capacities, and also as ambassador (13-15). The Caesar mentioned in *l.*15 is Gaius (Caligula) whose presence in Germany in 39/40 was the most recent imperial venture there. The allusion to him merely as Caesar may be suggestive of *damnatio memoriae* (cf. *AE* 808, n. ad loc.). We can thus date Theophilos' embassy there, some 35 years before his death and the erection of this inscription. To have been an ambassador so long previously *may* allow the inference that Theophilos reached a considerable age. The Attic form ἄχρι (15) is prevalent in the NT: see BAGD, s.v., 1b.

Not only is Theophilos said to be προσηνής (16; for the form see Herrmann, 440) to his fellow citizens, but he is συμπαθής in relation to his wife (17). This example of that word needs to be added to MM's entry; in the NT it occurs only at 1 Pet. 3.8, and the treatment of the word in E.G. Selwyn's standard commentary is deficient. For ἀναγιγνώσκω, 'read aloud', the NT has plenty of instances, but in view of the date of the inscription the example should be noted in MM, s.v. As to the phrase ἀσκήσαντες βίον (23-24) BAGD, s.v. ἀσκέω, refers to Diognetus 5.2 and *SB* 1 (1915) 5100.4 (Abydos, n.d.) an epitaph for abbot David τὸν μοναδικὸν ἀσκήσας βίον . . . , 'who cultivated the monastic life'. For μαρτυρία — cf. L. Robert, *Hellenica* 13 (1965) 207 n.5 — note Tit. 1.13; 1 Jn. 5.9; 3 Jn. 12 in the NT.

19. A freedman's dedication for his patroness

Rome   II/III
ed.pr. — A. Stein, *BCAR* 56 (1928) 302-03, no.27 (fig.8) (*non vidi*)

> Γ(αίου) Φουλβίου Πίου
> τοῦ πάτρωνός μου
> Γ(αίος) Φούλβιος Εὐτυχής
> ἀπελεύθερος καὶ
> 5   πραγματευτὴς
> τὴν πατρώνισσαν

Bib. — L. Moretti, *IGUR* II.2 (1973) 1045; **I. Charles Univ.* 6, pp.26-27 (pl.2); cf. *SEG* 1304

Gaius Fulvius Eutyches, freedman and manager (honours) NN his patroness, wife (daughter ?) of Gaius Fulvius Pius my patron.

The woman's name is lost from the top line(s?) of the stone. Whether this inscription was an honorific text or an epitaph is uncertain, although the former is perhaps more likely. Editors have assumed that she was the wife of Pius and that

Eutyches may be understood to be 'the common property of both partners before the manumission' (Marek, *I. Charles Univ.*, p. 27; cf. Moretti, ad loc. But is there any reason why she could not have been his daughter? On this view Eutyches would have been manumitted by the father ('my patron'), and on the latter's decease Eutyches' client obligations were transferred to the daughter [as heir?].). For an example of someone who is a 'freedwoman of the two Scribonias' see the Latin funerary inscription rediscussed by H. Bloch, *HSCP* 86 (1982) 141-50 (fig. 1; Rome I²BC), a text of some historical interest by virtue of its mention of several people prominent in the late Republic. Other examples of πατρώνισσα include *P. Oxy.* 3 (1903) 478.27-28 (πατρω|νείσης Διονυσίας; 132AD), and *IG XIV* (1890) 1671 (Rome, n.d.). Although the term 'patroness' is not applied to them, it may not be inappropriate for the Greek women of status who supported Paul in his ministry (Acts 17.4, 12; cf. *New Docs 1976*, **69** *ad fin.*): patronage could be established not only by manumission but also by financial benefaction or social protection.

Eutyches' function in relation to his patron(s) was that of manager of the household, especially its finances (πραγματευτής = Latin *actor*). The post was usually held by slaves, but freedmen might continue in their posts in wealthier households: 'the very fact that freedmen remained in the positions they had occupied as slaves is a symptom of the deterioration of the social standing of freedmen in general' (Marek, 27). This text may be a useful example to bear in mind, therefore, when 1 Cor. 7.20-21 is being considered.

On patronage from Augustus to the Severi see R.P. Saller, *Personal Patronage under the Early Empire* (Cambridge, 1982), which includes discussion of the Latin terminology of patronage (7–39).

20. Letter promising money

Karanis
ed.pr. — *P. Wiscon.* 71, pp.119-22 (pl.26)

II

```
       Πτολεμαῖς        Κασσιαν[ῷ τῷ ἀδελ-]
       φῷ πλεῖστα χαίρειν. π[ρὸ μὲν ]
       πάντων εὔχομαί σε ὑγια[ίνειν. ἐ-]
       κομισάμην κεράμιν ἒ[ν ..... ]
   5   καὶ ἐπιστολὶν ἐν ᾗ γράφ[εις σε ]
       παραγεγονένε ἐν τῇ α. [..... .]
       ἐδύνου ἐν τῷ αὐτῷ ἀ[ναβῆναι ]
       πρὸς ἡμᾶς ἵνα καὶ ἡμεῖ[ς ..... ]
       λογήσομεν. τοῦτο γὰρ ἔχ[ει ἡδέως ]
  10   κατ' ὄψιν σε ἀσπάσασθαι. [ ἡὰν βού- ]
       λητέ σαι μεθ' ὑγίας ἄλλοτε ἐπι-
       παραγενέσθαι παρακαλῶ ἀνα-
       βῆναι πρὸς ἐμέ. ἡὰν εὔρω τινὰ
       τὸν δυνάμενον ἐνέγκε σοι τὸν
  15   χαλκὸν Πρόκλου πέμσω σοι διὰ
       αὐτοῦ, ἡὰν μή, ἡὰν ἀλλαγῇ
```

Λονγεῖνος, τοῖς ἐμοῖς λόγοις ἐρεῖ`ς΄
αὐτῷ καὶ λήμψῃ παρ' αὐτοῦ καὶ
γράψον μοι δι' αὐτοῦ καὶ δώσω αὐ-
20 τῷ ὅδε δραχμὰς τετρακοσίας
ἴκοσι τέσσαρες. ἀσπάζου Σαραπιά-
δα καὶ τὴν μητέραν αὐτῆς καὶ Βαυ-
κ̣α̣λᾶν καὶ τοὺς παρ' ὑμῶν πάντες κατ' ὄνομα. ἐρρῶσθέ σαι
25 εὔχομαι, κύριε. Μεχεὶρ ι̅ζ̅.

(*verso*) εἰς Καρανίδα   ＼ ╱   Κασσιανῷ Γεμέλλῳ
         ο̣ὐ̣ετερανῷ   ╱ ＼   ἀπὸ Πτολεμαίου ἀδελφοῦ.

The papyrus was largely cut-off regularly on all sides and folded both
horizontally and vertically. The *verso* (not included in the plate) has a cross in the
middle of *ll*.26-27. Read ἐπιστολήν or ἐπιστόλιον (5), πέμψω (15), πάντας (23-24);
αι for ε and vice versa. *Ed.pr.*'s insertion of μή before ἀλλαγῇ (16) has not been
retained: see below.

> **Ptolemaios to Kassianos his brother, very many greetings. Before everything**
> 5 **I pray you are in good health. I received one keramion . . . |and a letter in**
> **which you write that you had been present in the . . . You could at the same**
> **time have come up to us in order that we also . . . might converse (?). For**
> 10 **this is pleasant, |to greet you face to face. [If he wants] you to come on**
> **another occasion when you are in good health I urge you to come up to me.**
> 15 **If I find someone who can convey to you |Proklos' money I will send it to**
> **you via him; otherwise, if Longinos comes, you will speak to him with my**
> **words and receive (it) from him; and write to me via him and I will give him**
> 20 **|here 424 drachmai. Greet Sarapias and her mother and Baukalas and all**
> 25 **those with you individually. I pray you fare well, |lord. Mecheir 17 (= 11/12**
> **February).**
> **(*verso*) To Karanis. (*cross*) For Kassianos Gemellos, veteran, from Ptolemaios**
> **his brother.**

This letter has nothing particularly unusual about it, but illustrates well the
problem of conveying safely money and other goods in antiquity. Cf. *O.Florida*
(1976) 15.5-7 (Edfu, II) — quoted at *New Docs 1976*, **17**, with the comments on
the collection for the Jerusalem Church (Acts 11.27-30) — and *New Docs 1976*, **84**,
ll.13-14 (IV). In the present letter Ptolemaios asks his brother, if a carrier cannot
be found, to get a certain Longinos to advance the money which Ptolemaios will
repay upon his return. That travel is not easy, nor an everyday event for the bulk
of people in antiquity, is clearly implied in Ptolemaios' gentle upbraiding of his
brother for not visiting him when he was in the vicinity.

A few philological points relevant for the NT may be listed *en passant*. ἀναβαίνω
πρός τινα (12-13; restored at 7-8), cf. Acts 15.2 (cf. *New Docs 1976*, **15** for a further
example). At *l*.7 the construction without ἄν is paralleled at Mt. 26.9: cf. BDF 358

(noted by Sijpesteijn, p.121). ἀλλάσσω occurs here (16) with a secondary meaning 'change (location), arrive': the NT does not attest this sense, but it should perhaps be mentioned in a revised MM entry. In a note to me K.L. McKay points out that ἀλλάσσω can mean 'come/go to' as well as 'from' although the meaning is not common. There is no need for the editorial insertion of μή at *l*.16. What is unusual, perhaps, is the use of the passive, unless ἀλλαγῇ is a passive form for a middle meaning, 'move oneself'. He compares ἀπαλλάσσεσθαι at Acts 19.12. The wording of τινὰ | τὸν δυνάμενον (13-14) is curious. On κατ' ὄνομα (cf. 3 Jn. 15) see *New Docs 1976*, **15** ad fin., **19**, *l*.16. In the present letter Ptolemaios begins by calling Kassianos ἀδελφός (largely restored at *l*.1, but cf. *verso l*.27), and concludes by calling him κύριος. *P.Wiscon.* includes a number of other letters where this combination occurs: 72.2-3 (provenance unknown, II), τῇ ἀδελφῇ | καὶ κυρίᾳ (wife ?); 73.1-2 (Oxyrhynchite nome, II); 74.1, 22 (provenance unknown, III/IV); 75.14 (provenance unknown, IV). Note also the phrase (largely restored) in an instruction for payment, 63.1 (Oxyrhynchos, 9/8/410), concerning which *ed.pr.* (p.93) speaks of Phoibammon asking 'his "brother"' to provide payment. The phrase can appear in letters which are Christian (e.g., *New Docs 1976*, **85**) as well as in those which are not (e.g., *New Docs 1976*, **20**; both these examples are IV).

The cross on the *verso* is not a Christian symbol, but appears on the address section of other letters (e.g. *P.Wiscon.* 73, verso *l*.24); it indicates where the letter is to be tied when folded ready for dispatch (cf. Deissmann, *LAE*, 182 n.24, with an example on p.179). At *New Docs 1976*, **85** it occurs in the middle of a word, κυρίῳ μου ἀδελ Χ φῷ, κτλ, but I was in error to suggest that it may be felt to have a Christian significance there.

21. Five letters of Sempronius from a family archive

Provenance unknown Late II

ed.pr. — P.J. Sijpesteijn, *ZPE* 21 (1976) 159-181, nos.5 (pl.2), 6a-b (pl.3), 7a-b.

5. Σεμπρώνι[ος]   Σατορνίλᾳ τῇ μητρὶ καὶ κυρίᾳ
   [πλεῖσ]τα   χαίρειν. πρὸ τῶν ὅλων ἐρρῶσθέ σε εὔ-
   [χομαι,] ἅμα δὲ καὶ τὸ προσκοίνημά σου ποιοῦμε ἡμερησίως
   [παρὰ τ]ῷ κυρίῳ Σαράπιδι. θαυμάζω πῶς οὐκ ἔγραψάς μοι
  5 οὔ[τ]ε [δ]ιὰ [Κ]έλερος οὔτε διὰ Σεμπρων[ί]ου· παραγενάμ[ε]νος
   γὰρ ἀπὸ τῆς ἀποδημείας εὗρον αὐτοὺς καὶ ἐπυνθανόμην
   δι' ἣν ἐτείαν οὐκ ἐκομείσαντό μ[υ] ἐπιστόλιον. ἔφασαν διὰ
   τὴν ἀ[π]οδημείαν. μαθὼν δὲ περὶ τῆς σωτηρία[ς] ὑμῶν
   ἀμεριμνότερος ἐγενάμην. διὸ ἐρωτηθεῖσ⟨α⟩, ἡ κυρία μου,
  10 [ἀνόκνως μ]οι γράφε περὶ τῆς σωτηρίας σου. ἐκομ[ισ]άμην
   [ἐπιστόλιον] διὰ Σωκράτους κὲ [ἕ]τερ[ο]ν μικρὸν διὰ Ἀν[τω]νιανοῦ·
   [καὶ ἐπιστό]λιον Ἑξᾶτο[ς] ἐκομ[ισ]άμην, ἄλ]λο δὲ ἐκομ[ισάμη]ν Λω-
   [βώτου. ἔγραψά]ς μοι κ[αὶ] περ[ὶ] . . . . .
      (*ll*.13-19 omitted as too fragmentary)

20 [. . . . .]ψα . [.] . κ . . Σεμπρ[ων]ίῳ γὰρ εἰ κε[
    [. . . . .] . οιτων ἐμόν ἐστιν τ[ὸ π]ρονοῆσαι, ἄ[λλο]υ ἐστ[ὶ]ν
    [τὸ . .]ούσασ[θ]ε πρὶν τοῦ χρόνου τὰ τοιαῦ⟨τ⟩α . [.] . μετα
    [. . .]εχι οὖν ἐστὶν ἐλάχιστον πρᾶγμα. ν[ῦ]ν γράφω σοι
    [ὅπως] μνη[μονεύῃς αὐ]το[ῦ·] νῦν γὰρ κωφῷ σοι ἔγραψεν.
25 [καὶ ἔ]γραψας π[ερὶ] τούτων τὴν δευτέραν ἡμῖν ἐπισ-
    [τολήν. γρά]φω περὶ τ[ούτων·] καὶ γὰρ ἐβουλόμην πᾶν ποιῆσε
    κὲ ἐλθῖ[ν] πρὸς ὑμᾶς πρῶτον μὲν προσκυνῆσέ σου τὸ ἀγαθὸν
    καὶ φι[ι]λότεκνον ἦθος, δεύτερον κὲ περὶ τούτων. οὐ νῦν
    δὲ [.]ν εὗρον ἀφορμ[ή]ν, ἀλλὰ πρὸς ἀποδημίαν ὢν ἔγραψά
30 σοι περὶ αὐτῶν τούτων. ἄσπασε Μάξιμον καὶ τὴν σύν-
    [βιον α]ὐτοῦ καὶ Σεμπρώνιον τὸν Κύριλλον καὶ Σατορνῖλον
    [καὶ Γέ]μελλον καὶ Ἰ[ού]λιον καὶ τοὺς αὐτοῦ καὶ Ἑλένην καὶ τοὺς
    [αὐτ]ῆς καὶ Σκυθικὸν [καὶ] Κοπρῆν, Χαιρήμονα, Θερμοῦ-
    θιν καὶ τὰ πεδ[ία] αὐτῆς.   ἔρ⟨ρ⟩ωσό μοι, ἡ [κ]υρία [μ]ου,
35   διὰ παντός.
    Ἀπόδ(ος) Μ[α]ξίμῳ παρὰ Σεμπρωνί[ου]
        ἀδελφοῦ.

6a. [Σ]εμπρώνιος   Σατ[ορ]νίλᾳ τῇ μητρεὶ
     [κ]αὶ κυρί[ᾳ μ]ου [πλεῖσ]τα χαίρ[ειν.]
     [π]ρὸ τῶν ὅλων ἐ[ρ]ρ[ῶ]σθέ σε εὔχο[μαι με-]
     [τ]ὰ κὲ τῶν γλυ[κ]οι[τά]των ἀδε[λφῶν μου, ἅ]μα
  5 [δ]ὲ κα[ὶ] τὸ [π]ροσκύνημα ὑμῶ[ν ποιοῦμε ἡ]με-
     [ρ]ησίως παρὰ τῷ [κ]υ[ρίῳ] Σε[ρά]πιδι. ε[ὑρὼν τ]ὸν
     πρὸς ὑμᾶς ἐρχόμενον ἀνα[πλέ]ον[τα ἠπιγό]μην
     δι' ἐπειστολῆς ἀσπάσα[σ]θε ὑμᾶς. ἐρ[ωτη]θεῖσ⟨α⟩, ἡ
     κυρία μου, ἀνόκνως [μ]οι γρά[φ]ε[ι]ν π[ερὶ] τ[ῆ]ς σω-
 10 τ[η]ρία⟨ς⟩ ὑμῶν, εἵνα ἀ[μερι]μν[ότ]ερα δι[άγω]. περὶ
     [τ]ῶν ἱματίων μ[ου ἄλλοτε γράψ]ω σ[οι . . . .] . .
         (*ll.*12-15 omitted as too fragmentary)
 16 [.]νου. ἄσπασε Μ[άξιμον καὶ τὴν σύμβιο]ν αὐτοῦ
     κ[αὶ Σα]το[ρ]ν[ῖ]λον Κέλ[ερα ± 12]σοι γρά-
     [ψω π]ε[ρ]ὶ αὐτο[ῦ] κοὺ δ[± 15] αιθε
         (*ll.*19-26 omitted as too fragmentary)

6b. Σεμπρώνιος   Μαξίμ[ῳ τῷ ἀ]δελφῷ
     πλε[ῖ]στα χ[αίρε]ιν. [π]ρὸ τ[ῶν] ὅλ[ων]
     ἐρρῶσθέ σε εὔ[χο]με. ἐ[κ]ομεισάμην σου
 30 ἐπιστόλιον δι' [οὗ] μοι γρ[άφ]ει[ς] δ[ύ]ο ἐπισ-
     τολάς μοι ἀπεσταλκένε. ἴσθι, ἄδελφε, ὅτι
     μείαν μόνην ἐκομεισάμην. γ[ράφε]ις μοι
     περὶ Λωβώτου [ὥ]ς πρ[.]ασε[.] οὐκ ἔστιν
     εὐχερὲς παντὶ ἀνθρώπῳ τ[ὰ πλεῖ]στα δοῦνε.

35 διὰ τὸν σκυλμὸν σοι πλ .[.] ι.[. . .] μὴ με
   μεμφοῦ ὡς ἀμελοῦντα· κατ[.] . . . [. . .]
   τὰ μὲν ἔστην [δι'] ἀσχολία[ν παρ' ἐμῷ]
   πάντα δὲ ὅσα μο[ι εἴ]ρηκας ἐπλ[ήρ]ω[σα,]
   τάχιον δὲ διὰ .[. . .] πέμ[π]ετέ σοι. [ἀσ]πάζ[ομαι]
40 τὴν σύμβιό[ν σου] καὶ [τὰ] τ[έ]κν[α σο]υ.
                    ἔρρω⟨σ⟩ο μ[οι, ἄδελφε.]
              (Continued in the left margin)
   ὃν ποῖς μοι βαρυγαύτην πρὸς ὃν πεποίηκας [±24]ς πορφυρᾶς
              ἔχοντα προσποδω κεὶς τὸ τραχήλιν κεὶς τὰ χιρίδια
   ἁπλοῦς π. . . . .τρα γενέστω τὰ κεὶς ὀσφυ[

45 ['Απόδ(ος) Μαξίμῳ ἀδελφῷ π(αρὰ) Σ]εμπρωνίου.

Col.2

7a. [Σεμπ]ρώνιος   Σατ[ορνί]λῳ τῷ ἀδελφῷ
                    χαίρειν.
    ἐκομεισάμην σου δύο [ἐ]πειστολάς, μείαν μὲν πε-
    ρὶ ὧν ἐδήλωσα τῷ ἀ[δ]ελφῷ Μαξίμῳ, ἐτέραν δὲ
  5 περὶ τῆς κυρίας ἡμῶν μητρὸς ὡς κεινδυνευ[ο]υσά-
    σης αὐτῆς καὶ ἀκμὴν δειακατεχομένη`ς´ τῇ νωθρί-
    ᾳ. γείνωσκε οὖν, ἀδε[λ]φέ, ἱκανῶς με ἀγων[ι]ᾶν
    ἅμα μηδὲ τὰς νύκ{κ}τ[α]ς κοιμώμενον ἄχρε[ι]ς οὗ
    μου δηλῶσῃς πῶς δι[ά]γει ἐν τούτῳ τῷ ἀέρι. μὴ λη-
 10 ρήσεις ἄχρι οὗ εὕρῃς τὸν πρὸς ἐμὲ καταπλέοντα.
    παρηγόρησον τὸν ἀδελφὸν Μάξιμον ὡς ἐὰν δύ-
    νῃ. ἔγραψ[α] καὶ Οὐαλερίῳ τῷ ἀδελφῷ περὶ τούτου. ἐλπί-
    ζω δὲ [ὡς] καὐτὸς οὐκ ἀγνοεῖ πῶς χαλεπῶς
    περὶ [. . .]ς διάγωμεν ἀλλὰ τί ἐκ τούτου ὠφε-
 15 λῆσε δυνηθησόμεθα; οὐ γὰρ μόνος αὐτῆς ἐσ-
    τερή[θη ἀλ]λὰ καὶ πάντες ἡμεῖς. δι⟨ὸ⟩ οὖν ὡς μη-
    δὲν δυν[αμέ]νας ποιῆσαι [ἀ]λλ' οὐδὲ [ὀ]φέ-
    λῃς τὰ ἀν[θ]ρ[ώ]πινα φρονεῖν ἐξερέτως
    ἐν τυούτῳ κερῷ. ἔρ⟨ρ⟩ωσό μοι.

Col.3

7b.
 20 Σεμπ[ρώνιος]   Σατ[ο]ρ[νίλᾳ]
    τῇ μητ[ρ]εὶ   χαί[ρ]ειν.
    λαβὼν ταῦτα γρά[μ]ματα
    αὐτῆς ὥρας δήλω[σ]όν μοι
    πῶς διά[γ]εις, οὐκ ὀλίγως γὰρ
 25 ἀγωνιῶ μέχρει οὗ μάθω
    τὰ περὶ σοῦ. περὶ γὰρ τοῦ ἀ-
    δελφοῦ [μ]ου Μαξίμ[ου] νῦν

σοι γράψ[ω] ὅπως αὐ[τ]ὸν πα-
ρηγορή[σ]ῃς. οὐκ ἰ.ˊδ[.] ἐκ πε-
30 ρεισσοῦ ωκω γάρ, φ[η]σιν, αὐτὰ τὰ υδ..α ἀλλὰ ἡ τ[ο]ῦ κερου
ἀκερία οὐκ ἐᾷ με .ι..ενό-
μενος μὴ ἐκ τῆς λύπης
εἰς ἄλλο τι καὐτὸς [ἀπ]οτˊρˊα[[ρ]]πῇ.
35 οἶδα γὰρ ὅτι καὶ σὺ αὐτὴ ὑπὲρ
αὐτὸν λυπῇ ἀλλά, δέσπ[οι]να,
νῆψον διὰ τὰ ἀδέλφιά μου
καὶ το⟨ῦ⟩το ἔδι ὅτι ἴσως π[εφ]ίλη-
κε [τὰ]ς θυγατέρ[ας] καὶ [...]..
40 ἀδελφὴν Σιβό[ρ]ραν [ἀ]λλὰ
τί δυνάμεθα πρὸς ἃ̣ [ὁ θεὸς] ο[ὐ]
δύναται; ἔρρωσό μοι.

(*verso*)
    [ἀπ]όδ(ος) [Ο]ὐαλερίωι ἀδε[λφῶ]ι [καὶ Σατορ]νίλωι ἀδελφῶι π(αρὰ)
        Σεμπ[ρωνίου .]

The middle of no.5 (*ll*.13-19) is badly damaged and has been omitted here; so too no.6a-b (*ll*.12-15; *ll*.19-25).
Bib. — no.7a-b repr. as *P.Wiscon.* 84, pp.177-79 (pl.39)

(5) Sempronius to Satornila his mother and lady, very many greetings. Before all things, I pray you are faring well and at the same time I make obeisance for you daily before the lord Sarapis. I am wondering why you did not write
5 **to me |either via Celer or via Sempronius. For when I turned up after my absence I found them and sought to learn the reason why they did not bring a letter for me, they said, 'Because of your absence'. But when I learned about your health I became less anxious. Accordingly, my lady, since you've**
10 **been asked, |write to me without delay about your health. I received a letter via Sokrates and another brief one via Antonianos, and I received a letter from Hexas and another from Lobotes. You wrote to me as well about . . .**
15,20 **|. . . |. . . (*l*.23) . . . is no small matter. Now I am writing to you so that you may be mindful of him. For now his letters have been falling on your deaf**
25 **ears. |And you wrote the second letter to me about these matters. I am writing to you about these things. For I also was wanting to do all I could and to come to you first to do obeisance to your good and childloving disposition, and second concerning these matters. But I have not found an occasion, now,**
30 **but while I was on a journey I wrote |to you about these very matters. Greet Maximus and his wife, and Sempronius, Kyrillos and Satornilus and Gemellus and Julius and his family, and Helen and her family, and Skythikos and Kopres, Chairemon, Themouthis and her children. Fare well, my lady,**
35 **|always. Give to Maximus from Sempronius his brother.**

(6a) Sempronius to Satornila my mother and lady, very many greetings. Before all things I pray you are faring well with my sweetest brothers; and

5 at the same time | also I make obeisance for you daily before the lord Sarapis.
When I found the man who is coming to you sailing upstream I made haste
to greet you by letter. Since you've been asked, my lady, write to me without
10 delay about your health, | so that I may continue to keep less anxious.
15 Concerning my clothes I will write on another occasion to you ... | ... (*l.*16)
Greet Maximus and his wife and Satornilus Celer, ... I will write to you
about him ...

(6b) (*l.*27) Sempronius to Maximus his brother, very many greetings. Before
30 all things I pray you are faring well. I received your | letter in which you write
that you have sent me two letters. Know, brother, that I received one only.
You write to me about Lobotes that ... it is not easy to give the most to every
35 person. | Because of the vexation for you ... do not blame me for being
uncaring ... I set some matters beside me because of my busyness, but
everything that you have said to me I have fulfilled, and they will be sent to
40 you quickly via ... I greet | your wife and your children. Fare well my
brother. (*Left margin*) As for the garment which you are making for me for
which you have made [the border?] of purple, with fringes both on the collar
and the sleeves ... let it be on the loincloth (?) ... [Give to Maximus, my
brother from S]empronius.

(7a) (*col.*2) Sempronius to Satornilus his brother, greetings. I received your
two letters, one concerning the matters which I have clarified to our brother
5 Maximus, and the other | concerning our lady mother that she is at risk and
still in the grip of her illness. Know therefore, brother, that I am considerably
worried and that at the same time I am sleepless at night until you make clear
10 to me how she is faring in this climate. Do not waste time | until you find
someone who is sailing down in my direction. Console our brother Maximus
as best you can. I wrote also to Valerius our brother about this. I hope that
he does not fail to appreciate how badly we feel about ... but what help will
15 we be able to provide by this? | For he is not the only one who has been
deprived of her, but all of us. Accordingly, therefore, treat us as unable (to
do anything), but you ought not to think in human terms ('be humble' —
ed.pr.; 'think humanly in excess'(?) — *P.Wiscon.*), particularly at this
moment. Farewell.

20 (7b) (*col.*3) | Sempronius to Satornila his mother, greetings. When you receive
this letter at the same time clarify for me how you are keeping, for I worry
25 a lot | until I hear news concerning you. About my brother Maximus now I
30 will write to you that you may console him ... | ... (*l.*31) but the
inappropriateness of the occasion does not allow me ... lest out of grief he
35 too may turn away to something else. | For I know that you yourself as well
grieve for him; but, lady, exercise self-control because of my brothers. And
40 this was necessary because he loved equally his daughters and [his (?)] | sister
Siborra. But what can we do in a situation where [God] is powerless?
Farewell. (*verso*) Give to my brother Valerius and my brother Satornilus from
Sempronius.

The family archive of which the above texts form part consists of nine letters in all, written on six papyri. The full list is:

1a. *SB* 3.1 (1926, repr. 1974) 6263.1-17 (II), Sempronius   )   *ed.pr.*, H.I. Bell,
    to Satornila   )   *Rev. Ég.* 1 (1919)
  b. *SB* 6263.18-31, Sempronius to Maximus   )   204-06
2. *P.Mich.* 3 (1936) 206 (*ed.pr.*, J.G. Winter, *CP* 22 [1927] 254-56; = *SB* 4
    [1931] 7357; II), Longinus Celer to Maximus
3. *P.Mich.* 3 (1936) 209 (late II/early III), Satornilus to Sempronius
[4. *PSI* 8 (1927) 943 (provenance unknown, II?), Maximus to Korbolon]
5. *P.Mich.* inv. 192, Sempronius to Satornila   )
6a. *P.Mich.* inv. 280.1-26, Sempronius to Satornila   )
  b.   280.27-45, Sempronius to Maximus   )   printed
7a. *P.Wiscon.* 84, col.2, 1-19, Sempronius to Satornilus   )   above
  b.   84, col.3, 20-43, Sempronius to Satornila   )

H.I. Bell treated 1a, b, 2-4 in S. Morenz (ed.), *Aus Antike und Orient. Festschrift Wilhelm Schubart zum 75. Geburtstag* (Leipzig, 1950), 38-47 (*non vidi*); but Sijpesteijn, 169, regards no.4 as not belonging to the group. The members of the family, as we can reconstruct it, are: Satornila, her son Sempronius Maximus, and his four brothers, Maximus Celer (whose unnamed wife is mentioned), Satornilus Celer, Longinus Celer, Valerius. For comments on these see ibid, 169-70. The surviving letters allude to other correspondence between family members (e.g., 6b). Reference (usually greetings) is made to nearly two dozen others and their families (ibid., 171 n.11, for a full list). The three papyri which each carry two letters emanate from Sempronius, from which Sijpesteijn deduces (ibid., 171) that he may have been 'parsimonious'. This need not be the only way to see it, but simply with the opportunity afforded by a departing traveller he sent two letters (or three in the case of no.7, for the remains of *col.*1 survive as ten end-lines, and as no.7a, *l.*12 and the address on the *verso* of 7 shows it was addressed to Valerius). Sempronius himself appears to have been travelling about — a civil servant perhaps? (ibid., 170) — but based at Alexandria, the latter being inferred from his use of the *proskynema* formula (no.5, *ll.*3-4; no.6a, *ll.*4-6); on this see Z. Aly, *Ét.Pap.* 9 (1971) 165-219, cf. *New Docs.* 1976, **16**. For the particular association of Sarapis with Alexandria note *P.Oxy.* 3239, *col.*2, *ll.*31-32, which includes the following 'definition' in an alphabetic glossary (late II): ὁ Σάραπις Ἀλεξανδρείαν κοσμεῖ. The noun used in connection with gods in Egypt is not associated exclusively with Sarapis, however. A number of 'acts of adoration' to Pan are attested in inscriptions, e.g., *I.Pan* 18 (Mons Porphyrites, 4/7/29AD), 51.19, 23-25 (Wadi Semna, 26/5/11AD), 52 (almost entirely restored; Wadi Semna, principate of Tiberius), 66 (Wadi Menih, 29/4/44AD; here performed by someone 'for my good friend Leonidas son of Areios'), 81 (Abydos, I or II). In his discussion of *I.Pan* 22, an inscription on an altar dedicated to Εἴσιδι Μυριω|νύμῳ (Mons Porphyrites, 137/8) Bernand quotes two examples of *proskynema* inscriptions addressed to Isis 'of a myriad names', (on the latter epithet see especially *P.Oxy.* 11 [1915] 1380. 190-220 [early II], and cf. briefly *New Docs* 1976, **2**, p.16). *SB* 11066 (provenance unknown, III) is a private letter in which Isis is the object of the *proskynema*.

It is a pity that the length of the letters precludes the reprinting here of the entire archive — nos. 1a and b are reprinted with discussion in Deissmann, *LAE* 192–97

— and in view of the length of the ones which have been included comments have been restricted to a minimum to allow the letters to speak largely for themselves. Nos.5 and 6.6-8 illustrate well the way in which people will write a letter simply because someone is travelling to the addressee's home. This may in part account for some of the repetition from one letter to another (especially no.5 and 6a), though this is not to be confused with the stereotyped formulae which are a conventional feature of private letters (opening greeting, wishes for health, salutations to others, farewell, etc.). *New Docs. 1976*, **16** is a letter devoid of any real content, and perhaps it was written simply to keep in touch with the addressee even though there was no particular news for the writer to include at the time the courier happened to be leaving. Cf. also *SB* 11243, a virtually complete brief letter (provenance unknown, III) containing nothing but greetings. Another aspect of letter sending is illustrated in *P.Laur.* 44 (Oxyrhynchite nome ?, VI), a Christian letter in which the writer says: γεγράφηκα τάδε ἵνα παραγγείλω | τοῖς ἐρχομένοις μὴ δοῦναι τὰ γράμματά τινι, εἰ μὴ τοί γε εἰς τὰς χεῖρας ὑμῶν, κτλ, (3-4), 'I have written this to instruct those who are coming not to give the letter to anyone except in fact into your hands'. (This letter includes another clause of interest. *Ll.*5-6 read: κύρι' ἄδελφε, ἔξοτε ὁ θεὸς ἐπεσκέψατο | καὶ ηὑρέθην εἰς μέσον ἀνθρώπων οὐ καλῶ[ν], κτλ, 'Lord brother, since God looked after me and I was found in the midst of wicked men . . . ' For ἐπισκέπτομαι here see BAGD, s.v., B, especially Acts 15.14. For the passive of εὑρίσκω see BAGD, s.v., 1b, expecially Acts 8.40.) To return to the archive, the extended list of greetings at the end of no.5 (on such lists see *New Docs 1976*, **15**) includes two women and their families (*ll.*32-33, 33-34): are these more women who are in charge of their *oikos* (cf. comments in **3** above)? It is hardly possible to say here, but the very possibility should not be ruled out entirely. For the apparent fatalism in no.7b, *ll.*40-42 — note that ὁ θεός is restored without comment by *ed.pr.* — one might compare the formula θεοῦ θέλοντος which occurs in both non-Christian and Christian documents (cf. *New Docs. 1976*, **15**). Cf. *P.Oxy.* 1 (1898) 115.9-10 (II), a letter of consolation (discussed by Deissmann, *LAE* 176-78) containing the statement ἀλλ' ὅμως οὐδὲν | δύναταί τις πρὸς τὰ τοιαῦτα.

A few philological items may be noticed briefly. MM, s.v. ἀκμήν, discuss the adverbial accusative use of this noun, and although the Atticists' condemnation of it in the sense 'yet, still' is mentioned, no documentary examples are provided. BAGD, s.v., follows suit. Letter no.7a, *l.*6 provides a clear-cut example, thus affording a parallel to the sole NT use at Mt. 15.16 (it is a *v.l.* at Heb. 5.13). The adjective ἀμέριμνος (no.5, *l.*9; no.6, *l.*10) is well attested in the papyri already, but for the phraseology of 1 Cor. 7.32 the wording of the two new letters may be particularly compared. BAGD attests no papyrus examples of the idiom εὐχερές ἐστιν + infin. (no.6b, *ll.*33-34); it is found in ECL (though not NT) and so should be noted s.v. εὐχερής, 1. For νήφω in the same figurative sense as found in the NT (1 Thes. 5.6, 8; 1 Pet. 1.13; 4.7; 5.8) note no.7b, *l.*37. With the wording at no.6b, *l.*37 τὰ μὲν ἔστην . . . [. παρ' ἐμῷ] cf. Lk. 9.47, ἔστησεν αὐτό (sc. παίδιον) παρ' ἑαυτῷ. φιλέω of familial love (no.7b, *ll.*38-39) may be noted. Sempronius speaks of 'τὸ' ἀγαθὸν | καὶ φ[ι]λότεκνον ἦθος (no.5, *ll.*27-28): for this compound adjective (used primarily of women; cf. **80**) cf. Tit. 2.4. The example is well worth adding to MM.

Finally, one sentence from no.3 (*P.Mich.* 3.209) may be drawn to readers' attention. In this letter which contains much flattery, Satornilus tells Sempronius, οἶδας γάρ, ἄδελ|φε, ὅτει οὐ μόνον ὡς ἀδελφόν σε ἔχω ἀλλὰ | καὶ ὡς πατέρα καὶ κύριον καὶ θεόν (*ll.*11-13).

22. The Christian (?) letters of Paniskos

Eight letters survive of a late-III archive which have attracted much attention since their first publication in 1927. The corpus, reprinted as *P.Mich*.3 (1936) 214-221, consists of six letters from a soldier, Paniskos, five to his wife Ploutogeneia and one to a 'brother' Aion; to these are added a very scrappy seventh letter, and finally a letter from Ploutogeneia to her mother. F. Farid, *MPL*, pp.109-17, surveys modern discussions of these documents, of which Paniskos' letters at least have been accepted as Christian by some and rejected by others. Naldini includes several of them in his collection of Christian letters, nos. 14-17. Farid draws attention to the differences of phraseology in references to god(s) in these letters: some use the plural, e.g. *P.Mich.* 214.4-6, εὔχομε . . . καθ᾽ ἑκάστην ἡμέραν παρὰ ταῖς θεοῖς πᾶσι (cf. *ll.*14-16), while others employ the singular, e.g., *P.Mich.* 216.3-6, εὔχομαι . . . παρὰ τῷ κυρίῳ θεῷ (similarly at *P.Mich.* 219.2-3).

Paniskos was illiterate, hence he will have found professional scribes to write his letters for him. Farid shows by analysis of other verbal features in the letters that the writer of *P.Mich.* 216 also wrote 218 and 219. And it is in just these three letters that the singular use of θεός occurs. Thus when Paniskos wanted a letter written to his wife he found a scribe and told him the 'gist' of what he wanted included. The writer then formed this into a letter using the phrases he was accustomed to employ himself. 'The content is the client's, the form is the writer's' (Farid, 116). The particular wording, then, may inform us about the religious adherence of the scribes whose services he used, rather than about Paniskos himself. (This solution has been raised independently and more briefly in E.A. Judge/S.R. Pickering, *JbAC* 20 [1977] 53.) Farid believes (117) that the writer of *P.Mich.* 216, 218 and 219 was a Christian, but thinks we must remain uncertain whether Paniskos himself was or was not. In fact, however, it is most probable that he was not Christian, for otherwise he might have ensured that he found someone who would take care to represent his monotheistic sympathies more consistently.

The argument advanced by Farid is of importance for its general application to other documents written for illiterates which appear to contain a Christian content.

23. Fourfold reimbursement

Provenance unknown   11/2/143
ed.pr. — W.L. Westermann, *JEA* 40 (1954) 107-11

(Ἔτους) ἕκτου Ἀντωνείνου Καίσαρος τοῦ κυρίου Μεχεὶρ ἑπτακαιδεκάτῃ.
παρερχομένου Καλλινείκου γενομένου κωμογραμματέως προσ[[ ]]-
ελθόντος τε Καλλινείκου   μεθ᾽ ἕτερα Εὐδαίμων Καλλινείκῳ εἴ[[π]]-
πεν· τί δοκήσας ἄπορον ἄνθρωπον ἔδοκας εἰς λιτουργίαν; αἴτιος
5 αὐτῷ φυγῆς ἐγένου αἴτιος τοῦ πραθῆναι τὰ ὄντα αὐτῷ. ἐνέχῃ
[ἐ]πιτείμοις. ἐν τῷ ταμείῳ τὰ τειμήματα ἀποδώσεις ἀλλὰ καὶ τούτῳ
τὸ τετραπλάσειον ἢ ὅσου πέπραται τὰ ὑπάρχοντα αὐτοῦ.

Papyrus regularly cut off on all sides, with six vertical folds. *Verso* blank. Read
ἔδωκας (4).

Bib. — *SB* 6 (1958) 9315; **P. Wiscon.* 81, pp.169-70 (pl. 37)

**During the sixth year of Antoninus Caesar the lord, Mecheir 17th, Kallinikos
former village secretary being present, and Kallinikos having approached (the
tribunal), after other matters Eudaimon said to Kallinikos: 'What were you
thinking of that you gave a man without means over to a liturgy? Since you
5 were to blame | for his flight you were to blame for the sale of his possessions.
You are subject to penalties. You will pay the fines at the treasury, but also
to this man four times as much as that for which his possessions were sold.'**

This document appears to be a copy of the sentence or extract from the trial by
Valerius Eudaimon, prefect of Egypt, of a village scribe for wrongfully designating
for a liturgy a man belonging to the official class of ἄποροι who were granted
immunity from such public services. Sijpesteijn's new reading at the beginning of
*l.*5 (αὐτῷ φυγῆς in place of *ed.pr.*'s ἀ[δι]κία[ς] ταύτης) allows us to reconstruct the
events a little more clearly. When proposed for a liturgy the *aporos* fled — on this
common phenomenon in Roman Egypt note N. Lewis, *JEA* 23 (1937) 63-75 — and
his possessions were sold. Sijpesteijn suggests that the man sought redress after
Kallinikos had ceased to be village secretary. R. Taubenschlag, *JJP* 10 (1956) 553,
thinks that the liturgy in this case may have lain in the area of collection of some
money tax. Eudaimon's term of office as Prefect of Egypt under Antoninus Pius
is documented by several other papyri, including *P.Oxy.* 1.40 (reprinted above at
2). On his career see Westermann, 109-11. To illustrate the background to this text
we may note *P. Wiscon.* 85 (Oxyrhynchos, late II/early III), a (draft ?) list by the
secretary of Oxyrhynchos in which he nominates duly qualified men (δίδωμι τὰ
ὑπογε|γρ(αμμένα) εὔπορα, 3-4) to supervise field irrigation. Information about those
designated for service includes parentage, age, and value in money terms of their
property.

Concerning the flight of *leitourgoi* note *P.Berl.Leihg.* 46 (district of Themistos,
after 17/4/136), part of a file with copies of memoranda (including a prefectural
edict) belonging to the district *strategos* which relate to the attempt to trace two
sitologoi of Theadelphia. The edict (*ll.*41-51) may be quoted by way of example.

Μάρκος Πετρώνιος Μαμερτῖνος ἔπαρχος Αἰγύπ(του) λέγει·
Τοὺς ὑπογεγραμμένους σιτολόγους διατάγματι γραμ-
ματέα σιτολόγων καὶ φύλακα, ὥς φησιν Οὐέγετος ὁ καὶ
Σαραπίων ὁ τῆς Θεμίστου μερίδος στρατηγὸς ἀναπεφευ-
45 κέναι, κελεύω ἐντὸς ἡμερῶν εἴκοσι ἐμφανεῖς γενομέ-
νους ἐπὶ τῶν τόπων λόγον ὑποσχεῖν ἢ εἰδέναι, ὅτι
ἀναζητηθέντες τῆς δεούσης ἐπιστροφῆς τεύξονται.
   Εἰσὶ δέ· Χαιρήμ(ων) γρα(μματεὺς) σιτολόγ(ων) κώμης Θεαδελφείας
παραδοθεὶς Σώτᾳ Πτολεμαίου φύλακι ἕνεκα κεφαλαίων
50 ἀνηκόντων τῷ χειρισμῷ. Σώτας φύλαξ ὁ παραλαβὼν
τὸν Χαιρήμονα.   κ (ἔτους) Φαρμ(οῦθι) ϛ̄.

**Marcus Petronius Mamertinus prefect of Egypt says: those listed below,
(appointed)** *sitologoi* **by edict, a secretary of the** *sitologoi* **and a guard, since
Vegetos (also called Sarapion),** *strategos* **of the district of Themistos, says**
45 **they have fled, |I order that they appear within twenty days at their locations
to furnish an account; or that they (should) know that when they have been
searched for they will meet with the necessary attention. They are:
Chairemon, secretary of** *sitologoi* **of the village of Theadelphia, handed over**
50 **to Sotas, son of Ptolemaios, guard, because of sums of money |involving his
financial administration; Sotas, guard, who received Chairemon into custody.
20th year, Pharmouthi 6.**

For comment on the individuals and other aspects of this case see *ed.pr.*, pp.148-
52. With διάταγμα here (42) cf. the only NT occurrence, τὸ δ. τοῦ βασιλέως
(Heb. 11.23). As for ἐπιστροφή (47), BAGD, s.v., 1, note one ECL passage where
the meaning 'attention' is found; and this is the sense in which it occurs in the
papyri. Whether the word in its only NT occurrence, ἐκδιηγούμενοι τὴν ἐπιστροφὴν
τῶν ἐθνῶν (Acts 15.3) need mean as much as 'conversion' is at least worth querying.
For a complaint against unjustified enrolment in a liturgy note *SB* 11222
(Panopolis, 1-24/7/332).

To return to *P.Wiscon.* 81, while the term λειτουργία is so frequent that it need
not detain us as a NT parallel here one word does require comment. τετραπλάσιος
is not itself found in the NT but MM, s.v. τετραπλόος (-οῦς, BAGD; only at
Lk. 19.8) give two examples of it as the nearest they could come to attesting
τετραπλοῦς from documentary texts. Those two inscriptions are *SIG*[3] 880.80 (Pizus,
202) and *OGIS* 665.30 (48/9AD). The only other documentary examples known to
me of this rare word are *SB* 5.3 (1950) 8248.30 (I) and *P.Wiscon.* 81 (listed in *WB*
and Foraboschi as *SB* 9315). As for documentary attestations of the synonym
τετραπλοῦς, I am not aware of any epigraphical examples but there are two in the
papyri, published too late for MM to note. *PSI* 9 (1929) 1055.13-14 (Arsinoite
nome, 265) includes the phrase τοῦ τετραπλοῦ μισ|θοῦ; it is noted in BAGD, s.v. In
addition, *P.Rein.* 2 (1940) 117 (provenance unknown, III fin.) is a fragmentary
letter in which the writer says 'do not neglect to write me a letter knowing that if
you do anything, you receive it fourfold' (λαμβάνεις | αὐτα [τ]ετραπλᾶ, *ll.*13-14).

That the two adjectives are synonymous is shown by comparison of the wording
of *P.Wiscon.* 81.6-7 with Zacchaeus' comment at Lk. 19.8, ἀποδίδωμι τετραπλοῦν.
His undertaking to provide fourfold recompense is not to be thought of as an
arbitrary figure. Reference to Ex. 21.37 and 22.1, which speak of fourfold
restitution, are not relevant to Zacchaeus' case; for this was a standard proportion
in some parts of Roman Law, and he was a petty Roman functionary (noted briefly
by J.M. Creed, *Comm.* [1930], ad loc.; I.H. Marshall, *Comm.* [1978], p.698; cf.
J.D.M. Derrett, *Law in the New Testament* [London, 1970] 283-85). In particular,
poena quadrupli was a penalty laid down for extortion, and in view of Zacchaeus'
comment εἴ τινος τι ἐσυκοφάντησα, ἀποδίδωμι τετραπλοῦν (Lk. 19.8) it is very
probable that we have a reference to it here, as R. Taubenschlag notes (*The Law
of Greco-Roman Egypt in the Light of the Papyri, 332BC–640AD* [Warsaw, 1955[2];
repr. Milan, 1972] 552-53). Zacchaeus is thus offering to provide restitution in the
same proportion as he would have been liable to under Roman law if he had been

brought to court. (In passing Taubenschlag, ibid., mentions an edict of Eudaimon, referred to in *P.Oxy.* 2.237, col.8 *verso l.*18 (128AD), which provided a *poena sycophantiae* for Egypt.)

On ἀρχιτελώνης (used of Zacchaeus, Lk. 19.1) see briefly **2** where some other ἀρχ-compounds are discussed.

24. Reminder of an order for goods

Provenance unknown   III/IV
ed.pr. — *P.Wiscon.* 62, pp.91-92 (pl.17)

Πρὸς ὑπόμνησιν ἐντολικὸν
παρ' ῭Ανρου
πρὸς ὑπόμνησιν ᾿Αλεξάνδρου
δοκοὶ δ᾿ σάμβαθα ὀνάρου β᾿
5   σ[ ] [ ]κεραι δ᾿ ἀμοίγδαλα ω̅
κωροίναι β᾿.

The papyrus was folded four times, both horizontally and vertically. At *l.*4 read οἰναρίου.

> **As a reminder of the orders from Anras, as a reminder for Alexander: 4
> 5 beams, 2 sambatha of wine, |4 . . . , 800 almonds, 2 (shepherd's) crooks (?).**

The document is insignificant in itself, but its vocabulary has some features of interest for the NT. ὑπόμνησις is not common in the papyri: MM, s.v., provide only one example (IV) and devote the rest of that entry to ὑπόμνημα, which is found far more frequently. (The latter means 'memorandum' most often, e.g., *P.Wiscon.* 48.22 [provenance unknown, II]; 54.23 [Arsinoe, 27/6/116]; but in inscriptions it occurs as a funerary formula, e.g., *MPR* 1 [Tomis, III-IV] — reprinted in this volume at **110**.) *Spoglio* provides four examples of which *SB* 4 (1931) 7475.8 (Ombos, VI/VII) is an inscription (= G. Lefebvre, *Recueil des inscriptions grecques chrétiennes d'Égypte* [Cairo, 1907; repr. Chicago, 1978], 561); in the case of *P.Ryl.* 4 (1952) 606.6 (provenance unknown, late III) the context where the word occurs in this business letter is extremely fragmentary; note also *SB* 3 (1926) 7033.28 (Lykonpolis, 481). The new Wisconsin papyrus with its two examples provides a phrase similar in meaning to ἐν ὑπομνήσει, used at 2 Pet. 1.13 and 3.1; at 2 Tim. 1.15 the phraseology is different (ὑπόμνησιν λαβών τῆς . . . πίστεως), and this affects the meaning of the noun slightly.

The noun δοκός is well attested in the papyri — *P.Mil.Vogl.* 281.6 (Tebtynis, II) provides another 1977 example — and MM's papyrus examples need no supplementation. In addition to MM's one inscription, *SIG*² 587 (Eleusis, 329/8; not repr. in *SIG*³), we may note *IG* II/III² .2 (1913, repr. 1974) 463 (Athens, 307/6), a long text which deals with the specifications for a contract for repair of the walls of Athens. L.B. Holland, *AJA* 54 (1950) 337-56, discusses several of the technical terms in this document. At *ll.*61-62 a contrast is made between δοκοί and δοκίδες: καὶ ἐπ[ιθ]ήσει δοκοὺς εἰς τοὺς στό[χ]ους. οὐ μὴ καταστέ[γ]αστα[ι], στεγάσει δοκί|σιν καὶ ἐπιβλῆ[σ]ιν, κτλ, 'he shall place large beams on the pilasters. Where it is not roofed over he shall roof it with small beams and slats.' Holland (351) calculates that the δοκοί (which here act as lintels), 'with a span of seven feet, would probably be eight to twelve dactyls wide and high'. In contrast the δοκίδες are clearly smaller beams (Holland 351-52). This epigraphical example thus underscores MM's comment very well, that the hyperbolic force of δοκός at Mt. 7.3-5 (= Lk. 6.41-42) should not be softened.

Returning to *P.Wiscon.* 62, the translation (by *ed.pr.*) of κορώνη as shepherd's crook is certainly one possibility; but it could refer to a number of other items in such a varied list, e.g., a door handle, or the curved end of a plough-pole (see LSJ, s.v.).

25. Sailing in stormy weather

Acts 27 records the shipwreck during storm of the boat carrying Paul, his entourage and guard. Recent discussion of this incident in the light of a classical precedent (Antiphon, *On the Murder of Herodes*) has sought to elucidate the theological import, implicit in Luke's narrative, of the preservation of Paul and those with him (G.B. Miles/G. Trompf, *HTR* 69 [1976] 259-67: it is a 'telling confirmation of Paul's innocence', p.264).

P.Oxy. 3250, a freight contract dated 63AD, emphasizes that the ship's captain carries final responsibility for the safety of the goods he is transporting between certain cities on the Nile. One particular clause reads: ... καὶ μὴ ἐξέστω αὐτῷ νυγτοπλοεῖν μηδὲ | χειμῶνος ὄντος. ἀνορμίτω καθ' ἑκάστην ἡμέραν | ἐπὶ τῶν ἀσφαλεστάτων ὅρμων ... (*ll.*22-24), 'Neither is he allowed to sail at night nor during stormy weather. And he is to drop (?) anchor each day at the safest anchorages ...' (On the form ἀνορμίτω — from the new verb ἀνορμέω (?) which ought to mean 'weigh anchor' — see *ed.pr.*, p.123, n. ad loc.) Such sailing regulations affecting shipping on the Nile have precedent in Ptolemaic times (*P.Hibeh* 2[1955] 198. col.5, *ll.*111-22 [provenance unknown, reign of Ptolemy Philadelphus (probably)], perhaps an attempt to minimize piracy), and is known from IIAD (*P.Ross.Georg.* 2 [1929, repr. 1966] 18.24-34 [Fayum, January(?) 140]). Now, the Nile is not the Mediterranean or the Adriatic, but ships' masters who travelled in larger seaways than the Nile — and note anyway that the port of origin of the ship in Acts 27 is Alexandria: see v.6 — must have been under some kind of contract to ensure the safe arrival of their cargo. While Luke's focus in this section is entirely upon a passenger in chains who takes over the running of the ship, background features in the narrative of Acts 27, such as the risktaking of the helmsman and owner (implied at 27.11-13), are illustrated by documents such as the one from which this extract comes.

In the present context of a comment on Acts 27 we may note the occurrence of κουφίζω (figurative; the only NT example, Acts 27.38, is literal; the verb is not rare outside the NT) at *P.Berl.Leihg.* 28 (district of Herakleides, c.170). This papyrus consists of extracts from two official letters dealing with an error in taxation. The nominative participle occurs at the end of the second, καὶ κουφιζόμεναι ἐπὶ τ[ῆ] παραδοχῇ | π[υρ(οῦ)], 'and alleviations (of tax) for the rebate of [... artabas] of corn' (*ll.*19-20).

26. Reclining at the Passover meal
(cf. *New Docs 1976*, 1)

At the end of the entry in *New Docs 1976* which discussed 'invitations to the *kline* of Sarapis', a suggestion was put forward (p.9) concerning the occurrence of the Greek custom of reclining at the Last Supper (Jn. 13.22ff., especially vv.23, 28). E. Ferguson (per litt., 27/8/82) points out to me that '. . . the Mishna (*Pesahim* 10) and Talmud (b. *Pesahim* 108a) specify that the meal is to be taken reclining. It might be thought that this evidence is too late to confirm first-century practice; but the reason given for this posture in the Talmud, namely as a sign of freedom, is such a thoroughly Greek reason that one should conclude that the practice dates from the Hellenistic period'.

Relevant to the same entry — although I have only seen a synopsis — is D.E. Smith, *Social Obligation in the Context of Communal Meals: A Study of the Christian Meal in 1 Corinthians in comparison with Graeco-Roman Communal Meals* (Diss. Harvard, 1980). J.-M. Dentzer, *Le motif du banquet couché dans le Proche-Orient et le monde grec du VIIe au IVe siècle av. J.-C.* (*BEFAR*, 246; Rome, 1982), may also be registered here — *non vidi*.

C.-H. Kim, *JBL* 94 (1975) 391–402, discusses papyrus invitations; *New Docs 1976*, 1 updates his list of Sarapis invitations by 50%.

H.B. Schönborn, *Die Pastophoren im Kult der ägyptischen Götter* (*Beitr. zur kl. Phil.*80; Meisenheim am Glan, 1976), suggests briefly (30-32) that the *pastophoroi*, a class of religious officials in Egyptian cults, participated in *klinai*. For a Christian *pastophoros* ('sacristan') mentioned in a letter — Naldini, no.43; IV — see Schönborn, 45 n.2.

In *MPL*, pp.85-97, F. Dunand and J. Schwartz offer re-evaluation of *P. Lond*. 2 (1898) 429, a memorandum concerning banquets: written in 85 short lines it mentions costs and amounts of wine, bread and vegetables. The frequent use of the term καθαρά for 'pure bread' in this text is mentioned and comparison made (pp.90-91) with the LXX references to 'shewbread' (e.g., Ex. 40.21, ἄρτους τῆς προθέσεως). But the text is unlikely to have any Christian affinity, and Dunand/ Schwartz conclude that it relates to pagan marriage banquets.

27. A verbatim copy of an agreement
(cf. *New Docs 1976*, 26)

P.Mich. 667 (Aphrodite, mid-VI) is an agreement (ὁμολογία) concerning a lease of land which Aurelios Phoibammon — known from over a dozen other papyri; see *ed.pr.*, p.89 — rents from a monastery called after Psentuses, τοῦ αὐτοῦ ἁγίου μοναστηρίου καλουμένου Ψεντουσῆτος (*l.*4). In fact, he negotiates with the board of management of another monastery from which Sijpesteijn (ibid.) infers that 'the monastery of Psentuses was economically dependent on the bigger, more important monastery of Apa Surus'.

The document specifies that the agreement has been 'written in two copies identical in tenor' (δισσὴν | γραφεῖσαν ὁμότυπον, 24-25; tr. *ed.pr.*). In a legally binding document such as this the replication of the exact wording would be imperative. For the notion of τύπος as a verbatim copy (not simply an approximation in wording) and its bearing on the letters in Acts 15.23-29 and 23.26-30, see E.A. Judge's discussion in *New Docs 1976*, **26**. In this context we may note also Buresch, *Aus Lydien*, no.46 (pp.89-106), a battered inscription (Kula, in Lydia, c.250-70) recording parts of two rescripts from the proconsul Maximilianus to the Asiarch Domninus Rufus. At *ll.*22-24 the text reads: ἀπεθέμη[ν ἀ]ντίγραφ[ον τ]ῶν ἐπιστολῶν | [-?-] αὐθεντι[κὴ]ν ἐπιστολ[ὴν] τὴν ἐπι|[σταλεῖσαν . . . , 'I deposited a copy of the commands . . . the original command which was written . . .' For the meaning of ἐπιστολή here — synonymous with ἐντολαί, *mandata* — see Buresch, p.105. The adjective αὐθεντικός is worth adding to BAGD, s.v., for only papyrus references are included to illustrate the ECL passage mentioned there.

B. MINOR PHILOLOGICAL NOTES

28. ἀγγαρεύω

This verb — treated in Deissmann, *Bible Studies*, 86–87 — appears at the head of two statements itemizing the requisitioning of donkey drivers (cf. *New Docs 1976*, **9**, pp.43-44) at the port of Pisai from 11-20 Phaophi and 21-30 Phaophi respectively: λόγος ὀ[νηλα]τῶν ἀν⟨γα⟩ρε[υθέντων] | ἐν ὅρμῳ Πισ[ά]ϊ [τ]ῶν ἀ[πὸ ια´] Φαῶφ[ι] | ἕως κ´ (*P.Berl.Leihg.* 43A.1-3, 43B.1-3; Arsinoite, end II). MM, s.v., include no papyrus examples from this period, so this new attestation is worth note. The documentary examples illustrate well how the word is 'officialese', and carries no pejorative connotation as the NT passages (Mt. 5.41; 27.32 = Mk. 15.21) could be misinterpreted as implying (cf. *New Docs 1976*, **9**, p.42).

29. ἀθέτησις

J.G. Keenan, *Akten des XIII. Internat. Papyrologenkongresses, Marburg/Lahn 2-6 Aug. 1971*, edd. E. Kiessling/H.-A. Rupprecht (Munich, 1974) 211-14 (= *SB* 11041), has re-examined *P. Tebt.* 2 (1907) 586, which was described but not fully published in the original volume. This document preserves portions of 20 lines of an anachretic loan — whereby the creditor accepts in lieu of interest the right to live in a dwelling owned by the debtor — and in *ll*.17-18 we read ἀναδέδωκα τὸ δάνειον ... | καὶ ἀθέτησιν καὶ [ο]ὐδὲν καθότι πρόκειται. The usual legal phrase referring to annulment of a contract is εἰς ἀθέτησιν καὶ ἀκύρωσιν (cf. MM. s.v. ἀθέτησις; Keenan refers to *P. Yale* 1 [1967] 63.11n., which gives several references, although the phrase in *P. Yale* 63 is different again); and Deissmann, *Bible Studies*, 228-29, has discussed it in relation to Heb. 7.18 and 9.26 (the latter has the phrase εἰς ἀθέτησιν). This papyrus is worth notice for NT philology in view of its date (20/21); three of MM's examples are II, the fourth late IBC.

30. ἀντικύριος

appears for the first time in *P.Oxy.* 3239 (later II), an alphabetic glossary with definitions of some kind, though its precise function is unclear (see *ed.pr.*, pp.90-91). At col.2, *l*.45 the diplomatic transcription is υπηρ ετης αντι κυριος which *ed.pr.* interprets as ὑπηρέτης ἀντικύριος. There are of course parallel formations, such as ἀντιβασιλεύς (= *interrex*); cf. ἀντιβασιλεύω, 'reign as a rival king' (Jos. *BJ* 4.7.1); and in the NT, ἀντίχριστος (1 Jn. 2.18, 22; 4.3; 2 Jn. 7). Cf. ἀντίθεος (examples cited at BAGD, s.v. ἀντίχριστος).

Col.2, *l*.21 from the same list may also be noted, in connection with the Isis aretalogies treated at *New Docs 1976*, **2**. Here the reading is Ἶσις ἡ μεγάλη [ἐ]λπίς. As *ed.pr.* notes, this way of speaking of Isis does not occur in the aretalogies or magical papyri. The phrase provides a useful parallel to 1 Tim. 1.1 where Christ is spoken of as τῆς ἐλπίδος ἡμῶν; cf. Col. 1.27. MM provide no examples to illustrate this usage of ἐλπίς.

31. ἀντιλογία

Two Byzantine loans, *P.Mich.* 669 (Aphrodite, 12-13/9/529, or 514) and 670 (Aphrodite, 527) include the formulaic phrase whereby the debtor agrees to repay the loan 'without any argument'. At *P.Mich.* 670 a soldier, Flavius Samuel, borrows grain from a land entrepreneur, Aurelius Phoibammon, and agrees to the terms (non-repayment in time will compound his previous mortgage indebtedness to Phoibammon) [ἄν]ευ τινὸς ἀντιλογίας (*l*.16). Two other papyri help to document the gradual loss of Samuel's holding to Phoibammon, *P.Michael.* (1955) 43 (Aphrodite, 8/6/526) and 44 (Aphrodite, 19/7/527). On Phoibammon and these three papyri see J.G. Keenan, *BASP* 17 (1980) 145-54.

In *P.Mich.* 669 a woman (possibly two: see *ed.pr.*'s n. to *ll*.1-2) lends money at 12½% interest to three men (one is a πρεσβύτερος, *l*.3). They agree to repay the money whenever the lender requires it, and accept the interest terms χωρὶς πάσης | ἀντιλογίας (*ll*.14-15). This phrase provides an exact parallel to the wording at Heb. 7.7, although finances are certainly not the subject there. Similarly, at Heb. 6.16 the phrase πάσης . . . ἀντιλογίας πέρας is to be taken in a general way.

These two examples may be added to MM's entry to illustrate the continuity of the formula from the Augustan period through to VII. In fact, the phrase appears in the Ptolemaic period as well: further examples, including some from IIIBC and IIBC are listed in *WB* I.1 (1924), *WB* Suppl. 1 (1969), and *Spoglio*.

32. αὔξησις

P.Mich. 659.227-28 (Aphrodite, VI[1]) speaks of τοῦ κινδύνου μειώσεως ἤτοι αὐξήσεως | δημοσίων τελεσμάτων, 'the risk of the lessening or increase of public taxes'. MM note one inscription only attesting αὔξησις, and no papyri; BAGD follows suit. The example in this late papyrus illustrates the rare NT occurrence in the parallel passages Eph. 4.16, πᾶν τὸ σῶμα . . . τὴν αὔξησιν τοῦ σώματος ποιεῖται . . . (where the genitive is objective, as in the papyrus), and Col. 2.19, πᾶν τὸ σῶμα . . . αὔξει τὴν αὔξησιν τοῦ θεοῦ (where the genitive is subjective). *WB* has a few attestations of αὔξησις in texts ranging in date from IBC–VI. I am unaware of any inscriptions where the word appears, apart from that listed in MM, s.v.

As for μείωσις, this papyrus reference is worth noting for the sole ECL attestation in BAGD, although the Diognetus phrase (μ. τῆς σαρκός) is figurative. Neither *WB* nor *Spoglio* has any examples and I am unaware of any epigraphical attestations.

33. βραβεῖον

J. Pouilloux, *BCH* Suppl. IV, 103-21, publishes an inscription which lists tasks taken on by various individuals for the Pythian Games at Delphi in 247/6 (?); *l*.40 reads, τὰ βραβεῖα Πλείστιος μνᾶν αἰγι[ναίαν c.16/17*l*.], 'for the prizes, Pleistios — one Aiginetan mina.' This is the earliest epigraphical attestation of the word, which occurs frequently in agonistic inscriptions of the Roman Imperial period. *BE* 236 (cf. *SEG* 762) is a useful note on the term, which refers to the victory prize in a contest. The βραβεῖα in view here must be bronze, given the price (so *BE*). To the few examples in MM we may add the following reference, in addition to the passage above (BAGD, s.v., has scarcely gone beyond MM for non-literary sources). *P.Princ.* 2 (1936) 75.13 mentions τὸ τῆς οἰκοδεσποτείας βραβεῖον in a fragmentary horoscope (provenance unknown, 138-61).

As for the verb (NT, only Col. 3.15), the reference MM give to *P.Par.* (1865) 63.70, λόγῳ τινὶ ταῦτα βραβευθῆναι is superseded by *UPZ* 1 (1922-27) 110.70 (note also *l.*161 of that text); so too their *P.Leid.B.* (1843) 22 = *UPZ* 1.20.22. The verb appears also in *P.Cairo Masp.* 2 (1913, repr. 1973) 151.222-23 (Antinoe, 15/11/570), a lengthy will in which the hope is expressed κ[αὶ] εἴη [βεβαία (*sc.* ἡ διαθήκη), ὑπὸ] Ῑυ τῶ ⲕⲱ κ(αὶ) θ̅ω̅ ἡμῶν καὶ [ἀεὶ φυλαττομένη, 'and may the will be valid, forever watched over by Jesus our Lord and God'. It is attested as well in another Byzantine text (a contract) from the same town, *P.Cairo Masp.* 3 (1916) 353.31 (12/11/569). I know of no epigraphical attestations of the verb.

MM's entry on the verb mentions the occurrence of the noun at *P.Oxy.* 7 (1910) 1050.11 (II/III), a very broken expenditure account for public games at Oxyrhynchos. Add to this the comment in *BE* (1963) 221 on the occurrence of the noun βραβευτής in an inscription from N-E Lydia (61/60 or 31/30) that the title is well known in Lydian villages. Two 1977 examples of this are Buresch, *Aus Lydien*, no.6, *l.*12, and no.23, *l.*13. βραβευτής appears at *ll.*84, 86 in the Beroian gymnasiarchal law (c. 168-48BC) discussed elsewhere in this volume (**82**).

No documentary examples of καταβραβεύω (NT, Col. 2.18) have been found to add to the sole reference in MM, s.v. (T.K. Abbott in the *ICC* Comm. gives two literary sources).

34. γένημα

MM's entry on this word (following Deissmann, *Bible Studies*, 109–10, 184) is excellent: the noun is related to γίγνομαι, not γεννάω. A further example from a fragmentary papyrus (provenance unknown, III) referring to a ship's cargo may be noted: P.J. Sijpesteijn, *Aeg.* 52 (1972) 137 no.22 (= *SB* 11037), *l.*2. In the NT the Gospels use the word literally (Mt. 26.29 = Mk. 14.25 = Lk. 22.18; Lk. 12.18), and the sole other usage, at 2 Cor. 9.10, is metaphorical (τὰ γ. τῆς δικαιοσύνης ὑμῶν), for which no parallel has yet been noticed (for καρπός exhibiting metaphorical development — in several directions — note especially Heb. 12.11, καρπὸν εἰρηνικὸν . . . δικαιοσύνης).

35. γυμνός

Towards the end of a chatty letter, *P.Wiscon.* 73 (Oxyrhynchite nome, end II) a certain Didymos asks the addressee, Hephaistion, to 'purchase a tunic for Thermouthis: she has nothing to wear', Θερμούθι κιθῶ|να ἀγόρασον. γυμνή ἐστιν (19-20). For this use of γυμνός in the NT cf. Jn. 21.7, or perhaps Mt. 25.36, 38, 43, 44; Jas. 2.15.

This papyrus letter contains several verb forms worth brief comment (cf. *ed.pr.*'s notes ad loc.). *Ll.*5-6, ἑωρτὴν ἤξαμεν λαβόν|τες σου τὸ ἐπιστόλιον, 'we had a party when we received your letter'. For this sigmatic aorist form of ἄγω cf. B.G. Mandilaras, *The Verb in the Greek Non-Literary Papyri* (Athens, 1973) §306.1.

*Ll.*7-9, ἡμῶν πάντες ἔρρωνται καί| πλεῖον ἴσχυκαν λανβόντες σου τὰ | γράμματα, 'all of us are well and even more so after receiving your letter': Sijpesteijn suggests that here may be an example of an aorist in -κα; but K.L. McKay points out to me that it is a genuine perfect — see his discussion of the ending -αν for -ασι in *BICS* 27 (1981) 24 (with p.44, where the view of Mandilaras, §307-309 is rejected, and pp.31-32 where aorist/perfect confusion is also rejected). On the insertion of the nasal in λανβόντες (= λαβόντες) *ed.pr.* refers to Gignac I, 118. *Ll.*13-14 περὶ τούτου οὐδὲν | ἐτέλεσθαι, 'concerning this (viz., the purchase of some mixed produce) nothing has been finalized'. Here, for the augment in place of the reduplication (= τετέλεσται), *ed.pr.* refers to Mandilaras, *Studies in the Greek Language* (Athens, 1972), 12f. (*non vidi*).

36. διαρρήγνυμι

MM provide one example only (quoted in BAGD, s.v.), dated 389, where the verb is used of tearing clothing. The NT uses it with such an object, and also of breaking chains (Lk. 8.29). *P.Mich.* 659 (Aphrodite, VI¹) employs the verb in the literal sense of tearing up a receipt and a security: ἔδοξεν τό τε ... ἐντάγιον ... καὶ τὴν ἀσφάλειαν ... διαρραγῆναι (*ll.*126-130). Though late, this example is worth noting for a revised MM entry, and for BAGD.

37. διαστολή

P.Mich. contains several attestations — all Byzantine in date, from Aphrodite — of this word in its common meaning of 'description'. At 662.41 (VII) the document speaks of the new owner's purchase of part of a house κατὰ τὴν ἀνωτέραν διαστολήν 'according to the description above'. The same phrase occurs at 665.65 (613-41), another sale of parts of a house; and a similar formula at 663.11-12 (VI) allows the confident restoration of διαστολήν in *l.*12. Another variation appears at 670.8 (527), a loan of grain, καθὼς πάσ[ας] διαστολάς, 'in accordance with all the memoranda'. *P.Berl.Leihg.* 38 (Theadelphia, mid-II), a summary of silver transfers to the public bank, includes the word at *l.*3.

These examples do not help us with the NT usage of διαστολή; at Rom. 3.22 and 10.12 it means 'distinction, difference', while 'distinctness' in musical notes is the sense required at 1 Cor. 14.7. MM, s.v., confessed themselves unable to illustrate this NT usage from the papyri; no papyrus or epigraphical example has come to my attention. BAGD, s.v., may be misleading when it includes 'inscr., pap.' at the head of that entry. No specific documentary example is referred to, and the allusion is merely to the meaning found commonly, though not in the NT.

38. διηνεκής

The NT uses this adjective only in Heb., where it occurs in the stock phrase εἰς τὸ διηνεκές, 'forever, constantly' (7.3; 10.1, 12, 14). *P.Mich.* 659.201-02 (Aphrodite, VI¹) has the similar but more fulsome phrase ἐπὶ τὸν ἑξῆς | ἅπαντα καὶ διηνεκῆ χρόνον, 'for all continually succeeding time', in part of a settlement which deals with the use of a land holding. Similar phrases occur at *P.Mich*. 662.15 (VII) and 664.10, 19 (585 or 600), two documents of sale from Aphrodite. The adverb (ECL, only 1 Clement) occurs at *P.Mich*. 659.271, and also in a Roman-period honorific inscription for a benefactor from Ainos in Turkish Thrace (*BE* [1972] 275).

39. διϊσχυρίζομαι

P.Mich. 659 (Aphrodite, VI) is a very lengthy record of the settlement of a dispute between two parties, the heirs of a man who had died 19 years previously and a couple who argue that money was owed to them by the deceased. The beginning of the document is not extant but at *ll*.7ff. mention is made of the production by the heirs of a notice of a deed of sale concerning a property. The notice validated the sale, ἐκεῖθεν διϊσχυριζόμενοι (sc. the heirs) | καὶ κατασκευάζοντες ὡς, κτλ, 'from that fact confidently affirming and maintaining that' (14-15, trans. *ed.pr.*) if the sale had not gone through no validation would have been added to it.

This text provides the first papyrus attestation of this verb (so *ed.pr.*, p.14); no occurrence in inscriptions is known to me. MM lack an entry for the word, which is rare but classical. Writers of the Koine period use it occasionally (Josephus, Aelian, Dio); and it is found in Lk.-Acts. Lk. 22.59 employs it of someone insisting that Peter was one of the disciples; Acts 12.15 of Rhode maintaining that she is not hallucinating but that it is Peter at the door. Acts 12.5D includes the following addition, ἔλεγεν γὰρ ὁ Παῦλος μένειν οὕτως κάθως ἐπίστευσαν διϊσχυριζόμενος, the 'probable' source of which, according to J.H. Ropes (Jackson/Lake, *Beginnings of Christianity*, I.3. *Text*, n. ad loc.), is 1 Cor. 7.8, 20, 24, 40. The word provides an illustration of Sijpesteijn's observation (*P.Mich*. 13, p.xi) on 'the revival [in later Byzantine documents] of words common in older times but not used in the centuries immediately following Christ's birth'. On this subject generally see H. Zilliacus, *Zur Abundanz der spätgriechischen Gebrauchssprache* (*Comm. Hum. Litt. Soc. Scient. Fennica*, 41.2; Helsinki, 1967).

40. εἰκῇ

I.Tyre 1.17 has brief texts on two faces of a sarcophagus, (A) εἰκῇ· οὐ δύνη ἀνῦξε (= ἀνοῖξαι); (B) † σώριν Ἐλιοῦτος ἀσ|προπολίσας †, 'In vain, you cannot open (it); Sarcophagus of Elious, incense-seller'. For the female trader cf. Lydia at Acts 16.14, and the discussion at **3**. Rey-Coquais (ad loc.) draws attention to εἰκῇ here, conforming to biblical usage. Rom. 13.4; Gal. 3.4; 4.11 must be meant, but nowhere in the NT is the adverb used absolutely. MM offer only papyrus examples to illustrate the word.

41. ἐκτιτρώσκω

This verb is not itself found in the NT, although the noun occurs in Paul's striking metaphor at 1 Cor. 15.8, ἔσχατον δὲ πάντων ὡσπερεὶ τῷ ἐκτρώματι ὤφθη κἀμοί. *P.Tebt.Tait* 40 (Tebtynis, II) is a fragmentary portion of a herbal in which ἐκτρῶσαι occurs at *l*.2, although the context is irrecoverable. MM, s.v. ἔκτρωμα, offer no documentary attestations of the noun — though they note the occurrence of ἐκτρωσμός — and only one of the verb (which is picked up at BAGD, s.v. ἐκτιτρώσκω). BAGD, s.v. ἔκτρωμα, has noted *P.Tebt*. 3.1 (1933) 800 (= *CPJ* 1 [1957] 133; Samareia (?) (Fayum), 17/7/153 or 15/7/142 BC), but the meaning given there, 'premature birth', is doubtful. This papyrus, whose central portion is lost, is a petition from a Jew ([Ἰου]δαίου, *l*.3), Sabbataios, whose pregnant wife had been attacked and injured by a certain Joanna — also Jewish, judging by her name. As part of his allegation Sabbataios says that his wife has taken to her bed and is suffering terribly as a result of the blows and her fall, and κινδυνεύει [ὅ] ἔχει ἐγ γ[α]στρὶ | παιδίον ἔκ[τ]ρωμα γί[νεσ]θα[ι] | μετάλλαξαν τ[ὸ]ν βίον, 'the child which she is carrying is at risk of becoming a miscarriage and dying' (*ll*.29-31). For similar language in another complaint about assault on a pregnant wife note *P.Mich*. 5 (1944) 228 (Karanis, 47AD), where the effect of the attack is such 'that the child within her has been aborted dead', ὥσ|ται παρ' αὐτῇ ἐκτέτρωται {αὐτὴν} τῶι (*read* τὸ) | βρέφος νεκρόν (*ll*.20-22). Questions to oracles concerning such matters as a safe pregnancy appear to have been common: a papyrus fragment of the *sortes Astrampsychi*, *P.Oxy*. 38 (1971) 2833 — see further **8** in this volume — includes the answer ἐκτίτρωσκι καὶ κινδυνεύει at *col*.2, *l*.22. These examples of the verb may be added to BAGD, s.v.

BE (1955) 189 reports the occurrence of the noun ἔκτρωσις in an inscription (Smyrna (?), II) detailing ritual prohibitions on access to a Dionysiac association until purification is achieved: *l*.5 of this metrical text reads: ἔκτρωσίν τε γυναικὸς ὁμοίως ἤματα τόσσα, 'and the miscarriage/abortion of a woman, likewise four days'. *BE* notes that, like φθορά, ἐ. can mean 'miscarriage' as well as 'induced abortion'.

42. ἐμπεριέχω

ECL has this only at 1 Cl. 28.4 (of God). In participial form the verb appears twice at *P.Mich*. 659.286, 295 (Aphrodite, VI[1]) where two individuals acknowledge that they have executed the settlement ἐπὶ πᾶσι τοῖς ἐμπεριεχομένοις αὐτῇ ἐπερω-τήμασι καὶ ὁμολογ[ήμασι], 'in accordance with all the pledges and agreements embraced by it'.

43. ἐξαποστέλλω

An inscription from Delphi (145-125BC) republished as Nachtergael, *Galates* no.80 (pp.492-93), mentions that when envoys were sent by the city to the association of artists (πρε]σβευτᾶν ἐξαποσταλέντων [ὑ]πὸ τᾶ[ς] πόλιος τᾶ[ς] Δελφῶν ποτὶ τὸ κ]οιν[ὸν τῶν τεχνιτᾶν, *l*.1) for a conference concerning the winter *Soteria* festival games, the *technitai* agreed to certain requests καὶ ἐξαπέστειλαν τοὺς ἀγωνιζομέ[νους τῶι θεῶι δωρεὰν τού[σδε], 'and sent the following people [names listed below in the text] who would compete gratis in honour of the god' (*l*.4). These examples are perhaps worth adding to MM. Cf. Acts 7.12, (Jacob) εἰς Αἴγυπτον ἐξαπέστειλεν τοὺς πατέρας ἡμῶν . . . , and other NT references listed at BAGD, s.v., 1b.

The triple compound συνεξαποστέλλω occurs at Nachtergael no.36, *l*.2 (Delphi, July-December 168BC). A Hellenistic coinage (LSJ attest it twice in Polybios, once in Diodorus), it does not occur in the NT, but might be noted for MM, s.v. ἐξαπο-στέλλω or συναποστέλλω. For ἀποστέλλω ἐπὶ + acc. note that the inscription listed by MM, s.v., and BAGD, s.v. 1bγ, as Preisigke/*SB* 174 (IIIBC) is reprinted as *I.Pan* 77 where the date given is 217-204BC. The same phraseology (partly restored) occurs in no.84 (same date), while ὁ συναποσταλείς occurs in the similarly-worded no.85 (210-204BC). Note Bernand's comment on *I.Pan* 86.5-6, ὁ ἀπεσταλμένος, that the verb is used 'to designate the sending of a subordinate by his superior' (p.256). That inscription is also of Ptolemaic date (2/10/130BC), and this group of examples taken with his comment underlines the especial appropriateness of this verb and the related nouns so frequently employed in the NT. συναποστέλλω may be noted also in an honorific inscription for three judges, *SEG* 226.9 (Thessaly, 150-30).

Nachtergael's monograph is specifically concerned with two questions, a historical analysis of the Galatian (Celtic) invasion of Macedonia and Greece between 280-78, and a study of the *Soteria*, a festival instituted at Delphi in memory of the Greek victory against this new barbarian invasion. It was in response to being blocked in this direction that some of the Galatians moved to Asia Minor. Nachtergael consciously excludes any treatment of the latter group. A major appendix to his work (pp.391-519) prints the nearly 90 epigraphical texts (or relevant parts of them) which bear on the Delphic *Soteria*.

44. ἐξουδενέω

appears in a mutilated letter, *P.Laur.* 39.7 (Arsinoite nome, II init.), αὐ]τὸ ἐξο[υ]δενῶν ἀνήρ τις δέξω τῶν ἐν τῶι Προφή||[τη ... It is not easy to see what this means, perhaps 'Though (?) I despise it as a man I will give an indication (δείκνυμι ?) of the things in the Prophet ... (?)'. This spelling of the verb appears only at Mk. 9.12 in the NT, although the variant -ουθενέω is also attested. The -δ- spelling appears to have arisen as a consequence of the revival (Atticistic ?) of οὐδείς as a rival to οὐθείς. Gignac, I, p.97, notes that οὐθείς etc., is attested from 328BC, but becomes rare after IIAD with only a few Byzantine examples known. The -θ- spelling of the verb occurs more commonly in the NT — both forms are subject to the additional complexity, whether -εω or -οω is original. J.A.L. Lee points out to me that both -δ- and -θ- forms occur in the 'W' version of the *Vita Aesopi*, which exhibits a tendency to shorten and 'tidy up' the more authentic tradition preserved in 'G' (late I/II). The latter has one example of the -θ- verb, none of the -δ- alternative (references in BAGD, svv.). This slight papyrus example should be added to a pool of these words when an attempt is made to sort out the relationship between the various orthographical forms for NT textual criticism.

45. ἐξουσία

MM's entry for this noun offers attestations for a range of uses, over a dozen from papyrus texts but only one inscription. For the meaning 'the authorities' found in Rom. 13.1-3 (as also at Lk. 12.11 and Tit. 3.1) they offer two papyrus parallels. Two epigraphical examples, known from last century, could well have been included to round out the picture. *CIG* 3 (1828-77, repr. 1977) 4441 (Adana, n.d.) includes the warning at the end of a gravestone inscription for a woman that if anyone else is buried here καὶ λόγον ὑφέξεται τῇ ἐξουσίᾳ. (For this use of ὑπέχω — more commonly active in such formulae — cf. MM, s.v., to which this example could be added to help illustrate Jude 7, δίκην ὑπέχουσαι.) J.G.C. Anderson, *JHS* 19 (1899) 112 no.97 (Inler Katrandji, Galatia, probably 140) begins, after the dating formula: Βρόμιος | Βασίλου ὁ μέγας ἀνὴρ [. . . τῇ] βουλῇ εὐχαριστεῖ | . . . . . καὶ ταῖς ἐξουσίαις, 'Bromios son of Basilos the great man gives thanks to the council . . . and to the authorities'. The text goes on to provide that the man's heirs should burn a sheepskin each month as an offering. Published too late for MM to include was *SEG* 2 (1925) 384 (Dyrrachion [Belgrade], n.d.) an epitaph on a sarcophagus which read at *ll.*9-11: [ἐγὼ δὲ] πολλὰ περειπλεύ|[σας κὲ] πολλὲς ἐξουσείες | [ὑπ]ηρετήσας, κτλ, 'and I, after having sailed about a great deal and served many magistrates . . .' *BE* 523 mentions these examples in the context of reporting a revised reading for an inscription from Lamos in Cilicia: the suggested restoration is μήτ' ἐπ' (ἐ)ξου[σίαν *or* -σίας].

Turning briefly to a far more common use of ἐξουσία, note *P.Laur.* 23 (Arsinoite nome, II/III), a fragment from a land register which lists names in alphabetical order with the declared property of each. In the case of Herakles, son of Herakles, ἐξουσ[ί]αν ἔδωκ(εν) υ[ἱῷ –?–] ἀδελφ( ) σὺν καὶ τ[–?–] | κληρονόμ( ) ἀπὸ γέν[ους –?] (*ll.*34-36). The loss of the right side of the text makes exact reconstruction uncertain, but it appears that Herakles granted authority to his son, sibling(s?) and hereditary heir(s?), perhaps to manage his property. For the wording in *l.*34 cf. Jn. 1.12, ἔδωκεν αὐτοῖς ἐξουσίαν . . .

46. ἐπανόρθωσις

2 Tim. 3.16, πᾶσα γραφὴ . . . ὠφέλιμος . . . πρὸς ἐπανόρθωσιν, κτλ, is the only NT attestation of this noun. MM, s.v., record four figurative and one literal example of the word. *P.Berl.Leihg.* 44 (Theadelphia, 157/58) is a proposal made by ten farmers of the village concerning the appointment of those authorized to settle an adjustment to the rent and taxes payable on land which they have leased and which they are working in conjunction with others. Their request is 'for correction of the corn rent and the taxes in kind and silver — which are not small — applying to us and to our fellow farmers', εἰς ἐπανόρθωσιν τῶν ἡμεῖν τε καὶ | τοῖς συνγεωργοῖς ἡμῶν ἐξακολουθούντων ἐκφορίω(ν) | σιτικῶν τε καὶ γενῶν καὶ ἀργυρικῶν φόρων οὐκ ὀλίγων | ὄντων, κτλ (5-8). *Ed.pr.* discusses the term ἐπανόρθωσις (p.139) and provides some further attestations.

From the preceding verse (3.15) the phrase ἱερὰ γράμματα may also receive a brief comparative note in this context. BAGD, s.v. βίβλος, attest the phrase ἱερὰ β. in magical papyri. To these examples may now be added *AE* 840 (Birbat Markos, lower Nubia, 29/3/111). This complete inscription defines certain territorial boundaries, which the prefect of Egypt had required the commandant of a cavalry cohort to establish. The decision is settled κατὰ τὴν ἱερὰν βίβλον (*ll.*11-12). Quite what this phrase refers to is unclear to me (I have been unable to see the *ed.pr.*, G. Geraci, *Dehmit* [1973] pp.69-89).

47. ἐπαρχεία

Normally this word is a Greek equivalent of *provincia*, thus Acts 23.24 (of Cilicia), cf. 25.1, τῇ ἐπαρχείῳ (sc. χώρᾳ), where the noun is a *v.l.* But at *P.Mich.* 659.45 (Aphrodite, VI¹) the context requires a less widespread 'district' to be in view: προσεληλυθέναι δὲ | πολλάκις καὶ τῷ τῆς ἐπαρχείας ἄρχοντι | περὶ ταύτης τῆς αἰτίας, κτλ, '(They proved that) . . . they had often approached the official at the head of the district regarding this reason . . .' (trans., *ed.pr.*). See Sijpesteijn's reference (p.15) to further discussion of the meaning of this word. H.J. Mason, *Greek Terms for Roman Institutions* (*Amer.Stud.Pap.* 13; Toronto, 1974) includes discussion of ἐπαρχεία at pp.135-36; but this work is to be used with caution: note some trenchant criticisms in reviews by T. Drew-Bear, *CPh* 71 (1976) 349-55, and J. Marcillet-Jaubert, *BASP* 14 (1977) 51-56.

48. ἐπιμαρτυρέω

In a document recording a deposit of land (one aroura) which the recipient undertakes to return upon demand and for which he pledges his whole property (*P.Mich.* 671; Aphrodite, mid-VI), the man authorizes his security 'with my own subscription followed in order by those of the customary witnesses bearing witness' (μεθ']| [ὑπογραφ]ῆς ἐμῆς καὶ τῶν ἑξῆς συνηθῶν ἐπιμαρτυρ[ούντων] | [μαρτύρ]ων, κτλ *ll.*20-22). MM provides one example of this verb, and a couple of -τυρομαι, which has the stronger force 'call someone to bear witness'; BAGD has one further example, from the same century as the *P.Mich.* text. While it could not be said to be common in the papyri, further attestations exist. In fact *WB* lists several Ptolemaic examples; two further texts from VI are *P.Michael.* (1955) 41.70 and *SB* 6 (1958) 9051.16.

Sijpesteijn notes (p.111) 'that the importance of this papyrus lies in its mention of a παραθήκη'; see his discussion for bibliography. While still occasionally used as late as VI, the institution is rarely attested after IV. This noun — equivalent in meaning to παρακαταθήκη which is a *v.l.* in the NT — occurs only in the phrase τὴν π. φυλάσσειν and only in the Pastorals: 1 Tim. 6.20; 2 Tim. 1.12, 14. I have not seen C. Spicq, *Rev.Bib.* 40 (1931) 481-502, but his discussion in his 1947 *Commentary* on the Pastorals is excellent (pp.214-15 and especially pp.327-35). This phrase is being used figuratively, but the writer is clearly drawing on the literal usage found in such papyrus documents as *P.Mich.* 671.5. In fact, at *ll.*10-12, *ed.pr.* reads ὁμολογῶ . . . | . . . τὴν προδεδηλωμ[ένην ἄρουραν] | [φυλάξαι], κτλ, 'I acknowledge . . . that I will keep safe the previously referred-to aroura'. The restoration of φυλάξαι is made by analogy with other texts: Sijpesteijn (p.114) instances *BGU* 3 (1903) 729.10-14 (provenance unknown, 3/10/144 BC). MM, s.v. παραθήκη, includes a range of attestations of the noun, though none of the particular phrase occurring in the Pastorals.

49. κατ' ἐπιταγήν

Düll, *Götterkulte*, no.224, pp.390-91, is a dedicatory inscription to the goddess Nemesis (Stobi, c.200):

> Θεᾷ Νεμέσει κατ' ἐπιταγή[ν]
> Τ. Μέστριος Λόγος.

Titus Mestrius Longus (set this up) to the goddess Nemesis in accordance with (her) injunction.

Such actions resulting from a divine command are frequently attested: MM and BAGD provide a number of other epigraphical examples of the phrase. The NT usage of this noun — confined entirely to Paul and the Pastorals — bears out very consistently this usage of a divinely-originated injunction. κατ' ἐπιταγήν at Rom. 16.26, 1 Tim. 1.1, and Tit. 1.3 are explicit (as MM note) because of the following reference to God in each case. 1 Cor. 7.25 fits in with this group, too: ἐπιταγὴν κυρίου οὐκ ἔχω. At Tit. 2.15, μετὰ πάσης ἐπιταγῆς, BAGD's translation 'impressiveness' obscures the connection a little: Titus is urged to speak, etc., 'with all commandment', viz., with the authoritativeness derived from his being under divine injunction. For 1 Cor. 7.6, οὐ κατ' ἐπιταγὴν (λέγω), and 2 Cor. 8.8 (same wording) BAGD claim that the phrase takes on another meaning, 'say as a command'. If by this BAGD means 'I, Paul, am not commanding you', then it is an unpersuasive softening of the usage; and MM are surely correct in their suggestion that the same connotation of a divine command is present in both these passages. It is of course true that there are examples of ἐπιταγή which do not imply any divine involvement. But in the case of the letters under Paul's name the usage is consistent.

Buresch, *Aus Lydien*, has two other examples of the formula. No.35 (pp.73-76) is a dedication of an altar (Maionia, 177): Λοῦκις Μάρκο|υ κατ' ἐπιτα|γὴν τοῦ θεο|ῦ ὑπὲρ τῆς | σωτηρίας Διεὶ Τερμαίῳ ἀ|νέστησεν (date), 'Lucius son of Marcus set up (this) for Zeus Termaios in accordance with the god's order, for his salvation.' Another text from Maionia with this formula is printed in the course of his discussion of no.45 (p.87). Another example from 1977 publications is *SEG* 824 (Nikomedia in Bithynia, Roman period), a dedication to Agdistis written on a small statue of the seated goddess.

50. εὐσχημόνως

A decree for Athanadas of Rhegion (Delphi, c.150/49), reprinted as Nachtergael, *Galates* no.70 (pp.484-86), includes as one of the grounds for honouring him that 'during his stay (in Delphi) he behaved well and decently', ἔν τε τᾶι ἐπιδαμίαι ἀνε|στράφη καλῶς καὶ εὐσχημόνως (*ll.*7-8). Cf. the comparable περιπατεῖν εὐσχημόνως at Rom. 13.13 and 1 Thes. 4.12. The example is worth adding to a revised MM entry, as also is εὐσχημόνως τὸ ζῆν ἕξεις (*P. Vindob. Salomons* 1 = **8** above). For ἀναστρέφεσθαι καλῶς cf. Heb. 13.18. As for ἐπιδημία the noun is listed by BAGD as occurring once (figuratively?) in ECL, although the participle is used a couple of times in Acts (2.10; 17.21; cf. 18.27D).

51. ἐφόπτης

I. Charles Univ. 7 (pp.28-29, pl.3; cf. *SEG* 1303) is a fragmentary list of names, both male and female (Samothrace or Asia Minor (?) [ed.], not before II/III), possibly part of the membership of a religious association. Marek infers this from *l.*4, . .]φανος Παπᾶ ἐφοπτ, an abbreviation for ἐφόπτης. The letters -οπτ are unclear, being written above the line in small size. ἐφόπτης is a rare form of ἐπόπτης: for the false aspiration on the related verb see Gignac, I, 136-38. At least one other instance of this spelling is known in the phrase ἐφόπται εὐσεβεῖς at *IG* XII.8 (1909) 205.3 = *SIG*³ 1053 (Samothrace, post 90BC). Here and in several other examples the noun refers to a certain grade of initiate in the mysteries. The noun μύστης occurs together with it at *IG* I² (1924) 6.49-53 = *SIG*³ 42 (Athens, pre-460BC) — a law concerning the Eleusinian Mysteries — and Plut. *Alk.* 22.3 where Alkibiades is charged in 415BC with illegally τοὺς δ᾽ ἄλλους ἑταίρους μύστας προσαγορεύοντα καὶ ἐπόπτας. The occurrence at C. Michel, *Recueil d'inscriptions grecques* (Paris, 1900; repr. Hildesheim, 1976) 1141.1 (Samothrace, IIBC), ἱεροποιοὶ καὶ μυστηρίων ἐπόπται, provides a grammatical parallel (noted by MM) to 2 Pet. 1.16. This phrase, ἐπόπται γενηθέντες τῆς ἐκείνου μεγαλειότητος, provides the sole occurrence of the noun in the NT (for a related verb, ἐποπτεύω, note 1 Pet. 2.12, 3.2). Commentators appear fairly agreed that the terminology of mystery cult is being drawn on here; so it is not really appropriate to equate the noun with αὐτόπτης, as C. Bigg does (*I.C.C.*; Edinburgh, 1902², ad loc., referring to Lk. 1.2). Just as in a mystery cult the title ἐπόπτης indicates a certain status vis-à-vis other members, so here Peter bases his claim to authority on the special experience accorded to him. For examples of the noun and related verb in the Greek Bible, ECL, and elsewhere, see Deissmann, *LAE*, 347, 418.

In alluding to the transfiguration here in 2 Pet. the noun μεγαλειότης is used, which is also found in Luke's account (9.43) of the reaction to the healing of the boy with the unclean spirit. It is a way of referring to a divinity by describing one of his attributes (cf. the use of ἡ δύναμις) and clearly imputes divine status to Christ. But it should not be thought that this is a semitism *tout court*. For at Acts 19.27 Ephesian Artemis is referred to with the same word.

52. ζυγός

This word at Rev. 6.5 refers to the yoke or arms of a pair of scales, and hence the scales themselves. For another example of this sense in the papyri note *P.Mich.* 659.144 (Aphrodite, VI¹), where two people acknowledge receipt of τὰ λοιπὰ | νομίσματα δεκατέσσαρα παρὰ κεράτια | πεντηκονταὲξ ζυγῷ δημοσίῳ, 'the outstanding 14 nomismata less 56 keratia by the public scales'. (*Ed.pr.* renders the last two words with 'the public standard'.) The phrasing is repeated at *ll.*288-89 and 297-98.

53. θυρωρέω

The verb is not found in the NT, although the noun in -ρος occurs both of men (Mk 13.34, Jn 10.3) and a woman (Jn 18.16, 17). MM refer to other female door-keepers: *BGU* 4 (1912) 1061.10 (provenance unknown, 25/1/14BC); *P. Ryl.* 2

(1915) 136.6 (provenance unknown, 34AD; text has θυλουρόν). S. Daris, *Stud. Pap.* 13 (1974) 39-43 (pl.) has published a fragmentary statement of expenses (= *SB* 11169) which at *ll.*9,10 and 13 refers to Βερενείκη παιδίσκη [| ᾿Αθηναίδι θυρωρούση . . [| . . . | . . . | Ἄβη ἀραβίσσῃ θυρωρο[ύσῃ. The three women are clearly slaves, and the function of two is defined by the participle. Should we think of the παιδίσκη Rhode at Acts 12.13 as a θυρωρός as well in view of what she does?

54. κακολογέω

MM suggest (s.v.) that in the NT this verb always seems to be used in its 'weaker' sense, 'speak evil of'. This is not really correct: on all four occasions (Mt. 15.4 = Mk. 7.10 = Ex. 21.17; Mk. 9.39; Acts 19.9) the sense of 'abuse, revile, slander' is quite appropriate; and it is hard to find any examples outside the NT where the meaning is clearly stronger. Of classical references cited by LSJ, s.v., all are from the orators; one may note in particular the verb occurring in section 5 of [Lysias] 8; cf. κακῶς λέγετε at sections 19 and 20. The title of this speech is, 'An accusation of abuse against fellow members of an association', κατηγορία πρὸς τοὺς συνουσιαστὰς κακολογιῶν.

The verb appears in papyrus petitions occasionally where the complainant accuses someone of verbal and/or physical assault. G. Geraci, *Aeg.* 50 (1970) 43-45, pl. (= *SB* 11018) has published what remains of eight lines of a petition (Oxyrhynchos?, I/II) containing at *ll.*2-3,] με κακολογοῦσα πολλὰ |] καὶ ἀσχήμονα ἄλλα, κτλ.; here a woman is the cause of complaint. This phrase, with variations, seems to have been fairly standard in these documents: MM quote *P. Ryl.* 2 (1915) 150.9 (40AD) which employs the same words, and *BGU* 6 (1922) 1247.10 (Syene or Ombros, c. 149/8), ἐλοιδόρει με π[ο]λλ[ὰ κ]αὶ ἀσχήμονα. (The sole NT use of ἀσχήμων, 1 Cor. 12.23, applies it to a rather different context. MM's citations, s.v., one of which is the *P. Ryl.* passage above, do not provide useful illustrations.)

In sum, the NT use of κακολογέω is not 'weaker'; how it differs from the papyrus examples and the classical orators is simply that it is not used in a context of litigation. Acts 19.9 is the text that perhaps comes closest to this: it is the sort of comment that could have appeared in a papyrus petition.

55. κανών again (cf. *New Docs 1976*, 9)

P. Mich. 664 is an early Byzantine document recording the sale of a share of a corn measure (Aphrodite, 585 or 600). At *l.*27 κανών is used in the sense of 'assessment, schedule'. This attestation is an example of the regular Byzantine use, now seen to be related to the IAD instance cited in *New Docs 1976*, 9 as explaining 2 Cor. 10.13.

Note also *P.Str.* 657 (provenance unknown, end VI) a tax receipt in which the writer notes ἐδεξάμην | καὶ ἐπληρώθην παρὰ σοῦ ὑπὲρ τῆς ἐλεημοσύνης᾿ ὑπὲρ κανόνος | τῶν παρελθόντων χρόνων, κτλ (*ll.*2-4), 'I received from you and have been paid for alms-giving for the assessment of bygone times . . .' Are the words written above the line, ὑπὲρ τῆς ἐλεημοσύνης, a clarificatory gloss for ὑπὲρ κανόνος? *Ed.pr.* offers no comment on the exact position of the superior words, and *P. Stras.* lacks plates.

It seems hardly appropriate to consider a tax assessment as 'alms-giving', if that is the meaning of ἐλεημοσύνη here. MM, s.v., offer only one papyrus attestation of this noun, to which the *P.Stras.* example should be added, as also to BAGD, s.v. For ἐ. = 'alms-giving' in the NT note Mt. 6.2-4 and the several references from Lk./Acts listed in BAGD.

SB 11023 (provenance unknown, 423-25) is a certificate for a ship's cargo in which a man swears the standard oath by almighty God and the emperor that he has loaded his freight on to τὸ] τεταγμένον πλοῖον ἀπὸ κανόνος (*l.*8).

56. κολλουρίδιον

A short mid(?)–IAD papyrus letter of unknown provenance published by J.O'Callaghan, *APF* 22/23 (1973) 271-74, pl. (= *SB* 11064), contains a surprising number of rare words, one of which is worth brief notice here. After the introductory greeting Thaesis asks her brother Harmiysis to buy (?) κολλουρίδια τετρώβολον [ἐ]ν οἰκίᾳ [(3). The context is not full enough to allow us to be sure whether the request is for bread rolls or eye-salve, although the editor prefers the former. The noun is not attested in LSJ or the Suppl., but κολλούριον, 'eye-salve', occurs at Rev. 3.18. On the spelling -λουρ-/-λυρ- see G. Mussies, *The Morphology of Koine Greek as used in the Apocalypse of St. John* (*NovT Suppl.* 27; Leiden, 1971) 24-25. In fact, κολλούριον is itself a diminutive, so this new word is really a double diminutive.

At *l.*7 there is a reference to τὰ βάτα, 'blackberries', a very rare word (see LSJ, s.v.). Cf. in the NT ἡ βάτος, 'bramble', at Mk 12.26 (where the word is masculine); Lk. 6.44 (metaphorical); 20.37; Acts 7.30, 35.

57. κτήτωρ

This word — NT, only Acts 4.34 — is more common (so, F.F. Bruce, *Comm.*) than MM's entry or BAGD, s.v., may lead some to think. *P.Mich.* 13 comprises 15 Byzantine documents from Aphrodite, nearly all of which involve financial dealings (leases, sales, loans). κτήτωρ, 'owner', occurs at 667.3 (mid-VI), 668.1, 10 (9/7/542 or 557), and is restored at 671.3 (mid-VI). *WB* and *Spoglio* have a good number of attestations.

The lawyer (νομικός) who drew up 668 (a receipt for rent) is Pilatos (*l.*9). He is known from a number of other texts from this period: see *ed.pr.*, p.97 and add to his list *P.Lond.* 5 (1917) 1661.29 (553), mentioned by MM, s.v. Πειλᾶτος. But the name is not common in the papyri; see *NB*, and Foraboschi (svv., Πειλᾶτος and Πιλᾶτος), nearly all of whose references are to this individual. Paul's reference to Ζενᾶν τὸν νομικόν (Tit. 3.13) is more likely to be to a man with experience in Greek law (rather than Jewish law); the note in C. Spicq's *Commentary* (1947) is very useful. The name Zenas, probably an apocopated form of Zenodoros, is attested several times for Egypt (see *NB* and Foraboschi), but is also found in similar quantity in Vidman's *Index cognominum*, CIL VI. 6.2 (Rome), a good proportion of which Vidman regards as servile in origin. The name does not occur in the indexes to *CIJ* or *CPJ*.

58. λύτρον

A brief glance at this word provides a useful illustration of the need to revise MM. Their entry to this noun quotes an inscription printed in Buresch, *Aus Lydien* (p.197), reported by Deissmann *LAE* (4th edn., p.328n. and fig.60). But before the relevant fascicle of MM appeared this inscription had already been re-edited by W.H. Buckler, *ABSA* 21 (1914-16) 181-83 (cf. W.M. Calder's review of Deissmann in *CR* 38 [1924] 29-30). The inscription should read: Γαλλικῶ Ἀσκληπίας | κώμης Κερυζέων πα(ι)δίσκη (Δ)ιογένου | λύτρον, 'Galliko, female slave of the Asklepian village of the Keryzeis (dedicates this as) a ransom of Diogenes'. Above the text stands the god Men. Buresch's comments on several of the words in the inscription are superseded by this re-edition. As Buckler notes, ethnic names like Galliko used as servile names should not occasion surprise. He suggests (p.183) that the propitiatory ransom was made by the slave 'on behalf of some sinful relation'. See his comments as well on sacred villages belonging to a sanctuary of Asklepios.

Clearly MM did not know Buresch's book at first hand; and it is curious that Deissmann referred to the reprinting of the inscription on p.197 of Buresch. For while it is printed there, it appears with further comment on pp.86-89 as no.45. Furthermore, to illustrate the word in the Galliko text on p.87 Buresch reprints another 'ransom' inscription, to which Deissmann and MM make no allusion.

Ἔτους σκζʹ· Ἀρτεμίδω[ρο-
ς Διοδότου καὶ Ἀμιὰς
μετὰ τῶν συνγενῶν ἐξ ἰδό-
των καὶ μὴ ἰδότων λύτρ-
5 ον κατ' ἐπιταγὴν Μηνὶ
Τυράννῳ καὶ Διὶ Ὀγμην-
ῷ καὶ τοῖς σὺν αὐτῷ θεοῖ[ς.

Year 227 (= 143AD). Artemidoros son of Diodotos and Amias with their relatives, both those who are aware and those who are not (?), (dedicated this as) a ransom, in accordance with an injunction, to Men Tyrannos and Zeus Ogmenos and the gods in his company.

This second inscription is well worth adding to MM's entry, for the singular use of λύτρον is attested far less often than the plural. For the singular in the NT note Mt. 20.28 = Mk. 10.45, λ. ἀντὶ πολλῶν. With the clause in *ll*.3-4 cf. Mt. 13.13-14.

The chain from Buresch to Deissmann to MM carries on to BAGD, which refers, s.v., to an 'inscr. in K. Buresch, Aus Lydien 1898 p.197', as well as to literary references to illustrate the singular use of the noun. While Deissmann could be excused for ignorance of Buckler's war-time re-edition in an English journal, it is at least surprising that MM were not aware of it.

59. μετέπειτα

MM, followed by BAGD, mention *OGIS* 1 (1903) 177.14-15 as their only documentary attestation of this word to illustrate the sole NT occurrence at Heb. 12.17. This text (= *SB* 5.3 [1950] 8886) is an honorific inscription from Dime, dated to 16/9/95BC. *WB* had given two other references, *P.Cair.Masp.* 2 (1913) 166.22 (Antinoe, 15/3/568), and *BGU* 1 (1895) 163.12 — though the word appears to be entirely restored here. To these we may now add *SEG* 406 (Tomis, III¹), a metrical epitaph for a certain Markellos who says that after living 30 years, μετέπειτα τε|λευτοῦν (5-6).

60. μήτηρ

Two figurative uses of this noun from 1977 publications may be mentioned here briefly (for a third note *I. Charles Univ.* 11, quoted at **15**, section 3; for a fourth — μ. = the Church — see brief comment at **103**). MM, s.v., provide no useful examples apart from an illustration of Rom. 16.13 ('his mother and mine'). At Rev. 17.5 'Great Babylon' is called ἡ μ. τῶν πορνῶν, the implication being that this city is the one which has given birth to/nurtured vice.

C. Naour, *ZPE* 24 (1977) 265-71, no.1 (pl.8) (= *SEG* 938) has published an honorific inscription for a female benefactor called Lalla (Tlos, c.150). The beginning and ending of this text are lost, but towards the end of the extant portion ἡ πόλις cried out at an assembly to the priest of the Augusti to propose a motion 'that they should call Lalla mother of the city', ὥστε χρηματίζειν τὴν Λάλλαν | [μη]τέρα πόλεος . . . (*ll.*16-17). For this title see the references cited by Naour, 271 n.22. Cf. the use of the title πρώτη γυναικῶν, mentioned at *New Docs* 1976, **25 bis**.

A lengthy Latin inscription from Ravenna, dated 7/6/287 or 290 or 293, provides a list of members of an association: A. Donati, *Epigraphica* 39 (1977) 27-40 (= *AE* 265). Members are listed according to their title: *fabri*, *patrones*, *matres* (five women), *amatores* (twelve men, 'sympathisers'), *scriba*, *ordo* (i.e., rank and file members). On the term *amatores* see Donati, 39 and n.17.

61. μισθόω

The verb is common enough in papyrus lease documents, whether in the active or the middle. *P.Wiscon.* 52 (4/10/32) is one of the earliest such land leases from Karanis (see *ed.pr.*, p.55, for references to earlier examples). Here a certain Euphranis certifies that he has leased land (ἐμίσθ[ωσε]ν, 2) on his mother's behalf to NN for three years. The regular term for the lessee is the perfect middle participle, ὁ μεμισθωμένος (*ll.*[12], 18 [19-20], 21); cf. K.L. McKay, *BICS* 27 (1981) 41-42. These examples are worth noting simply because of their earlier date than the texts cited in MM, s.v. Mt. 20.1, 7 (the only NT occurrences) use the middle of hiring workmen.

62. οἰκονομία

This word appears at *P.Wiscon.* 55.1 (provenance unknown, II), an abrupt, anonymous instruction to another unnamed person:

Ποῦ εἰσιν αἱ οἰκονομίαι
τοῦ ἐποικίου; εὐθέως
οὖν πέμψατε᾿ δι' Εὐχαί-
του δυναμένο[υ] ἀπο-

5 λογίσασθαι ἀλλὰ
πάντως σήμ[ε]ρ[ον]
ἐπεὶ ἐνθάδε εἰσιν
οἱ ἐπισκέπται.

Where are the documents (*or* plans (?)) of (for) the village (*or* farmstead (?))?
5 **Send them straightaway via Euchaites who can render | an account; but at any**
rate (send them) today since the surveyors are here.

The plural of this noun occurs only at Diog. 4.5 in ECL, never in the NT. For the sense, 'arrangement, plan', see BAGD, s.v., 2a-c, for which the only relevant NT passages are Eph. 1.10, γνωρίσας ἡμῖν τὸ μυστήριον τοῦ θελήματος αὐτοῦ . . . εἰς οἰκονομίαν τοῦ πληρώματος τῶν καιρῶν; and 3.9, ἡ οἰκ. τοῦ μυστηρίου. Given the proximity of μυστήριον in both places Paul appears to be applying the same particular (theological) weighting to οἰκονομία.

Two other words in this text may hold us briefly. The absolute use of ἀπο-λογέομαι (*ll*.4-5) is found in the NT at Lk. 21.14; Acts 26.1; and Rom. 2.15. In the first two there is a legal context, while at Rom. 2.5 Paul has taken over legal terminology for an extended metaphor. The more general sense of the verb, as found in this papyrus text, is illustrated by 2 Cor. 12.19. For πάντως (*l*.6) as a strong affirmative note the examples in MM and BAGD, s.v., 1 (but the latter's differentiation of 1 Cor 9.22 — s.v., 4 — for this sense is unwarranted).

63. οἰοσδήποτε

The NT has οἰῳδηποτοῦν (the variant -δηποτε is attested) only in Jn 5.4, a verse which is subject to textual doubt (it reads like an explanatory gloss). Several examples of -δηποτε to add to MM, s.v. οἰοσδηποτοῦν, are *P.Mich.* 659 (Aphrodite, VI¹), *ll*.207, 236, 243, 251; 662 (Aphrodite, VII) *ll*.24, 40; 672 (Aphrodite, VI), *l*.4 (restored).

64. ὀψάριον

occurs in a list of food disseminated to five individuals, *P.Wiscon.* 60.12 (provenance unknown, III): Φανίᾳ | ὀψάριν | ᾠὰ χήνια δ | κίτρια β (*ll*.11-14), 'to Phanias: fish, 4 duck eggs, 2 citrons' (tr. *ed.pr.*). For the spelling of ὀψάριον here cf. D.J. Georgacas, *CP* 43 (1948) 243-60. In view of the Synoptic parallels ὀψάριον means 'fish' at Jn 6.9, 11; 21.9, 10, 13; and this is probably the preferable sense for the new papyrus, in view of the singular form. But it is not the only possible sense, as MM's entry attests.

65. ὀψώνιον

A IAD letter — noteworthy in that it is exactly dated, 17/11/93 (or probably 94 — *ed.pr.*) — has ὀψώνιον at *ll.*4, 5, 6, 9, 12, 22 (*P.Wiscon.* 68; Theadelphia?). Diotimos confirms in his letter to Isarous that he has received the 'allowance' paid at various intervals for Aphrodite, who is apparently staying with him. The allowance is normally paid in coin, but on two occasions payment in kind is involved (wool, and a chiton). We are clearly well away from the military context which appears to have been the primary usage of this word (see BAGD and MM). The writer uses the phraseology ἐκο|μ[ισάμ]ην . . . τοῦ πρώτου ὀψωνίου (δραχμὰς) κβ 'I received 22 dr. as the first allowance' (*ll.*1-4); cf. 2 Cor. 11.8, λαβὼν ὀψώνιον. At *ll.*4-5 Diotimos has used the dative instead of the genitive; this interchange is an indication of the gradual disappearance of the dative. ὀψώνιον occurs in two other *P.Wiscon.* texts: 78.108, a lengthy account (Philadelphia, Feb./March 248BC) where the plural is used of 'wages' paid for the care of kids; and 80.187, a customs account (Bacchias, 1/10/114) where the word is used of the salary fr two archers.

At the end of this letter note the greeting 'to your mother' καὶ τοὺς ἐν οἴκῳ πάντας (*ll.*20-21). For ἐν οἴκῳ cf. Jn 2.1, and particularly 1 Cor. 11.34; 14.35. The same phrase appears at *P.Wiscon.* 69.16 (Philadelphia, 2/5/101), at the conclusion of another letter.

66. πανοικεί

This adverb (NT, only at Acts 16.34) and its variants πανοικεσίᾳ/-ησίᾳ are found in a number of papyrus letters of II and IIIAD, as part of a concluding greeting formula. In addition to examples in MM note *P.Stras.* 652, portions of four business letters addressed to one man, Apollonios, by two or three different writers. The word occurs — abbreviated twice as πανοικ(εί) at the conclusion of three of the letters (*ll.*21, 43, 77), and *ed.pr.* has restored it at the end of the other one (*l.*9). In their note on the word (p.77) the editors refer to further examples.

67. παρασκευή

Although this noun is employed in the NT, Jewish writers and ECL to refer to Friday as a specifically Jewish and Jewish Christian usage, no documentary occurrences of the word with this meaning have been noticed hitherto. No examples occur in either *CIJ* or *CPJ*; nor do *WB* and *Spoglio* provide any help. *SEG* 728 is a short inscription in a cave from Benler in Ionia (n.d., *ed.pr.*) whose wording runs:

> Μητρᾶς *(vac.)* τῇ ἀγα-
> θῇ ΠΑΡΑ
> ΣΚΗ

Ed.pr. raises the possibility — it is no more than that — that the capitalized letters may be an abbreviation for παρασκευή and mean 'Friday'.

68. πιστός = **Christian**

The absolute, active use of this adjective in the NT is common enough, especially in the singular (BAGD, s.v. 2); for the plural note Acts 12.3D; 1 Tim. 4.3,12; at Acts 10.45 it is used of Jewish Christians. MM report the view of H. Lietzmann that π. has this meaning also at 1 Cor. 7.25, but it is not persuasive (cf. BAGD, s.v., la, α). About one in six of the inscriptions in *I.Tyre* 1 uses πιστῶν in various brief epitaph formulae to indicate that the deceased are Christians. Rey-Coquais interprets the word, which occasionally stands alone (39B, 64, 99, 107C, 192) to mean 'belonging to the community of the faithful'. Two other anonymous epitaphs are nos. 32 and 57. For τόπος π. note 37, 66, 68, 90 (οἰκὶν π.), 91B, 93, 94, 96, 141, 160, 172. Only twice (26, 174) in the forty-odd examples in this volume is the singular πιστοῦ used.

One interesting group throws up an example of the continuing status cleavage between free and slave Christians in the later Empire. No.44 reads P πιστῶν † | ἐλευθερικό(ν), nos.45 and 46 are very similar; but no.47 has † πεδαρικόν †. In the latter case while πιστῶν does not appear it is in other respects (e.g. the shape of the stone — see pl.43.1-3) identical with and adjacent to nos. 45 and 46. Of the three other examples which illustrate this status distinction continuing to be observed in death, nos. 131 and 132 are Christian: † Δεσποτικόν and [Πα]ιδαρικόν respectively — both belong to the same monument, and it is not impossible that a cross should also be restored at the front of the word in no.132 by analogy with no.131. The third example is Samaritan, no.168 : Σαμαριτῶν ἐλευθέ|ρων.

The text on the sarcophagus of no.134 reads, † τόπος πιστῶν· Μηνᾷ τραπεζίτη †. Rey-Coquais (ad loc.) draws attention to the fact that a certain Menas, reader of the Church of Tyre, was excommunicated by Epiphanius for his Monophysite beliefs. But whether this is his tomb is impossible to say. For Christian bankers note also from this volume of inscriptions from Tyre no.137, where the man has in addition the trade of purple-dyer, ἀληθεινόβαφος. Two other Christian bankers were noted at *New Docs 1976*, **87**.

SEG 662 (Syracuse, after 402) provides another example of the term in an epitaph for Eutychia ἡ πιστή. *AE* 128 reprints a Latin epitaph from Rome for a teenager which begins *hic dormit virgo fid[e]|lis Aurelia Maxima M. f.*, etc.

69. πλάνη

This word provides a clear example of how MM is unfortunately invested with more final authoritativeness than its authors ever envisaged for it. MM, s.v., provides only one papyrus example, *BGU* 4 (1912) 1208.6 (27/6BC), where it is partly restored and is taken to mean 'deceit'. This is the sole documentary text alluded to in BAGD, s.v., whose entry shows the popularity of the word in ECL. The meaning of πλάνη as found in the NT, 'error, delusion' (Mt. 27.64; Rom. 1.27; Eph. 4.14; 1 Thes. 2.3; 2 Thes. 2.11; Jas. 5.20; 2 Pet. 2.18; 3.17; 1 Jn 4.6; Jude 11) is in fact attested by a number of papyri (no epigraphical examples are known to me): between them *WB* and *Spoglio* provide over a dozen references to the word, dated II–Byzantine. From 1977 publications *P.Wiscon.* 86 (Philadelphia, 244-46) includes the word in a petition by three brothers concerning a tax assessment based on an inaccurate reckoning of their landholding. 'The village registrar, possibly through error (ἴσως κα[τ]ὰ | πλάνην), assessed us in the posted list of individual taxpayers, etc.' (9-10; tr., *ed.pr.*). The same prepositional phrase occurs in C. Wessely, *Stud.Pal.* 20 (1921, repr. 1969) 85, page 1, *recto l.*7. This document is an account submitted to a *logographos* with details of payments made to certain people (a *paidagogos*, some *grammateis*, etc.). The scribe mentions money that was 'not spent at that time by mistake but is now being spent', μὴ ἀναλωθ(έντα) τότε κατὰ πλάνην | ἀλλὰ νῦν ἀναλισκόμ(ενα).

70. προθεσμία

Part of a register refers to some action (payment of money?), 'on the appointed day during the 13th year of Domitian, Tybi . . .' τῆ προθεσ(μία) ιγ (ἔτους) Δο(μιτιανοῦ) Τῦβι κατ[(*P.Laur.* 35, *recto l.*5; Arsinoite nome, 93-95). The abbreviation of προθεσμία is an indicator of the frequency of the noun in such a context. MM provide no epigraphical attestations, although Buresch, *Aus Lydien* — first published late last century, but apparently known to MM only via Deissmann, *LAE*: see MM, s.v. λύτρον, and **58** — includes as no.16 a sarcophagus from Gjöktsche Köy carrying a fragmentary inscription whose *l.*3 Buresch reads as νομι(?)]κὴν προθεσμ[ίαν . . . , presumably some reference to the fact that the heir of the deceased has to make some offering on the customary appointed day. The presence of προθεσμία only once in the NT (Gal. 4.2) illustrates the danger of thinking (even subconsciously) that NT word frequencies may roughly approximate to those in other literary or documentary sources.

71. προκόπτω

L. Robert, *R.Phil.* 51 (1977) 12, n.36 (cf. *SEG* 1242) corrects the inscription on a gem published last century, to read εὐτύχως πρόκοπτε (previously ἀπο-) ὁ φορῶν, 'may the wearer prosper happily'. This verb occurs in the Classical period as well as later (where it is intransitive), but the noun προκοπή is a Hellenistic coinage. Both words are frequent enough in Hellenistic and Roman times to express the idea of advancement, progress, success in one's career or in knowledge of virtue (cf. *BE* [1973] 501). While in the earlier period the Greeks lacked a specific noun to allow them to speak of 'progress' the notion is discussed, especially in scientific fields; and there is a clear link made by several writers in antiquity (e.g. Hesiod, Lucretius) between scientific progress and moral degeneration. On this see E.R. Dodds, *The Ancient Concept of Progress and other essays on Greek Literature and Belief* (Oxford, 1973) ch.1; cf. K. Thraede, 'Fortschritt', *RAC* 8(1972) 141-82.

For further discussion of the terms see L. Robert, *Études anatoliennes* (Paris, 1937; repr. Amsterdam, 1970) 228, n.7. His pp.227-28 examine the notion of being 'known to the Augusti': part of a text is given there (B. Latyschev, *Inscriptiones antiquae orae septentrionalis Ponti Euxini graecae et latinae*, I [Petersburg, 1916²; repr. Hildesheim, 1965] 79), *ll.*6-7 of an honorific inscription for a man μέχρι τᾶς τῶν Σεβαστῶν γνώσεως προκό[ψ]αντος, 'who advanced as far as the knowledge of the Augusti'. This same passage is considered by Deissmann, *LAE* 378 n.6 (cf. 181

n.15), who also draws attention to the use of γνῶσις as a parallel to Phil. 3.8 (acquaintance with Christ, not knowledge about him). Robert (1977) has further bibliography. The best NT parallel to the gem inscription is 2 Tim. 3.9, ἀλλ' οὐ προκόψουσιν ἐπὶ πλεῖον (cf. the use of the noun at 1 Tim. 4.15).

72. πρωτεύω

This verb is a NT hapax at Col. 1.18, ἵνα γένηται ἐν πᾶσιν αὐτὸς πρωτεύων, but is not uncommon elsewhere, and is found from Classical Greek authors through to Byzantine documents. Although MM, s.v., do not crystallize the point their three late Roman/early Byzantine examples reveal a use of this verb as a title, whether denoting real political leadership in a city or acting as an honorific. This more specific use is attested also by some of the classical literary, and epigraphical references in LSJ, s.v. As an honorific term πρωτεύοντι (dative, *l*.3) occurs in *P.Laur.* 27 (Arsinoe, 487-91) as part of the titulary of a count (κόμες), Flavius Eustochius, in a fragmentary document of surety (ἐγγύη). W. Michaelis, *TDNT* 6 (ET, 1968) 882 n.3, thinks that πρωτεύων at Col. 1.18 'cannot be a title here, since the verbal function of the saying is evident'. Even if the participle does have a verbal function there, that need not exclude its also being felt as a title. But further, does it have a verbal force here anyway? It is true that Col. 1.18 may be grouped with other NT passages to illustrate γίνομαι + part. (cf. BDF 354); but the intervening ἐν πᾶσιν goes closely with γένηται and has the effect of detaching πρωτεύων somewhat from its close liaison with γένηται. Although πρωτεύω does occur in a more general sense, given the overall hymnic section of Col. 1.15-20 perhaps πρω-τεύων is not accorded its full weight by modern commentators who merely relate it back to πρωτότοκος earlier in v.18 and v.15. Lightfoot offered no comment on πρωτεύων in his Commentary; E. Lohse's note (*Comm.*, ad loc) does not take us far; nor does the most recent detailed commentary on Col. (P.T. O'Brien; *Word Bib. Comm.*: Waco, 1982) address itself to this possibility.

Returning to *P.Laur.* 27 two other features of this document require notice. The oath is sworn by θεὸν παντοκρ[άτορα . . . (*l*.5). *Ed.pr.* has restored the remainder of the oath in conformity with extant standard formulae, an example of which may be found at *New Docs 1976*, **27**. On the epithet παντοκράτωρ cf. *New Docs 1976*, **86**.

The *verso* of this papyrus contains three lines of writing, and two further hands are in evidence in addition to the two on the *recto*. *Ed.pr.* suggests that *verso ll*.1-2 may be a memorandum or perhaps the remains of a probably Christian letter. The second line reads π(ρὸς) ἅγι(ον) Ἠλίαν ἐλθῖ(ν) (καὶ) ἴαμα τοῦ Ἰσὰκ υἱὸν Ἰακώβου ἁγί(ου) (καὶ) ὑπ(ὲρ) εὐημερίας, 'To come to the church of St. Elias and (get) healing for Isak son of holy James and for his good health.' This use of ἴαμα is rare — more commonly it means 'medicine, remedy' — but is found on an inscription from Epidauros listing cures effected by Apollo and Asklepios (*IG* 4.951.2 = *SIG*³ 1168), as noted by MM and BAGD, apart from the thrice-repeated phrase χαρίσματα ἰαμάτων in 1 Cor. 12 (vv. 9, 28, 30).

73. ῥάκος

To the four examples in MM, s.v., we may add *P.Stras.* 647.2, ῥάκος εἰς ἔμπλαστ[ο]ν (*sic*), 'a patch for plaster' (i.e. for healing wounds), in a fragmentary military account (provenance unknown, II¹). This example is closer in time to the NT than those in MM; cf. Mt. 9.16 = Mk. 2.21. This example of ἔμπλαστρος may be added to BAGD (ECL only), along with the further papyrus reference given by *ed.pr.*, n. ad loc.

74. στοιχεῖ μοι

P.Mich. 13 attests this construction thirteen times — once restored, 671.24 — all in Byzantine financial documents (VI-VII): see index to that volume for the references. The NT uses this verb with the dative but not in the impersonal construction found commonly in Byzantine papyri, which MM abundantly attests but BAGD does not (beyond a general allusion). It is the norm in these Byzantine texts for a personal subject to coexist in the sentence along with the impersonal construction, showing that στοιχεῖ μοι has become so formulaic that its grammatical force has entirely ceased to be felt. As an example note *P.Mich.* 669.19, 21, 22 (Aphrodite, 12-13/9/529 or 514), a loan agreement where each of the three debtors (Victor, son of Besarion, *presbyteros*; Senouthes, son of Apollos; Apollos, son of Dioskoros — on the name Apollos see *New Docs 1976*, **50**; several more examples may be noted in the indexes to *P.Mich.* and *P.Wiscon.*, all Byzantine in date except *P.Wiscon.* 46 [22/1BC]) signifies his agreement by adding the formula after his name. In the NT the passages which perhaps most nearly approximate in sense to this impersonal use are Gal. 6.16 and Phil. 3.16, possibly also Gal. 5.25.

75. συγκληρόνομος

The suggestion was made in *New Docs 1976*, **85** that the occurrence of this word in a pre-Byzantine letter (*PSI* 8 [1927] 972; re-ed. J.R. Rea, *Chr. d'Ég.* 45 [1970] 363-68 [= *SB* 10841]) could be an allusion to the fact that the two people involved were believers (cf. Rom. 8.17). MM., s.v. συνκλ- provides an example of the stock formula in Byzantine sale documents whereby the vendor undertakes that neither he nor his heirs and co-heirs will hinder the purchaser's full use of the item bought. *P.Mich.* provides four examples of this phrase, τῶν μετὰ ἐμὲ κληρονόμων ἢ συγκληρονόμων: 662.45-46 (Aphrodite, VII), 663.17 (Aphrodite, VI; partly restored), 664.28-29 (Aphrodite, 585-600), 665.69-70 (Aphrodite, 613-41). The close conjunction of the two nouns in this formula is of some interest for Rom. 8.17; whereas Heb. 11.7, 9 provides no such parallel.

Apart from these texts and *P.Mich.* 672.3, κληρονόμος is attested extremely frequently (21 times) in *P.Mich.* 659, a lengthy document detailing the settlement (διάλυσις) of a long-standing financial dispute. This papyrus, of over 360 lines on 28 sheets of papyrus, is, 'apart from tax-lists, the longest papyrus known to me even though it is incomplete at the top' (*ed.pr.*, p.x). In connection with the wording of Rom. 8.17, εἰ δὲ τέκνα, καὶ κληρονόμοι, cf. *l.*60 of this papyrus where 'Victor and Senouthes undertake business for Apollos, Paul and Maria τέκνων καὶ κληρονόμων of John of pious memory'.

76. συμπλήρωσις

The related verb occurs in a few places in Lk./Acts, either of (the occupants of) a boat being swamped with water (Lk. 8.23), or of time (Lk. 9.51; Acts 2.1 — both use the infinitive as a noun). Some late examples of the noun occur in *P.Mich.*: 659.144 (Aphrodite, VI[1]) where people have received an amount εἰς συμπλήρωσιν τῆς τιμῆς, 'in fulfilment of the price' (the same phrase again at *ll.*289 and 298; 666.32 (Aphrodite, VI) a lease in which the tenant agrees to provide certain payments in kind, ὑπὲρ τῆς συμπληρώσεως τοῦ φόρου, 'for the completion of the rent'. MM, s.v. συμπληρόω, have a few examples of the noun in this sense. The verb is attested rather less frequently than the noun in the papyri, as *WB* and *Spoglio* make clear.

77. συναντάω

P.Laur. 45 (Hermopolite nome (?), VI/VII) is a letter from a village official requesting that a κολλητίων (military policeman) be sent to his village because the soldiers responsible for collecting tax (in kind) have not been co-operative. The first six lines read:

                                    χμγ
Βο[υ]λόμ[ενο]ς καταλαβεῖν τὴν κώμην, ἀπολυθεὶς παρὰ τῆς σῆς λαμπρότητος,
συνήντησάν μοι οἱ στρατιῶται οἳ καὶ ἀπαιτηταὶ τῆς προειρημένης
κώμης Τάλκεως, καὶ ἀπὸ τῆς πρώτης ἡμέρας ἐν ᾗ κατείληφα
5 τὴν κώμην οὐκ ἐδυνήθην, ὡς χρή, ἀπαιτῆσαι, διὰ τὸ μὴ ἐμὲ ἔχειν
τι[νά], καθὼς γρά[φω α]ὐτῇ, εἰ μὴ μόνον ἕνα.

Wishing to make a check of the village, when I was released from your Serenity, there met me the soldiers who are also the tax-gatherers of the aforesaid village of Talkis, but from the first day on which I have made my check of the village, I have not been able to make demands as I ought, because of my not having anybody just as I write to (you) yourself, except one person only.

συναντάω is not especially rare and is found several times in the NT with the same dative construction as occurs in this text (Lk. 9.37; 22.10; Acts 10.25; Heb. 7.1, 10). It may be noted for MM's entry, however, all of whose examples with this construction are IIIBC. The continuity of usage over a longer period deserves to be noticed.

The verb ἀπαιτέω is common enough (see MM, s.v.), but we may note here the term ἀπαίτης, yet another word designating tax-gatherers. It does not appear in the NT, but MM, s.v. ἀπαιτέω, ad fin., note one much earlier example. In addition to the one in this Byzantine document, *ed.pr.* (n. ad loc.) refers to two other papyri (VI) where it is found.

For the abbreviation χμγ see **104**.

78. συνωμοσία

Neither MM nor BAGD provide any papyrus attestations to this noun, though MM adduces two inscriptions. *P.Mil.Vogl.* 287 is a very fragmentary copy of a report of proceedings (provenance unknown, II). Although too mutilated to allow much restoration of its subject matter, the word occurs at *l.*9, σ]υνωμοσίας (genitive singular). In the NT, only at Acts 23.13.

79. φιλόθεος

Neither MM nor BAGD provides any documentary attestations for this adjective, which in the NT is found only at 2 Tim. 3.4 where it provides an adversative contrast to φιλήδονοι in one of the NT vice lists. In fact the word occurs on an inscription from Ajas Ören in Lydia which Buresch published late last century (*Aus Lydien*, no.39, pp.79-83, a work with which MM appear to have had no direct acquaintance):

<blockquote>
Τατ]ιανὸς Γλαῦκος καὶ ᾿Αμμιανὴ φι-
λό]θεοι Μηνὶ Μοτυλείτῃ εὐχαριστ-
ία]ν ἔθοντο, εὐχόμενοι ἀεὶ ὑπὲρ
θ]ρεπτῆς γένει πρώτης Σαβείν[ης
5   ἥνπερ σώσειες σύ (?).
</blockquote>

Tatianos Glaukos and Ammiane, pious ones, rendered thanks to Men 5 Motuleites, constantly praying for Sabeine their eldest foundling. | May it please you to save her(?).

On the form ἔθοντο see Buresch, pp. 79-80, where parallel formations in the LXX and NT are noted; on the epithet of Men here, ibid. pp. 81-83. For the common use of εὐχαριστία here cf. Buresch, no.36 (pp. 75-76) where the participle occurs in a dedication to Hosios and Dikaios to fulfil a vow from a woman grateful for her powers of sight being healthy (ε]ὐχαριστοῦ[σα ὑπὲρ] | [ὑγιοῦ]ς ὁράσεως (3-5)). On Hosios and Dikaios see briefly *New Docs 1976*, **7**. Buresch no.23 (Arpaly in Lydia) is a fragmentary honorific decree set up by the foreign residents (κάτοικοι) of the town, who conclude the text by saying that their decree is to be valid for all time, and is to be inscribed, so that the benefaction (?) of such men and ἡ τῶν κατοίκων εὐχαριστία may remain (*ll.*16-19). For the meaning 'gratitude' in this last example cf. Acts 24.3. On *threptoi* see M.R. Flood, *Epigraphic Evidence for Family Structures and Customs in Asia Minor during the Early Roman Empire* (Diss., Macquarie, 1978) 95–153.

80. φιλοστοργία in epitaphs from Asia Minor

Arsada (Lykia)   Late Hellenistic
ed.pr. — C. Naour, *ZPE* 24 (1977) 276-79, no.6 (pl.10)

AI   [. . . . . .]ανις Αρμ[. . . . .]ιου ἐπὶ τῷ ἀγ[δρὶ]
        [αὐτῆς Ἀ]ρτεμη καὶ Ἀρτεμης καὶ Ἑρμαῖο[ς]
        [καὶ . . .]ς καὶ Ὀσονοα ἐπὶ τῷ πατρὶ Ἀρτε-
        μη φιλοστοργίας ἔνακεν θεοῖς ἥρωι.

B 5 [θύ]σουσι δὲ οἱ υ[ἱοὶ α]ὐτοῦ κατ' ἐνιαυ[τὸν]
        ἐν τῷ Ἀρτεμισίῳ μηνὶ δεκάτῃ *vacat*
        [τ]ομίαν· ἐὰν δὲ μὴ θυσῶσι, ἁμαρτωλο[ὶ]
        [ἔ]σθωσαν θεῷ καὶ ἡρώων.

AII   Ὀσονοα ⟨Ἀ⟩ρτεμε{με}ους
  10 ἐπὶ τῷ ἑαυ[τ]ῆς ἀνδρὶ καὶ
        ἀδελφ[ῷ --- καὶ ---]βορις
        καὶ Ἀρτεμης ἐπὶ τῷ πατρί.

Two sides (A, B) of a limestone block, side A containing two texts (I, II). The wording of *l*.11 is largely lost because the horizontal bar of a cross was later incised across it (*ed.pr.*'s pl. is very clear).
Bib. — *BE* 469; *SEG* 907

(*AI*) **[NN] for her husband Artemes, and Artemes and Hermaios . . . and Osonoa for their father Artemes, deceased, for the sake of heartfelt love to**
5 **the gods. |(*B*) And his sons shall sacrifice annually during the month Artemision on the tenth (day) a victim; but if they do not sacrifice let them be accounted sinners against god and the dead. (*AII*) Osonoa daughter of**
10 **Artemes |for her own husband and brother . . . and Artemes for his father.**

Side A preserves two epitaphs, the first for a certain Artemes from his wife and children, the second for Artemes' son from his wife (who is also his sister; she is also the daughter of Artemes) and their children (one of whom in turn bears his grandfather's, and perhaps father's, name). Other examples of marriage between siblings are known from Asia Minor: Naour, 278 n.49, refers to *TAM* 2 (1944) 593, 636 (both from Tlos). Side B is a surprisingly spare example of a frequently-attested prescription: in the first month of the town's calendar (= July) the sons are to ensure that a sacrifice is made. τομίας (7) probably refers to a gelded male animal, perhaps a pig. The ἁμαρτωλός clause (7-8) is very common in Lykia, often in the singular; θεῷ does not need to be altered to θεῶν (Naour, 278 and n.48). Cf. Naour no.11 (= *SEG* 909; Arsada, Roman period), which warns that if any other corpse is interred in the grave ἁμα[ρτωλὸς] | ἔσται θεοῖς πᾶ[σι] | *vacat* καταχθονίοις.

The noun φιλοστοργία is not found in the NT, although it is used of Christians in ECL (see BAGD, s.v.); the adjective φιλόστοργος only at Rom. 12.10, τῇ φιλα-δελφίᾳ εἰς ἀλλήλους φιλόστοργοι. L. Robert's book-length critique of *MAMA* 8 (1962) in *Hellenika* 13 (1965) devotes several pages (38-41) to the occurrence of these words in inscriptions; the reference ought to be included in BAGD's entry to these two words (the only item given is C. Spicq, *Rev.Bib.* 62 [1955] 497-510, an excellent survey covering LXX, Philo, Josephus and other hellenistic literary attestations, as well as papyri and inscriptions, these latter concentrating on honorifics which are thus largely ignored here). Robert shows with reference to a series of Cilician texts from *MAMA* 8 that the words can be used in a variety of familial loving relationships: conjugal, mother for child, child for parents. Thus a man honours his wife [φ]ιλοστοργίας καὶ | [ε]ὐνοίας ἕνεκεν (235); a son honours his mother using the same phrase (392; rather more restored). In these the woman is praised because of the affection she has exhibited towards them during her lifetime. A decisive example is 394 where four sons honour τὴν | [ἑ]αυτῶν μητέ[ρ]|α σωφρο-σύνη[ς] | [κ]αὶ φ[ιλ]ο[σ]τ[ο]ργία[ς] | [ἕ]νεκεν, for *sophrosyne* is essentially a feminine virtue. The fullest study of the word is H. North, *Sophrosyne. Self-Knowledge and Self-Restraint in Greek Literature* (Ithaca, 1966), which supersedes the references given in BAGD, s.v. σωφροσύνη. She includes a chapter (pp.312-79) on the term in patristic literature. For the adjective used in connection with a male slave see **15**. In contrast 367 is a text in which the husband and two brothers honour a woman φιλοστοργί|ας καὶ μνήμης | ἕνεκεν; in view of the companion noun μνήμη here φ. must refer to the affection of the surviving people for the deceased to which they wish the epitaph to bear witness. Note also 391, where a woman is honoured by her children φιλοτεκνία[ς] | ἰδίας μητρὸ[ς] καὶ | στοργῆς ἑαυ[τῶν] χάριν — ἑαυτῶν is Robert's correction for *MAMA*'s ἑαυ[τοῖς] — 'because of the maternal love which their own mother showed and because of their own affection (i.e. for her, presumably)'. (For φιλοτεκνία here, cf. the adjective at Tit. 2.4. The same verse contains another NT *hapax*, φίλανδρος. To MM's few references add Buresch, *Aus Lydien*, p.14, no.11, a Roman epitaph from Philadephia in Lydia for a wife who lived three years with her husband ἄγνως καὶ φιλάνδρως [*ll.*3-4].) For the combination φίλανδρος καὶ φιλότεκνος in an epitaph for a woman (Pergamon, time of Hadrian) see Deissmann, *Bible Studies* 255–56, and *LAE* 314–15. Furthermore, Robert provides examples of the adjective in epitaphs: Stratonike is φιλόστοργος to her children (247); a father's epitaph from Rome for his child (aged one year and 40 days), Πριμιτείβῳ γλυκυ|τάτῳ τέκνῳ καὶ φι|λοστόργῳ, κτλ (*IG* XIV.2 [1890] 1967); and a third text whose lacuna he corrects to read φιλόστ[οργος] εἰς γονῖς, 'loving to his parents'. To this collection of texts a further example, from 1977 publications, may be added. In a metrical epitaph for four brothers, their aunt and a slave (Raffeiner, *Sklaven*, no.49), who perhaps were all killed in one incident and thus buried together (on the burial of slaves in family graves see **14**), the woman is spoken of (*l.*5) as γνωτή θ' Ἡράκλεια φιλοστόργοιο τεκούσης 'and Herakleia sister of their (i.e., the brothers', mentioned earlier in the text) beloved mother' (Sidon?, II/III). Two other examples may be noted, both superlatives: *IGRR* 1 (1911, repr. 1964) 1082 = *SB* V.3 (1950) 8291 (Alexandria, Roman period), Τι(βέριον) Κλαύδιον Ἀπίωνα | τὸν πάντα ἄριστον καὶ φιλοστοργότατον | ἀδελφῶν | Κλαυδία Φιλορωμαία (the readings here supersede those of *CIG* 3 [1853, repr. 1977] 4689); and *OGIS* 1 (1903, repr. 1970) 331.46-47 (Pergamon, IIBC), where Stratonike, mother of Attalos III Philometor is said by him to be φιλ[ο]|στοργοτάτη δὲ διαφερόντως πρός τε τὸμ πατέρα μου καὶ πρὸς ἐμέ. (Spicq, 498, mentions that Philo uses the superlative of Abraham *qua* father, *de Abra.* 198.)

One very noticeable feature emerges about the epigraphical usage of these words. They are used always to refer to the heartfelt love shown by or directed towards a mother or wife, or in one case towards a father by an infant. While the context of all these epitaphs — *OGIS* 331 is the only non-epitaph among them — is different from Paul's series of admonitions in Rom. 12.9-16, in view of the large number of examples from Cilicia Paul is most unlikely to be unaware of the usage.

When we turn to consider the papyrological occurrences of these words some differences may be discerned. The adjective is used of Isis in the very important *P.Oxy* 11 (1915) 1380.12, 131 (cf. *I.Kyme* [1976] 41.20-21 = *New Docs 1976*, **2**, p.19), where Isis sees it as one of her roles to promote φιλοστοργία within families. The adverb -γως at *P.Oslo* 3 (1936) 80.3 (provenance unknown, after 161) recurs in a report of legal proceedings whose context is too mutilated for us to do more than note the occurrence. (MM give two other references, s.v. φιλόστοργος.) *Spoglio* III, s.v., registers the verb once, and several instances of the noun; further references for the latter are listed in *WB* and *WB* suppl. I (1940-1966), 2.Lief. (1969), s.v. Some instances of the noun merit brief comment. In a badly-damaged papyrus will, *P.Oxy.* 3 (1903) 495.12 (181-89) Petosorapis leaves his estate to his son Epinikos, but until the latter is of age the father's sister, Apollonous, is to administer the inheritance, treating him with μητρικῇ φιλοστοργίᾳ. In two other wills, *P.Oxy.* 490.4 (124AD) and 492.6 (130AD), a woman in each case leaves her estate to Dionysios (another minor), and to two brothers respectively, κατὰ φιλοστοργίαν. *P.Oxy.* 494.6 (156AD) is a copy of a will in which Akousilaus grants freedom to five slaves κατ' εὐνοίαν καὶ φιλοστοργίαν, 'in view of their goodwill and affection for me'. (Cf. *P.Oslo* 3 [1936] 129.15 [Antinoopolis, III], where φιλοστοργίας occurs in a damaged deed of emancipation.) A similar phrase is to be found at *P.Grenf.* 2 (1897) 71.12 (Great Oasis, 244-48), a deed of gift by which a father cedes property to two sons εὐνοίας χάριν καὶ φιλοστοργίας; on the connection between these two nouns see Spicq, 502. Five of these six texts are wills or will-related documents; in three, women are involved in the relationship expressed by φιλοστοργία. (The *P.Oxy.* editors understood the phrases to mean that the deceased bequeaths his/her gift to someone 'in view of the affection he has shown to me'; but surely the reverse is true, as Robert [above] has demonstrated for epitaphs, that the legacy is made 'in view of my affection for him'? K. L. McKay, in a note to me, writes: 'From a quick check of LSJ, s.v. κατά, I find κατ' εὐνοίην used in Herodotus clearly referring to the goodwill of the subject of the verb, and κατ' ἔχθραν, κατ' ἔχθος, κατὰ φθόνον, καθ' ἡδόνην, κατὰ φιλίαν all referring to the attitude of the subject. The examples given in BAGD also seem to have this implication. In the wills quoted there seems to be no contextual reason to take it as referring to the attitude of the object. . . . Following the classical (and other) examples I think that the natural presumption of κατά plus an anarthrous accusative of a feeling or emotion noun must be that it refers to the attitude of the subject. If the opposite is intended it seems to me that further definition is required [e.g., an article and a genitive: κατὰ τὴν εὐνοίαν αὐτῶν]'.) Two of the texts — four, if the ones mentioning slaves are included — relate to family members (*P.Oxy.* 495; *P.Grenf.* 2.71). In the case of some of these papyri, where family relationship is not in view (and perhaps the slave texts), is φιλοστοργία being used in a vaguer sense? Such a more general meaning appears to be in evidence at *P. Tebt.* 2 (1907) 408.5-10 (3AD), a letter in which the writer says, παρακαλῶ σε περὶ υἱῶν | μου τῆι φιλοστορ|γίᾳ τῶν περὶ Σωτή|ριχον μὴ ἐᾶσαι | πυρὸν αὐτοῖς δοθῆ|ναι, 'I entreat you about my sons, not to allow that, out of their regard for Soterichos and his people, wheat be given them' (*ed.pr.*; cf. their note to *ll.*7-10). In another letter as well, *P.Flor.* 3 (1915) 338.10-12 (Arsinoite nome, III) only men are involved in the relationship implied by φιλοστοργία, and the sense is vaguer: καὶ νῦν τάχα ἡ σὴ | σπουδὴ καὶ φιλοστοργεία κατανεικήσῃ τὴν ἐμὴν [[. . .]] ἀκαιρείαν, 'and now quickly your good will and regard will overcome my tactlessness'. The first two nouns form a hendiadys; for σπουδή in the sense here cf. 2 Cor. 8.16; cf. MM., s.v., 3. (In passing, for ἀκαιρία cf. MM, s.v. ἀκαίρως: only the adverb appears in the NT, at 2 Tim. 4.2. This MM entry illustrates further the need to update their dictionary. Fasc. 1 of *VGT* appeared in 1914, thus too early to note this *P.Flor.* text. The 1930 one-volume complete dictionary included virtually no changes to the separate fascicles. Thus for words at the beginning of the alphabet MM was already 15 years out of date by the time the complete dictionary appeared. (Cf. C. J. Hemer, *NovT* 24 [1982]101.)

Some differences thus appear to be emerging between the usage of φιλοστοργ-words in Asia Minor and Egypt; indigenous cultural factors as well as the different types of document may largely account for this. Whereas in the former region women are with one exception involved in the relationship (that exception involves an infant), and always familial ties are in view, in Egypt the pattern of usage is not so tightly consistent and the meaning appears to be more generalized in some instances. A larger, socio-linguistic question emerges from this brief study, which can be no more than adumbrated here. Are there words (or images) employed by Paul which can be shown by external evidence to be used predominantly of either males or females? If so, does Paul consistently adhere to the usage found outside the NT and ECL, or does he deliberately create a new dimension for these words — as he does with his application of cultic terms to non-cultic contexts — and apply them to his addressees in such a way that it may be surmised that he is consciously ignoring, at the verbal level, sex-role distinctions? A sensitive philological investigation along these lines could prove illuminating for our understanding of Paul's own perception of differences in sex-roles in his own day.

We have here another example to illustrate the need to update MM. Their composite entry on φιλόστοργος and related words provides no documentary attestations for the adjective (although the *IG*, *IGRR*, and *OGIS* texts cited above were already available); it highlights how MM's focus was not primarily upon epigraphical evidence, but upon the papyri, from which no examples of the adjective have yet been found, to my knowledge.

The name Eustorgia occurs at *I.Tyre* 176; the woman was Christian.
I.Pamphyl.dial. 146 and 154 (both from Belkis-Camiliköy, near Aspendos, IIBC) are two epitaphs, the first for two brothers described as φιλάδελφοι, the second for two sisters, φιλάδελφαι. Brixhe points out (ad loc.) that although this adjective is very frequent in texts from Egypt, its rarity in Asia Minor makes a striking contrast (*MAMA* 8 [1962] 132.13 is mentioned by Brixhe as the only other example known). 1 Pet. 3.8 is the only NT occurrence, where it is used figuratively of fellow-believers, but we should note that this letter is directed to people in Asia Minor.

81.　χλευάζω

This verb appears in the NT only at Acts 17.32 (at 2.13 διαχλευάζω is to be read, not the simple verb), for which MM, s.v., offers two late papyrus attestations. *P.Cair.Masp.* 1 (1911, repr. 1973) 67092.9-10 (Aphrodite, 21/9/553) is a petition from a woman jilted by her prospective husband in which she says, 'And now I have been mocked by him', νῦν δὲ ἐχλευάσθην | παρ' αὐτοῦ. *PSI* 5 (1917) 481.9-10 (provenance unknown, V/VI) is a letter in which it is mentioned that 'the very magnificent Taurinos came here from the Lykoi(?) and made himself a mockery, bringing neither the cooking things nor, etc.', ἦλθεν ἐνταῦθα Ταυρῖνος ὁ μεγα-λοπρεπέστ(ατος) | ἐκ τῆς Λύκων χλευάσας ἑαυτὸν καὶ μηδὲ τὰ μαγιρικὰ ἐνέγκας μηδὲ | κτλ. However, the Jewish complaint to Trajan quoted in MM, s.v. Ἰουδαῖος is certainly earlier than the Byzantine examples, and should be requoted in a revised MM entry for the verb. BAGD, s.v., would then need to alter its comment 'late pap.'. To these scant attestations we may now add *P.Laur.* 43 (provenance unknown, V²), a fragmentary letter in which the writer says, 'And if you are not willing but mocked not me but yourselves, send...' εἰ δὲ | οὐ θέλεις ἀλλ' ἐχλευ|άσατε οὐκ ἐμὲ ἀλλ' ἑαυτοὺς | πέμψατε, κτλ (*ll.*9-12).

82.　A gymnasiarchal law from Beroia

In *Ancient Macedonia* II, 139-50 (3 pl.), J.M.R. Cormack has published the legible portion of this long inscription, 'probably the most important to come from Beroia' (139). Cormack printed the first 34 lines of side A of the stele — originally there were 106 — and side B (110 lines). *SEG* 261, following *BE* (1978) 274 (pp.431-35), includes some new readings and what can be made out of A.35-51. The subject matter of this text, which is not conclusively datable (167–148BC, Cormack; mid-IIBC, *SEG*), has no particular relevance for NT studies, but it does contain items of philological interest for that area of work. A number of these are listed fairly baldly below. Several words in this text should be added to MM entries in view of the date of the inscription, or because MM have only papyrological attestations; similarly, BAGD.

ἀρρωστέω (B. 17) — only at Mt. 14.14D; for other documentary examples see MM, s.v. ἄρρωστος; several instances of the verb and the noun in -ία are listed in the index to *SIG³*. The adjective is found at *P.Cair.Masp.* 2 (1913; repr. 1973) 151.185, 192; and (largely restored) at *P.Cair.Zen.* 1 (1925; repr. 1971) 59018.5 (= *SB* 3 [1926; repr. 1974] 6710) and *SIG³* 620.10 (Tenos, 188BC).

ἀτακτέω (B. 22, 99) — the usage in the inscription does not afford a parallel to 2 Thes. 3.7, for at both places in the former the idea is that of being disobedient: at *l.*22 the gymnasiarch is authorized τῶν | [π]αιδῶν τοὺς ἀτακτοῦντας μαστιγῶν καὶ τῶν παιδαγωγῶν if they are slaves or to fine them if they are of free status; at *l.*99 ἐὰν δὲ μὴ πειθαρχῇ ἢ ἀτακτῇ τι he is to be flogged by the gymnasiarch. The notion of unruliness applying here is relevant to the adjective ἄτακτος at 1 Thes. 5.14 (cf. C. Spicq, *Studia Theologica* 10 [1956] 1-13).

ἐμφανίζω + dat. (B. 18) — cf. Acts 23.15; 24.1; 25.2, 15 where the construction is expanded with a ὅπως clause or κατά/περί + gen.

εὐταξία (B. 47, 48 [probably an engraver's error for εὐεξίαν], 55) and φιλοπονία (B. 47, 56) — the gymnasiarch has to arrange competitions for good physical condition (εὐεξία), discipline (εὐταξία) and industriousness (φιλοπονία). The second of these terms is found in ECL at Ign. *Eph.* 6.2; the verb related to the third at *2 Cl.* 19.1.

ἱεροσυλία (B. 100) — the noun is not NT; for the adjective note Acts 19.37. The inscription reads ἐὰν δέ | [τ]ις κλέψῃ τι τῶν ἐκ τοῦ γυμνασίου, ἔνοχος ἔστω ἱεροσυλίαι: for this conjunction of the word with κλέπτω cf. Rom. 2.21-22, κλέπτεις ... ἱεροσυλεῖς (though the passages are not of course formally parallel).

κυριεύω + gen. (B. 87) — cf. Lk. 22.25; Rom. 6.14; 7.1; 2 Cor. 1.24.

μελετάω + infin. (B.10) — the NT uses this verb in the sense found here (μ. ἀκοντίζειν δὲ καὶ τοξεύειν) but the construction at 1 Tim. 4.15 is different. BAGD, s.v., differentiates the meaning at Acts 4.25 more appropriately than MM.

νοσφίζω (A. 31) — used absolutely (in the gymnasiarch's oath) as at Tit. 2.10; MM cite an exactly parallel phrase from another oath: *P.Petr.* 3 (1905) 56(b) *l*.10 (after 256BC).

ὀλιγωρέω + gen. (B. 19) — MM include only one epigraphical example, nearly 400 years later in time than the Beroian text. Neither the papyrus examples nor the epigraphical text cited by MM attest ὀ. + gen., the construction of the NT *hapax* at Heb. 12.5 (quoting Prov. 3.11), μὴ ὀλιγώρει παιδείας Κυρίου; the Beroian text reads, ἐὰν δέ τις δοκῆι ὀλιγωρεῖν τῶν παιδοτριβῶν, κτλ.

πειθαρχέω + dat. expressed or implied (A. 13; B. 7, 8-9, 99) — the construction is common enough (NT, at Acts 5.29; 27.21; Tit. 3.1); these examples predate by more than two centuries MM's attestations.

ὑπὸ τὴν ῥάβδον μαστιγούτω (B. 9; the verb again at B. 22, 70, 99) — for ῥάβδος as a rod for punishment see LSJ, s.v., 7; for the metaphorical use in the NT note 1 Cor. 4.21, ἐν ῥ. ἔρχεσθαι. Three of the occurrences of μαστιγόω in the text refer to beating for disobedience; at B. 70 μ. is a way of punishing those who cheat in athletic competition (for this usage see BAGD, s.v., 1 ad fin.).

As part of his oath the gymnasiarch undertakes to act impartially: οὔτε φίλωι χαριζόμενος οὔ|τε ἐχθρὸν βλάπτων παρὰ τὸ δίκαιον, κτλ (A. 29-30; cf. B. 50-51 where the judges for the εὐταξία competition [see above] are required to swear δικαίως κρίνειν ... οὔτε χάρι|[τ]ος ἕνεκεν οὔτε ἔχθρας οὐδεμίας). The clause should not be taken to imply a forswearing of the standard Greek notion of individual morality involving doing good to one's friends and harm to one's enemies. The latter works primarily on the personal level; here the men are acting in an official capacity.

Two other words from this text, βραβευτής (B. 84, 86) and πολιτάρχης (A. 42 [in *SEG*], B. 110) receive brief attention at **33** and **5** respectively. One and possibly two words are first attested in this inscription: λυμαγωνέω (B. 69) and ἐπεγδύομαι (B. 1; but the first letter is in doubt and ἀπεγδύομαι is possible).

83. Moral terms in the eulogistic traditon

The many inscriptions registering public tributes to the character of notable citizens (cf. **18** above) provide an indirect approach to the question of the socio-cultural position of the Pauline churches in the Greek cities of the Roman empire. The array of moral ideals involved has been drawn into a systematic order, along socio-linguistic lines, in the light of the *Moralia* of Plutarch, by C. Panagopoulos, *Dialogues d'histoire ancienne* 5 (1977) 197–235 (cf. *SEG* 1289). The system of public eulogies is the principal ideological regulator in Greek society under the Empire (p.233). It interprets and applies the social position which the notable citizens established through benefactions (p.198). But to what extent do its ideals correspond with those of the churches?

Of some 75 eulogistic terms examined by Panagopoulos, fewer than half are found in the NT, and then often as *hapax legomena*, and mostly in Acts, Hebrews or the Pastoral Epistles (notable Titus). Many more occur in the later ECL, and they are more frequent there. The Pauline *homologoumena*, by contrast, have relatively little in common with the eulogistic canon. A careful exploration of this gap could reveal whether we are witnessing a deliberate confrontation or simply a non-congruence of ideals.

Noticeably under-represented in the NT are the fields of compounds in εὐ- and φιλ-, which often give expression to the prevailing nexus between aesthetic and moral approval (e.g. εὐκοσμία, εὐνομία, εὐταξία, φιλοδοξία, φιλοκαλία). (For φιλ-compounds that do find a place see *New Docs 1976* **46, 47, 48**; and above, **79, 80**.) Whole categories of terms of merit as defined by Panagopoulos are missing from the NT, notably the language of courage (ἀνδρεία, ἀνδραγαθία, φιλοπονία) and of general excellence (ἐξαίρετος, διαφερόντως, ἀπρόσιτος). It is noteworthy that some of the α- privative terms in these fields do go over (ἄμεμπτος, ἀνέγκλητος, ἀνεπίλημπτος) as also do those from the field of benefaction itself (ἀφειδία, ἀφθονία). Many eulogistic terms are of course developed by Paul in distinctive ways (e.g., δικαιοσύνη, ζῆλος, πίστις, σοφία), so that their place in the competition for civic honour seems to be lost sight of. Some other interesting absentees from the NT are the two adjectives (derived from the virtues of domestic animals) ἥμερος and προσηνής, and the great classical ideal of ὁμόνοια (consensus), frequent otherwise in ECL; see further E.A. Judge, *Rank and Status in the World of the Caesars and St Paul* (Christchurch, N.Z., 1982) 22–23.

On the points of congruence see now F.W. Danker, *Benefactor: Epigraphic Study of a Graeco–Roman and New Testament Semantic Field* (St Louis, 1982), especially 317–392. There may well, however, be no respect in which the emphasis in the two literatures fully corresponds. On the many fundamental differences between Pauline thought and that of the Stoics see J.N. Sevenster, *Paul and Seneca* (Leiden, 1961). L. Moretti, *RFIC* 105 (1977) 5–11, observes the early use of the benefactor title for their own citizens by the cities of Asia Minor, and in *Athenaeum* 65 (1977) 82–87 traces the similarities between this ideology and that of the early Stoics (cf. *SEG* 1255).

(E.A. JUDGE)

84. Greek names of Latin origin

The fact that 30 of the 91 personal names in the Pauline connection are of Latin derivation poses tantalizing questions to those interested in the social pattern of the Pauline churches. It has usually been taken for granted that it arises from the free use of Latin names by Greeks, and does not therefore indicate Roman citizenship. But the proportion is ten times as high as for non-Romans with Latin names in the first-century texts collected in the series beginning with V. Ehrenberg/A.H.M. Jones, *Documents Illustrating the Reigns of Augustus and Tiberius* (Oxford, 1955²). Morever, the *cognomina* amongst the Pauline Latin names correspond quite closely with the names favoured by Greeks acquiring Roman citizenship through service in the auxiliary forces, or through emanicipation from slavery to a Roman. NT social history must therefore face the possibility that the churches drew heavily upon those classes of lower-level Greeks whom Roman patronage was systematically advancing to citizenship during an era when eminent members of the ruling classes in the Greek cities were still by no means regularly granted Roman citizenship. Did the NT people then enjoy civil rank but not social status? See E.A. Judge, *Rank and Status in the World of the Caesars and St Paul* (Christchurch, N.Z., 1982) 12–14.

The first Greek documentary collections I have noticed which show a proportion of Latin names corresponding with the Pauline one are the catalogues of manufacturers' signature on Corinthian lamps of II/III assembled by P. Bruneau, *BCH* 95 (1971) 437–501 and 101 (1977) 249–295 (cf. *SEG* 35), and the Roman imperial lamp signatures registered in the report of the Chicago excavations of the sanctuary of Poseidon at Isthmia, O. Broneer, *Isthmia III : Terracotta Lamps* (Princeton, 1977) (cf. *SEG* 36). A total of 48 names occurs (counting twice names that are in both lists, though G. Joyner tells me that if it is the distinctive clay which determines 'Corinthian' attribution of a lamp it is likely to be artificial to separate Coirinth from Isthmia), of which as many as 18 may be of Latin derivation. The ratio *praenomina : nomina : cognomina* gives an even closer parallel with the Pauline connection — Corinth has 4:3:11 compared with the Pauline 7:5:18. Seven Latin names are common to the lamps and to Paul (Lucius, Marcus and Quintus amongst the *praenomina*; Crescens, Rufus, Secundus and Tertius amongst the *cognomina*), but only one Greek name (Carpus). One ought of course to expect Latin names in a Roman colony: in the case of the Pauline connection, Corinth supplies a ratio of Latin to Greek names of 10:7, compared with 6:5 for the list in Romans 16, and 0:19 for the eastern Aegean seaboard (Troas, Ephesus, Colossae, Laodicea, Crete).

Do the Latin names in Paul then signify Roman citizenship? In the case of *praenomina*, probably not: the handful of 'first names' still in use in Latin were quickly taken over as Greek names at an early stage of Roman contact. But the much more distinctive and legally essential *nomina* (family names) should be assumed to signify citizenship, especially in the case of women (who normally had no other name). *Cognomina* (the now normal 'additional names') ought also to be considered as possibly signifying citizenship, though we know some (notably Rufus) which established themselves too soon in Greek for this to be likely. Only those formal documents that record full names can ordinarily distinguish Greeks with Roman citizenship from those without, and even there one must allow for the possibility of someone explicitly registered as a Roman nevertheless using the Greek form of name (personal name followed by father's name in the genitive), as in *IG* II² (1931) 1961, *l.*71 (40 BC); this Greek pattern may itself of course involve Latin names, as in *l.*69.

G. Daux, 'L'onomastique romaine d'expression grecque' (*Onomast. lat.* 405–417), deals with the problems of nomenclature arising for Greeks who acquired Roman citizenship, and notes (410) amongst a series of issues the need to determine when the practice arose of members of Greek states assuming Roman names without citizenship. The same CNRS colloquium also heard reports on two projects which may ultimately provide the material for answering our Pauline question: an Onomasticon of the Roman Empire, for which A. Mócsy reported progress especially for the Danube provinces (*Onomast. lat.* 459–463); and a 'Lexicon of Greek Personal Names' down to mid–VII reported on by J.K. Davies (465–473), for which the first regional volume (the Aegean islands and Cyrenaica) has been subsequently projected for completion in 1983, for publication by Oxford.

Onomast. lat. includes a section on onomastics of the Christian period, which brings out the limited impact of Christianity on nomenclature. Contributors are I. Kajanto, 'The emergence of the single name system' (419–430); H.-I. Marrou, 'Problèmes généraux de l'onomastique chrétienne' (431–435); Ch. Pietri, 'Remarques sur l'onomastique chrétienne de Rome' (437–445); N. Duval, 'Observations sur l'onomastique dans les inscriptions chrétiennes d'Afrique du Nord' (447–456).

(E.A. JUDGE)

85. Asynkritos

S. Mitchell, *AS* 27 (1977) 77-79, no.9 (pl.14) = *SEG* 841, is an honorific inscription of Roman Imperial date from Ankara set up for a man by his tribe. The man had held various posts, including that of phylarch ἀσυνκρίτως | [κ]αὶ μεγαλοπρεπῶς, 'incomparably and magnificently'. Neither of these adverbs occurs in the NT although an example of the related noun and adjective respectively is found.

In the NT Ἀσύγκριτος appears only as a personal name, at Rom. 16.14, although Ignatius and Hermas employ it as an adjective. Given its meaning, one might expect that as a name the word was largely reserved for those of servile status (cf. Chrestos). Apart from the NT occurrence H. Solin, *Die griechischen Personennamen in Rom. Ein Namenbuch* (Berlin, 1982) III, 1274 notes two further examples from Rome, dated I² and 250-350 respectively. L. Vidman, *CIL* VI.6 *Indices* fasc.2 (1980), s.v., includes six other incomplete names under this lemma as possible candidates for the name Asynkritos. Lest we think of it as a servile name *tout court*, *P.Oxy.* 12 (1916) 1413.21-22 includes mention of Ἀριστίων ὁ καὶ Ἀνδ[ρό-νει]κος Ἀσ[υ]γκρί|[του] in a report of proceedings to the Senate (270-75): Aristion is appointed to provide oil for gymnasial purposes on a certain day of the month. He — and almost certainly his father, therefore — cannot have been of servile status, but belonged to a background of some wealth and prominence in the IIIAD Oxyrhynchus community. Similarly, *P.Lips.* 1 (1906) 98 col.1, *l*.2 (provenance unknown, IV) mentions [Σ]ερῆνος Ἀσυγκρίτου in a list of allotments of tax-collectors (ἐξάκτορες). Serenos' very presence in this list indicates that he is not a slave, and the inference is not improbable that his father is to be similarly viewed. BAGD, s.v., mentions several of these documentary examples. The similar name Ἀσυγκρίτιος is probably not to be taken as a variant of it: its slightly more frequent occurrence is attested in *NB* and Foraboschi for the papyri, and the Vidman and Jory/Moore indexes to *CIL* VI (parts 6 and 7 respectively). Given the paucity of documentation of this name the question must remain open whether Asynkritos was first employed in the Roman period as a (rare) servile name which by III/IV had passed across to use — fairly uncommon still — by those of higher status.

Turning to the other adverb in the Ankara inscription the adjective μεγαλοπρεπής occurs only once in the NT, at 2 Pet. 1.17, φωνῆς ἐνεχθείσης αὐτῷ τοιᾶσδε ὑπὸ τῆς μεγαλοπρεποῦς δόξης, 'when a voice of such a kind was conveyed to him (i.e., Jesus) by the majestic glory'. The last phrase in this clause is a rare periphrasis for God, and is certainly Semitic in tone. *1 Clement* employs the same phrase at 9.2, and uses the adjective on several other occasions (see BAGD, s.v.). In the papyri the adjective — not infrequently superlative — and its related noun (-πεια) and adverb is largely an honorific title: see *WB* III.2 (1929) p.197, and *WB* Suppl. 1 (1940-66), 3 Lief. (1971) p.386, where most of the examples listed are V-VII. *Spoglio*, s.v., does not differentiate the honorific from the less common 'ordinary' use. For an adverbial example of the latter note *OGIS* 56.53, a priest's decree from Kanopos (IIIBC; three copies of this trilingual text have been found — see Dittenberger's notes), reprinted as *SB* V.3 (1950) 8858. At *P.Tebt.* 1 (1902) 33.6 (112BC) a visitor is to be received μεγαλο{υ}πρεπέστερον, 'with special magnificence'. *MPR* 72 is an epitaph (Axiopolis, V-VI) for the daughter of Gibastes τοῦ μεγα[λ]ο-πρ(επεστάτου) κόμ(ητος), 'the most magnificent count.'

86. Tychikos

The great majority of the epigraphical attestations of this not very common name — *pace* G. Daux, *BCH* 78 (1954) 393 — come from Rome; as Vidman's *Index Cognominum* to *CIL* VI (vi.2) makes clear about ¼ of these identify a servile origin. *F.Delphes* III.4.471 is a dedication from Delphi (I or II) set up by a slave: Τυχικὸς Τ. | [Φ]λ. Μεγαλι|[ν]οῦ δοῦλος | (*crescent moon*) | [Δι]ὶ Υψίστ[ῳ]. A possible alternative restoration in the last line could be [θεῷ]ι. Pouilloux notes (p.151) that *Zeus/Theos Hypsistos* normally refers to the God of the Jews, but this is not necessarily the case: see *New Docs 1976*, **5**. The crescent moon suggests that the god Men is here being invoked, in which case Tychikos may be a slave from the East living at Delphi with his master (Pouilloux, ibid.).

C. BIBLICAL AND RELATED CITATIONS

87. Some recently published fragments of the Greek Old Testament

Over the last two decades K. Treu has identified and/or published the *ed.pr.* of over two dozen papyrus and parchment fragments of the LXX, a little over half belonging to the Berlin collection. Brief reference was made to some of the publications in *MPL* 2 (1977) 251, and this provides the *prophasis* for drawing these texts to the attention of readers who are not primarily papyrologists, textual critics, or Septuagintalists. Not all the texts warrant reprinting, but some descriptive comment is offered on each. Accents and breathings have been added where *ed.pr.* was a diplomatic text. A small number of apparent typographical errors in the original publications have been silently corrected here. The order in which the texts are listed below follows that of the LXX. The following articles by Treu are referred to in the catalogue, for those who wish to pursue further details or check texts not printed below.

(a) 'Das Berliner Genesis-Fragment P.17035', *Actes Xe Congrès international de Papyrologues, Varsovie-Cracovie 3-9 Sept. 1961* (Warsaw, 1964), 209-13;
(b) 'Majuskelbruchstücke der Septuaginta aus Damaskus', *Akad. der Wiss. in Göttingen, 1 : phil.-hist. Kl., Nachrichten* 6 (1966) 203-21;
(c) 'Neue Berliner Septuagintafragmente', *APF* 20 (1970) 43-65 (pl.1-7);
(d) 'Zwei weitere Berliner Septuagintafragmente', *Akten des XIII. Internationalen Papyrologenkongresses Marburg/Lahn 1971* (Munich, 1974), 421-26;
(e) 'Vier Wiener Septuagintafragmente', *JÖB* 23 (1974) 1-9;
(f) 'Varia Christiana', *APF* 24/25 (1976) 113-27 at 117-20 (nos. 2 and 3; pls. 13, 15).

Where the references to van Haelst, Aland, *Repertorium*, and Turner, *Typology*, are lacking it is to be understood that the text was published too late for inclusion in those works (Aland records papyri only, not parchment texts).

1. Gen. 10.12-13 (Treu (b), 205): Qubbat al-ḥazna, Damascus, IX; parchment section of one leaf from a codex. The *recto* alone is known from a photograph, but the *verso* ended at Gen. 10.20 (B. Violet identified the text at the turn of the century but never published it). Some ten lines are extant, with 8-10 letters per line. Treu calculates that the codex had two columns of 18-20 lines each per page, the original dimensions of which were c.24B x 32Hcm. (the surviving piece is 12 x 16). No special readings in the fragment.
   Van Haelst, 9; Turner, OT5A.
2. Gen. 19.11-13, 17-19 (Treu (c), 46-47, pl. 1a, b): provenance unknown, III (init.?); fragment (3.7B x 6.2Hcm.) from the middle of a leaf of a papyrus codex, originally c.27-28 lines in one column per page.

verso . . . .

[μικρο]ῦ ἕως [μεγάλου καὶ παρελύ-]   19.11

[θησαν] ζητοῦν[τες τὴν θύραν, εἶπαν]   12

[δὲ οἱ] ἄνδρες π[ρὸς Λωτ ἔστιν τίς]

[σοι ὧδ]ε γαμβρο[ὶ ἢ υἱοὶ ἢ θυγατέ-]

5 [ρες; ἢ ε]ἴ τίς σοι ἄλ.[λος ἔστιν ἐν τῇ πό-]

[λει, ἐξά]γαγε ἐκ [τοῦ τόπου τούτου· ὅτι]   13

[ἀπόλ]λυμεν ἡ[μεῖς τὸν τόπον τοῦ-]

[τον, ὅ]τι ὑψ[ώθη   ]

. . . .

recto . . . .

            ] καὶ εἶ[παν]   17

10 [σῶζε τὴν σεαυτοῦ ψυχή]ν· μὴ π[ερι-]

[βλέψῃς εἰς τὰ ὀπίσω] μηδὲ στῇ[ς ἐν]

[πάσῃ τῇ περιχώρῳ· ε]ἰς τὸ ὄρος σ[ώζου,]

[μήποτε συμπαραλη]φθῇς· ε[ἶπεν]   18

[δὲ Λωτ πρὸς αὐτούς Δέ]ομαι, ἐ[πειδὴ]   19

15 [εὗρεν ὁ παῖς σου ἔλεος ἐ]ναντίο[ν σου]

[καὶ ἐμεγάλυνας τὴν δικαι]οσύν[ην σου,]

[ὃ ποιεῖς ἐπ' ἐμέ, τοῦ ζῆν] τὴ[ν ψυχήν]

. . . .

Two variants in the *recto* may be mentioned. At *l*.10 σῶζε needs to be restored for reasons of space in the line, not σῶζων. This accords with Origen's text. Of rather more interest is *l*.14 where a space has been deliberately left after δέομαι: κύριε has been omitted. Is this due to pious 'embarrassment' of the scribe (analogous to pronouncing יהוה as *adonai*), or was he working from a copy which at this point had the Hebrew Tetragrammaton (Treu, 47)? If the latter did he omit it because he did not understand it, or leave a space for the Hebrew to be inserted later? *P.Oxy.* 4 (1904) 656 (late II/III), which preserves parts of four leaves from a papyrus codex of LXX Gen. (= van Haelst 13), provides a useful comparison. In four places (*ll*.17, 122, 155, 166) the word κύριος referring to God was omitted, and at all these points except *l*.122 a second hand wrote it in unabbreviated (pl.2, which includes *l*.166, shows this very clearly). According to C.H. Roberts, *Manuscript, Society and Belief in Early Christian Egypt* (London, 1979) 76-77, this codex is probably Jewish, for whereas in a Christian text the abbreviated κ̅ς̅ would normally occur, here the space was left blank 'as though in expectation of a second hand inserting the Hebrew Tetragrammaton.' Occasionally the Greek letters ΠΙΠΙ were used to copy the form of the Hebrew letters (see B.M. Metzger, *Manuscripts of the Greek Bible* [New York, 1981] 35). On *nomina sacra* in pre-Christian LXX papyri, and LXX papyri of II/III, see respectively F. Bedodi, *Stud.Pap.* 13(1974) 89-103, and S. Jankowski, *Stud.Pap.* 16(1977) 81-116.

P.Berl. 17213; van Haelst, 15; Aland AT10; Turner, OT11A.

3. Gen. 36.14-15, 23-24 (Treu (a), 209-13): provenance unknown, c. 500; section (4.6B x 3.5H cm.) from the middle of a leaf of a parchment codex, containing originally 35-40 lines. To highlight its divergences from the LXX the latter is printed beside the fragment.

recto   o]υτο[ι   .... οὗτοι δὲ υἱοὶ Ἐ-   14

]μα θυγατρο[ς   λιβέμας θυγατρὸς Ἀνὰ τοῦ υἱοῦ Σεβεγών,

γυν]εκος Ησαυ· κα[ι   γυναικὸς Ἡσαύ· ἔτεκεν δὲ τῷ

Ησα]υ τον Ισους κα[ι   Ἡσαὺ τὸν Ἰεὺς καὶ τὸν Ἰεγλὸμ

5   τ]ον Κορα· και ο[καὶ τὸν Κόρε. οὗτοι οἱ ἡγεμό-   15

]οι των υιων Η[σαυ   νες υἱοῦ Ἡσαύ. υἱοὶ Ἐλι-

]πρωτοτοκο[φὰς πρωτοτόκου Ἡσαύ...

verso   ]κα[ι   .... καὶ Μαννάχαθ

]βαλ· και Σ[καὶ Γαιβήλ, Σὼφ καὶ

]· και ουτοι υι[οι   Ὠμάν. καὶ οὗτοι υἱοὶ Σε-   24

]ι· και Ανα· ουτ[ος   βεγών· Αἰὲ καὶ Ὠνάν· οὗτός ἐστιν

5   ]ευρεν τους η[ὁ Ὠνᾶς ὃς εὗρεν τὸν Ἰαμεὶν

ερ]ημω· οτε εν[εμεν   ἐν τῇ ἐρήμῳ, ὅτε ἔνεμεν τὰ

]ς Σεβωων το[υ   ὑποζύγια Σεβεγών τοῦ πατρὸς

In these 14 part-lines there are as many as 16 readings which differ from the LXX. Seven of these occur in other texts, while nine are not elsewhere attested (five of these being proper names). The fragment displays points of contact with other Greek translations of the Hebrew OT, those of Aquila, Symmachos and 'Theodotion'. On these three, and particularly the problems associated with the latter, see S. Jellicoe, *The Septuagint and Modern Study* (Oxford, 1968) 76-99; and especially D. Barthélemy, *Les devanciers d'Aquila* (*VT Suppl.* X; Leiden, 1963). All three were made in II — 'Theodotion' in earlier form may go back to I — and were included by Origen the following century in his Hexapla. Jerome comments on the textual problem in Gen. 36.24 (*verso ll.*4-7), and discusses the versions of the LXX and the other three: σὺν τοὺς ἡμίν (Aquila), τοὺς ἡμίν (Symmachos), τὸν ἰαμίν (LXX, 'Theodotion'): *liber Hebraicarum quaestionum in Genesin* (Migne, *PL* 23.993f.). Our fragment thus adheres at this point to Symmachos, and reflects an attempt to convey more accurately the Heb. *iamin*. In these same lines of the fragment note also *l.*4 Ανα, which accords with Heb. *ānāh* (Αἰνάς, Aquila; Αἰνάν, 'Theodotion'; Symmachos not attested; Ὠνάν, LXX). Treu says (211) that the first letter of *l.*7 is definitely not α and therefore the word of which ς is the probable last letter is ὄνους (so Aquila), not ὑποζύγια (LXX) or βουκόλια ('Theodotion'). The word following that is not paralleled in the other versions in the form found here, nor can it have been occasioned by the Hebrew: LXX/Aquila/ 'Theodotion' all have Σεβεγών, Heb. *zibᵉʿon*. At *verso l.*2 καί is attested elsewhere by a few MSS; so too the καί before οὗτοι at *recto l.*5 with a few versions against LXX/Heb. At *recto l.*2 there is not enough room for Ἀνὰ τοῦ υἱοῦ Σεβεγών after θυγατρὸ[ς, even if the definite article were omitted and υἱοῦ abbreviated. For other variants and idiosyncrasies in this parchment see Treu's detailed apparatus (212-13).

What may be concluded about the character of the text is not altogether certain. Nine divergences from the LXX appear to reflect an attempt to render

the Hebrew more accurately (*recto ll*.1, 2, 3, 5, 6; *verso ll*.2, 4, 5, 7). On the other hand four readings are not supported by the Hebrew (*recto ll*.4, 5; *verso ll*.2, 7): see Treu, 212. Treu suggests that the fragment may cohere more with the textual tradition associated with Symmachos, than with any other.
P. Berl. 17035; van Haelst, 22; Turner, OT15A.

4. Ex. 5.14-17; 6.22-25; 7.15-17 (Treu (c), 47-50, pl.3): provenance unknown, IV; a single leaf (*P. Berl.* 11766) and a still-connected double leaf (*P. Berl.* 14046) from a small parchment codex. One column of twelve lines to the page whose dimensions are 7.8B x 9H cm. The three leaves are almost intact; but eight leaves are missing between leaves 1 and 2, and a further six between 2 and 3. Treu calculates that at most this codex could have contained the whole of Exodus: 400 pages of this size would have been needed. The text is good, avoiding special readings found in B : leaf 2 *recto l*.33 (Ex. 6.23) τόν omitted before Ἐλεαζαρ; leaf 3 *recto l*.50 στήσῃ against ἔσῃ (B).
Van Haelst, 32; Turner, OT23A. See below, no.5.

5. Ex. 34.18-20 (Treu (c), 51-52, pl. 4a): provenance unknown, IV; ten of an original twelve lines in one column per side of a leaf from a small parchment codex (7.4B x 7.4 surviving height). Noted briefly by O. Stegmüller, *Berliner Septuagintafragmente* (*Berliner Klassikertexte*, 8; Berlin, 1939) no.24, where the date suggested was V/VI; but Treu thinks (51, n.1) IV is more appropriate, and draws attention to the similarities with no.4 above (page size, hand, substance). He is not sure, however, that it can be demonstrated that nos.4 and 5 are from the same codex. The present fragment accords more with B against AFM *et al.*, although note *verso l*.14 (Ex. 34.19) where it goes against B in omitting πᾶν before πρωτότοκον, and has μόσχο(ν) instead of the usual μόσχου in the same line. The link with B on the whole does not appear consistent with the pattern of readings in no.4 above, but is probably not sufficient a factor — given the amount of text surviving — to allow a firm answer on whether the two pieces are from a common codex.
P. Berl. 16990; van Haelst, 41; Turner, OT29A (who treats it as a separate codex from no.4 above).

6. Ex. 34.35–35.8 (Treu (c); 52-53): provenance unknown, III/IV; four fragments of a leaf from a parchment codex, with 20 lines in one column on either side (extant dimensions, 5B x 11H cm.). On the whole the text follows the majority of witnesses, avoiding unusual readings. But note *recto l*.14 (Ex. 35.2) where σάββατα ἀνάπ]αυσις κ͞ω conforms with B (σάββατον, ἀναπαύσεις τῷ κ͞ῳ, A *et al.*).
P. Berl. 14039; van Haelst, 42; Turner, OT29B.

7. I Kings 18.26-33; 18.41–19.2; 20.11-14, 22-26; 22.6-10 (Treu (b), 205–10): Qubbat al-ḥazna, Damascus, V/VI; portions of three leaves from a parchment codex, palimpsest (Arabic text written crosswise over the Greek). One column survives (via a copy) of an original two, containing 34 lines. Original page size 22-25B x 30H cm. Text identified by B. Violet (see no.1 above); now lost. On the whole the text coheres with B against A, but avoids peculiarities of both (see Treu, 20b, for details).
Van Haelst, 73; Turner, OT49A.

8. Esther 8.10–12a, 12b-d (Treu (b), 210-11): Qubbat al-ḥazna, Damascus, V/VI; one leaf from a parchment palimpsest codex, Arabic written crosswise over the Greek. Originally 24 lines in a single column; surviving dimensions 13.5B x 14.5H cm. Now lost. The text is good, although note *verso l*.18 (Est. 8.12c), κάρπον for κόρον. This is the first passage to be found from this OT book in a codex.
   Van Haelst, 78; Turner, OT51B.

9. Judith 2.19 (Treu (b), 211): Qubbat al-ḥazna, Damascus, V; a leaf from a parchment palimpsest codex (Arabic above the Greek). The text (now lost) of only one side still available from a copy (see no.1); but the fragment appears to be from a codex, and is so treated by Turner. This is one of only two occurrences of this OT book in a codex.
   Van Haelst, 79; Turner, OT51C.

10. Ps. 31.9b–10b (Treu (e), 3-4): provenance unknown, VI/possibly VII; fragment (5.6B x 7.4H cm.) from a papyrus codex. Only a few letters are still visible on the *recto*, and it is uncertain whether it preceded or followed the *verso* (of which parts of seven lines remain). The latter contains Ps. 31.9b-10b, and Treu calculates that if the *recto* preceded it Ps. 31.2b would fall at *ll*.10f.; if it followed the *verso*, Ps. 32.6b would occur there (*l*.10 has only]ομα at the end of the line, and each of these two verses contains a form of στόμα). No particularly noteworthy variants.
    P. Vindob. G. 29491.

11. Ps. 36.4-8, 18-23 (Treu (d), 422-25): Hermopolis Magna (Fayum), IV. This small piece (4B x 7H cm.) with portions of twelve lines *recto* and *verso* is interesting beyond its size because it is part of a papyrus codex leaf published 40 years ago by Stegmüller (above, no.5), no.8, pp.20-25. That sheet contained Ps. 35.12–36.10, 14–25 (*P. Berl.* 6747 = 2046 Rahlfs). From an original 33-34 lines 25 survived and Stegmüller calculated that the page size had been 22B x 24H cm. (but Turner, *Typology*, 172 n.230, says this size is unparalleled). The new fragment (*P. Berl.* 6785) fits with Stegmüller's *recto ll*.12-22, *verso ll*.10-21. Printed below is the new fragment in italics, the lines being filled out by Stegmüller's text.

recto
    12 καὶ π[οι]μανθήσῃ ἐν τῷ πλούτῳ αὐτῆς· (4a)κ[α]*τατρύφησον*
                τοῦ κ̄ῡ, (4b)καὶ δώσι σοι τὰ ἐτήματ|*ά σου*
            τὰ αἰτήματα τῆς καρδίας σου. (5a)*ἀποκάλυψον* | *πρὸς κ̄ν̄ τὴν*
    15   ὁδόν σου |
            (5b)καὶ [ἔ]λπισον ἐπ' αὐτὸν καὶ αὐτὸς ποιήσ[ει] (6a)κ|*αἰ ἐξοίσι ὡς*
                φῶς τὴν δικαιοσύνην [σου] |
            (6b)[καὶ τὸ κρίμα σου] ὡ[σ]εὶ μεσημβρίαν. (7a)ὑπο|*τά[γη]θι τῷ κ̄[ῳ̄]*
                [καὶ] *ἱκέτευσον αὐτόν·* |
    20 (7b)[μὴ] *παραζήλο[υ]* ἐν τῷ κατευοδωμέν[ῳ] *ἐν τῇ ὁδῷ*
    20a | *αὐτοῦ,*
            [ἐν ἀ]νθρ[ώ]πῳ ποιοῦντι ἀνομίας. (8a)[π]*αῦσαι ἀπὸ*
                ὀργῆς καὶ ἐν[κατ]άλι[π]ε *θυμό(ν),*

verso

10 (18b)καὶ ἡ κλ[ηρον]ομία αὐ[το]ῦ εἰς τὸν αἰῶνα ἔ[στα]ι· (19a)[οὐ καταισ-]
| χυνθήσοντε κερῷ πονηρῷ
(19b)καὶ ἐν λιμ|ῷ χορτασθήσοντε. (20a)ὅτι οἱ ἁμαρτω[λοὶ]
| ἀπολλοῦνται,
(20b)οἱ δὲ ἐχθρ[οὶ] κ̅υ̅ ἅμα τῷ δοξασθῆναι καὶ ὑψωθῆνε
15 (20c)ἐκλιπόν[τες] ὡσεὶ καπνὸς ἐξέλειπαν.
(21a)δανείζετα[ι] ὁ ἁμαρτωλὸς καὶ οὐκ ἀποτείσι, (21b)ὁ δὲ
| δίκαιος οἰκτείρι καὶ διδοῖ·
(22a)ὅτι οἱ εὐλ[ο]γ[οῦν]τες αὐτὸν κληρο[ν]ομήσουσιν [γῆν,]
(22b)οἱ δὲ κατα[ρώ]μενοι αὐτὸν ἐξολ[ο]θρευθήσον[ται.]
20   (23a)π[αρ]ὰ κ̅[υ̅]

[τ]ὰ δια[βήματα] α̅ν̅ο̅υ̅ κατευθύνεται,

It is common for copies of OT poetical books to contain two margins, the second for the latter half of the verse. Here, however, there are three margins, for the longest lines extend a considerable way back into the left margin. Furthermore, at *recto l.*20a and *verso l.*20 the end of the previous line has turned over to conclude on a line of its own. It is usual, too, for the first half-verse to begin on the left margin. But this codex leaf is quite idiosyncratic in that this practice is observed only at *verso ll.*16, 18 (vv. 21a, 22a). In fact, the second half of the verse commonly starts at the left margin, the verse beginnings occurring at various places inside the line, thus failing to attract the prominence which might be expected. Treu draws the inference that the writer of this text divided the verselets differently: note particularly *recto ll.*12-14 (Ps. 36.4), and *verso ll.*12-15 (Ps. 36.20). So dissimilar does the hand appear to be between *recto* and *verso* that one might consider that different scribes had been at work, were it not for the striking verse division format (Treu, 423). The unusual arrangement of the text may be a clue that this codex was used in a liturgical context (ibid., 421).

The eccentric arrangement of the text on this leaf discourages one from giving much weight to the textual variants it contains, especially at *verso l.*12 (Ps. 36.19b) where καὶ ἐν λιμῷ occurs for καὶ ἐν ἡμέραις λίμου. At *recto ll.*13-14 (Ps.36.4b) τὰ ἐτήματα ... τὰ αἰτήματα may not be dittography (note the different spelling): although it would be ungrammatical, v.5 may have been thought by the scribe to start at the beginning of *l.*14. Treu comments on several other textual points.
Van Haelst, 142(2); Aland, AT63; Turner, OT90 (listing the Stegmüller text, but not mentioning the new fragment).

12. Ps. 39.3-6 (Treu (c), 53-54, pl.5): provenance unknown, Byzantine date; a single leaf of papyrus, not from a codex since the *verso* is blank. Full height survives, but not full breadth (7.2B x 8.8Hcm.): eleven lines of text spaced unevenly down the page. The sole indentation occurs at *l.*5 for the half-verse 4b. Division markers indicate the beginnings of vv. 5, 6 (*ll.*7, 10).

κα]ὶ ἀνέγαγέν με ἐκ κ λάκκ[ου ταλαιπωρίας]   39.3

καὶ] ἀπὸ πηλοῦ ἠλύος κ[αὶ---

κα]ὶ κατηύθυνεν τὰ [διαβήματά μου]

κα]ὶ ἐνέβαλεν ἰς τὸ σ[τόμα μου ᾆσμα καινόν,]   4

5   ]   ὕμνον τῷ θῷ [ἡμῶν·

ὅ]ψοντε πολλοὶ καὶ φο[βηθήσονται καὶ]

ἐ]λπ[ιοῦ]σιν ἐπὶ κ̅ν̅#μακ[άριος ἀνήρ, οὗ ἐστιν]   5

τ]ὸ ὄνομα κ̅ς̅ ἐλπίως αὐ[τοῦ καὶ οὐκ ἐνέ-]

βλεψεν εἰς ματεότη[τας καὶ μανίας]

10   ψε]υδος#πολλὰ ἐποίησ[ας---   6

].. καὶ τοῖς διαλογισμ[οῖς

The very defective orthography, the failure to observe with any consistency the verselet divisions on new lines, and the fact that the text is written on one side only, creates a presumption that the text may have served as an amulet; no folding on this papyrus can be detected, however. Private edification rather than use in a liturgical context was its probable function (Treu, 54). Extracts from Psalms were very popular on amulets: nearly ¼ (43 out of 158) Psalms passages inventoried by van Haelst are amulets; and this constitutes slightly more than ⅓ (43 out of 118) of all the amulets he lists. As to the spelling in this text, at *l.*2 read ἰλύος, *l.*8 κ̅ς̅ for κ̅υ̅, *l.*10 read ψευδεῖς. If *l.*21 contained all the LXX text between ἰλύος and καὶ κατηύθυνεν, viz., κ[αὶ ἔστησεν ἐπὶ πέτραν τοὺς πόδας μου, the lines must have varied considerably in length (contrast *ll.*8-9 where ἐνέ|βλεψεν is split between the lines).

On the difficulties in determining from a fragment with one side blank whether it is part of a codex see Turner, 9-10.

P. Berl. 17098; van Haelst, 144; Aland, Var. 9.

13. Ps. 51.4-7; 52.2-5 (Treu (c), 55-56, pl.6); provenance unknown, VI/VII; lower third of a parchment codex leaf, 5.9B x 8.9H cm. The fragment was referred to briefly by Stegmüller (above, no.5), no.25; but Treu thinks (55, n.1) the date may be somewhat earlier than the VI/VII proposed there. Ten of c. 32 lines per side are extant. Treu holds that the text shows more affinities with the 'lower Egypt' group of readings (B, S, etc.) than with those from Upper Egypt (group U). There are both links with and divergences from the fourth-century minuscule 2013 (*P.Lips.* 1 [1906] 32). Treu's apparatus is excerpted here: *recto l.*2 (Ps.51.4) ἐξηκ[ονήμενον with B, S against ἠκονήμενον 2013 *et al.*; *verso ll.*11, 16 (Ps. 52.2, 4) ἀγαθ]όν against χρηστότητα 2013; *verso l.*15 (Ps. 52.4) ἐπὶ] τὸ αὐτό with S, 2013, ἅμα other texts: *l.*15 ἐταρά[χ]θ[ησαν] 2013, ἠχρεώθησαν other texts; *l.*19 (Ps. 52.5) βρώσει B, S *et al.*, ἐν βρώσει 2013 *et al.*

P. Berl. 16703; van Haelst, 156; Turner, OT102A.

14. Ps. 77.48-52, 60(?)-66 (Treu (e), 4-6): provenance unknown, end IV; a small fragment (2.7B x 4.5H cm.) from a parchment codex leaf containing parts of 11 and 12 lines respectively on each side. Originally the codex had room for c. 28-30 lines. The length of text per line varies considerably, following sense phrases. At hair-side *l.*22 (Ps. 77.66a) αὐτοῦ accords with S *et al.* against B *et al.* (αὐτῶν). It is not clear whether *l.*13] ν εισ [is part of v.61b (καὶ τὴν

καλλόνην αὐτ]ῶν εἰς χ[εῖρας ἐχθροῦ]), in which case *l*.12 (neither of whose two surviving letters is certain) is v.61a. Alternatively *l*.13 is in fact part of v.61a καὶ παρέδωκεν εἰς αἰχμαλωσίαν τ]ὴν εἰσχ[ὺν αὐτῶν] (εἰσχύν : itacism for ἰσχύν), in which case *l*.12 would be part of v.60b, and v.61b has been omitted by the writer between *ll*.13-14.
P. *Vindob. G*. 35781.

15. Five citations from Ps. 117 and 122 (Treu (f), 117-19; cf. *MPL* 2 [1977] 253): provenance unknown, V/VI; single leaf of papyrus (37.2B x 13.5H cm.) complete on three sides (loss to upper edge). Note the defective orthography, e.g., *l*.3 κάρ = γάρ; γαθός = καθώς; *l*.4 μελλοτῶς = μελῳδός; read o for ω and vice versa, ι for ει.

]μων ἐν εὐφροσύνῃ ἐκάλεις τα... [

δοξάσοντες αὐτὸν τὸν δεσπότην Χριστ[ὸ]ν ὅτι ἐφάνησαν ο θεαριν[
οὐ κὰρ ἀπόσετε ὁ θεὸς πάντωτε· τοὺς εἰς αὐτὸν ἐλπείσοντε[ ] γαθὸς καὶ εἶπεν
ὁ μελλοτῶς [Δ]αυίδ᾽, ὅτι ἐν θλίψει ἐπεκαλεσάμην τῶν κ[ύρι]ων καὶ   117.5
                                                    ἐποίκουσέν μ[ου
5 εἰς πλατισμὸν [κα]ὶ ὅτι κύριος ἐμοὶ βοηθὸς καὶ οὐ φοβη[θήσομαι τί   6
                                                    πο]ιήσει μοι
   ἄνθρωπος κ(αὶ) ὅτι ἀγαθὸν ἐλπίσιν ἐπεὶ κύριων ἢ ἐλπείσιν ἐπ᾽ [ἄ]ρχοντα   9
                                                    καὶ πάλιν
   ἐν ἑτέρῳ λέγει κύριος ποιμένειν με καὶ οὐτέ με ἰστερέσει καὶ ὅτι   22.1,3
                                                    ὁτήγησέν [με
   ἐπ[ὶ] τρίβ[ο]υς δικαιοσύνης ἕνεκεν τοῦ ὀνόμα[τος] αὐ[τοῦ]

You called in joy ... intending to glorify Christ himself as Master because they seemed ... For God will not reject at any time those who hope in him. For just as the lyric poet David also said, 'In distress I called upon the Lord
5 **and he heard me | for my enlargement' (*cf. RSV*, 'and set me free'), and 'The Lord is my helper, and I shall not fear what man will do to me', and 'It is better (*lit*. good) to hope in the Lord than to hope in a ruler'; and again he says in another place, 'The Lord shepherds me and will not fail me'; and, 'He guided me upon the paths of righteousness for his name's sake'.**

   The fact that each citation is introduced by ὅτι may suggest a theological treatise — a sermon, even — rather than a liturgical text. It is not an amulet (Treu, 119). Since the text could not have concluded like this it must be an excerpt from a work which carried over to at least another sheet, since the *verso* contains an unrelated text. May the contents have been devoted to proving from Psalms that Jesus was the Christ? For δεσπότης = κύριος in the NT note Jude 4, and cf. 2 Pet. 2.1.
   All the textual variants in the Psalms quotations are attested elsewhere. In *l*.3 the phraseology has a biblical ring to it, but no actual quotation is involved. Of the quotations only Ps. 117.6 appears in the NT (at Heb. 13.6).
P. *Berl*. 2791.

16. Ps. 143.7-13; 145.8–146.6; Ode 1 (= Ex. 15.1-19).8-15; Ode 2 (= Deut. 32.1-43) .32-39 (Treu (b), 212-15): Qubbat al-ḥazna, Damascus, IX/X; bilingual Greek and Arabic text on two still-connected double leaves from a parchment codex. Between leaves 1 and 2 there are four pages missing, and a further six are lost between leaves 3 and 4. The pages are virtually complete, with 21 lines in a single column. The beginning of Ps. 146 (leaf 2, *recto l.*14) is indicated by the numeral ρμς´ out in the left margin. The scribe has observed the usual two margins (see no.11 above), a new line beginning a verse or verselet even if blank space is left on some lines at the end of a verse or verse section. Although there is no lacuna Ps. 145.8b, κύριος σοφοῖ τυφλούς is absent from the text at the beginning of the second leaf. Treu suggests (212) that v.8b may have preceded v.8a; but it may simply be that the scribe's eye wandered and missed one of the four adjacent lines beginning with κς. The Psalms passages show most variation from L(VIAD), the Odes appear to stand closest to 55(XAD). Insofar as it is recognizable the Arabic text corresponds to the Greek (Treu, 212). Van Haelst, 237; Turner, OT161A.

17. Ode 1 (Ex. 15.1-19).1-2 (Treu (c), 50): provenance unknown, VI/VII; a complete single papyrus leaf (13.3B x 9H cm.) with an unrelated text (a list or calculation) on the *verso* which is probably dated VI; the *recto* text was written after the *verso*. The biblical text is written in eight lines generally with *nomina sacra* abbreviated (but note *l.*7, θς τ[ο]ῦ πατρός, Ode 1.2). Textually the papyrus coheres with A.
P. Berl. 16158; van Haelst, 242; Turner, OT25A (he says that the number of lines to the page is 15, but it is not clear whence he derives this).

18. Ode 12.3-5 (Treu (d), 425-26): Hermopolis Magna (Fayum), VI/VII; eleven lines of a papyrus leaf (extant size 11B x 9H cm.) written perpendicularly to the fibres on the *verso*; *recto* blank. Treu calculates that 6-7 lines are missing before the surviving passage, and that therefore the page contained originally 16-17 lines. Three leaves of this size would have been required to record the entire Ode. The subject of this Ode, the 'Prayer of Manasseh', is derived from 2 Chron. 33.1ff. (note especially vv. 18-19 which refer to the Prayer), and the influence of biblical phraseology is marked. But it is the only Ode incorporated with the Psalms which is not repeated direct from other OT books. Since at least codex Alexandrinus (V) it was connected with the other Odes at the end of Psalms. This is the first papyrus attestation of it to have been found.
P. Berl. 17097; van Haelst, 251.

19. Prov. 4.26–5.8; 6.8a–16 (Treu (b), 215-17): Qubbat al-ḥazna, Damascus, V; two pieces from a parchment book-binding, the second an almost complete leaf. Identified but not published by B. Violet (above, no.1). Two leaves are missing between the two survivors, each page originally containing one column with 27 lines written in the usual pattern of two margins common for OT poetical books (see no.11 above). Textually no consistent affinity is apparent: leaf 2 *verso l.*16 (Prov. 6.14) διεστραμμένη καρδία with B against S, A; but *l.*27 (Prov. 6.16) κς with S, A against θεός B. Note three minor idiosyncrasies: leaf 2 *recto l.*10 (Prov. 6.8b) τε for δέ; leaf 2 *verso l.*4 (Prov. 6.11a) ὡς for ὥσπερ; *l.*26 (6.16) ἐπὶ πᾶσιν for πᾶσιν.
Van Haelst 253; Turner, OT165A.

20. Two citations from Prov. 6 (Treu (f), 119-20; cf. *MPL* 2 [1977] 253): Fayum, c.V; a badly damaged fragment (9.7B x 7.5H cm.) of papyrus blank on the *recto*, the *verso* containing parts of seven originally quite long lines. The only reasonably clear section of text is *ll.*4-7, the first three of which cite Prov. 6.9 (*l.*4), 10 (*ll.*5-6). The text in which these quotations occur is probably therefore a theological tract (sermon, perhaps?) dealing with sloth. Judging by the restoration needed to complete the Prov. citations the original breadth may have been as much as 30 cm. Treu therefore doubts that this was a codex, suggesting it was a single sheet. Leaving aside the fact that the *recto* is blank — on this see no.12 above, *ad. fin.* — papyrus codices of this breadth are known: Turner, *Typology*, 14, table 1 group 1, lists six with breadth of 27 + cm., ranging in date from IV-VIII. (In four of these the dimensions have been reconstructed.) In all but one of the six the calculated height is greater than the breadth. If our papyrus is to be thought of as a codex having a breadth of c.30cm., therefore, its height may have been anything up to 40cm.
P. Berl. 6776.

21. Prov. 23.26-27, 31-32 (Treu (c), 56-57, pl.4b): provenance unknown, V/VI; a small parchment fragment (10.7B x 3.9H cm.) from a codex, paginated 119/120 (although only the latter number on the *verso* is still recognizable). Treu estimates that in the 118 preceding pages the remainder of Prov. up to 23.26 could have been accommodated. Text written in sense lines in a single column. The transposed word order in *l.*3 of the *recto* (printed below) warrants attention.

recto   οἱ δὲ σοὶ ὀφθαλμοὶ ἐμὰς [ὁδοὺς]   23.26
      τηρείτωσαν: ἀλλότ[ριος]
     [πίθος γ]ὰρ τετρημέ[νος ἐστὶν οἶκος,] 27
     [καὶ φρέαρ σ]τεν[ὸν---

      . . . .

Here S has ἐστιν τετρημένος; further, the scribe, realising he had no room for ἀλλότ[ριος] after οἶκος inserted it above in the space at the end of *l.*2. But these two words are reversed in other witnesses, and while Treu's reconstruction is plausible it is not necessarily the case that the scribe intended οἱ. ἀλλ.; for ἀλλ. may have been omitted accidentally and inserted in the convenient space in the line immediately above where it ought to have occurred.
P. Berl. 16991; van Haelst, 257; Turner, OT167A.

22. Cant. 2.1-6; 2.17-3.2; 5.8-13 (Treu (b), 217-19), Qubbat al-ḥazna, Damascus, IV/V; fragments of three parchment leaves from a palimpsest codex, Arabic written crosswise over the Greek. Now lost, and only the hair-sides were photographed at the turn of the century (see no.1 above). Since the height (but not the breadth) of the first and third leaves is fairly well preserved we know there was one column with 21 lines per page (of the second leaf only eleven lines survive). Treu calculates that the preceding Canticle would not have required two full pages. The book of Canticles, then, began at about mid-page, and therefore another work may be assumed to have preceded it in this codex.

In the first two lines of the first leaf (Cant. 2.1-2) the possibilities allowed by space show that the scribe has omitted several words, probably owing to homoeoteleuton:

$$\text{Ἐγὼ ἄν[θος τοῦ πεδίου, κρίνον}$$
$$\text{ἐν μ[έσῳ ἀκανθῶν.}$$

Between these lines τῶν κοιλάδων. Ὡς κρίνον has been omitted. Again, at *ll.*10-11 on the same page (Cant. 2.3) Treu suggests that the restoration

$$\text{καὶ καρπὸ[ς αὐτοῦ ἐν λάρυγγί μου}$$
$$\text{γλυκύ[ς}$$

is required; i.e., γλυκύς has been removed from its more usual position after αὐτοῦ. Before *l.*6 on the third leaf Cant. 5.9a has been omitted owing to vv. 9a and 9b beginning with the same form of words. In this line as well σου is omitted before ἀπό.

Van Haelst, 268; Turner, OT174A.

23. Cant. 5.13–6.4 (Treu (c), 57-58, pl.7a): provenance unknown, IV; most (6B x 9.3H cm.) of a parchment codex leaf (originally 7.5B x 10H cm.) broken into two fragments. The single column has 17 lines to the page (although of hair-side *ll.*1-2 nothing is decipherable). The usual two margins occur (see no.11). At hair-side *l.*15 (Cant. 5.16) the last word appears as γλυκασμο'ς: the scribe realised his error in writing the singular, added the iota in a small superior letter, but forgot to cross out the sigma. The next line reads [και ολος] υμνημα; the reading in Rahlfs is ἐπιθυμία, but there is not enough room to fit the prepositional prefix inside the bracketed section, and in any case the end of the word is different.

    P. Berl. 18196; van Haelst, 270; Turner, OT175A.

24. Job 7.9b–10, 14 (Treu (e), 6-7): provenance unknown, VI; very short scrap (6.8B x 1.5H cm.) from a parchment codex, containing parts of three lines on the hair side, and parts of two lines on the flesh side. Only five whole words survive. The lacuna between the two sides suggests that there were originally c.19 lines to the page. Treu assumes a single column to the page in his calculation that Job would have filled 225 pages in a codex with the original dimensions of 16B x 21H cm., and that therefore this book may have formed the entire contents of the codex. But too little remains for us to be confident that there was only a single column.

    P. Vindob. G. 35767.

25. Job 31.32-34, 39-32.1: see **99**.

26. Wisd. 10.19–11.11 (Treu (b), 219-21: Qubbat al-ḥazna, Damascus, V/VI; an almost complete palimpsest leaf from a parchment codex, now lost. Over the biblical text is written a passage from Aristotle, *de interpretatione* 6-8 (17a35-18a16). For a classical text to be written over a biblical one is much less common than the reverse phenomenon (although patristic texts are written over biblical texts, most notably the fifth-century Codex Ephraemi rescriptus [C]). The biblical text consists of one column of 26 lines written in stichic form (i.e., each verselet begins a new line, any requiring more than a single line being indented on the second). The text is fairly unremarkable; note, however, the

omission of κύριε after ὕμνησαν at hair-side *l.*7 (Wisd. 10.20).
Van Haelst, 278; Turner, OT179A.

27. Jer. 2.2-3, 8-9; 2.16-19, 24-26; 2.30-32, 37-3.1; 3.6-7, 12-13; 3.18, 24-25 (Treu (c), 60-65, pl. 1c, 2): provenance unknown, III; fragments of five successive leaves of a papyrus codex (largest fragment — no.3 — c.9.5B x 9.2H cm.). Originally 37 lines per page in a single column. Two and a half pages would be needed to cover the text up to fragment 1; i.e., one leaf is lost from the start, and fragment 1 belongs to the lower half of the second leaf. The surviving leaves would then constitute the 2nd to 6th leaves of a quaternion (4 sheets, 8 leaves, 16 pages) which eventually became the standard 'gathering' in codices. Codices consisting of gatherings of folded single sheets ('ones') through to eights (and possibly nines) are discussed, along with single-quire codices (where all the sheets are placed on top of one another and folded to form a single gathering) by Turner, *Typology*, 55-71.

   Nomina sacra are mostly abbreviated, but not consistently so, e.g. *l.*6 Iηλ (Jer. 2.3) and probably also at *ll.*65 (Jer. 3.6), 69 (3.16), but *l.*44 Ἰσραηλ (2.31). At *l.*18 (Jer. 2.17) the reading ἐνκαταλιπεῖν is idiosyncratic (καταλιπεῖν elsewhere); in *ll.*56-57 (Jer. 3.1) word order differs from other witnesses: πρὸς | αὐτ[ὸν ἔτι ἀνακ]άμψῃ. At *ll.*53f. (Jer. 3.1, γυναῖκα ἑαυτοῦ; αὐτοῦ, *alii*) and *l.*63 (Jer. 3.6, ὅ[σα; ἄ, *alii*) the papyrus accords with minuscule 538 (XII) and thus provides important evidence for the early occurrence of these readings. Special readings of A and S are avoided. This text is our oldest papyrological witness to the preserved sections of Jeremiah. *P. Chester Beatty* VII (containing Jer. 4.30–5.1 and 5.9-14, 23-24 on parts of two leaves) is also III (966 Rahlfs).
   P. Berl. 17212; van Haelst, 303; Aland, AT138; Turner, OT201A.

28. Jer. 25.10-12 (Treu (b), 221); Qubbat al-ḥazna, Damascus, VI (?); one side only (flesh side?) surviving via a copy made by B. Violet (see no.1 above) of a fragment (14B x 15.5H cm.) from a parchment palimpsest, now lost. Arabic text written over the Greek. Two columns on the page, but it is uncertain how many lines originally the full page contained (the fragment has 5 and 4 lines respectively in the two columns). Variant readings of S, A, B are avoided.
   Van Haelst, 310; Turner, OT204C, who regards it as being from a codex.

29. Jer. 41.3, 10f.; 42.9f., 16f. (Treu (e), 7-9): provenance unknown, IV (early rather than late); fragment (3.2B x 8.7H cm.) of a still-connected double leaf with eight lines on the inner column of a two-column parchment codex. Each column originally contained 26 lines. The gap in text between the two leaves shows that another double leaf must have occurred between them. Roughly 250 pages would have been needed for this codex to contain the entire book of Jeremiah. Treu considers this to be an early parchment witness to Jer. (he refers to two others of rather later date also in the Vienna collection: *P. Vindob. G.* 39774, V; *P. Vindob. G.* 26093, V/VI); but papyrus fragments from III are known (above, no.27).
   P. Vindob. G. 19891.

   On the lexicography of the LXX in the papyri note most recently F. Vattioni, *Stud.Pap.* 19(1980) 39-59, which restricts itself to the Pentateuch. While not primarily concerned with the papyrus texts J.A.L. Lee draws upon documentary parallels in his *A Lexical Study of the Septuagint Version of the Pentateuch* (*Septuagint and Cognate Studies*, 14; forthcoming, Chico, 1983).

88. Miscellaneous quotations from Psalms

Biblical citations in Christian inscriptions in late antiquity and the early Byzantine period are quite common. Two which may receive passing mention here are *CIMAH* I.23 (St-Maurice, Canton Wallis, Switzerland, c.600), which quotes Ps. 22.1-2 in Latin on a brick (*ed.pr.*, 1954: for details see Jörg, p.81); and *SEG* 987 (= J.-P. Rey-Coquais, *AArchSyr.* 26 [1976] 38-39, no.5), a medallion from Laodikeia in Syria (n.d., *ed.pr.*) quoting Ps. 90, ὁ κα|τοικῶ|ν ἐν βο|ηθίᾳ. *MPR* 32 is a fragment of a vase (Tomis, V-VI) which includes wording from Ps. 26.1, † Κ(ύριο)ς φωτισμός μ[ου κ(αὶ) σωτήρ (μου), τινα φοβηθή]σομε; Barnea thinks that the text enables us to identify the function of this vase as a receptacle for holy water. Barnea considers that on *MPR* 34 the four letters surviving on a piece of white marble, ἄρτω[ν, may form part of a quotation from Ps. 131.15-16 (Tomis, V-VI).

89. More Light on the Greek Text of Daniel

The book of Daniel in Greek survives in two distinct versions, the original LXX and the later translation attributed to Theodotion. For reasons that are still a matter of conjecture, Theodotion's version has almost completely ousted the LXX from our MS tradition. The LXX survives in only one Greek MS, Cod. Chisianus of X AD (= 88). Until 1931 there was no other witness to this text except the Syro-hexaplar (= Syh), the Syriac translation of Origen's mighty Hexapla. In that year came the discovery of a papyrus codex, *P. Beatty* IX/X (= Papyrus 967(-8), containing, besides parts of other books, Daniel 3.72–8.27 in a version of the same text-type as 88. This material, now in Dublin, was edited by F.G. Kenyon in 1937-8.

Subsequently (but unfortunately not in time for Ziegler's Göttingen edition of 1954) further leaves of this codex were found in the Köln collection, and these combine with the Dublin leaves to make a complete text of Daniel. In 1977 W. Hamm completed publication of the Köln text, together with the already-published *P. Beatty* material and a detailed commentary, in the third of a series of volumes, as follows:

A. Geissen, *Der Septuaginta-Text des Buches Daniel, Kap. 5–12, zusammen mit Susanna, Bel et Draco, sowie Esther, Kap. 1,1a-2,15, nach dem Kölner Teil des Papyrus 967* (*Papyrologische Texte und Abhandlungen* 5; Bonn, 1968)

W. Hamm, *Der Septuaginta-Text des Buches Daniel, Kap. 1–2, nach dem Kölner Teil des Papyrus 967* (*Pap. Texte und Abh.* 10; Bonn, 1969)

W. Hamm, *Der Septuaginta-Text des Buches Daniel, Kap. 3–4, nach dem Kölner Teil des Papyrus 967* (*Pap. Texte und Abh.* 21; Bonn, 1977)

(Note also a further part of this papyrus, published as: P.L.G. Jahn, *Der griechische Text des Buches Ezechiel nach dem Kölner Teil des Papyrus 967* [*Pap. Texte und Abh.* 15; Bonn, 1972].)

In these volumes, then, we have the full text of a valuable witness to the non-Theodotionic text of Daniel. The codex is dated to II or III[1] (Geissen 18; Hamm [1969] 18), and so not only predates Cod. 88 by many centuries but is also older than Syh (early VII), and the Hexapla itself (mid-III). The text shows none of the hexaplaric corrections found in 88 and Syh, and seems to be less influenced by the

Theodotion text than they are. In short, this text brings us a great deal nearer to the original LXX version, which in turn is important for the light it may throw on the Hebrew/Aramaic text.

The new text is rich in variants, many of which are valuable. The following is a brief sample. At 3.1 the reading τὸ πλάτος αὐτῆς πηχῶν δώδεκα is likely to preserve a better text than all the rest of the tradition, including MT, all of which give the width of the statue as 6 cubits. As Hamm points out ([1977] 135), a statue 60 cubits high and 12 broad matches the proportions of the human frame, whereas one 60 cubits high and 6 broad is grotesque. Similarly 2.1 ἐν τῷ δεκάτῳ ἔτει (ἐν τῷ ἔτει τῷ δευτέρῳ 88 Syh Theod. = MT) presupposes a Hebrew text different from and probably more original than MT. Instances in which 967 gives a more original form of the LXX than 88 are 2.40 πρίζων (δαμάζων 88, cf. λεπτύνει καὶ δαμάζει Theod.), 3.2 ἐστήρισεν (ἔστησεν 88 = Theod.). In various places 967 offers a more popular Koine word or form than 88, which has evidently undergone some revision in the interests of 'better' Greek. E.g. 6.18 νήστης (νῆστις 88), 7.16 προσῆλθα (προσῆλθον 88), 12.13 ἀπωθοῦ, apparently 'push off!' (ἀναπαύου 88), 5.13 εἰσηνέχθη (εἰσήχθη 88; this example from J. Smit Sibinga, *Mnem.* 25 (1972) 313).

A number of quotations from the book of Daniel appear in the NT. It is one of the long-standing puzzles of LXX studies that these quotations, along with those found in other writers such as Hermas and Clement, mostly follow the Theodotion text, which ought not to have been in existence if the traditional date for Theodotion (II) is correct. Thus Mark 14.62 cites Daniel 7.13 in the form μετὰ τῶν νεφελῶν, agreeing with Theodotion against LXX ἐπὶ τῶν ν. (For further examples see S. Jellicoe, *The Septuagint and Modern Study* [Oxford, 1968] 87.) This state of affairs has led to many hypotheses, but the best answer to the puzzle has been provided in recent years by D. Barthélemy in his epoch-making work, *Les devanciers d'Aquila* (Leiden, 1963). The 'Theodotion' text of Daniel belongs to the 'καίγε' group of recensions produced in Palestine not later than IAD and designed to bring the Greek text into closer conformity with the original Hebrew/Aramaic. Papyrus 967 of course has little new to offer here; it simply confirms, for an earlier date, the separation between the LXX and 'Theodotion' texts.

(J.A.L. LEE)

90. 'Daniel in the Den' on a belt buckle

Nax, Canton Wallis (Switzerland)   VI
ed.pr. — M.-R. Sauter, *Vallesia* 15 (1960) 262f. (fig. 17); *non vidi*

　　　† *qui liberasti Danielum de lacu[m?] leone rquimbtibiriio.*

Bronze buckle, text written around three outside edges, which frames a central panel depicting Daniel flanked by two lions. The reading after *leone* is very difficult.
Bib. — *C. Jörg, *CIMAH* I.18, pp.72–73 (pl.10, fig.21)

(cross) You who freed Daniel from the lion's den...(?)

Daniel was a popular subject for portrayal in the early Christian centuries: Jörg refers to E. Diehl, *Inscriptiones latinae Christianae veteres* 2426e (Yugoslavia, n.d.), 2427a (North Africa, n.d.). Reference to him in connection with prayers for the dead is also attested (Jörg, 73). This might encourage us to read the last group of letters as something like *requiem tibi Riio*, though the final four letters provide no sense. For the biblical allusion cf. Dan. 6.27.

91. Some recently published NT fragments

Of the NT fragments identified by K. Treu over the last twenty years the majority have been written on parchment, and the great bulk of them belong to the Berlin Collection. The mention of some of the publications in Treu's article, *MPL* 2(1977) 251, provides the *raison d'être* for collecting this large group here. But in contrast with the entry on LXX fragments (**87**, above) it was decided to reprint all the NT texts (most with minimal comment) in order to make them more accessible. Accents and breathing have been added where *ed.pr.*'s text was diplomatic. A small number of apparently typographical errors in *ed.pr.* have been corrected silently here. Two as yet unidentified Christian texts are included — they may not be biblical texts — in the hope that this may prove a stimulus to their identification. Well over one hundred of the entries in van Haelst's *Catalogue* comprise Christian fragments which as yet can only be given a general definition, 'prayer, liturgical passage, homily', etc. M. Naldini (per litt. to E.A. Judge) is preparing a corpus of fragmentary papyri covering patristic/Christian literary adespota. The following articles by Treu are referred to in the list below:

(a) 'Ein neues neutestamentliches Unzialfragment aus Damaskus (= 0253)', *ZNW* 55 (1964) 274–77;

(b) 'Griechisch-Koptische Bilinguen des Neuen Testaments', in *Koptologische Studien in der DDR*. Special number of *Zeitschrift der Martin-Luther-Universität, Halle-Wittenberg*, 14 (1965) 95–123, especially 100–04;

(c) 'Neue neutestamentliche Fragmente der Berliner Papyrussammlung', *APF* 18 (1966) 23–38 (pl. 1–4);

(d) 'Ein weiteres Unzialpalimpsest des Galaterbriefs aus Damaskus', *Stud. Evang.* 5 (1968) 219–21;

(e) 'Drei Berliner Papyri mit Nomina sacra', *Studia Patristica* 10 (1970) 29–31 (2 pl.); the second of these was subsequently identified (by C.H. Roberts) and published in revised form by Treu in *APF* 21 (1971) 82;

(f) 'Papyri und Majuskeln', in *Studies in New Testament Language and Text. Essays in Honour of G.D. Kilpatrick*, ed. J.K. Elliott (*NovT Suppl.* 44; Leiden, 1976) 373–86, especially 379–86.

(Note also Treu's 'Neutestamentliche Unzialfragmente in einer Athos-Handschrift (0167, Lavra Δ61)', *ZNW* 54 (1963) 53–58; cf. 55 (1964) 133. He publishes five small fragments from four leaves of a parchment codex, which contain various verses from Mk. 6, not reprinted below. On uncial texts see also his 'Remarks on some uncial fragments of the Greek New Testament', *Studia Evangelica* 3.2 (1964) 273–81.)

As well as references to van Haelst, Aland *Repertorium*, and Turner the Gregory/Aland sigla are provided.

1. Mt. 10.17-20, 21-23; 10.25-27, 28-32 (Treu (c), 25-28, pl.1): Hermopolis Magna, c. 300; portion of a parchment leaf (5.7B × 9.2Hcm.) from a codex, containing two columns on either side, each originally of 23 lines. 17 and 13 lines survive flesh-side (= recto), 14 and 17 lines hair-side (= verso). A later hand wrote 10.33 on the upper edge of col.2.

*recto, col.*1

```
[        ἀνθρώ]πων· πα-        10.17
[ραδώσουσιν] γὰρ ὑμᾶς
[εἰς συνέδρι]α, καὶ εἰς
[τὰς συναγ]ωγὰς αὐτῶ‾
5 [μαστιγώ]σουσιν ὑμᾶς·
[καὶ ἐπὶ ἡ]γεμόνων καὶ        18
[βασιλεω]  σταθήσεσθε
[ἕνεκεν] ἐμοῦ, εἰς μαρ-
[τύριον] αὐτοῖς καὶ τοῖς
10 [ἔθνεσ]ιν. ὅταν δὲ παρα-      19
[δῶσιν] ὑμᾶς, μὴ μεριμνή-
[σητε τί] λαλήσητ[ε]· δοθή-
[σεται γ]ὰρ ὑμεῖν [ἐν ἐ]κεί-
[νῃ τῇ] ὥρᾳ τί λα[λήσητε·]
15 [οὐ γὰρ ὑ]μεῖς ἐσ[τε οἱ λα-]   20
[λοῦντ]ες, ἀλλὰ τ[ὸ π‾ν‾α]
[τοῦ π‾ρ‾ς] ὑμῶν [        ]
```

*col.*2

```
σουσιν αὐτού[ς. καὶ]        21,22
ἔσεσθε μεισο[ύμε-]
20 νοι ὑπὸ πά[ντων]
διὰ τὸ ὄνο[μά μου·]
ὁ δὲ ὑπομ[είνας εἰς]
τέλος, οὗ[τος σωθή-]
σεται. ὅτ[αν δὲ διώ-]        23
25 κωσιν [ὑμᾶς ἐν τῇ]
πόλει [ταύτῃ, φεύγε-]
τε εἰς [τὴν ἄλλην ἐὰν]
δὲ ἐν [τῇ ἄλλῃ ἐκδιώ-]
ξου[σιν ὑμᾶς φεύγε-]
30 τε [                    ]
    ·  ·  ·  ·  ·  ·
```

*verso, col.*1

```
[αὐτο]ῦ, καὶ ὁ δοῦλος        25
[ὡς ὁ κ‾]ς‾ αὐτοῦ.
[εἰ τὸν ο]ἰκοδεσπότη‾
[        ]βουλ ἐκάλε-
35 [σαν, πόσ]ῳ μᾶλλον
[τοὺς οἰκια]κοὺς αὐτοῦ.
[μὴ οὖν φο]βηθῆτε         26
[αὐτούς· οὐδ]ὲν γάρ ἐ-
[στιν κεκαλυ]μμένο‾
40 [ὃ οὐκ ἀποκα]λυφθή       27
[σεται καὶ κρυ]πτὸν ὃ
[οὐ γνωσθήσε]ται. ὃ         27
[λέγω ὑμῖν ἐν] τῇ σ-
[κοτίᾳ εἴπατε]  [ . . ]
    ·  ·  ·  ·  ·  ·
```

*col.*2

```
45 τὸν δυνά[μενον καὶ ψυ-]     28
χὴν καὶ σ[ῶμα ἀποκτεῖ-]
ναι ἐν γεέ[ννῃ. οὐχὶ δύο]     29
στρουθία ἀσ[σαρίου πω-]
λοῦνται; καὶ[ ἓν ἐξ αὐτῶν]
50 οὐ πεσεῖται ἐ[πὶ τὴν γῆν]
ἄνευ τοῦ πα[τρὸς ὑ-]
μῶν. ἀλλὰ κα[ὶ αἱ τρίχες]     30
τῆς κεφαλῆς[ ὑμῶν]
πᾶσαι ἠριθμημ[έναι εἰ-]
55 σίν. μὴ οὖν φο[βεῖσθε·]      31
πολλῶν στρουθ[ίων]
δ[ιαφέ]ρετε ὑμ[εῖς. πᾶς]      32
[οὖν ὅσ]τις ὁμο[λογήσει]
[ἐν ἐ]μοὶ ἔνπ[ροσθεν]
60 [τῶν ἀ]νθρώπ[ων, ὁμο-]
[λογ]ήσω [            ]
    ·  ·  ·  ·  ·  ·
```

On the basis of the hand Treu notes that this piece belongs to the same codex as *PSI* 1 (1912) 2 and 2 (1913) 124 — Lk. 22.44-56, 61-63. *Nomina sacra* are handled inconsistently: abbreviated at *l*.32 and virtually certainly also at *ll*.16,17 given the amount of available space (the later addition of 10.33

employs shortened forms as well); but full forms at *ll*.1,51,60. (For other examples of such inconsistency see nos.7,10,13 below.) At *ll*.4,33,39 a short superior bar does duty at the line end for a final *nu* (cf. no. 10 below). For this feature see K. McNamee, *Abbreviations in Greek Literary Papyri and Ostraca* (*BASP* suppl. 3; Chico, 1981) 116.

Textually the passage accords overall — although not everywhere — with D which embodies several readings influenced by phraseology in the synoptic parallels. E.g., *ll*.3–4 εἰς [τὰς συναγ]ωγάς D (cf. Mk. 13.9; Lk. 21.12), ἐν + dat. *alii*; *l*.6, ἡγεμόνων D (cf. Mk. 13.9), ἡγεμόνας δέ *alii* (some omit δέ); *ll*.6–7, καὶ [βασιλέω]ν (cf. Mk. 13·9) omitted by D, καὶ βασιλεῖς *alii*; *l*.7, σταθήσεσθε D and some others (cf. Mk. 13.9), ἀχθήσεσθε *alii ll*.48–49, [πω]λοῦνται D, πωλεῖται *alii*. Against this adherence to D note *l*.17, ὑμῶν omitted by D; *l*.47, ἐν γεέ[ννη], εἰς + acc. D; *l*.48 ἀσ[σαρίου], D.

P. Berl. 11863; Gregory/Aland 0171; van Haelst, 356(1); Turner, NT Parch. 15A (who dates text III/IV).

2. Mk. 5.26–27, 31 (Treu (c), 28–29, pl.2b): provenance unknown, VI; small scrap (8.4B × 3H cm.) of parchment from a codex originally possessing 17–18 lines to the page. Portions of three lines only survive on either side. Two little survives for anything to be said about its textual affinities.

recto

```
.   .   .   .   .   .
[            καὶ] μηδὲν ὠφε-      5.26
[ληθεῖσα ἀλλὰ μᾶλ]λον εἰς τὸ
[χεῖρον ἐλθοῦσα,] ἀκούσα-        27
[σα                        ]
.   .   .
```

verso

```
.   .   .   .   .   .
5  βλέπει[ς τὸν ὄχλον συνθλί-]    31
   βοντά σ[ε, καὶ λέγεις, τίς μου]
   ἥψατο; [                     ]
.   .   .   .   .   .
```

P. Berl. 14045; Gregory/Aland 0263; van Haelst, 389; Turner, NT Parch. 27B.

3. Lk. 7.20–21, 34–35 (Treu (c), 29–30): provenance unknown, VI; fragment (2.8B × 5.5H cm.) from the lower edge of a parchment codex leaf, parts of five lines from an original c.24 surviving. The gap in text between the two sides means that each page must have contained two columns; it is the inner column on each page that remains. There is insufficient wording to allow us to say any more than that it does not belong to the Alexandrian (or H) group of texts.

recto

```
.   .   .   .   .   .   .
[      ἐρ]χόμε[νος, ἢ ἄλ-]        7.20
[λον προσ]δοκῶμ[εν; ἐν]           21
[αὐτῇ δ]ὲ τῇ ὥρα[ ἐθερά]
[πευσε]ν πολλοὺς [ἀπὸ νό-]
5  [σων κ]αὶ μαστίγ[ων        ]
```

verso

```
.   .   .   .   .   .   .
[          ] φά[γος καὶ]           34
[οἰνοπότη]ς, φίλ[ος τε-]
[λωνῶν κα]ὶ ἁμαρτω[λῶν.]
[καὶ ἐδικα]ιώθη ἡ σ[οφία]         35
10 [ἀπὸ τῶν τέ]κνων[      ]
```

P. Berl. 16994; Gregory/Aland 0265; van Haelst, 410; Turner, NT Parch. 45A.

4. Lk. 10.19–22 (Treu (a)): Qubbat al-ḥazna, Damascus, VI[1]; portion of a parchment codex leaf with an Arabic religious text written over the Greek (but not properly a palimpsest: Treu, 275). The full height (31 cm.) survives but not the full breadth (9 cm.; originally 25 cm.). Treu calculates that in this format of 14 lines in one column per page c.250 leaves would have been needed to contain Luke entire: all four gospels could scarcely have been included in this codex.

recto

πατεῖ]ν ἐπάνω	10.19
ὄφεω]ν καὶ σκο[ρ-	
πίων], καὶ ἐπὶ πᾶ[σαν	
τὴν δύ]ναμιν το[ῦ	
5 ἐχθρο]ῦ· καὶ οὐδ[έν	
ὑμᾶς ο]ὐ μὴ ἀδικ[ήσει.	
Πλὴν ἐ]ν τούτῳ [μὴ	20
χαίρετ]ε ὅτι τὰ π[νεύ-	
ματα ὑ]μῖν ὑπο[τάσ-	
10 σεται], χαίρετε δ[ὲ	
ὅτι τὰ] ὀνόματα ὑ[μῶν	
ἐγράφ]η ἐν τοῖς [οὐ-	
ρανοῖ]ς·	
Ἐν αὐτ]ῇ δὲ τῇ ὥρ[ᾳ	21

verso

15 ἠ]γαλλιάσα[το τῷ	
π]νι ὁ ῑς κα[ὶ εἶπεν,	
ἐ]ξομολογ[οῦμαί	
σ]οι, περ, κε [τοῦ οὐ-	
ρ]ανοῦ καὶ τ[ῆς γῆς,	
20 ὅ]τι ἀπέκρυ[ψας	
τ]αῦτα ἀπὸ [σοφῶν	
κ]αὶ συνετ[ῶν καὶ	
ἀ]πεκάλυψας αὐτὰ	
ν]ηπίοις· [ναί, ὁ πηρ,	
25 ὅ]τι οὕτως [ἐγένε-	
τ]ο εὐδοκί[α ἔμπρο-	
σ]θέν σου·	
Καὶ] στραφεὶ[ς πρὸς	22

Nomina sacra are not always abbreviated, e.g., *ll*.18–19, and in particular contrast π]νι (16) with *ll*.8–9 where Treu restores πνεύματα unshortened in view of the amount of space. *Ll*.13 and 27 end short and have punctuation marks, thus indicating the sense break for the start of the new verse in the line following each. Textually the passage usually avoids special readings such as those of D (*ll*.2, 2–3, 8–9, 12–13, 21–22), but with D and a few others it adds δέ at the beginning of Lk. 10.21; and at *l*.28 it employs the longer Byzantine text for the start of Lk. 10.22.

Gregory/Aland 0253; van Haelst, 416; not listed in Turner.

5. Lk. 20.19–25, 30–39 (Treu (c), 30–32, pl.2a): provenance unknown, VI; two fragments from the upper part of a parchment codex leaf, surviving dimensions 14B × 14·5H cm. Both sides still contain portions of 20 of the original 33–34 lines, mostly only a few letters per line, however. Traces of two letters at the top of the hair-side are suggestive to Treu of a heading (or a page number?). The initial letter of *l*.34 is larger and stands out into the margin: it carries an embellishment line above it. This same device needs to be restored at *ll*.5, 10 and 39 to provide space for the required number of letters: they too coincide with what was clearly regarded as the start of new sections (note how *l*.9 ends short — the end of Lk. 20.20 — and similarly *ll*.33, 38).

recto

[ἐπιβ]αλεῖν [ἐπ' αὐτὸν]   20.19
[τὰς χεῖρας ἐν αὐτῇ τῇ ὥρ]ᾳ· καὶ [ἐφοβήθη]
[σαν τὸν λαόν·   ἔγνωσ]αν ὅ[τι πρὸς αὐ-]
[τοὺς εἶπεν τὴν παραβολὴν] ταύ[την.]

5 [Καὶ παρατηρήσαντες ἀπέ]στιλα[ν ἐγκαθέ-]   20
[τους ὑποκρινομένους ἑαυτ[οὺς δικαίους]
[εἶναι ἵνα ἐπιλάβω]νται α[ὐτοῦ λόγου]
[ὥστε παραδοῦναι αὐτ]ὸν τῇ ἀρχ[ῇ καὶ τῇ]
[ἐξουσίᾳ τοῦ ἡγεμόνος.]

10 [Καὶ ἐπηρώτησαν αὐτὸν λέγοντες, δι]δ[ά-]   21
[σκαλε, οἴδαμεν ὅτι ὀρθῶς λέ]γει[ς]
[καὶ διδάσκεις καὶ οὐ λαμβάνεις πρόσ]ω-
[πον, ἀλλ' ἐπ' ἀληθείας τὴν ὁδὸν τοῦ] θ̅υ̅
[διδάσκεις· ἔξεστι] ἡμ[ᾶς Κ]έσαρει   22

15 [φόρον δοῦναι ἢ οὔ;] κατα[νοήσ]ας δὲ   23
[αὐτῶν τὴν πανουρ]γίαν εἶ[π]εν π[ρὸς]
[αὐτούς, δείξατέ μοι δη]νάριον. ο[ἱ δὲ ἔδειξαν] 24
[καὶ εἶπεν, τίνος ἔχει εἰ]κόνα καὶ ἐ[πιγραφήν;]
[οἱ δὲ εἶπαν, Καίσαρο]ς· ὁ δ[ὲ] εἶπ[εν πρὸς]   25

20 [αὐτούς, τοίνυν ἀπό]δο[τε] τ[ὰ Καίσαρος]

. . . .

verso

[καὶ ὁ δεύτ]ερος κ[αὶ ὁ τρίτος ἔλαβεν αὐ-]   30,31
[τήν, ὡσαύτ]ως δὲ κ[αὶ οἱ ἑπτὰ οὐ κατέλιπον]
[τέκνα καὶ] ἀπέθ[ανον. ὕστερον καὶ ἡ γυνὴ]   32
[ἀπέθαν]εν· ἡ[γυνὴ οὖν ἐν τῇ ἀναστάσει]   33

25 [τίνος αὐ]τῶν [ἔσται γυνή; οἱ γὰρ ἑπτὰ ἔσχον]
[αὐτὴν γ]υναῖ[κα. καὶ εἶπεν αὐτοῖς ὁ ι̅ς̅, οἱ]   34
[υἱοὶ το]ῦ αἰῶ[νος τούτου γαμοῦσιν καὶ γα-]
[μίσκ]ονται. Οἱ [δὲ καταξιωθέντες τοῦ αἰ-]   35
[ῶ]νος ἐκ[εί]ν[ου τυχεῖν καὶ τῆς ἀναστά-]

30 [σ]εω[ς τῆς ἐκ νεκρῶν οὔτε γαμοῦσιν οὔτε]
γαμ[ίζονται· οὐδὲ γὰρ ἀποθανεῖν ἔτι δύ-]   36
να[νται,   τῆς ἀνα-]
στά[σεως υἱοὶ ὄντες.]
‾Ὅτι δὲ ἐ[γείρο]ντ[αι οἱ νεκροί, καὶ Μωϋσῆς ἐ-] 37

35 μήν[υσεν] ἐπὶ τ[ῆς βάτου, ὡς λέγει κ̅ν̅]
[τὸ]ν θ̅ν̅ Αβρααμ [καὶ θ̅ν̅ Ισαακ καὶ θ̅ν̅ Ιακωβ·]
[θ̅ς̅] δ[ὲ ο]ὐκ ἔστιν [νεκρῶν ἀλλὰ ζώντων·]   38
[πάν]τες γὰρ αὐ[τῷ ζῶσιν.]
['Απ]οκριθέντε[ς δέ τινες τῶν γραμματέων]   39

40 [εἶ]π[αν,] διδ[άσκαλε,   ]
[. .] . [   ]

. . . .

Textually the fragment adheres to the Alexandrian (H) group of witnesses and does not reflect the Koine text. In *l*.3 (Lk. 20.19), e.g., G *et al.* omit τὸν λαόν. Even so the remaining text is too short to fill up the available room in the line. The text avoids readings and word order found in D (*ll*.2, 11, 12, 14–15, 15, 17, 18, 20, 21–22, 27–28). At *l*.32 the usual text of Lk. 20.36, ἰσάγγελοι γάρ εἰσιν, καὶ υἱοί εἰσιν θ̄ῡ, will not fit into the space available between δύνανται and τῆς ἀναστάσεως. Twelve letters of *l*.32 out of a maximum of 28–30 for the line are certain because of the preceding and following lines. Treu suggests that the scribe jumped in error from εἰσιν to εἰσιν, thus omitting καὶ υἱοί εἰσιν (so D and a few others): this would mean fitting in 19 letters. Another possibility is that εἰσιν was omitted both times and υἱοί abbreviated as ῡῑ (= 19 letters). καί was presumably not abbreviated here, since it is not shortened elsewhere in the text. For full textual apparatus see Treu, 32.

NT MSS with so many lines are not common, according to Treu. A check through Turner's Table 16 (pp. 101 ff.) allows us to modify this claim a little. Thirty-three lines is an arbitrary figure, but if we list all NT codices containing as many (or more) lines to the page (or column) as this Luke fragment there is a remarkably clear-cut difference between the proportion of the papyrus and parchment representatives. Turner's table contains just over 80 NT papyrus codices, and twice that number of NT codices made of parchment.

NT papyrus codices

$\mathfrak{P}^1$	— Mt., *P.Oxy.* 1 (1898) 2, III, 33*ll*.
$\mathfrak{P}^4$	— Lk., *MIFAO* 9 (1893) p.215 + *Rev.Bib.* 47 (1938) pp.5ff., III or III/IV, 35*ll*. (2 cols).
$\mathfrak{P}^{15,16}$	— 1 Cor./Phil., *P.Oxy.* 7 (1910) 1008, 1009, IV (Turner), 37–38*ll*.
$\mathfrak{P}^{27}$	— Rom., *P.Oxy.* 11 (1915) 1355, III, 41*ll*. (?).
$\mathfrak{P}^{30}$	— 1,2 Thes., *P.Oxy.* 13 (1919) 1598, III/IV, 33*ll*.
$\mathfrak{P}^{37}$	— Mt., *P.Mich.* 3 (1936) 137, IV, 33*ll*.
$\mathfrak{P}^{38}$	— Acts, *P.Mich.* 3 (1936) 138, III/IV, 37*ll*.
$\mathfrak{P}^{40}$	— Rom., *P.Baden* 4 (1924) 57, V/VI?, 33 + *ll*. (?).
$\mathfrak{P}^{45}$	— Gospels + Acts, *P.Chester Beatty* 2 (1934), III, 39*ll*.
$\mathfrak{P}^{51}$	— Gal., *P.Oxy.* 18 (1941) 2157, IV/V, 38*ll*. (?).
$\mathfrak{P}^{64,67}$	— Mt., *HTR* 46 (1953) 233 + R.Roca-Puig, *Un pap. gr. del. evang. de S. Mateo* (Barcelona, 1962²), II, 36–39*ll*. (?) (2 cols?).
$\mathfrak{P}^{69}$	— Lk., *P.Oxy.* 24 (1957) 2383, III, 48–50*ll*.
$\mathfrak{P}^{74}$	— Acts/Cath.Epp., *P.Bodmer* 17 (1961), VI or VII, 31–35*ll*.
$\mathfrak{P}^{75}$	— Lk., Jn, *P.Bodmer* 14, 15 (1961), III (Turner), 38–45*ll*.

NT parchment codices

7	— Mt. (Lectionary), *P.Vindob.G.* 2324 a-k, VI/VII (Turner), 33*ll*. (2 cols).
17B	— Mt., Leningrad Pub.Lib.Gr. 277 + Harris, *Sinai* 7, VI, 34*ll*. (*2 cols*).
43	— Lk., Paris Copt. 129 (+ BM + Vienna holdings), VI, c.35*ll*. (2 cols).
50A	— the text presently being discussed.
71,104	— Acts/1 Pet., *Stud.Pal.* 11 (1911) 59c, VI, c.35*ll*. (2 cols).
84	— 1 Cor., *Paris Copt.* 129, IX/X, 35*ll*. (2 cols).
105A	— 2 Pet., *P.Ryl.Copt.* 20, VI, 36*ll*. (2 cols).

Discounting the three Coptic Texts in the latter group leaves us with a ratio of 14:4 Greek papyri:parchments of the NT (i.e. more than 3:1). In Turner's list six further NT papyrus fragments have 30 lines on one or more surviving pages; there are 8 more for the parchment texts. If we add these figures together 20 NT papyrus texts of 30+ lines compares more closely with 15 parchment examples (including the Coptic Texts). But the ratio is still 4:3. Is the date differential a relevant factor in this disparity? Almost all the NT papyrus codices of this size are earlier than the earliest parchment ones.

P.Berl. 17034; Gregory/Aland, 0266; van Haelst, 421; Turner, NT Parch. 50A.

6. Jn 1.30–32 (Treu (b), 100–04): Fayum, VI; parchment fragment of a codex leaf containing Jn 1.16–18 in the Fayumic dialect of Coptic, and Jn 1.30–32 in Greek on the hair-side. This is the first occurrence of this passage from Jn to be discovered in this particular Coptic dialect, although the extract is known in Bohairic and Sahidic versions (Treu, 102). E.M. Husselman, *The Gospel of John in Fayumic Coptic* (*P.Mich.Inv. 3521*) (Ann Arbor, 1962), has published 29 fragmentary leaves from a single-quire papyrus codex which preserves parts of Jn 6.11–15.10. Turner, 57–60, discusses single-quire codices, but does not include this example in his Table 6 (p.60). On the Coptic versions of the NT see B.M. Metzger, *The Early Versions of the New Testament* (Oxford, 1977) 99–152. Only the Greek text of the new fragment is printed below.

γέγο]νεν,	1.30		Ιη]λ̅· διὰ	
ὅτι]πρῶ-		10	το]ῦτο ἠλ-	
τό]ς μου ἦ(ν).			θ]ον ἐγὼ	
κἀ]γὼ οὐκ'	31		ἐν ὕδατι	
5 ἤ]δειν αὐ-			βαπτίζω(ν).	
τ]όν· ἀλλ᾿·ἵ-			καὶ ἐμαρ-	32
ν]α φανε-		15	τύρησεν	
ρ]ωθῇ τῷ			Ἰωάννη[ς	

Both versions abbreviate *nomina sacra*. The Greek text (5.3B × 21H cm.) accords with the majority of old Uncials. Treu's article (95–100) is very informative about the relationship between the two languages in bilingual NT texts. Because Greek was the language of the dominant culture in Egypt, and since for Christians it was virtually a sacred language (because of the LXX and NT), it is normally possible to conclude that translators of Greek texts into Coptic and users of bilingual texts were themselves Copts (Treu, 97).

P.Berl. 5542; Gregory/Aland 0260; van Haelst, 431; Turner, NT Parch. 54A.

7. Jn 1.30–33 (Treu (e)): provenance unknown, VI/VII; fragment (4.5B × 6.5H cm.) of a small parchment codex leaf (full size originally calculated as 7.5B × 10H cm.). Treu's revised text is printed below.

recto

ἀνὴ[ρ ὃς ἔμπροσ-]	1.30	ἵνα φαν[ερωθῇ]	
θέ μ[ου γέγονεν,]		[τῷ Ι]η̅[λ, διὰ τοῦ-]	
ὅτι π[ρῶτός μου]		[το ἦλθον ἐγὼ ἐν]	
ἦν. κἀγ[ὼ οὐκ ἤ-]	31	[ὕδατι βαπτίζω(ν).]	
5 δειν αὐτό[ν, ἀλλ᾿]		10 [καὶ ἐμαρτύρησε(ν)]	32

verso

['Ιωάννης λ]έγω(ν)
[τεθέαμαι τὸ] π̄ν̄ᾱ
[καταβαῖνο]ν̣ ὡς
[περιστε]ρὰ̣ν̣ ἐξ οὐ-
15 [ρανοῦ,] καὶ ἔμει-
[νεν ἐπ'] αὐτόν.
[κἀγὼ οὐκ ἤ]δ̣[ειν]   33

— — — — —

An embellished cross stands above the text on the flesh-side — perhaps a place-marker. Treu calculates that at ten lines per page some eight leaves preceded this one, i.e., an entire quaternion from a codex containing Jn. On quaternions and other sizes of codex 'gatherings' see Turner 55–71. *Nomina sacra* are not treated consistently by the scribe: abbreviated at *ll*.7, 12, but full form at *ll*.14f. A blank space in *l*.4 marks the beginning of v.31; so, too, *l*.32 ends a little short and v.33 begins on a new line. Textually the fragment avoids the special readings of Sinaiticus; at *l*.13 ὡς occurs instead of ὡσεί (𝔓⁶⁶ and the Koine text).

The dimensions of the codex to which this leaf belonged put it into group XIV (Miniature) in Turner's classification of parchment codices by size (table 2, pp.29–30). This group comprises ¼ of the parchment codices tabulated by him (he includes 165 examples in the whole table, roughly ⅛ of known Greek and Coptic parchment codices). The dimensions of some in group XIV are considerably smaller than this one (the smallest codex on parchment he includes is the Cologne Mani [IV or IV/V], 3.5B × 4.5H cm.). In contrast, the corresponding group 11 in Turner's Table 1 (papyrus codices tabulated by dimension, pp. 14–22) has only ¼ as many examples, although Turner has listed 220 papyrus texts in that table altogether.
P. Berl. 6790; van Haelst, 432; Turner, NT Parch. 54B.

The other two unidentified texts published by Treu (e) are reprinted here with the hope that re-exposure may stimulate a further attempt to place them. Treu's publication includes plates.
(i) *P. Berl.* 6781 (provenance unknown, VI); fragment (8B × 7.4H cm.) from a papyrus codex with parts of 6–8 lines surviving. Following the *nomen sacrum* in *l*.13 is a space (to mark a sense break? — see the Jn text immediately above). Van Haelst, 1126.

recto

].̣.̣[.̣].̣.̣
]ακοαι δ αι παρ
].̣.̣ των αυτου
]λης ει νυ̣ν̣
5] ωνεποσ
]αρ̣αμουαν
]ως ουσ̣αι

verso

ν [.̣.̣.̣].̣υ.̣.̣[
τινδιοπα̣ [
10 καλεσαντ[
αξιους τη̣ [
νον ως δε[
κ̄ω̄ δαὶ̣ [
ειναι τ[
15 .̣.̣ α[

(ii) *P. Berl*. 16704 (provenance unknown, Byzantine period): parchment fragment (5B × 3.5H cm.) probably from a codex with parts of 6–8 lines. Read ἐπιτελεῖτε or -ται (3), χαίρομεν or -ωμεν (10), ματαιότητα (12). At *l*.12 *nu* has been added as a correction above the line. In view of the first person plural forms at *ll*.4–10 Treu thinks this may be a liturgical piece. Van Haelst, 888.

recto

```
 ] . και χαρ[
 ]μονος θ̅ς̅ κεφ[
 ]τηριον επιτελιτε[
 ]ειδομεν οτησει[
5 ]αυγκρ . [
   ] . [
```

verso

```
                ]σιν[
   ] . φιλανθρ[
   ]ωφητεσκαη . [
10 τ]ου θ̅υ̅ χερωμε[ν
   ]τε και ουκ ην[
   ]τηⁿ ματεωτητα[
   ]εναιτια[
   ] . ε[
```

8. Jn 8.19–20, 23–24 (Treu (c), 33): provenance unknown, V; inner edge of a small parchment codex leaf containing 7 of an original 18 lines (present dimensions 3.6B × 4.3H cm.).

recto

```
  ·   ·   ·   ·   ·   ·   ·
   ἤδειτε, [καὶ τὸν π̅ρ̅α̅ μου]   8.19
   ἂν ἤδειτ[ε.]
   Ταῦτα τὰ ῥ[ήματα ἐλάλησεν]   20
   ἐν τῷ γ[αζοφυλακίῳ]
5  διδά[σκων ἐν τῷ ἱερῷ·]
   καὶ οὐ[δεὶς ἐπίασεν αὐτόν,]
   ὅτι οὔπ[ω              ]
  ·   ·   ·   ·   ·   ·   ·
```

verso

```
  ·   ·   ·   ·   ·   ·   ·
   [        κ]άτω ἐσταί,   23
   [ἐγὼ ἐκ τῶν ἄν]ω εἰμί· ἐγὼ
10 [οὐκ εἰμὶ ἐκ το]ῦ κόσμου
   [τούτου. εἶπον ο]ὖν ὑμῖν   24
   [ὅτι ἀποθανεῖσθε] ἐν ταῖς
   [ἁμαρτίαις ὑμῶ]ν· ἐὰν
   [γὰρ μὴ πιστεύσ]ητε ὅτι ἐγώ
```

Despite the small amount of surviving text it clearly sides with the Alexandrian (or H) group. The space at the end of *l*.2 with the large initial T out in the margin (*l*.3) indicates a sense break (see no.6 above). At 8.23 the scribe has omitted a clause accidentally: between εἰμί and ἐγώ in *l*.9 should occur ὑμεῖς ἐκ τούτου τοῦ κόσμου.
P. Berl. 14049. Gregory/Aland 0264; van Haelst, 449; Turner, NT Parch. 59A.

9. Rom. 3.23–25, 27–30 (Treu (f), 379–86): Fayum, V init.; ten lines in one column surviving on either side of a two-column parchment codex which originally had 26 lines per column. Dimensions of the full page, 14B × c.20H cm. What makes this text all the more interesting is that another leaf from the same codex had already been published: Treu recognized its connection with *MPER* 4 (1946) 42 (*P. Vindob. Gr.* 36113), containing Rom. 2.21–23; 3.8–9. Both leaves are printed below with Treu's revised readings included in the older fragment.

leaf 1 recto

πτειν κλέπτε[ι]ς; ὁ   2.21,22
λέγων μὴ μοι[χεύει(ν)
μοι[χε]ύεις; ὁ [βδελυσ-
σόμε[νος τὰ εἴδωλα
5 ἱεροσυ[λεῖς; ὃς ἐν νό-   23
μ[ῳ καυχᾶσαι, διὰ τῆς
π[αραβάσεως ...
. [

verso

ὅτι ποιήσωμεν τὰ   3.8
10 κακὰ ἵ]να ἔλθη ἐφ' ἡ-
μᾶς τὰ] ἀγαθά; [ὧ]ν τὸ
κρίμα ἔνδικό]ν ἐστι(ν)·
τί οὖν; προεχό]μεθα;   9
οὐ πάντως· προ]η-
15 τιασάμεθα γὰρ 'Ιο]υ-
δαίους ...   ].

leaf 2 recto

... καὶ ὑστερο]ῦ[ν   3.23
ται τῆς δόξη]ς το[ῦ
θῦ, δικαιούμ]ενοι   24
δωρεὰν τῇ α]ὐτοῦ
5 χάριτι διὰ τῆς] ἀπο-
λυτρώσεως] τῆς ἐ(ν)
Χῶ Ῑυ· ὃν προέ]θετο   25
ὁ θ̅ς̅ ἱλαστήριο]ν δι-
ὰ πίστεως ἐν τ]ῷ αὐ-
10 τοῦ αἵματι, εἰς ἐ]νδι

verso

λα] δ[ιὰ νόμου πίστε-   27
ως.] λο[γιζόμεθα γὰρ   28
δικαι[οῦσθαι πίστει
ανον [χωρὶς ἔργων
15 νόμ[ου. ἢ 'Ιουδαίων   29
ὁ θ̅ς̅ [μόνον; οὐχὶ
καὶ [ἐθνῶν; ναὶ καὶ   30
ἐθ[νῶν ἐπείπερ
εἷ[ς ὁ θ̅ς̅ ὃς δικαιώ-
20 σ[ει ...

Treu's finely developed discussion shows that between Rom. 3.9 and 3.23 in
this codex there are c.52 lines missing. He calculates that the ten extant lines
of the new piece belong to the middle of the leaf, and that the two leaves are
successive, probably forming a connected sheet. Furthermore, the preceding
section of Romans would have fitted on to three leaves of this size (i.e. 14B ×
c.20H cm.) and allowed room for a title. Consequently our leaves are nos. 4
and 5 of a codex, being thus the centre sheet of a quaternion. But Treu goes
further. He suggests that this codex must have begun with Romans and
therefore these leaves belong to the first quaternion in the codex. Romans
would have required 48 pages (i.e. three quaternion 'gatherings') of the above
dimensions, the entire Pauline corpus c.480 pages (30 'gatherings'). This would
have been an impressive size for a codex (Turner, 83, mentions that the largest
sizes of the V–VI Tura papyrus codices — gatherings in quaternions — is
480pp.) and it is most unlikely that the whole NT was included. Romans would
thus be the most plausible starting point for the codex (Treu, 382). But his
calculation (382) of the proportional size of Romans is astray. Romans
constitutes not ¹⁄₁₀ but slightly more than ⅕ of the Pauline corpus, or if Heb.
is added, slightly more than ⅙. (This calculation is made on the basis of the
number of pages of NT text in Nestle/Aland[26].) Even if we work with the latter
fraction only some 18 or 19 quaternion gatherings would be required, i.e. 288
or 304 pages. So while Treu's suggestion that the codex contained the Pauline
material alone is not ruled out, it is not an inevitable conclusion to draw, given
that larger codices of similar format and period survive. Furthermore, there are

other variables in the make-up of codices which can never be excluded when one is attempting a reconstruction on the basis of a very small surviving portion of a codex. In particular, some codices are known to have been made up of a variety of quite disparate texts. The 'Apology of Phileas', *P. Bodmer* 20 (see **106** below) belongs to a composite codex which includes some NT texts, Melito, a hymn fragment, OT verse texts and the *Nativity of Mary*: see Turner, 79–80, Table 12, for details, and pp. 79–82 for discussion of composite codices. Another example represented elsewhere in this year's volume of *New Docs* is *P. Barc.* which includes both Christian (a Latin antiphonal psalm) and Classical (Cic., *in Cat.*) texts: see **92** below. Another variable which cannot be settled when only a small amount survives is whether the gatherings are all of uniform size (in the case of the 'Romans' codex under discussion, e.g., whether all gatherings were quaternions). On this see Turner, 57, 61 (gatherings of twos and threes are usually mixed with gatherings of other sizes). For some examples of Christian parchment codices which have quaternions but not exclusively so, note Turner, 61, Table 8, Parchment nos. 2, 3; *P. Bodmer Composite*, mentioned just above, is a papyrus codex with gatherings of fours and threes (Turner, 62, Table 9).

As to textual points note ἐφ' ἡμᾶς (*ll*.10–11 on the first leaf). Rom. 3.8: the codex provides a very early witness to this reading which is not common and elsewhere confined to much later texts. In the second leaf at *l*.8 (Rom. 3.25) διὰ τῆς πίστεως occurs in B and the Koine text-group. Further, at *l*.18 (Rom. 3.30) the longer reading ἐπείπερ should be preferred (on the basis of the amount of space available), and accords with Western (D, G) and Koine readings against εἴπερ S, A, B, etc.

P. Vindob. Gr. 26083; Gregory/Aland 0219; van Haelst, 494 (*MPER* 4.42); Turner, NT Parch. 81.

10. Gal. 1.9-12, 19-22; 4.25-27, 28-31 (Treu (c), 33-35): Fayum, V; three parchment fragments from the one codex, two belonging to the middle and lower half of the same leaf (*P. Berl.* 6791, eleven lines, 3.2B × 5.9H cm.; *P. Berl.* 6792, seven lines, 2.8B × 5.6H cm.). The third piece (*P. Berl.* 14043, 3.5B × 14.2H cm.) comprises 20 lines from the upper outside edge of another leaf. When complete this codex had 25 lines in each of two columns per page. Turner, 161, NT Parch. 93B, reconstructs the original height of the codex as 20 cm., but no accurate idea of the breadth can be retrieved. Between the two surviving leaves occurs a lacuna, the text of which would require five leaves; Treu suggests that we may have the first and seventh leaves of a quaternion.

leaf 1 recto

. . . . .				
[γ]ελ[ίζεται παρ' ὅ]	1.9	10	λος οὐ[κ ἂν ἤμην.]	
παρε[λάβετε,]			[γ]νω[ρίζω δὲ ὑμῖν,]	11
ἀνάθ[εμα ἔστω.]			[ἀδ]ελφ[οί, τὸ εὐ-]	
Ἄρτι γ[ὰρ ̅α̅ν̅ο̅υ̅ς̅]	10		αγγέλι[ον τὸ εὐ-]	
5 πείθω [ἢ τὸν ̅θ̅ν̅;]			αγγελισ[θὲν]	
ἢ ζητ[ῶ ̅α̅ν̅ο̅ι̅ς̅]		15	[ὑ]π' ἐμοῦ [ὅτι]	
ἀρέσκ[ειν; εἰ ἔ-]			[οὐκ ἔστιν κ[ατὰ]	
τι ἀνθρ[ώποις]			[α]νον· οὐ[δὲ γὰρ]	12
ἤρεσκ[ον, ̅χ̅υ̅ δοῦ-]			[ἐ]γὼ παρ[ὰ]	

verso

```
        .    .    .    .        .    .
        [        ]  . . [        ]                    ["Επειτα ἦ]λθον εἰς              21
20      [        ἀπο]στόλω⁻              19          [τὰ κλί]μᾳτᾳ [τῆς]
        [οὐκ εἶδο]ν· εἰ μὴ                  30      [Συρίας] ᾳᾳ[ὶ τῆς]
        ['Ιάκωβο]ν τὸν ἀ-                          [Κιλικ]ίας. ἤμη[ν]              22
        [δελφὸ]ν τοῦ κ̅υ̅.                           [δὲ ἀγ]νοούμε-
        [ἃ δὲ γρά]φω ὑμῖν,        20                [νος] τῷ προσ-
25      [ἰδοὺ ἐν]ώπι̣[ον]                            [ώπῳ] ταῖς ἐκκ[λη-]
        [τοῦ θ̅υ̅] ὅτι οὐ ψεύ-              35      [σίαι]ς τῆς 'Ιουδαί-]
        [δομαι.]                                     [ας τ]ᾳῖς ἐν Χ̅[ῷ]
```

leaf 2 recto   *verso*

```
        [ . . ]ρ[ . . . . . . . ]        4.25         [        ἐ]πᾳ[γγε]              28
        [ὅρ]ο[ς ἐστὶν ἐν]                            [λί]ας [τ]έκ[να]
        [τῇ] 'Αραβίᾳ· [συν-]                         [ἔσ]ται· ἀλ[λ' ὥσ-]           29
40      [στ]οιχεῖ δὲ [τῇ]                    60      [πε]ρ τότε [ὁ κα-]
        [νῦ]ν Ι̅λ̅η̅μ̅· [δου-]                          [τὰ] σάρκα [γεν-]
        [λεύ]ει γὰρ μ[ετὰ]                           [νη]θεὶς ἐ[δίω-]
        [τῶ]ν τέκν[ων]                               [κεν] τὸν κ[ατὰ π̅ν̅α̅,]
        [αὐ]τῆς.[·]ἡ δ[ὲ ἄ-]              26        [ο]ὕτως κ[αὶ νῦν.]
45      [νω Ι̅]λ̅η̅μ̅ ἐλ[ευ-]                  65      [ἀ]λλὰ τί λέ[γει ἡ]            30
        [θέρ]α ἐστίν, [ἥ-]                           [γ]ραφή; ἔ[κβαλε]
        [τις ἐ]στὶν μ̅[η̅ρ̅]                           τὴν πα[ιδίσκην]
        [πάν]των ἡμῶ[ν·]                             καὶ τὸν [υἱὸν]
        [γέγρα]πται γάρ·              27            αὐτῆς· [οὐ γὰρ]
50      [εὐφρά]νθητι,                        70      μὴ κλη[ρονομή-]
        [στεῖρ]α ἡ οὐ τί                            [σ]ει ὁ ὑἱ[ὸς τῆς]
        [κτου]σα· ῥῆξο⁻                              παιδίσ[κης με-]
        [καὶ βόη]σον, ἡ                              τὰ τοῦ [υἱοῦ τῆς]
        [οὐκ ὠ]δίνου                                 ἐλευ[θέρας.]
55      [σα· ὅτι] πολλὰ                      75      διό, ἀ[δελφοί,]              31
        [τὰ τέκν]ᾳ τῆς                              οὐ[κ        ]
        .    .    .    .                            .    .    .    .
```

Nomina sacra are often abbreviated but, as has been noticed for some other texts (e.g. no. 7 above; cf. no. 13 below), not consistently. Treu implies that υἱός (partly or entirely restored at *ll*.68, 71, 73) is not shortened because it does not refer to Christ. This distinction does hold good frequently, but as a criterion to differentiate the practice within this text it is clearly invalidated by Gal. 1.10 (*ll*.4, 6, 8). Here ἄνθρωπος is abbreviated twice (in view of the available space) and written in full once; all three words refer to mankind in general. *Ll*.20, 52 have examples of the superior bar at line end as an equivalent for final *nu* (cf. no.1 above).

The textual affinities of this Galatians codex fragment lie with the Alexandrian (H) group. Western readings are avoided as are those of idiosyncratic MSS.

Gregory/Aland, 0261; van Haelst, 517; Turner, NT Parch. 93B.

11. Gal. 3.13–17 (Treu (d)): Qubbat al-ḥazna, Damascus, V; leaf from a parchment uncial palimpsest (Arabic written above) discovered and photographed, but not published, by B. Violet in 1901 (see **87**, no.1). Text now lost. 18 lines are legible of a 20-line single-column page (no photo was made of the other side of the leaf).

ετε ἀλλήλοις.	5.13	λέγω δὲ πνι περιπα-	16
Ὁ γὰρ πᾶς νόμος ἐν ἑ-	14	τεῖτε καὶ ἐπιθυμία(ν)	
νὶ λόγῳ πεπλήρω-		σ[αρ]κὸς οὐ μὴ τε-	
ται, ἐν τῷ, ἀγαπήσεις		λ[έσητ]ε. ἡ γὰρ σὰρξ	17
5 τὸν πλησίον σου	15	ἐ[πιθ]υμεῖ κατὰ τοῦ	
ὡς σεαυτόν.		πν[ς], τὸ δὲ πνα κατὰ	
Εἰ δὲ ἀλ[λή]λους [δ]άκνε-	15	τῆ[ς σαρκός,] ταῦτα	
τε κα[ὶ κατεσθίετε,		γὰ[ρ ...	
βλέπ[ετε μὴ ὑπ᾽ ἀλ-		. . . .	
10 λήλων ἀναλώθ[ητε.	20	. . . .	

The text is good, and belongs to the Alexandrian group, following S, B against Western readings at *ll*.3 (πληροῦται D *et al*.), 4 (D omits ἐν τῷ), 6 (ἑαυτόν in F, G, *al*.), 7 (D, F, G have ἀλλήλους after κατεσθίετε), 9–11 (the same trio have ὑπ᾽ ἀλλήλων after ἀναλωθῆτε). New sense sections are indicated at *ll*. 2 and 7 by the larger initial letter, which is also moved a little out into the margin, both the immediately previous lines ending short (cf. no. 7 above).

Gregory/Aland 0254; van Haelst, 521; not listed in Turner.

12. 1 Tim. 1.4–5, 6–7 (Treu (c), 36): Fayum, VI; upper part of a parchment double leaf (i.e. a sheet), each 9 cm. wide with the fold-mark and holes (for stitching?) visible. The second leaf is entirely blank. The first preserves seven of an original c. eleven lines. Surviving height (max.), 8 cm.; i.e., the original format was nearly square. The text is thus to be situated within Turner's class XIV (Table 2, p.29; see above, no. 7). On parchment codices with fairly square dimensions see Turner, 31. On the sense break markers in *ll*.1, 13, 14, see no.14 below.

recto

χουσιν μᾶλλον´´	1.4
ἢ οἰκονομίαν θῡ	
τὴν ἐν πίσ[τει·]	
τὸ δὲ τέλ[ος τῆς]	5
5 παραγ[γελίας ἐσ-]	
τὶν ἀγ[άπη ἐκ κα-]	
θα[ρᾶς]	
· · · · · · ·	

verso

νες ἀστοχήσαν	6
τες ἐξετράπτησαν	
10 εἰς ματαιολογίαν,	
θ[έ]λ[ο]ντες εἶναι	7
[νομοδ]ιδάσκαλοι,	
[μὴ νοοῦν]τες´´ μή-	
[τε ἃ λέγουσιν]´´ μή-	
[τε]	
· · · · · ·	

No clear-cut textual affinities are apparent. Treu suggests that the unskilled hand may indicate that the text is a school exercise or a writing specimen. Other school exercises which use biblical or related Christian texts are:—

1. Paris Louvre inv. *MND* 552 E, F (B. Boyaval, *ZPE* 17 [1975] 145–50 [pl.5b]) two wooden tablets (7.5B × 19H cm.) with Ps. 92 entire; provenance unknown, IV[1]; van Haelst, 205.

2. Paris Louvre inv. *MND* 552, H, I, K, L (B. Boyaval, ibid. 225–35, pl. 7–8), five (*sic*) wooden tablets (13.5B × 18H cm.) with Ps. 146 entire on tablet I face 2 and tablet H. (Other tablets contain a miscellany of non-Christian texts, including a table of fractions and a list of proper names. Three different hands are in evidence: the pupil, Aurelius Papnouthion [who signed his name in three places], wrote out the Psalm.) Provenance unknown, IV init.; van Haelst, 239.

3. Paris Louvre ined., wood tablet with beginning of Lord's prayer (Mt.); Antinoopolis, date unclear, *non vidi*; van Haelst, 349.

4. *P. Vindob. L.* 91 ined., papyrus text in Latin with part of Lord's prayer written out twice: probably a school exercise; Fayum, V/VI, *non vidi*; van Haelst, 1206.

5. *P. Oxy.* 2 (1899) 209, papyrus (25.1B × 19.9H cm.) whose *recto* includes Rom. 1.1–7 in eleven lines: probably a school exercise although an amulet has also been suggested as its function; Oxyrhynchos, IV; Gregory/Aland 𝔓[10]; Van Haelst, 490; Aland, pp.228, 357 (large bibliography provided); cf. Turner, 209.

6. *P. Amh.* 1 (1900) 3b, papyrus text with Heb. 1.1: probably a writing exercise, although an amulet has also been suggested as its function; Fayum, end III; Gregory/Aland 𝔓[12]; van Haelst, 536; Aland, pp.231, 360 (bibliography provided).

7. *P. Heid.* 1 (1905) 5, papyrus (17.5B × 18H cm.) whose *recto* contains a sacred onomasticon, transcribing into Greek Hebrew words from the Bible; *verso* blank; school exercise or amulet(?); provenance unknown, end III/IV init.; van Haelst, 1136.

8. W.E. Crum, *The Monastery of Epiphanius at Thebes, 2. Coptic Ostraca and Papyri* (New York, 1926), no. 589; Coptic ostrakon with eleven lines of text: fragment of a homily or a school exercise(?); van Haelst, 1098.

P. Berl. 3605; Gregory/Aland 0259; van Haelst, 531; Turner, NT Parch. 100B.

13. 1 Tim. 1.15–16 (Treu (c), 36–37, pl.3): provenance unknown, c. VII; strip of parchment 12B × 7.5H cm. with text in two columns of six lines each; hair side blank. A cross is written above col.1. The orthography is very poor: note too the inconsistent treatment of *nomina sacra* at *l*.3 (cf. nos.7, 10 above).

col.1	†		*col.2*	
[πισ]τὸς ὠ λλόκος		1.15	ὁμ πρῶτός ἱμιν	
καὶ πάσης ἀποτοχῆς			ἐγώ, ἀλὰ διὰ τᾶτο	16
ἄξιος, ὅτι Χριστὸς Ῑϲ			ἐλεήθην, ἵνα ἐν ἐ-	
[ἦλθεν] εἰ[ϲ τ]ὼν			10 μοὶ πρότῳ ἐνδί[ξη-]	
5 [κόσμον ἁμα]ρ-			τε Χϲ [Ῑϲ] τὴν [ἄπα-]	
[τωλοὺς σῶσαι·]			[σαν μακροθυμίαν]	

This parchment may well have served as an amulet: the text would be appropriate and its being written in two columns would have allowed a fold in the middle. Van Haelst lists 118 Christian amulets in his *Catalogue*, nearly 10% of his total inventory.

P. Berl. 13977; Gregory/Aland 0262; van Haelst 532; Turner, NT Parch. 100A ('*not* a codex').

14. Heb. 10.10–12, 28–30 (Treu (c), 37–38, pl.4): Fayum, VII; papyrus fragment (5.3B × 11.2H cm.) from the inner side of a codex leaf; 15 and 17 lines *recto* and *verso* respectively survive from an original 32 in two columns to the page.

recto

    · · · · · ·

    ασμε[νοι ἐσμὲν διὰ]   10.10
    τῆς προσ[φορᾶς τοῦ]
    σώματο[ς Ῑυ Χ̄υ ἐφά-]
    παξ˙˙ κα[ὶ πᾶς μὲν]   11
5   ἱερεὺς ἕσ[τηκεν κα-]
    θ᾽ ἡμέραν [λειτουρ-]
    γῶν κα[ὶ τὰς αὐτὰς]
    προσφέρ[ων θυ-]
    σίας˙˙ αἵ[τινες οὐδέ-]
10 ποτε δύν[ανται πε-]
    ριελεῖν ἁ[μαρτίας·]
    αὐτὸς δὲ μ[ίαν ὑπὲρ]   12
    ἁμαρτιῶ[ν προσε-]
    νέγκας θ[υσίαν εἰς]
15 τὸ διηνε[κὲς   ]
    · · · · · ·

verso

    · · · · · ·

    [ἀθετή]σας   28
    [τις νόμον] Μωϋσέ
    [ως χωρὶς ο]ἰκτειρ-
    [μῶν ἐπὶ] δυσὶν
20 [ἢ τρισὶν] μάρτυσιν
    [ἀποθνήσ]κει˙˙ πόσῳ   29
    [δοκεῖτε] χείρο-
    [νος ἀξιω]θήσεται
    [τιμωρία]ς ὁ τὸν ῡν
25 [τοῦ θ̄υ κα]ταπατή-
    [σας καὶ τὸ] αἷμα
    [τῆς διαθ]ήκης κοι
    [νὸν ἡγη]σάμενος˙˙
    [ἐν ᾧ ἡγι]άσθη˙˙
30 [καὶ τὸ π̄]ν̄α τῆς
    [χάριτος ἐ]νυβρίσας
    [οἴδαμεν] γὰρ τὸν   30
    · · · · · ·

Treu says that papyrus codices of the NT containing two columns are rare in contrast to parchment examples. Turner's table 16 makes this very apparent. Of the 83 NT papyri he lists (the Gregory/Aland list has reached nearer 100 by now) only five have two columns (taking 𝔓⁶⁴ and 𝔓⁶⁷ as part of the same codex). Contrast the NT parchment codices: he inventories 162 of which 66 have two columns and another nine may do so — almost half the full number he includes.

The textual affinities of this fragment are not easy to classify. There are links with both Alexandrian and Byzantine text groups. It does not attest readings of distinctive witnesses such as D. At Heb. 10.10 πολλάκις is omitted between αὐτὰς προσφέρων (*ll*.7–8): this omission is not elsewhere attested. Note the superior double stroke at the end of words in *ll*.4, 9, 21, 28, 29 — markers to indicate a sense break.

P. Berl. 6774; Gregory/Aland 𝔓⁷⁹; van Haelst, 540; Aland p.315; Turner, 𝔓⁷⁹.

Brief notice may be added here of the two most recently published NT papyrus texts: C. Gallazzi, *ZPE* 46 (1982) 117–22 (pl.3), has published two fragments

surviving from two separate leaves of a codex (Medînet Mâdi, III/IV) which
contained the Pauline epistles. Frag. 1 (5B × 7.2H cm.) has Eph. 1.11–13, 19–21
(this is our only papyrus witness to these verses of Eph.); frag. 2 (2B × 4H cm.)
has 2 Thes. 1.4–5, 11–12 (the earliest papyrus witness to these verses of 2 Thes.).
The text appears to be Alexandrian. C. Römer has published in *P. Köln* 4 (1982)
170, pp.28–31 (pl.1b), a fragment from a codex leaf containing parts of Philemon
(vv.13–15, 24–25; provenance unknown, early III). This is our earliest witness to
that NT letter. The fragment has been allocated the number 𝔓⁸⁷ by the Institut für
neutestamentliche Textforschung, Münster. These texts will be considered further
in a later number of *New Docs*. I am grateful to S.R. Pickering for drawing them
to my attention. He has also informed me of J.R. Royse, *Scribal Habits in Early
Greek New Testament Papyri* (Diss., Graduate Theological Union, 1981), which
studies in detail 𝔓⁴⁵, 𝔓⁴⁶, 𝔓⁴⁷, 𝔓⁶⁶, 𝔓⁷², 𝔓⁷⁵.

A considerable number of the texts listed here contain *nomina sacra*. In addition
to bibliographical items mentioned at *New Docs 1976*, **69,** note the following:
G. Howard, *JBL* 96 (1977) 63-83, a thought-provoking discussion of the Tetragrammaton and the NT; and C.P.H. Bammel, *JTS* 30 (1979) 430–62, on abbreviations used in fifty-century scriptoria. Neither of these articles shows acquaintance
with S. Brown, *Stud.Pap.* 9 (1970) 7–19, however, who, in his consideration of the
origin of *nomina sacra*, makes an important critique of the earlier views of L.
Traube and A.H.R.E. Paap.

S.R. Pickering has provided the following description of an as yet unpublished
fragment of Acts in the Macquarie papyrus collection. The papyrus of the Acts of
the Apostles held by Macquarie University (*P. Macquarie* inv. 360, of unknown
provenance) consists of two pieces. The main fragment is 9.6cm. high x 1.8cm.
broad. It is a portion of a leaf of a codex, with text lost at top, bottom and both
sides of the fragment. On the front, written at right angles to the direction of the
fibres, are the remains of 13 lines from Acts 2.30–37; on the back, parallel with the
fibres, are the remains of 12 lines from Acts 2.46 (45? — the first line has small
traces only. Which verse it belongs to depends on where in the codex leaf the
fragment is to be located.). The handwriting is neat, medium-sized, with some
cursive elements. A dating of c.200 seems possible, with the necessary palaeo-
graphical qualifications understood. Three *nomina sacra* are preserved ($\overline{\pi\rho[\varsigma}$, $\overline{\chi\rho\nu}$
and $\overline{\iota]\eta\nu}$), and others can be assumed for the lost portions of the pages. The size
and spacing of letters vary, so that the number of letters lost on either side of the
fragment cannot be ascertained definitely. It is clear, however, that between *l*.11
and *l*.12 of the front the text contained more script than the text and apparatus of
Nestle-Aland²⁶ can supply, suggesting a scribal error or alteration or an unusual text
tradition at this point. Otherwise the text accords closely with that of NA²⁶ and may
be categorized as 'Egyptian' or 'Alexandrian', with due allowances being made for
the imprecision of these terms. On the other hand, certain 'Western' readings are
definitely excluded. (The second piece is a tiny fragment, 0.35 x 0.25cm — which
is height and which breadth have not been determined. It was found adhering to
the front of the main fragment. Parts of two unidentified letters are preserved on
either side. The ink and the papyrus material are like those of the main fragment,
suggesting that the smaller fragment belonged to the same leaf or another leaf of
the same codex.) The papyrus has been registered by the Institut für
neutestamentliche Textforschung, Münster, as 𝔓⁹¹.

92. A fourth-century hymn to the Virgin Mary?

Provenance unknown (probably Egypt)   IV

ed.pr. — R. Roca-Puig, *Himne a la Verge Maria 'Psalmus Responsorius'.*
Papir llatí del segle IV (Barcelona 1965²)

leaf 1 *recto*
  psalmus responsorius

    pater, qui omnia regis,
    p⟨r⟩eco christi nos scias heredes.
    christus, verbo natus,
    per quem populus est liberatus.

5 *audiamus, fratres, magnalia dei.*
    primum dominus davit elegit,
    qui duodecim reges servire fecit.
    inde est progenies d(omi)ni mei
    iesum χρ(istu)m quem dicimus naξarenum,
10 *omnes profetae quem profetarunt,*
    dei filium venturum clamarunt.

    benedictus et potens est ipse pater.
    anna, quae sterilis dicebatur,
leaf 2 *verso*
    munus offerens d(e)o, sic revocatur.
15 *lacrumis diurno d(eu)m rogabat,*
    sterilitatem filiorum sibi im⟨probabat⟩.
    angelu[s] missus ad illam venit;
    orationem faciebat, sic illam invenit.
    vocem audibit, verbo concepit,
20 *inde maria virgo devenit.*

    claritas d(e)i demonstrabatur
    trima cum esset in templo data
    a parentibus, vota quia sic fecerant.
    cum sacerdotibus ibi fuit;
25 *plus patrem et matrem iam non requesibit.*
    quasi columba, sic ambulabat,
    et ab angelis manna [s]umebat.

leaf 2 *recto*
    duodecim annorum puella, tamen
    in templo reclusa magnificatur,
30 *et ab angelis diurno sic custoditur.*
    cum sacerdotibus diceretur
    de maria virgine 'sponso detur',
    viri prudentes sortes miserunt,
    ut, ostensa, iosepi daretur.

35 *ex{c}ierunt ambo de templo, pares.*
    tristis, iosep cogitare coepit
    de puella per sortem quae ad illum venit.
    animo suo dicere coepit:
    'si deo sic placet, quid faciam? tamen
40 *puella quam d(omi)n(u)s diligebat*
    custod[i]enda est mihi data', dicebat.

leaf 3 *verso*
    facta est ad fontem sola venire.
    vocem angelicam tunc ibi audibit
    et neminem v⟨i⟩dit.
45 *verbum in utero ferens, sic inde ibit.*
    spasmum passa, mirari coepit.
    reputans animo suo sic dicebat:
    'ego ancilla sum d(e)i', clamabat.

    gaudet maria per omnes dies.
50 *contigit iter dum pares agunt,*
    in rure devenerunt ambo. tamen
    'urguet me valde iosep', dicit,
    'quod in utero fero, foris prodire'.
    respicit locum, spelunc{h}am vidit
leaf 3 *recto*
55 *tenebrosam et obscuram, sic illoc ibit.*
    vox infantis mox audibatur,
    lux magna et praeclara illic videbatur,
    signum de caelo demonsʾsʾt⟨r⟩abatur;
    χρ(istu)s natus esse dicebatur.

60 *haec sunt gesta per omnia. tamen*
    signa de caelo graeci viderunt,
    cognoverunt esse iam χρ(istu)m natum.
    ex{s}ierunt, coeperunt ambulare.
    devenerunt tandem ad civitatem.
65 *vociti venerunt ad herodem:*
    latenter querebat interrogare
    '⟨re⟩x iudeorum si quando venit,
    ut ego ipse illum possim adorare'.

    inde reversi cum gratia. tamen
leaf 4 *verso*
70 *stellam ab oriente postquam viderunt,*
    quae praecedens eos, demonstrabat viam.
    venit ad locum et ibi stetit,
    d(e)i filium illic esse demonstrabit.
    introeuntes, puerum viderunt.
75 *prostrati, illum adoraberunt.*

    kandida munera offerebant,
    aurum tus et murram.
    cum gratia reversi per aliam viam.
    sensit {se} herodes delusum se esse;
80 *in bethleen misit, iratus valde;*
    omnes infantes illic attentabit,
    pro nomine χρ(ist)i, quem sic zelabit.
    vox plangentium illic sonabat,
    om⟨n⟩is mater pro filio plorabat.

leaf 4 *recto*

85 *latebat infans cum matre. tamen*
    angelus missus per somnum dicit:
    'ex⟨s⟩urge, iosep, et infantem sume;
    secede in aegypto, et esto ibi.
    querit infantem herodes', dicit,
90 *'ut scriptura profetarum adinpleatur:*
    ex aegypto vocabo electum meum —
    semitas ei rectas parat[[a]]*e'.*

    magnum mirabil{a}e signum ficit
    in galilea, qua primum ibit,

95 *nuptiarum votum, ibide⟨m⟩ fuit,*
    vocitus et ipse, sic illoc ibit,
    cum discipulis suis, quos sibi elegit.
    tunc ei dicitur: 'vinum non est'.
    respondit: 'mulier, mihi et tibi quid est?'
100 *aquae ministros ad se vocabit:*
    'metretas aquae inpl [
    sign[
    are[

(Leaf 5 *verso* and *recto* very fragmentary. There survive only the beginnings of some lines and the ends of others.)

The text above contains numerous emendations by *ed.pr.* and others. Note especially *l*.2, *peco* (*P.Barc.*), *peto* (Roca-Puig), *preco* (Barigazzi); *l*.16 *im* (*P.Barc.*), *imprecabatur* (Roca-Puig), *imputabat* or *improbabat* (Barigazzi); *l*.27 *umemac* (*P.Barc.*), *sumebat* (Roca-Puig). At *l*.47 where I have printed *reputans* *P.Barc.* reads *refugens*, and Roca-Puig proposes *refugiens*. The orthography shows some interesting features: *l*.6 *davit* — David; *–b–* appears frequently for *–v–* (e.g. *audibit*, 19); 'i' and 'e' are confused (*requesibit* for *requisivit*, 20); 'u' for 'i' (*lacrumis*, 15), etc.

Bib. — Roca-Puig's edition attracted many reviews, among which note particularly G. Lazzati, *Aeg.* 46 (1966) 120–23; C.H. Roberts, *JTS* 18 (1967) 492–94; W. Speyer, *JbAC* 10 (1967) 211–16. See further A.M. Emmett, *Proc. XIV Int. Cong. Pap.* (Oxford, 1975) 97–102; ead., *MPL* 2 (1977) 99–108; R. Seider, *Paläographie der lateinischen Papyri* II.2 (Stuttgart, 1981) 126–28, no.49 (pl.23).

Father, you who rule all things, I pray that you may know us as the heirs of Christ. Christ, born by the word, by whom (the) people have been set free.
5 **|Let us hear, brothers, the great deeds of God. First the Lord chose David, who made the twelve kings to serve him. From him is the generation of my**
10 **Lord whom we call Jesus Christ the Nazarene, |whom all the prophets foretold; they cried out that the Son of God would come. Blessed and powerful is the Father Himself. Anna, who was called barren, making an**
15 **offering to God was called back. |With tears daily she would implore God; she kept blaming herself for her barrenness of children. An angel was sent and came to her; she was praying, thus he found her. She heard his voice, she**
20 **conceived by the word; |thence the Virgin Mary came into being. The splendour of God was shown when at three years old she was presented in the temple by her parents, since they had thus vowed. She remained there with**
25 **the priests, | no longer now did she seek after her father and mother. Like a dove she used to walk about and to receive manna from the angels. As a**
30 **girl of twelve years, shut away in the temple, she was glorified |and by angels was guarded daily. When it was said to the priests about the Virgin Mary 'Let her be given to a bridegroom', wise men cast lots with the result that (when**
35 **the lot was) revealed, she was given to Joseph. |They both left the temple, united in marriage. Melancholy, Joseph began to reflect on the maiden who**

came to him by lot. He began to say in his heart, 'If such is the will of God,
40 what am I to do? |So the maiden whom the Lord loved has been given to me
to look after', he said. She went alone to a fountain. There, in that place she
45 heard the voice of an angel and saw nobody. |Bearing the Word in her womb,
so she departed the place. Feeling (the baby) leaping (within) she began to
marvel. After pondering in her mind, she spoke, 'I am the handmaid of the
50 Lord', she cried. Mary rejoiced every day. |It happened while the pair were
making their way they came together in(to) a rural place. 'I feel strongly
urged, Joseph', she said, 'to bring forth what I bear in my womb'. She looked
55 about the place and saw a cave, |shadowy and hidden, and she went into it.
Soon the cry of a baby was heard, a great and glorious light was seen there,
60 a sign was shown forth from heaven. The birth of Christ was announced. |All
these events took place. And Greeks saw the signs from heaven, they
recognized that Christ was now born. Out they went, they began to walk, and
65 at last they came to the town. |They were summoned and appeared before
Herod. He sought to interrogate them privately (saying), 'If the king of the
Jews has come, (tell me) that I myself may worship him'. They turned back
70 with the grace (of God). |Afterwards, they saw a star from the east which,
going before them, showed the way. It came to the spot and stopped there,
and showed that the Son of God was in that place. Going in, they saw the
75 boy. |They fell down and worshipped him. They offered splendid gifts, gold,
frankincense and myrrh. With the grace (of God) they returned by another
80 way. Herod realized that he had been deceived |and greatly angered sent into
Bethlehem. There he attacked all the infants for the sake of the name of
Christ of whom he was so jealous. The voice of weeping was heard there;
85 every mother was lamenting for her son. |The infant lay hidden with his
mother. An angel was sent in a dream, and said, 'Rise up, Joseph, and take
the infant; go away to Egypt, and remain there. Herod seeks the infant', he
90 said, |'that the scripture of the prophets may be fulfilled: out of Egypt shall
I call my chosen one — make straight his paths.' (Jesus) performed a great
95 miracle in Galilee, where he first went. |There was a celebration of a marriage
in that place and being invited he went there with his disciples, whom he chose
for himself. Then it was said to him, 'There is no wine'. He replied, 'Woman,
100 what is that to me and you?' |He summoned to him the servants of the water:
'Fill the measures of water . . .

The *Psalmus Responsorius* has been palaeographically dated to IV (IV, Roca-Puig, Seider; IV² E.A. Lowe *Codices Latini Antiquiores Suppl.* [Oxford, 1971] no.1782). It was written in early half-uncial script by a scribe who was at times careless (–im, *l*.16) and probably more at home with Greek than Latin (naζarenum, *l*.9; Greek *nomen sacrum* in the same line). The text forms part of a 'mixed' or 'composite' codex containing both Christian and non-Christian texts — an unusual occurrence (on such codices see further Turner, *Typology*, 79 ff.). The immediately preceding section of the codex was occupied by a copy of Cicero, *Cat.* I and II (on what survives see Roca-Puig, *Aeg.* 49 [1969] 92–104). The codex also contained some Latin hexameters on Alcestis. It contained Greek texts as well as Latin; some Greek liturgical items follow the *Psalmus* in the codex (see *MPL* 2 [1977] 99 n.3).

The *Psalmus* is rhythmical and also contains some rhyming sections: these aspects are thoroughly discussed by Roca-Puig in his edition. The first four lines are the keynote. They form an introduction which I have argued elsewhere (Emmett, 1975) may well have constituted a refrain, i.e., the responsorial element.

The surviving strophes begin with the letters of the alphabet in turn. We possess the A to M strophes complete (or nearly so) and fragments of the N, O and (presumably) P strophes. The *abecedarius* form normally comprised what a writer considered the manageable parts of the alphabet, sometimes omitting X, Y and Z (K. Thraede, *JbAC* 3 [1960] 159; H. Leclercq, *DACL* 1 [1907] 364). More literary *abecedarii* were composed by Hilary of Poitiers, and the *abecedarius* form was used by St. Augustine writing against the Donatists. *Abecedarii* were commonly used for mnemonic purposes. For another Latin example see the works of Commodianus (ed. J. Martin, *Corpus Christianorum*, series Latina, vol.128), and for a Greek one *P.Amh.* 1 (1900) 2, which is like our papyrus both in dealing in part with the life of Christ, and in its rather low literary quality. (For further references on acrostics/ *abecedarii* see Emmett, 1977, n.14; *P.Köln* 4 [1982] pp.35–56.)

The date of composition of the *Psalmus* could be III or IV. Since it draws on the early stanzas on the *Protevangelium* of James (II), it must postdate that work. Its other sources (discussed in detail by Roca-Puig) seem to have been Mt. (for strophes A, H, I, K and L) and Jn (for strophe M). There are also what Roca-Puig calls 'contacts' or 'affinities' with a Sahidic *Life of Mary*.

The subject matter of the *Psalmus* has been the focus of some controversy. Is it a Hymn to Mary, as was suggested by *ed.pr.*, and as the subject matter of the stanzas drawn from the *Protevangelium* would suggest? Or does it reflect Christ the Redeemer (*l.*4) or God the Father (*l.*1)? The fragmentary nature of the N, O and P stanzas and the loss of the rest (assuming that this writer, like most *abecedarius* writers, finished the alphabet so far as he could) make these questions difficult to answer with finality.

From strophes B to G we find a condensed version of the *Protevangelium*. The focus is on Mary and Anna as her mother, but the doxology with which B begins should be noted, with its relationship to the introductory four lines and to the first line. All these reflect the prayer to God the Father *omnipotens* (παντοκράτωρ) with which the *Psalmus* opens.

It would seem that in turn Anna, Mary, Joseph and Jesus are the focus of the subject matter of the *Psalmus* (which is almost pictorial in its elaboration of each episode), but the emphasis goes back to the power of God the Father (Emmett, 1977: 107). Each strophe has one central point or incident. Additional episodes found in the *Protevangelium* concerning Mary — her development up to her third year, the weaving of the veil and the visit to Elizabeth — are omitted. The result is a simple narrative which does not exalt the human participants but demonstrates the miraculous works of God. Averil Cameron has suggested to me (*per litt.*) that evidence from other sources (including mosaics) suggests that in this period the interest in Mary is primarily Christological, i.e., less for herself than for her role as vessel of the Incarnation. The suitability, therefore, of the title proposed by Roca-Puig needs to be carefully considered.

The birth and infancy of Christ are clearly the subjects of major emphasis in most of the strophes concerning Mary: C, D and E refer to Mary's youth and betrothal, F–K to her role in the Incarnation and birth of Christ. A crucial point is that the M strophe moves straight from the flight into Egypt to Jesus' first miracle (cf. Jn 2.1–11). If either Mary, or the early life of Jesus, were the primary subject of the *Psalmus* we would expect the occasion where Jesus, at twelve years old, lingers in the Temple (Lk. 2.41–51) to have been included. The fact that we pass straight to Jesus already established in his ministry, with his disciples chosen, suggests that it is the *miracle* which the writer wishes to emphasize. Mary is not even named (in the extant part of the M strophe), and though at Jn 2.3 it is Jesus' mother who tells him there is no wine, in the *Psalmus* we find the impersonal form *dicitur* (98).

Hymns and prayers as such addressed to Mary are generally later, after the fifth-century Christological controversies, as the following list of papyri demonstrates:

1. *P.Ryl.* 3 (1938) 470 (provenance unknown, III/IV on palaeographical grounds; IV suggested by subject matter). Prayer to the Virgin, θεοτόκος. Van Haelst 983.
2. *P.Bon.* 1 (1953) 9 (provenance unknown, III–IV, *ed.pr.*; proposed later datings discussed by van Haelst). Prayer to Virgin and Longinus followed by reference to Trinity. Van Haelst 893.
3. *P.Lit.Lond.* (1927) 235 (provenance unknown, V–VI). Hymn to Christ or the Trinity and the Virgin. Van Haelst 936.
4. *P.Aberd.* (1939) 4 (Upper Egypt?, VI (?)). Ostrakon. Hymn addressed directly to the Virgin. Van Haelst 841. (Cf. *P.Aberd.* 5, prayer or hymn celebrating the Annunciation: van Haelst 842).
5. *O.Stras.* (1923) 809 (probably Thebes, VI). Ostrakon. Prayer to the Virgin. Van Haelst 830.
6. *P.Rein.* 2 (1940) 63 (provenance unknown, VI). Three-line prayer to the Virgin. Van Haelst 970.
7. *P.Vindob.G.* 2616la (provenance unknown, VI). Hymn to God and the Virgin. Van Haelst 1024.
8. *O.Skeat Mich.* (1950) 14 (bought at Luxor, VI-VII). Hymn — *Trishagion* and address to the Virgin. Van Haelst 827.
9. *P.Berl.* 13220 (Hermopolis Magna, VI/VII). Hymn for the Visitation of Mary, paraphrasing Lk. 1.41ff., 43f. Van Haelst 878.
10. *P.Berl.* 21233: *ed.pr.* — K. Treu, *AFP* 24/25 (1976) 126–27, no.8 (provenance unknown, c.VI/VII). Hymnic prayer to the Mother of God. Not in van Haelst.
11. *P.Lond.* 3 (1907) 1029 (provenance unknown, VII). Hymn to the Virgin. Van Haelst 920.
12. *BKT* 6 (1910) 7.2 (provenance unknown, VII). Prayer (amulet) containing an invocation to the Virgin. Van Haelst 733.
13. *P.Amh.* 1 (1900) 9(b) (provenance unknown, VII-VIII). Prayer to the Virgin and Longinus. Van Haelst 846.
14. *P.Baden* 4 (1924) 65 (Qarara, VII-VIII). Amulet, with prayer to the Virgin. Van Haelst 860.
15. *P.Ryl.Copt.* 35 (Hermopolis Magna(?), X–XI). Hymn concerning the Virgin, divided into 4–line strophes (Arabic text on *verso*). Van Haelst 991.
16. *Crum C.Ostr.* (1926) 514 (Deir-el-Bahri, Byzantine). Hymn to the Virgin. Van Haelst 223.
17. *Crum C.Ostr.* (1926) 515 (Deir-el-Bahri, Byzantine). Hymn to the Virgin. Van Haelst 402.
18. *O.Tait* 1 (1930) Camb. 117 (provenance unknown, Byzantine). Hymn to the Virgin. Van Haelst 831.

19. *O.Tait* 1 (1930) Camb. 118 (provenance unknown, Byzantine). Hymn to the Virgin. Van Haelst 832.
20. *P.Edfou* (1937) 310 (Upper Apollonos, Byzantine). Invocation to the Virgin. Van Haelst 905.

On the general background of the development of the cult of the Virgin see Averil Cameron, 'The Theotokos in Sixth-Century Constantinople', *JTS* 29 (1978) 79–108.

The milieu of this text merits brief comment: this aspect particularly interests Roberts: cf. the general background afforded by his *Manuscript, Society and Belief in Early Christian Egypt* (Oxford, 1979) 6, 65 ff., and D. Bonneau, *REL* 45 (1967) 557. The audience was presumably one of Latin-speaking Christians — note the interesting *graeci* (*l.*61) for the *magoi* of Mt. 2.1. To the author 'Greeks' were presumably men from the East. Although the poem is in rather crude Latin, we note that it is copied in a codex with Cic. *Cat.*, which suggests literary tastes on the part of some at least of its audience. These, and other questions concerning the *Psalmus*, still await further elucidation.

(A.M. EMMETT)

93. A liturgical version of the Christmas Night Angels' song

Provenance unknown　　　　　　　　　　　　　　　　　　c. VI
ed.pr. — K. Treu, *APF* 21 (1971) 66 (pl. 4a)

Φ]ῶς ἄνοθην ἔλαμψεν . . . .
η . . . . δε . α . α . ἡμᾶς τὸν λόγον
τῆς πίστεως καὶ ἐκυραζεν ἡμὶν
τὸν ὕμνον τὸν ἀγγέλον· δόξαν
5 ἐν ὑψίστοις θεῷ τῷ σωτῆρι ἡμῶν.
ἀλληλούια

A complete papyrus leaf, 30B × 7H cm. Written perpendicularly on either side of the text are 7 and 4 lines, probably with no connection. The other side carries a three-line certificate. In *l.*1 read φῶς ἄνωθεν; ἐκήρυξεν or possibly ἔκραζεν (ἐκραύγαζεν?) at *l.*3 — see Treu's apparatus for discussion. *P. Berl.* 11842.
Bib. — K. Treu, *MPL* 2 (1977) 251; van Haelst, 875.

Light shone from above... us the word of faith and announced to us the 5 hymn of the angels: 'Glory |in the highest to God our Saviour. Alleluia.'

Luke's account of the angels singing on the night of Christ's birth (2.14) is frequently used in modified form in liturgical contexts. *P. Berl.* 13269, published in C. Schmidt–W. Schubart, *Altchristliche Texte* (*BKT* 6; Berlin, 1910) p.118, preserves a rather fuller paraphrase of Lk. 2.8–14 in the 13 lines which survive. That text (provenance unknown, c.VII: van Haelst, 727) uses the standard

Byzantine ὁ ἀσώματος (*l*.7) as an equivalent for ἄγγελος, although the latter also occurs (*ll*.2, 12).

In Treu's same article (pp. 60–62; pl. 1, 2) he publishes another longer, but much more fragmentary Christmas hymn (*P. Berl*. 8687; van Haelst, 872). This papyrus sheet (15.5B × 12H cm.; provenance unknown, VI/VII), has portions of 12 and 8 lines on *recto* and *verso* respectively. Its mention of the παρθένος (8, 11), Ἐμμαν[ουήλ] (14), and references to the joy of the world (καὶ τὰ πέρατ[α] εἰκουμένης ἀκαλλειᾶ[ται], 2) and festiveness (ἐωρτάσωμεν, 10), make fairly clear that the birth of Christ is the subject. At *l*.20, just as the text leaves off, a citation from Ps. 46.3 begins: ὅτι κύριος ὕψι[στος . . . . . None of the *nomina sacra* is abbreviated. The name Emmanuel occurs in the NT only at Mt. 1.23 (quoting Is. 7.14); it appears also in *l*.5 of *P. Berl*. 13269 (above).

The angelic doxology from Lk. 2.14 occurs in other parts of the liturgy as well. A single papyrus leaf complete in its width (30 cm.) but lacking top and bottom of the page (surviving height 19.5 cm.) is published in the same article by Treu (pp. 68–70; pl.5). In view of the attention paid to the Pentecost miracle (Acts 1–2), it is to be connected with the liturgy for Whitsunday. The *recto* contains 17 lines of Greek, the *verso* 17 lines of Coptic and some Arabic (provenance unknown, c.VIII; *P. Berl*. 13888; van Haelst, 880).

```
              ] [ ]    [ δόξα ἐν ὑψίσ]της θεῷ
  κὲ ἐπὶ κῆς· εἰρήνης· ἐν ἀθρ[ώ]π[ο]ις εὐτωκία  ✝
```

```
     ἀνβε ὠ θ(εο)ς ἐνν ἀλαλακ[μω]ν· κ(υριο)ς ν φωνῇ· σαλπινκη· κ(αι) ντως· επληρῶσθε
     τὴν· ὑίμραν· τῆς πεντηκωσ[   ] ἀπαστώ
  5  λισ· σιετάξατω· περιμένων· τὴν επαγελίαν· τοῦ πατρὼς· ὥπωε λήψ
     ασθε τήναμιν· ἐπελθων· της αυτων· τῶ ἁγίω πναῦματως· κ(αι) ἐκ(αι)νε
     τω ἔπνου· ἐκ τῶ οὐρανοῦ· ἕκως· εαυτου· τῶ ἁγίω πνᾶματως καθου
     αντου· κ(αι) ἡπλιστης· ἀναπαντς· αυτων· κ(αι) ἐλαλου(ν) τὰ· μεκαλῖα· τοῦ θου
     ἑτέρες· κρώτης· καθὼς· αυτης εϯτων· απωβεκ(αι)[ ]σ· σθε αυτης
  10 κ(αι) ἐκ(αι)νετω· μαρτερς· ἀπὼ εἱερου σαλημ ἕως ἐσχάτου· τοῦ τῆς κῆς
     ωϯ αὐτὼς ἐσϯν· ωσεη να ωϯων· το[υ θ]εου· κ(αι) πατρὼς· λώκως· ωπ
     ω σαρ κὼς· κ(αι) μετὰ σ[ ]κως· σήμερ[ ]ων· αυτων· σημρ ς κ(αι)νου
        μενων·    τοκ κοπ νως
  ————— ‖ ————— ‖ ——— ‖ ——— ‖ ——— ‖ ——— ‖ ———
     ϯτὰς νωερὰς· τηνάμῖς· μ ωρφωμη· κ[(αι)] τῶν λιτρωκι
  15 κῶν τακμάτων· ενι     πων· ἐνεσιν ἄκωντς· πᾶσαν ην
        ] [               ]εκαθεροὐτες· ειοὐρανίων
                          Χ]ερωβίμ ς·
```

...glory in the] highest to God and on earth peace, satisfaction among men. God went up with shouting, the Lord with the sound of the trumpet. And the 5 **day of Pentecost was fulfilled, just as the apostles | were instructed to wait for the promise of the Father in order that they might receive the power of the Holy Spirit coming upon them. And there occurred suddenly from heaven a sound of the Holy Spirit himself coming down (?); and all of them were filled**

10 **and spoke of God's great deeds with another language, just as...(?) |And they became witnesses from Jerusalem to the end of the earth that he is...(?) of God and Word of the Father from (?) flesh and with flesh. Today this very day has occurred...**

15 **(*cross*) the spiritual powers...(?) and of liturgical |arrangements... bringing all praise... heavenly... Cherubim...**

The use of the Coptic letter † (*ll.*9, 11) indicates that the writer is a Copt; that his understanding of Greek is minimal is apparent from his frequent faulty division of words. The latter suggests that he was copying from a version without word breaks. No doubt he was writing in accordance with how the words sounded to him. Note the following: the Lk. 2.14 doxology (*ll.*1–2) follows the Byzantine text-group in its use of εὐδοκία nom. instead of gen.; *l.*3 (Ps. 46.6), ἀνέβη ὁ θεὸς ἐν ἀλαλαγμῷ, κύριος ἐν φωνῇ σάλπιγγος; *ll.*3f. (Acts 2.1), καὶ ἐν τῷ συμπληροῦσθαι τὴν ἡμέραν τῆς πεντεκοστῆς; *ll.*4f., κάθως τοῖς ἀποστόλοις διετάξατο περιμένειν; *ll.*5f. (cf. Acts 1.8), ὅπως λάβωσιν (λήψεσθε?) δύναμιν ἐπελθόντος αὐτοῖς; *ll.*6ff. (Acts 2.11), ἐγένετο ἄφνω ... ἦχος αὐτοῦ τοῦ ἁγίου πνεύματος κατελθόντος (?); *l.*8, ἅπαντες; *l.*9, ἑτεραῖς γλώσσαις; *l.*10, ἐγένετο; *l.*10, μάρτυρες; *l.*11, ὅτι αὐτός ἐστιν ... λόγος; *ll.*11f., ὅπ|ως σαρκός; *l.*14, τὰς νοερὰς δυνάμεις; *ll.*14f., λειτουργικῶν ταγμάτων ... αἴνεσιν ἄγοντες; *l.*16, οὐρανίων. K.L. McKay suggests (in a note to me) that *l.*9 is a corruption of κάθως τὸ πνεῦμα ἐδίδου ἀποφθέγγεσθαι αὐτοῖς (Acts 2.4). 'The first αὐτῆς is simply misplaced and has η for οι; this leads to the loss of τὸ πνεῦμα. ε†των is no further from ἐδίδου than some of the other corruptions. If one ignores the (αι) after κ in απωβεκ(αι)[ ]σ·σθε, which seems to have no more justification than that κ(αι) occurs in three other places where they do make sense, απωβεκ[κε]σ[ε]σθε is a recognizable confusion of ἀποφθέγγεσθαι; and again αὐτῆς = αὐτοῖς'.

There are more echoes of biblical phraseology than have been noted above; but the writer himself is not alluding to all these. Rather, the liturgical section he has excerpted consists of a cento of passages, some varied slightly, others drawing directly whole phrases and clauses from Acts and elsewhere.

94. **The Syrian liturgy of St. James**
Tyre   Late Imperial
ed.pr. — J.-P. Rey-Coquais, *I.Tyre* 1.75, 76 (pl.47.2, 3)

Ἄνης, ἄφης,
ὑπέρβα, συνχώρησον
ὁ Θεὸς εἰς τὰ παραπτώματα
ἡμῶν {ἡμῶν}.

Two inscribed plaques belonging to the same monument, each used to close a funerary *loculus*. They share identical dimensions and were inscribed by the same hand.
Bib. — *D. Feissel, *BCH* 102 (1978) 548–50; *SEG* 997.

God, grant (eternal) rest, forgive, pardon, remit our sins.

Though edited as two separate texts by Rey-Coquais, the pair of stones has been persuasively shown by Feissel to require being read as one text, which draws on local liturgical wording. This passage from the Liturgy of St. James in turn draws on Mk. 11.25. The combination of ἄνης/ἄφης (both imperative, as are the other two verbs, ὁ θεός functioning as a vocative) is what indicates the connection with the Syrian rite; for other examples of the combination see Feissel, 549 and n.21 (Nubia, IX-XII; Thessalonike, late Imperial). For the meaning of ὑπερβαίνω here, 'pardon', note Micah 7.18 (LXX): τίς θεὸς ὥσπερ σύ; ἐξαίρων καὶ ὑπερβαίνων ἀσεβείας τοῖς καταλοίποις τῆς κληρονομίας αὐτοῦ. Feissel suggests (550) that this use of the verb is so exceptional that the inscription may be embodying a precise reminiscence of the Micah passage. The meaning is perhaps worth noting in BAGD and MM. The repetition of ἡμῶν in *l*.4 adds nothing to the meaning but was perhaps included for the visual symmetry of the whole text (Feissel, 549).

95. A Monophysite *Trishagion* in a hymn to Christ

Provenance unknown c.VII
ed.pr. — K. Treu, *NovT* 19 (1977) 142–49

	† ὁ δημιουργήσας τὰ πάν|τα	2	10	ἅγιος ἰσχυρός,	2
	Θς Λόγος	2		ὃν ἀπέκτει|ναν ἀθῷον	2
	ἐμ φάτνη | κεῖται	2		οἱ Ἑβραῖοι ἐπὶ | Πιλάτου·	2
	τεκθεὶς ἐκ τῆς | παρθένου·	2		τριήμερος ἀνέσ|τη·	2
5	ἅγιος ὁ Θς.	2		ἅγιος ἀθάνατος	2
	ὃν | Ἰωάννης καθεῖδεν	2	15	ὁ σταυ|ρωθεὶς δι᾿ ἡμᾶς	2
	ἐν Ἰορ|δάνῃ ⟨ποταμῷ⟩	2		σῶσαι κ[όσ]μον | βουλήσει.	3
	ἄνωθεν ἐλθότα |	2		ἐλ[έ]εσον ἡμᾶς. †	2
	ὑπ᾿ αὐτοῦ βαπτισθῆναι· |	2		ΙΣ ΧΣ ΝΙ ΚΑ	

A complete sheet of papyrus, 12.5B × 16.5H cm., written only on the *recto*. The text printed above is largely Koenen's but papyrus readings have been restored in place of the 'corrections' of the editors. The line arrangement of the hymn follows Koenen. In the text above vertical bars indicate the line divisions in the papyrus. Numbers on the right hand side of the text indicate the number of stresses to the line. *P. Berl.* 16389.
Bib. — *L. Koenen, *ZPE* 31 (1978) 71–76; the papyrus was originally dealt with in a 1941 dissertation by O. Stegmüller, but never published (Treu, 144, n.6); van Haelst, 886.

The creator of all things, God the Word lies in a manger born from the Virgin.
5 **Holy God, whom John saw at the Jordan (river) coming from above to be baptized by him.**
10 **Holy Strong One, whom though he was innocent the Hebrews killed in Pilate's day; on the third day he rose,**

15 **Holy Immortal One, crucified for us, to save the world by his will.**
    Have mercy upon us.
    JESUS CHRIST CONQUERS.

This papyrus copy of a liturgical text with a *Trishagion* refrain for the Sunday
after Epiphany predates by one or two hundred years a revision which has survived
in parchment MS Insinger 32, first published late last century (for details see Treu,
144 and n.7). The fact that it is a Coptic/Greek MS reflects the fact that Greek,
although traditionally used in services, was no longer understood, and so a
vernacular translation was added. Koenen had previously recognized the rhythmic
form of this hymn as it was known from the VIII/IX century MS (*P. Lugd.-Bat.*
17 [1968] p.38, n.22 — a parenthetical observation made in the course of his
discussion of *O. Zucker* 36, a Christian prose hymn (IV), first published by
F. Uebel, *Klio* 43-45 [1965] 395-409). In publishing the papyrus version Treu re-
organized the line length into three strophes concerned with Christ's birth, baptism,
and death and resurrection. Koenen (1978) largely accepted this but presented
further modifications to the structure. The form as printed above provides for
strophes of 4, 4, 3, 2 lines (all but *l.*16 with two stresses) interposed between each
of which occurs the *Trishagion* (2 stresses). This format thus has an introductory
four-line strophe (Christ as Creator and God become Man), followed by three
Trishagion strophes addressed to Jesus as baptized (4 lines), died/risen (3 lines),
crucified (2 lines). Koenen points out (75) that the length of the strophes may vary
considerably in *Trishagion* hymns. The one awkward feature of Koenen's revised
format is his addition of ποταμῷ in *l.*7 to ensure regularity of the scheme.
Appropriate though the word may be, it is nevertheless hard to imagine how it
could have been accidentally omitted by confusion with the surrounding words.

The writer of this hymn is an anonymous, but *l.*15 indicates that he was of
Monophysite inclinations (Koenen, 74-75). The addition of 'who was crucified for
us' after ἅγιος ἀθάνατος was a Monophysite addition to the *Trishagion* included
only in the 470s. (Theophanes, *Chron.* A.M. 5956 [ed. de Boor, 113]: Πέτρος ὁ
Κναφεὺς (bishop of Antioch) . . . προστίθησιν ἐν τῷ τρισαγίῳ ὕμνῳ τό· ὁ σταυρωθεὶς
δι' ἡμᾶς. I owe this reference to B. Croke. The claim that it was added as early as
431 is wrong — *pace* H. Chadwick, *The Early Church* [Harmondsworth, 1967] 208.
See in general B. Croke, *Byzantion* 51[1981] 127-28, on how the confusion arose.)
Opponents took this to mean that God was crucified. (A recently reprinted study
from early this century, J. Lebon, *Le Monophysisme sévérien* [Louvain, 1909; repr.
New York, 1978] devotes a few pages (483-86) to this addition to the *Trishagion*.)
In contrast to the papyrus, MS Insinger 32 has σαρκωθεὶς ὑπὲρ ἡμῶν at this point;
and Koenen argues that the interchangeability of such lines may reflect the
theological outlook of particular Christian groups who wished to use the hymn. It
is hard to say which version may be the prior one. Both texts have emanated from
Egypt, where the Monophysite movement was strong (on this see pp.580-81 of the
article by J. Moorhead, mentioned below). The wording in the Greek/Coptic
version goes back to 438, when the *Trishagion* originated in response to an
earthquake at Constantinople (Croke, 145). *P.Berl.* 21232 (see **100** below) contains
the word σταυροθίς at *l.*6, which may be suggestive of the *Trishagion*, although the
latter cannot be fitted into the context there.

Allusions to the NT in the hymn do not need to be spelled out in full here, but comment on a few words is in order. ὁ δημιουργήσας (1) of God occurs in noun form at Heb. 11.10, πόλιν ἧς τεχνίτης καὶ δημιουργὸς ὁ θεός, as well as having patristic, gnostic, and Byzantine attestation (see Lampe, s.v.). BAGD, s.v. δημιουργός, cite phrases from Aelius Aristides and the Hermetic corpus which parallel the first line of the text. The more usual NT word is κτίζω; note the parallel to the first line of our papyrus at Eph. 3.9, ἐν τῷ θεῷ τῷ τὰ πάντα κτίσαντι (cf. Rev. 4.11). The phrase θεὸς λόγος is not found in the NT, but Lampe, s.v. λόγος II, c, 2, provides patristic examples. For the wording of *l*.4 cf. Mt. 1.23 (citing Is. 7.14). Treu notes (147) that καθοράω (*l*.5) used of spiritual perception occurs at Rom. 1.20. At *l*.9 the papyrus reads ἐπ' αὐτῷ, MS Insinger ὑπ' αὐτοῦ. Treu thinks the former is to be preferred as a *lectio difficilior*, aiming to draw some emphasis away from Jesus' passive role at his baptism. But Koenen is right (72–73) that the words make little sense. The adjective ἀθῷος does not mean 'godless' here, but 'innocent', providing an exact parallel for Mt. 27.4. For the anti-Semitic attitude at a popular level among Christians reflected here in *ll*.11–12 cf. *New Docs 1976*, **61**, and the references given there.

Another Monophysite text published a few years earlier by Treu — *APF* 21 (1971) 78–79; pl.8 — may be mentioned here. *P. Berl.* 17612 (provenance unknown, c. VI) is an intercessory prayer on a single parchment leaf (10.4B × 11.6H cm.).

```
        | κ(αι) [
          τιζο[
          κ(αι) μαρ[
          Ου Στεφ[
    5     ρος καὶ [
          πρωτοδιακόνου κ(αι) πρωτω-
          μάρτηρος· πάντεος κ(αι) ἀρχη-
          γοῦ· κ(αι) τῶν ψυχολύτρων
          κ(αι) θεσπεσίων· προφητῶ(ν)
   10     καὶ ἀποστόλον κ(αι) τῶν ὑ-
          πὲρ Χ(ριστο)ῦ διεθληκότες· ἀήτ-
          τητον κ(αι) τροπεοφόρον μαρ-
          τήρων        ἐξερέτος
          Ἀββὰ Φιλοθ( ) ὀρθοδόξου ἀρχι-
   15     επισκόπου· κ(αι) ἀββὰ . . . . . .
          π(ατ)ριάρχης· σὺν ἀββὰ Σευήρῳ
          καὶ τοῦ ἐπισκόπου ῑῶ(αννου)
          . .τηριον
          ] απα τε τοννοιων
   20     ] . αηαλ . . .
                 ] . . [
                 ] . . [
```

5 (*l*.3) and of the martyr (?)... Stephen ... |...first deacon and first martyr and first leader among the ransomed souls and divinely inspired prophets and 10 |apostles (*gen. pl.* ?) and of those who struggled hard for the sake of Christ

and the unconquered and trophy-winning martyrs. Particularly (pray?) for
15 Abba Philoth(eos?) the orthodox arch|bishop and Abba... patriarch with
Abba Severos and bishop John...

The appeal to Stephen may have been preceded by a reference to John the
Baptist: at *l*.2 Treu suggests βαπ]τιζο- or φω]τιζο- as possible restorations. Severos
(465–539), patriarch of Syrian Antioch from 512–19 when he was exiled to Egypt,
was the most eminent of the Monophysite theologians (Chadwick, op. cit., 207).
His death in 539 provides a *terminus post quem* for this prayer. In view of the
reference to him at *l*.16, the Philotheos referred to (14) is very probably his
successor as leader of the Monophysite movement and bishop of Syrian Hierapolis
until his death in 523. To speak of Philotheos as orthodox (14) implies of course
that his church was too, and thus reflects in passing the theological polemic
occurring within Byzantine Christendom. An alternative identification for the
latter, suggested by Treu (79), could be the Bishop martyred at Antioch in 304
under Diocletian. B. Croke tells me that if the episcopal names are correct then the
patriarch whose name cannot be read at the end of *l*.15 'is most probably Timothy
IV (517–35), but it is odd that he doesn't come first in the list'. Croke also thinks
it possible that *l*.18 may indicate the place of the propitiation, and tentatively
suggests the restoration μαρ]τήριον.

The word ψυχόλυτρος (8) appears to be previously unattested; but cf. Ex. 30.12,
λύτρα τῆς ψυχῆς. At *l*.11 read διηθληκότων; the following words are also gen. pl.,
τροπαιοφόρος being a standard epithet for martyrs. Note the Attic spelling of
ἀήττητος (11-12).

With the allusion to Stephen as 'first martyr' in this prayer cf. *P.Laur.* 36
(provenance unknown, V) an account of expenses incurred 'at the festival of the
first martyr', ἐν τῇ ἑορτῇ τοῦ πρωτομ(άρτυρος) (*l*. 2; cf. *l*.7, πρωτ(ομάρτυρος)), the
festival of Apa Victor, and that of Apa Phoibammon. *Ed.pr.* notes (ad loc.) that
the μ in *l*.2 is not certain and τ might be a possible alternative. This could mean
that the word should be filled out as πρωτοτ(όκου), in which case the festival would
not be St. Stephen (Dec. 27 in the Coptic calendar), but the Nativity (Dec. 24–25).

Van Haelst lists six other Monophysite papyri in addition to *P. Berl.* 17612 (van
Haelst, 892).

1. *P. Lit. Lond.* (1927) 237 (provenance unknown, VI/VII); papyrus hymn in
   honour of Severos (van Haelst, 937).
2. *P. Flor.* inv. 534 — cf. L. Giabbani, *Aeg.* 20[1940] 17-18; G. Mercati, ibid.,
   212-13 — (Antinoopolis, VI), mention of Severos, probably the Monophysite
   (van Haelst, 755).
3. *P. Ryl.* 3 (1938) 466 (provenance unknown, VII); two Monophysite hymns (van
   Haelst, 978).
4. *P. Berl.* 7561 — = Schmidt/Schubart, *BKT* 6, p.121 — (Fayum, VII/VIII);
   communion hymn (?) concerning which Monophysite influence is not agreed
   (van Haelst 724 has references).
5. *P. Grenf.* 2 (1897) 113 (provenance unknown, VIII-IX), part of a litany;
   Monophysite character attributed to it because of the mention of the Patriarch
   Dioskoros (van Haelst, 913).

6. *P. Ryl. Copt.* (1909) 34 (Hermopolis Magna, X–XI), an amplified *Trishagion* as in the text with which this entry began; attributed to Peter I, Patriarch of Antioch, c. 450 (van Haelst, 990).

New Docs 1976 **94 bis** dealt briefly with a Monophysite inscription of Ezana of Ethiopia. This text is discussed further in the present volume **(117)**. Two short epitaphs from Tyre (*I. Tyre* 126, 134) may possibly have links with the Monophysite movement, though neither is explicitly Monophysite in its wording (so *ed.pr.*). The fullest recent study of Monophysitism is W.H.C. Frend, *The Rise of the Monophysite Movement* (Cambridge, 1972); the most recent discussion of one feature is J. Moorhead, *Byzantion* 51 (1981) 579–91. Moorhead argues against the generally received view that 'during the Arab invasions of Syria, Palestine and Egypt in the 630s and 640s the native peoples supported, or at least failed to oppose, the attackers, and that this was because imperial persecution of Monophysitism had occasioned great animosity between these peoples and their Byzantine overlords' (579). Early this century A.J. Butler had already opposed the 'Coptic betrayal' hypothesis in *The Arab Conquest of Egypt*, as P.M. Fraser notes in his introduction to the revised edition of Butler (Oxford, 1978²) vii–viii. Relevant to this question is *P.Madrid* 189 (Ben Hasan, VII), according to *ed.pr.* (P.J. Photiades, *Klio* 41 [1963] 234–36, pls.). She claimed that this semi-Greek, semi-Coptic text may have formed part of a special liturgy on the occasion of the Arab invasion in 640. But K. Treu, *Klio* 42 (1964) 337–39, has pointed out that, given the conservatism of the Eastern liturgy, it would be most surprising if such an *ad hoc* prayer were included. In re-editing the text Treu shows that it is in fact part of the 'Great Synapte', the antiphonal prayer between deacon and chorus at the beginning of the Mass. In that the scribe gets various Greek words wrong he is probably a Copt. Treu also provides an estimate of the original dimensions of the codex page from which this fragment comes. On this parchment see also H. Quecke, *Muséon* 78 (1965) 349–54.

Three other texts published in *APF* 21 (1971) by Treu may be mentioned here briefly. *P. Berl.* 16701 (van Haelst, 887) is the fragmentary conclusion — parts of four lines — of a hymn which may be addressed to Christ (Treu, pp.71–72; pl.4b). The last two lines of this parchment page (provenance unknown, c. VI; hair-side blank) read:]πάντα ὑπομείνας ἵνα | ---] η· κύριε δόξα σοι †. For ὑπομένω of Christ cf. Heb. 12.2. On p.75 he publishes *P. Berl.* 17090, a small fragment of a prayer from a parchment page written only on one side (provenance unknown, Byzantine date; van Haelst, 890). Parts of four lines survive: ἀδιαλ[είπτως in the first occurs in intercessory contexts in the NT (Rom. 1.9; 1 Thes. 1.2, 2.13, 5.17; the adjective at Rom. 9.2; 2 Tim. 1.3). The fourth line, where the text concluded, ends with φιλόθεος †: whether this is a name — see comment on *P. Berl.* 17612 above — or an adjective (only at 2 Tim. 3.4 in the NT; see **79**) is uncertain. If it is a name this text may be an intercessory prayer to the martyr under Diocletian. A not certainly Christian prayer survives in partial form as well (Treu, 70–71, pl.6a). This papyrus fragment (*P. Berl.* 16356; van Haelst, 885; 6.5B × 9.2H cm.) includes words like δε]όμεθα (1), ἱκετεύομε[ν (3; Treu notes that the term is common in non-Christian contexts), and τ]ῆς ζωῆ[ς] ἡμ[ῶν (?) (6; perhaps the strongest indication of a Christian origin for the text).

Van Haelst's *Catalogue* inventories over 300 liturgical texts (including hymns) and private prayers (nos. 720–1063).

96. A personal prayer and doxology in the shape of a cross

Tyre   Late Imperial

ed.pr. — J.-P. Rey-Coquais, *I. Tyre* 1.49, pp.32-33 (pl.45.1)

```
              ΧΕ
              O
    A         ΘС        ω
              Y
[Χ]E O ΘС     M   ΔΟΞΑ С
              Δ
    †         O          †    O[I]
              Ξ
              A
              СOI
```

A marble plaque, used to close a grave loculus.

This text Χ(ριστ)έ, ὁ θ(εό)ς μου, δόξα σοι, is written both horizontally and vertically with ΑΩ and crosses in the squares formed by the bars of the cross shape. The position of the letters of σοι reflects in each case the shape of the stone. There come together in this text both a personal address to Christ by the anonymous inscriber and a liturgical allusion.

97. A Byzantine letter quoting Paul

Provenance unknown   VI-VII

ed.pr. — K. Treu, *Studia Evangelica* 6 (1973) 533-36

```
     ]περὶ τοῦ εὐλαβεστάτου ἀββᾶ Πετρωνίου, ἵνα ὑποδείξῃς
     ]τοῦ αἵματος καὶ τὸ τοῦ ἐντέρου, δεινῶς γὰρ βασανίζεται.
     κόσ]μον τοῦτον. τὰ γὰρ μωρὰ ἐξελέξατο ὁ θ(εὸ)ς ἵνα καταισχύνῃ
     Χ]ριστόν, ὑμεῖς δὲ φρόνιμοι ἐν Χριστῷ. Ὁ θ(εὸ)ς ὤφειλεν
   5 π]ολλὰ ἔτη καὶ καλά, ὑγιαίνοντες ψυχῆς καὶ σώματος καὶ πνεύματος.
```

Five fragmentary lines of a papyrus sheet; *verso* blank. Diaeresis present above some iotas and upsilons. An apostrophe follows τοῦτον (3). Last syllable of πνεύματος written above the line. *P.Berl.* 13889.

Bib. - K. Treu. *APF* 22/23 (1974) 391; id., *MPL* 2 (1977) 251; *SB* 11144

> **. . . concerning the most reverend Father Petronios, in order that you indicate . . . of the blood and that of the intestine, for he is undergoing terrible torture. . . . this world. For it is the foolish things that God has selected in order that he might put to shame . . . Christ, but you are wise in Christ.**
> **5 Would that God had | . . . for many good years, (you) being healthy in soul and body and spirit.**

First, the pair of citations from 1 Cor. in *ll*.3 and 4. The wording of 1 Cor. 1.27 has been slightly altered, probably because of the particular context in which it is being applied here: τὰ γὰρ μωρά for ἀλλὰ τὰ μ.; τοῦ κόσμου is absent from the papyrus version no doubt because of the allusion to the *kosmos* at the end of the sentence immediately prior to this. The accusative κόσμον τοῦτον never occurs in the NT, although the genitive and dative forms do: Treu refers to 1 Cor. 3.19; cf. also 5.10, and several times in the Fourth Gospel. In *l*.4 the wording is identical with 1 Cor. 4.10, and Χ]ριστόν may well be the end of the previous phrase, ἡμεῖς μωροὶ διὰ Χ. Stylistically this would neatly pick up μωρά (3); but Paul's tone in the chapter 4 passage is out of place for what the writer of the papyrus appears to be discussing.

Further, there are fairly clear verbal echoes — we cannot call them as much as quotations — of the wording of Mt. 8.6, δεινῶς βασανιζόμενος, and of 1 Thes. 5.23 at *l*.5. In *l*.2 the metaphorical use of βασανίζω is the same as in the NT passage; cf. Rev. 12.2 where it is used in a childbirth context. The Thessalonians trichotomy has been discussed at *New Docs 1976*, **64**, where the order of the nouns, as here, is characteristic of Egyptian liturgies, although the type of document is quite different.

The size of the gap at the start of each line cannot be determined beyond conjecture: the present width of the papyrus is 15.5 cm. It is very hard to imagine how the lines could have run on with the mere addition of one or two words. Whether or not we postulate that the extant part of *l*.4 was preceded by the previous phrase from 1 Cor. 4.10 (given above), there must have been more room to complete the sentence begun in *l*.3. We may have surviving as little as half the original width of the papyrus sheet.

Treu suggests that the language of *l*.5 is suggestive of the closing wish for good health in private letters. This may be the case but does not put the question of genre beyond doubt. He takes the change from singular ὑποδείξῃς (1) to plural ὑμεῖς . . . ὑγιαίνοντες (4–5) to indicate that the writer is addressing either a monastic superior and his monks or a bishop and his clergy.

Early papyrus excerpts from the Corinthian letters are not common. Van Haelst 1217 is a fragment of a codex (V?) containing 1 Cor. 1.25–27; 2.6–8; 3.8–10, 20. 1 Cor. 1.27 does not appear again until a much later parchment (IX–XI; van Haelst, 503). In all, van Haelst inventories eight papyrus texts citing 1 Cor., dated IV–V and later (although his 505 — 1 Cor. 7.18–8.4 — may be III: see K. Aland, *Repertorium*, 235). There are some half-dozen fragments with parts of 2 Cor. (V–VI). Van Haelst lists no excerpts which include Mt. 8.6 before the tenth century.

As for early (II–III) patristic use of these passages, Mt. 8.6 is never drawn on, 1 Cor. 4.10 very rarely (once each in Ignatius and Origen), while 1 Thes. 5.23 thrice in each of Tertullian, Clement of Alexandria and Irenaeus, and sixteen times in Origen. But 1 Cor. 1.27 is worth a glance: twelve times in Tertullian, twenty times in Origen, once elsewhere in an anonymous (*Bib. Pat.* I. 446; III, 383). The passage in which this verse occurs has attracted those with a sociological interest in the NT (e.g., W. Wuellner, *Studia Evangelica* 6 [1973] 666–72). But one may also ask whether such passages were viewed with particular significance by Christians of particular localities over a range of time. In the case of Origen here perhaps one ought not to be surprised if Pauline comments relating to status in the Corinthian letters were lighted upon by the Alexandrian church. For a number of suggestive analogies between the two cities could be drawn.

In this papyrus only θεός is abbreviated as a *nomen sacrum*; Χριστός is left unabbreviated. Itacism in the latter should be noted (η for ι). On this spelling see *New Docs 1976*, **76**. Treu points out that we ought not particularly to expect πνεῦμα to be abbreviated here since it is not referring to the Holy Spirit. But note *l*.12 of the Hermas text discussed in **98** below, and cf. *P. Coll. Youtie* II (1976) 91.5 (= *New Docs 1976*, **64**) where the word is shortened.

Although the text was written in the sixth or seventh century, Treu links it back to the fourth century by his identification of Petronios. For the only *abbas* Petronios in Christian Egypt known to have gained senior office (testified to by the superlative εὐλαβέστατος; see Lampe, s.v., 1c) was the immediate successor of Pachomios. While still a relatively young man the latter founded the coenobitic way of life early in the fourth century at Tabennese. (An Anoubion ἀποτακτικὸς τοῦ μοναστηρίου of Tabennese is recorded (A, *ll*.17-18) as paying tax on the community's land in the Hermopolite nome in 367/8: *P. Berl.* inv. 11860 A–B, published by E. Wipszycka in *Le monde grec. Hommages à Claire Préaux* [Brussels, 1975] 625–36; cf. J. Gascou, *BIFAO* 76 [1976] 157–84 at 183–84.) Petronios was not one of Pachomios' first disciples; in fact he was a wealthy landowner who joined the *coenobium* only c.340 but was soon designated to be the founder's successor. Yet Petronios only exercised headship for some three months after Pachomios died of plague in May 346; for he too — like many others in the community — succumbed to its ravages. On Pachomios see, e.g., H. Leclercq, *DACL* XI.1 (1934) 1807–17 (s.v. Monachisme); D. Chitty, *The Desert a City* (Oxford, 1966) ch. 1–2 (Petronios, p.24); P. Rousseau, *Ascetics, Authority, and the Church in the Age of Jerome and Cassian* (Oxford, 1978) esp. Pt. I, ch. 2–3. On Pachomios' letters see H. Quecke, *Die Briefe Pachoms. Griechischer Text der Handschrift W.145 der Chester Beatty Library* (Regensburg, 1975).

Treu's hypothesis appears to be a very neat fit: someone is writing to offer what comfort he can to the monks who have seen their founder die and his successor about to follow in his wake. Thus Treu suggests that our papyrus may be a later copy of a fourth-century letter, preserved possibly in a literary work. This idea is at first sight attractive and if it should stand one may wonder whether the type of literature to have preserved such a mention of Petronios may have been a life of one of the Desert Fathers. Treu does not himself draw the inference, but if this letter were originally written in 346 while Petronios was ill (*l*.2), we would be provided with two certain NT quotations and two very probable echoes of NT language in the span of five fragmentary lines of a dateable mid-fourth century text.

But another interpretation of the fragment may be suggested. It is not at all certain that Petronios is the subject of βασανίζεται in *l*.2. This line may be referring to someone who now, in the sixth century, is very ill, and the writer reminds the addressee(s) of the example of Petronios two hundred years earlier who endured the plague. This could explain the present tense rather better. If the mention of Petronios is exemplary only, he cannot be regarded as the prime focus of the letter. That said, it should be pointed out that identifying *l*.2 with someone's illness is likewise not completely certain. Whether or not this alternative hypothesis has merit, it can be urged that the papyrus is not a later copy of a fourth-century letter, but original to VI–VII.

M. Naldini, *Il Cristianesimo in Egitto* (Florence, 1968), has collected nearly 100 private letters dating II–IV (some may be V) which he regards as Christian. Certainly the Christian attribution of some of his items is open to serious doubt: for particular criticism on this see E. Wipszycka, *JJP* 18 (1974) 302–21. Naldini offers a reply to her in *Civiltà classica e cristiana* 2 (1981) 167–76, and provides notes on Christian letters published since the appearance of his book. But even so the point needs to be made that there are less than two dozen Biblical citations and verbal echoes among that number of texts; and that number would be cut by half if one excluded reminiscences of biblical wording which are less than certain. Naldini discusses the question of such citations and echoes in his introduction, 48–55. For a critical evaluation of the subject see B.F. Harris, *Proceedings of the XIV International Congress of Papyrologists, Oxford 1974* (London, 1976) 155–60. Set out below in tabular form is a list of the relevant papyrus texts including more recently published pieces along with those discussed by Harris.

1. *Quotations*

P. Heid. 1 (1905) 6.7–10 (Naldini 41)	Prov 10.19 (close to LXX)	mid-IV
P. Lond. 3 (1907) 981.4–7 (N.51)	Is. 31.9b (LXX, freely)	IV

2. *Clear verbal echoes*

P. Harr. (1936) 107.4–7 (N.5)	Jn. 14.26, cf. 14.17	III init.
.7–12	1 Thes. 5.23; 3 Jn 2	
P. Oxy. 12 (1916) 1592.3–6 (N.31)	Lk. 1.46–47	III/IV
P. Heid. 1 (1905) 6.3–4 (N.41)	Phil. 3.20	mid-IV
P. Oxy. 8 (1911) 1161.1–4 (N.60)	Mk. 1.11; perhaps Eph. 1.6	IV
.4–7	1 Thes. 5.23	
SB 5 (1955) 7872.11–12 (N.75)	2 Tim. 1.16	IV
P. Herm. Rees (1964) 8.17–20 (N.83)	1 Tim. 6.11	IV
P. Stras. gr. inv. 1900.11	Gal. 6.18; Phil. 4.23;	mid-IV
(*ZPE* 18[1975] 317–23) (—)	1 Thes. 5.28, *al.*	

3. *Conjectural reminiscences*

P. Gron. (1933) 17.14–15 (N.24)	cf. Rom. 15.33; Lk. 1.28	III/IV
P. Oxy. 12 (1916) 1494.4–9 (—)	cf. Hos. 14.10; Mt. 3.3;	early IV
	Acts 13.10	
P. Heid. 1 (1905) 6.12–14 (N.41)	cf. Heb. 1.3; 2 Pet. 1.9	mid-IV
P. Oxy. 31 (1966) 2603.28–29 (N.47)	cf. Mt. 25.40	IV
P. Lond. 3 (1907) 981.8–11 (N.51)	cf. Rom. 1.8	IV
P. Iand. 2 (1913) 14.3–4 (N.59)	cf. Job 16.19; Lk. 2.14	IV
P. Oxy. 6 (1908) 939.3–4 (N.61)	cf. Tit. 2.11; 3.4	IV
SB 5 (1955) 7872.9 (N.75)	cf. Jn. 13.34	IV
P. Herm. Rees (1964) 9.16–20 (N.84)	cf. Lk. 11.28; Tit. 3.15	IV
P. Ross.-Georg. 3 (1930) 10.4 (N.90)	cf. 2 Cor. 1.3–4	IV/V
P. Oxy. 46 (1978) 3314.10–11 (—)	cf. Mt. 10.42; Mk. 9.41	IV
P. Oxy. 48 (1981) 3421.4 (—)	cf. 2 Cor. 1.3–4	mid-IV

4.   *Accepted by Naldini, but 'improbable' (Harris)*

P. Mich. 8 (1951) 482.14–17 (N.1)	cf. Ruth 1.16; Jn. 16.27	23/8/133
BGU 1 (1895) 27.8–11 (N.2)	cf. Mt. 4.20; Acts 15.4; 1 Cor. 12.18	II/III
P. Oxy. 31 (1966) 2603, esp. ll.3–6, 17–19 (N.47)	cf. 1 Cor. 13.13; Jas. 1.23	IV

(The first two are probably not Christian; the last is clearly so.)

A brief comment on this list is in order. First, the fact that there are actual citations and clear verbal echoes in a text makes conjectural reminiscences in the same papyrus more likely. This is relevant to *P. Lond.* 3.981, *P. Heid.* 1.6, *SB* 5.7872. Conversely, if the 'mirror' *topos* in *P. Oxy.* 31.2603 is not distinctively Christian (on this imagery see R.J. Mortley, *VC* 30 [1976] 109–20) it may encourage us to doubt that *ll.*28–29 contain a biblical reminiscence either; although it should be pointed out that the papyrus is undoubtedly Christian. *P. Ross.-Georg.* 3.10, included by Harris in the 'conjectural' group, should be treated, I suggest, as an 'improbable'. The same phrase occurs in *P. Oxy.* 48 (1981) 3421.4 (mid-IV), a letter which the editor regards as Christian apparently because of these words and its following phrase, εὔχομαι | τῷ πανελεήμονι Θεῷ | περὶ τῆς ἀδελφικῆς σου | διαθέσεως (3–6). *P. Oxy.* 3314 will be dealt with more fully in the next number of *New Docs*, but one may here raise the possibility that the text is Jewish. On this papyrus see most recently E.A. Judge, *Rank and Status in the World of the Caesars and St Paul* (*Broadhead Memorial Lecture no. 4*; Christchurch, 1982) 28–31.

The contrast between the thinness of the citations and echoes in these fourth-century texts and the superabundance of our papyrus fragment is manifest. The latter is a mere fragment of parts of five lines, yet it contains two NT quotations, and two virtually certain allusions to NT phraseology. While falling short of proof — few of the letters in Naldini are as ecclesiastical and sermon-like as this one — the contrast does add considerable weight to the suggestion that this document is no later copy of a fourth-century original, but a letter first written in the sixth century. From this it follows that the biblical allusions in these lines cannot be included among the small bulk of fourth-century citations and echoes; VI/VII is where they belong.

Fuller attention to papyrus private letters may be expected in *New Docs 1979*, where account will be taken of G. Tibiletti, *Le lettere private nei papiri greci del III e IV secolo d.C. Tra paganesimo e cristianesimo* (Milan, 1979). He lists all private letters within this time span and identifies those he regards as definitely pagan or definitely Christian. He treats Naldini no.44 (= *PSI* 7 [1925] 825) and Naldini no.66 (= *P.Oxy.* 14 [1920] 1775) as securely pagan (Tibiletti, pp.17, 19 respectively). A tabular comparative analysis of Tibiletti, Naldini, and G. Ghedini, *Lettere cristiane dai papiri greci del III e IV secolo* (*Aegyptus, suppl.*3; Milan, 1923) is provided by S.R. Pickering in his *Papyrology Newsletter* II.3 (Jan. 1983) 1–6, circulated within Macquarie University. B.F. Harris/S.R. Pickering, 'The Evidence of Papyri for Early Christianity in Egypt' (forthcoming in *ANRW*), surveys the pre-Constantinian period.

98. A private copy of the 'Shepherd' of Hermas

Fayum   not before V

ed.pr. — K. Treu, *VC* 24 (1970) 34–39

recto   *Mand.*

λαξη]ς. καὶ πᾶ[σι δὲ ἄφεσις ἔσ-   IV.4.4

ται, ἐ]ὰν τὰς ἐν[τολάς μου ταύτας

φυλά]σσουσι καὶ [πορευθῶσι ἐν τῇ ἁγ-

νότη]τι ταύτῃ [

5 Μακρ]όθυμος, φ[ησί, γίνου καὶ συνε-   V.1.1

τός, κ]αὶ πάντω[ν τῶν ἔργων τῶν

πονη]ρῶν κα[τακυριεύσεις καὶ

ἐργάσ]ῃ πᾶσαν δικαιοσύνην. ἐὰν   2

γὰρ μα]κρόθυ[μος ἔσῃ, τὸ π̅ν̅α̅ τὸ ἅγιον

10 τὸ κατ]οικοῦν ἐ[ν σοὶ---

verso

ξ̅β̅

---π]νείγεται γ[ὰρ ὑπὸ   3

τοῦ πονηρο]ῦ π̅ν̅ς̅, μὴ ἔ[χον τό

πον λειτουργ]ῆσαι τῷ κ̅[ω̅ κα-

θὼς βούλετ]αι, μιαιν[όμε-

15 νον ὑπὸ τῆς ὀ]ξυχολί[ας. ἐν γὰρ

τῇ μακροθυ]μίᾳ ὁ κ̅ς̅ [κατοικεῖ,

ἐν δὲ τῇ ὀξυ]χολίᾳ ὁ δ[ιάβολος.   4

ἀμφότερα οὖ]ν τὰ πν[εύματα

ἐπὶ τὸ αὐτὸ κα]τοικοῦ[ντα, ἀσύμ-

20 φορόν ἐστιν] καὶ πον[ηρὸν

ἐκείνῳ τῷ ἀ]νθρώπῳ[--

P. Berl. 5104. A portion (3.2B × 9.7H cm.) of the upper half of a leaf from a papyrus codex. About 11–12 lines are missing between *recto* and *verso*, the full page having 21–22 lines.

Bib. — K. Treu, *Kairos* 16 (1974) 103; id., *MPL* 2 (1977) 252

    (*recto*) **And to all people there shall be forgiveness if they keep these**
5 **commandments of mine and walk in this purity . . . |Be forbearing, he says,**
    and understanding and you will exercise mastery over all evil deeds and you
10 **will do all righteousness. For if you are forbearing the Holy Spirit |which**
    resides in [you] . . . (*verso*) p.62. . . . for it is choked by the evil spirit, since
15 **it does not have a place to serve the Lord as it wishes, (but) is defiled |by**
    sharp anger. For the Lord resides in forbearance, while the devil resides in
20 **sharp anger. So when both the spirits reside in the same place it | is**
    inexpedient and evil for that man . . .

    The 'Shepherd' is attested relatively frequently (17 times to date) in papyrus and parchment texts dated II–VI. Translation into several other languages (Coptic, Latin, Aethiopic) is another indication of its popularity. That it was included at the end of the NT in Codex Sinaiticus after *Ep. Barn.* is further testimony to the influence of the work in this period. (Sinaiticus breaks off about one-third of the way through Hermas, at *Mand.* IV.3.6.) Athanasius' Festal letter of 367 'expressly names the Didache and the Shepherd, with certain of the Old Testament apocrypha, as books not included in the canon but ancient and suitable to be read by catechumens' (Jackson/Lake, *Beginnings of Christianity*, I, vol.3. *The Text of Acts* by J. H. Ropes [London, 1926] xlviii, n.2). Yet the 'Shepherd' fell from favour almost totally in the following centuries, and is attested in only one MS of the Middle Ages (Athous, XV; contains *Mand.* XII.4.7–*Sim.* VIII.4.3; *Sim.* IX.15.1–30.3). All but one (*P.Mich.* 129) of the seventeen fragments are small, most coming from codices. Below is a tabulation in date order of the surviving fragments. Chapter divisions in M. Whittaker, *Der Hirt des Hermas* [Berlin, 1967²], are given in brackets. This list updates van Haelst and corrects a couple of minor points, as well as including the reference in Turner, *Typology*, where appropriate.

1. *P.Mich.* 130 (Fayum, end II), papyrus roll. *Mand.* II.6–III.1 (Whittaker, 27.6–28.1). The earliest surviving fragment of the work. *Ed.pr.* — C. Bonner, *HTR* 20 (1927) 105–16, republished in id., *A Papyrus Codex of the Shepherd of Hermas* (*Similitudes 2–9*) *with a Fragment of the Mandates* (*Univ. Michigan Studies, Humanistic Series* 22; Ann Arbor, 1934) 129–36. Van Haelst, 657.

2. *P. Mich.* 129 (Theadelphia, probably III²), papyrus codex, paginated. *Sim.* II.8–IX.5.1 (Whittaker, 51.8–82.1). The major papyrus text to survive, containing about one-quarter of the whole work, the only Greek witness to a considerable portion of *Sim. Ed. pr.* — Bonner, *A Papyrus Codex* ... (no.1 above), 1–126. Van Haelst, 660; Turner, *Typology*, no. 529.

3. *P. Berl.* inv. 5513 (Fayum, III), papyrus roll. *Sim.* II.7–10; IV.2–5 (Whittaker, 51.7–10; 53.2–5). *Ed.pr.* — H. Diels/A. Harnack, *Sitzb. Berl. Akad.* (1891) 427–31; repr. C. Schmidt/W. Schubart. *Altchristliche Texte* (*Berliner Klassikertexte* 6; Berlin, 1910), no.1, pp.13–17. Van Haelst, 662.

4. *P. Oxy.* 15 (1922) 1828 (III, 'probably' [*ed.pr.*]), parchment codex. *Sim.* VI.5.3, 5 (Whittaker, 65.3, 5). Identified by S.G. Mercati, *Biblica* 6(1925) 336–38. Van Haelst, 665 (see no.9 below); Turner, *Typology*, no. 533.

5. *P. Iand.* 1 (1912) 4 (Hermopolis Magna, III/IV), papyrus codex. *Mand.* XI. 19–21; XII.1, 2–3 (Whittaker, 43.19–21, 44.2–3). Identified virtually simultaneously by J. Lenaerts, *CE* 54 (1979) 356–58, and M. Gronewald, *ZPE* 40 (1980) 53–54. See below.

6. *P. Oxy.* 1 (1898) 5 (end III/IV init.; IV or V [Turner, *Typology*, no. 528]), papyrus codex. *Mand.* XI.9–10 (Whittaker, 43.9–10). Hermas cited in a work 'On Prophecy', possibly by Melito of Sardis. Identified simultaneously by F.C. Conybeare, *The Athenaeum* 9/7/1898, and A. Harnack, *Sitzb. Berl. Akad.* (1898) 516–20. Van Haelst, 682.

7. *P. Oxy.* 3 (1903) 404 (end III/IV init.), papyrus codex. *Sim.* X.3.2–5, 4.3–4 (Whittaker, 113.2–5, 114.3–4). The only Greek witness to this passage, almost at the end of the work. Van Haelst, 668; Turner, *Typology*, no. 536.

8. *P. Mich.* inv. 6427 (provenance unknown, IV init.), papyrus. *Mand.* I.1 (Whittaker, 26.1). Hermas cited in a liturgical prayer along with passages of Isaiah (40.16; 66.1). *Ed.pr.* — M. Gronewald, *ZPE* 14 (1974) 193–200. Van Haelst, 949a.

9. *P. Oxy.* 15 (1922) 1783 (early IV), parchment codex, palimpsest. *Mand.* IX.2–3, 4–5 (Whittaker, 39.2–3, 4–5). Van Haelst, 659, who mentions Mercati's suggestion that it is possibly the same codex as no. 4 above. But this is most unlikely. According to the editors of the two *P. Oxy.* texts 1783 is a 'round upright uncial of medium size', whereas 1828 has 'well formed rather small sloping uncials.' No photos included in *ed.pr.*, but 1783 has noticeably fewer letters per line, though note that no entire line of 1828 survives. Turner, *Typology*, pp.131–32, nos. 527, 533, dates 1783 to IV, 1828 to III.

10. *P. Oxy.* 9 (1912) 1172 (IV), papyrus codex, paginated 70/71. *Sim.* II.4–10 (Whittaker, 51.4–10). Van Haelst, 661; Turner, *Typology*, no. 530.

11. *P. Berl.* inv. 13272 (Hermopolis Magna, IV), parchment codex. *Sim.* V.1.5–2.2; V.2.4–6 (Whittaker, 54.5–55.2; 55.4–6). *Ed.pr.* — O. Stegmüller, *Aeg.* 17 (1937) 456–59. Van Haelst, 664; Turner, *Typology*, no. 532.

12. *P. Oxy.* 13 (1919) 1599 (IV), papyrus codex. *Sim.* VIII.6.4–8.3 (Whittaker, 72.4–74.3). Van Haelst, 667; Turner, *Typology*, no. 535.

13. *P. Hamb.* inv. 24 (provenance unknown, IV/V), parchment codex. *Sim.* IV.6–8; V.1.1–5 (Whittaker, 53.6–54.5). *Ed.pr.* — K. Schmidt/W. Schubart, *Sitzb. Berl. Akad.* (1909) 1077–81. Van Haelst, 663; Turner, *Typology*, no.531.

14. *P. Harr.* (1936) 128 (provenance unknown, V), papyrus codex. *Vis.* V.5–7 (Whittaker, 25.5–7). Identified by G.D. Kilpatrick, *JTS* 48 (1947) 204–05. Van Haelst, 656; Turner, *Typology*, no.526.

15. *P. Berl.* inv. 5104 (Fayum, V), papyrus codex, *verso* paginated 62. *Mand.* IV.4.4–V.1–2, 3–4 (Whittaker, 32.4–33.2, 3–4). Printed above in this entry. Van Haelst, 658; not included in Turner, *Typology*.

16. *P. Amh.* 2 (1901) 190 (provenance unknown, end V/VI init.), papyrus codex (7 fragmentary leaves), *Vis.* I.2.2–4, 3.1 (Whittaker, 2.2–3.1); III.12.3, 13.3 (Whittaker, 20.3, 21.3); *Mand.* XII.1.1, 3 (Whittaker, 44.1, 3); *Sim.* IX.2.1–2, 4–5 (Whittaker, 79.1–2, 4–5); IX.12.2–3, 5 (Whittaker, 89.2–3, 5); IX.17.1, 3–4 (Whittaker, 94.1, 3–4); IX.30.1–2, 3–4 (Whittaker, 107.1–2, 3–4). Only Greek witness of any size to final sections of the work. Van Haelst, 655; Turner, *Typology*, no. 525. See below, no. 17.

17. *P. Berl.* inv. 6789 (provenance unknown, VI), papyrus codex. *Sim.* VIII.1.1–12 (Whittaker, 67.1–12). *Ed.pr.* — Schmidt/Schubart *BKT* 6 (see no.3 above), no.2, pp. 17–20. Van Haelst, 666 (who mentions possibility that this and no. 16 are part of the same codex; but Turner, *Typology*, pp.131–32, nos. 525, 534, estimates that the number of lines per page in *P. Amh.* 190 could be nearly twice that for *P. Berl.* inv. 6789).

Two observations on the spread of passages. *Vis.* is attested in these papyrus and parchment finds only in two codices at the end of the period (nos. 14, 16). Virtually all the *Mand.* fragments are from a section between where Sinaiticus leaves off and Athous begins. No significance should probably be drawn from either point though, since these texts are chance finds and the scraps which survive mostly presuppose a considerably longer text.

To return to the Berlin text published by Treu. The appearance of the page number 62 on the *verso* is peculiar. The *recto* lacks a number. Sixty pages prior to this in the codex would not provide sufficient room to include the rest of the work up to this point. Turner, *Typology*, 76, instances a few codices where the leaves, not pages, are numbered, but in that case one should expect the first page (the *recto*), not the second, to carry the number. However, he also notes that some scribes only numbered the even page. But whether a combination of these two factors could explain the number on the Berlin text is still doubtful. Using Whittaker's text as a basis, my rough calculation is that c.75 pages (i.e. c. 37–38 leaves) would have been needed for the sections up to the surviving sheet. A further possibility is that the page number enumerates surviving pages from a damaged codex, as in the case of *P. Mich.* 129 (no.2, above; see Bonner, 8–9; and Turner, 75).

The text avoids the special readings which the Coptic and Latin translations presuppose (see Treu's apparatus, pp. 38–39). Note the indicative in *l*.3 where the subjunctive would be expected. Treu detects in the treatment of the *nomina sacra* the mark of a non-professional copyist. πνεῦμα is abbreviated (12) although it does not refer to the member of the Trinity; and one might expect ἄνθρωπος (21) to be shortened. 'Clearly it is a private copy from the time when the *Shepherd* is already in discredit' (Treu, 1970:37).

P. Iand. 1 (1912) 4 had lain long unidentified, but in 1979/80 two scholars independently recognised that it was a passage from Hermas. For the details see no.5 in the tabulation above. Only a few letters survive per line from 12–13 lines (a little over half the page) of a codex leaf. It is somewhat surprising that the text was not identified as Christian for so many years: the *ed.pr.*'s suggestion that it may have been a medical work may have caused it to be ignored. Abbreviated *nomina sacra* are visible in *verso ll*.2, 9. But the scribe was not consistent in his practice, e.g., *verso*, *l*.2 α͞ν͞ο[υς, but *l*.11 ἀνθρ[ώπους; *verso*, *l*.9, κ͞ε, but *l*.3 [θεοῦ] unabbreviated needs to be restored in view of the line length.

99. A homily attributed to Chrysostom

Fayum   V/VI
ed.pr. — K. Treu, *Studia Patristica* 12 (Berlin, 1975) 71–75

recto

Τοῦ μακα[ρίου Ἰ͞ω τοῦ Χρ]
ἐπισκ Κ[πόλεως λόγος εἰς]
τὸν ν̄ ψ[αλμόν ~   ]
Οἱ ζωγ[ράφοι μιμοῦνται]
5 τῇ τέ[χνῃ τὴν φύσιν, καὶ]
κ[εραννύντες τὰ χρώματα,]
ἀλ[λάσσουσι τὰς εἰκόνας]
τ[ῶν ὁρωμένων σωμάτων,]
κ[αὶ ποιοῦσιν . . . .]

verso
10 [. . . . . οὕ]τω δὴ
[καὶ οἱ προφῆται ζωγρ]άφοι
[τινές εἰσιν ἀρετῆ]ς [κα]ὶ
[κακίας. γράφουσι γὰρ κ]αὶ

P. Berl. 6788A, a double leaf from a papyrus codex. Only one leaf printed above, the second having so few discernible letters that it is not possible to determine its position in the codex relative to the first. Dimensions at largest point: 15B × 8H cm.

Bib. — K. Treu, *MPL* 2 (1977) 252, n.9; van Haelst, 635.

(*recto*) **The sermon of blessed John also called Chrysostomos, bishop of**
5 **Constantinople, on the 50th Psalm. 'Painters imitate | nature by their art, and**
by mixing colours change the forms of bodies which are seen and make
10 **. . . (*verso*) | . . . In this way, indeed, the prophets also are painters of good**
and evil. For they also paint . . .'

Although over 700 sermons and homilies of Chrysostom have survived (not
including a range of other works), this is only the fourth papyrus text attributed
to him to have been found. Brief though it be several features deserve mention. The
surviving fragment provides us with a three-line heading and the first few lines of
the homily (Migne *PG* 55, p. 565). The title is considerably abbreviated compared
to Migne's text: ὁμιλία εἰς ἐπιγραφὴν τοῦ ν΄ ψαλμοῦ καὶ περὶ μετανοίας, Δαυὶδ καὶ περὶ
τῆς τοῦ Οὐρίου. The papyrus implies λόγος instead of ὁμιλία (see Lampe, s.v. λόγος,
8). Furthermore, the details about Chrysostom himself must all be abbreviated as
is fairly common with patristic writers who were read a good deal. In fact,
'Chrysostomos' is a by-name accorded to him by a later age: during his life he was
usually known as John of Constantinople, the patriarchate of which he held from
398–404.

The gap in the text between *recto* and *verso*, when compared with Migne's text,
affords the calculation that the codex contained 20–21 lines per page. The reading
at *recto l.*7 ἀλ[λάσσουσι is preferred by Treu (*lectio difficilior*) to γράφουσι in Migne
(though the latter notes that two MSS attest the papyrus reading as well).

As with any popular author in antiquity, Chrysostom had works attributed to
him which are clearly not his. The homily on Ps. 50 is a case in point: its author
was an anonymous contemporary from the end of the fourth century. But it is
hardly a matter for surprise that the writer of this papyrus accepted John's
authorship. For it was included in a collection of 38 homilies translated into Latin
and known to Augustine in 422 (Treu, 73). In fact, of the other surviving papyrus
texts only one is certainly attributable to Chrysostom: *MPER* (n.s.) 4 (1946) 54
(*P. Vindob. G.* 26132B), 29th homily on Jn. This text (van Haelst, 632) is a single
sheet (Fayum, VI) which did not form part of a codex (Turner, *Typology*, p.132).
P. Ant. 3 (1967) 111 may be from his 44th homily on Mt., but certainty is lacking.
It comprises 24 fragments from a double-column codex (Antinoopolis, VI/VII; van
Haelst 633). Another pseudo-Chrysostom work, *On the beheading of John the
Baptist* (*P. Oxy.* 13 [1919] 1603), was identified independently by both A. Castig-
lioni, *Rendic. Ist. Lomb.* 52 (1919) 292–96, and R. Harris, *BJRL* 5 (1919) 386–87.

Treu had published earlier another fragmentary leaf (*P. Berl.* 6788) from the
same codex, containing Job 31.32–34, 39–32.1 (*APF* 20 [1970] 59, and pl. 7b). But
the connection between the two texts had not been easy to discern partly because
different scribes had written the portions. The fact that Job and a patristic homily
occur in the same codex may mean that the content of the third sheet, with only
a few letters remaining on either side, cannot be narrowed down to being a passage
of Chrysostom. By the same token, these three scrappy leaves are insufficient to
help us gauge with much hope of success what function such a codex may have had,
that it should contain such diverse works. We do not know of any works by John
relating to Job. And the fact that John's name and title are given in the heading
suggests that the rest of the codex did not contain his works alone, perhaps even
no other works by him. The only common thread which one might discern, and it

is tenuous enough, is that the codex comprised quotations of and patristic comments about OT Wisdom literature. The Job text is printed below.

recto

. . . .
[μο]υ π[αντ]ὶ ἐλθ[όντι]   31.32
[ἀνέῳκτ]ο.
[Εἰ δὲ καὶ ἁμαρ]τὼν ἀκουσίως ἔ-   33
[κρυψα τὴ]ν ἁμαρτίαν μου,
5 [Οὐ γὰρ διετρ]άπην πολυοχλεί-   34
[αν πλήθου]ς   τοῦ ἐξαγορεῦ-
[σαι ἐνώπιο]ν αὐτῶν,

verso

. . . .
. . [
καὶ ψ[υχ]ὴν [κ̄ῡ τῆς γῆς ἐκ]   39
10 λαβὼν ἐλ[ύπησα],
'Αντὶ πυροῦ ἄρα [ἐξέθοι μοι]   40
κνίδη,
> 'Αντὶ δὲ κριθῆ[ς βάτος.]
καὶ ἐπαύσατ[ο Ιωβ ῥήμασιν.] 32.1
15 ['Η]σύχασαν δὲ κ[αὶ   ]

On the whole the text follows B (IV), but the omission of μή before ἐξαγορεῦσαι accords with C (V, Ephraemi rescriptus). Note the awareness of verse and chapter divisions: verses begin on a new line out in the margin, even though much of the preceding line may be left blank (e.g., *recto l.*2, *verso l.*12); and before *verso l.*14 a *coronis* marks the end of the chapter. The number of lines per page can be calculated as 22–24, which accords reasonably well with the Chrysostom section of the codex.

Treu has published a lucid survey article, 'Papyri und Patristik', *Kairos* 16 (1974) 97–114, in which he compares the survival of Christian literary papyri with Classical Greek literary papyri. Included is a discussion of papyrus remains of a range of ECL and patristic texts. The ratio of Greek biblical (OT, NT) to non-biblical Christian (apocrypha, Fathers, hagiographical/martyrological, creeds, liturgies, magic, varia) papyri is almost 2:1.

100. Miscellaneous liturgical fragments

Although lack of space precludes reprinting here, a number of Christian texts (mostly liturgical in character) published recently by K. Treu deserve even brief mention. They appeared in either:
(a) 'Neue berliner liturgische Papyri', *APF* 21 (1971) 57–81 (pls.1-8); or
(b) 'Varia Christiana', *APF* 24/25 (1976) 113-27 (figs. 9-17).
Other texts from these articles have been noted above at **8, 87, 92, 93, 95**.

1. *P.Berl.* 1163 — Treu (a), pp.62-65, no.2 (pl.3) — (provenance unknown, V/VI). Epiphany (January 6) hymn with 45 lines of text extant and probably only the beginning missing. Celebrates Christ's baptism in the Jordan, drawing on the Gospel accounts, filled out with references to Psalms. Emphasizes the contrast between the majesty of the eternal Son of God and his humility in undergoing baptism. A succession of his miracles mentioned.

2. *P.Berl.* 16595 — Treu (b), pp.121–23, no.5 (cf. *MPL* 2 [1977] 253–54) — (provenance unknown, V/VI). Another Epiphany hymn, of interest musicologically because it employs vowel doublings to indicate note lengths to a singer (who must presumably already know the melody). *Recto* contains the Jordan baptism incident, while *verso* has Miriam's song (Ex. 15.20f.) after Israel was saved via the Red Sea. Paul mentions this event as a type of baptism (1 Cor. 10.1–2), and this is probably how the content of the two sides is related.

3. *P.Berl.* 21231 — Treu (b), pp.123–24, no.6 — (provenance unknown, IV/V). Prayer at the Eucharist? The text is very fragmentary but the presence of an imperative at *l*.12 is suggestive of a prayer. For *ll*.6–7,]. ἡμᾶς ἀλλή|[λους ---] . φιλήματι, Treu compares Rom. 16.16.

4. *P.Berl.* 17032 — Treu (a), pp.72–74, no.8 (pl.6b) — (provenance unknown, c.V/VI). Contents not fully clear, but in the 23 extant fragmentary lines the Sanctus anaphora can be discerned (*ll*.6–7) and the Words of Institution (*ll*.18–20). Treu notes that this text represents a relatively early and local Egyptian formulation of the anaphora.

5. *P.Berl.* 17449 — Treu (a), pp.75–78, no.10 (pl.7) — (Hermopolis, IV/V). *Verso* preserves the Great Doxology (*gloria in excelsis deo*).

6. *P.Berl.* 364 — Treu (b), pp.114–17, 127, no.1 (cf. *MPL* 2 [1977] 252–53) — (Thebes, V/VI). This preserves on stone another version of no.5. Cf. B.M. Metzger in *Studies in NT Language and Text. Essays in honour of G.D. Kilpatrick*, ed. J.K. Elliott (*NovT Suppl.* 45; Leiden, 1976) 301–12, who publishes a description of a Coptic Gospel of Matthew; the MS (IV/V) also contains the Great Doxology in Greek with a Coptic translation (Metzger, 309–12), whose wording is somewhat different from that surviving in Codex Alexandrinus. Is it a local Egyptian version?

7. *P.Berl.* 21232 — Treu (b), pp.124–26, no.7 — (provenance unknown, Byzantine). This text mentions the Trinity and the command to baptize, drawing on Mt. 28.19–20 in *ll*.8–11. It is possible that an anti-Arian polemic may be reflected in this fragment, given the presence of ὁμόδοξος (*l*.3), a specific term used of the Trinity which Arius rejected. Again, at *l*.5 the word ἀποίητος occurs, to which we may contrast Arius' view that Christ was a ποίημα. If no polemic is to be inferred, we may have a document giving advice to a baptismal candidate to avoid heresy (ἔρεσις, *l*.1).

D. ECCLESIASTICA

101. The earliest Christian silver hoard yet found

Two closely adjacent hoards of fourth-century date were found in 1974 and 1975 in and near the Roman town of Durobrivae, near Water Newton in England. This township grew up beside a military fort built during IAD to defend a bridge over the River Neve; but the town's suburbs sprawled over 100 hectares between the Flavian period and IV. The 1974 treasure included pottery, bronze and silver items, as well as the remains of a linen-lined leather purse, and 30 Roman gold *solidi* which range in date from 330-50 and emanated from widely distant mints (Nikomedia, Trier, Aquileia, Siscia, Thessalonike). Painter, *Water Newton Silver*, includes brief discussion of this hoard, but his pamphlet concentrates upon the 1975 find of 28 inventoried items (no.28 is a group of fragments), all but one (no.11, gold disc) being high quality silver bowls, dishes, cups and plaques. The importance of this hoard lies above all in the fact that it is 'the earliest known group of Christian silver from the whole Roman Empire' (Painter, 24).

(We may note here the discovery early this century of the so-called 'Great Chalice' of Antioch, a large silver cup embossed with 12 portrait figures representing Christ (twice), eight apostles, and two evangelists. It was found with six other silver objects in a well in Syrian Antioch. When first published (*ed.pr.* G.A. Eisen, *AJA* 20 [1916] 426–37; id., *The Great Chalice of Antioch*, 2 vols [New York, 1923]) it was treated as IAD. But while its Christian association is beyond doubt, the date proposed has been nearly unanimously moved forward to IV or V. The considerable debate about this work in the second quarter of this century has now largely died away; on balance, the cup is to be regarded as an authentic work of Christian art executed somewhere in Syria in IV or V, perhaps for use as a chalice.)

The Water Newton hoard was obviously buried with some care: there were no signs of its being dumped in haste or as being of no further use. Among possible reasons for the concealment, protection from damage or confiscation during the III/early IV persecutions directed against Christians — which culminated in the 'Great' Persecution under Diocletian in 303–04 — is not unlikely. Since the hoard includes some vessels made in III — the majority appear to be early IV — Painter suggests (20–21, 24) that the material was deposited in IV, earlier rather than later, or in any case not later than IV. A.C. Thomas, *Christianity in Roman Britain to AD500* (London, 1981) 119, prefers a date nearer to 350 plus. P. Salway, *Roman Britain* (Oxford, 1981) 340 n.1 (cf. 721 n.3), thinks it may have been hidden as a result of Constantius' edicts to demolish existing churches. (In fact, the wording of the source of this comment — Lact., *de mort. persec.* 15.7 — is *conventicula ...dirui passus est*, and the noun may refer merely to 'meeting places' used by Christians. Lactantius uses *ecclesia* elsewhere to refer to church buildings, e.g., 12.2, quoted below.)

Over half the items (17) are plaques: they are the first — so Painter, 22; but cf. *New Docs 1976*, 4 — examples found of Christian votive plaques, and are of the same type as pagan examples known all over the Empire: 'indubitably Christian in nature, but pagan in form' (Thomas, 31. He makes a direct comparison, 116–17, between no.12 [see below] and a contemporary pagan votive inscription found elsewhere in England.). They are dedications by individuals to God in recognition of and thanks for the fulfilment of some request. Of these plaques nos. 10, 13, 14, 16, 18, 19, 21, 22 all carry the ⳩ monogram, as does the gold disc (no.11). The style of this monogram on the latter, however, is distinctive, as it is also on some of the other items: they possess the so-called 'open' *rho*, i.e., the loop of the *rho* does not join back to the tail, but sometimes even curves away from it. The presence of this style of the monogram is one indication that the workmanship is Eastern, although the hoard was found in the far West of the Empire (Painter, 24). Examples with the 'open' ⳩ are nos.3 (large dish with ω following, but no A preceding the monogram), 8 (cup or bowl), 12 (plaque). A brief epitaph from Tomis (Constanţa), *MPR* 21 (V-VI), includes the open style ⳩ blended with the monogram cross, inside a *stephanos* from which trail two ivy leaves. Two other examples from the same provenance are included in *MPR*. No. 33 is a fragment of a table support which was a second-century votive offering, ὑπὲρ εὐχῆς; in V it was Christianized by the addition of crosses — including an open-style ⳩ — and names. The closest example in *MPR* to compare with the Water Newton find is no. 40, a large silver dish (.610m. in diameter) in the centre of which is a gilded A ⳩ ω (the *rho* is open); a Latin inscription encircles the monogram, and includes the name Paternus, who was bishop of Tomis under Anastasius I (491–518). Barnea dates this dish to the last decade of V (p.73), and regards it as the most important piece of worked precious metal to survive from Scythia Minor (p.220; see his discussion of this dish, pp.220-25).

Returning to the Water Newton plaques, three of them carry inscriptions, Latin in each case. No.12 reads *Iamcilla votum quo(d) promisit conplevit*, 'Iamcilla fulfilled the vow which she had promised' (for this reading of the name — Painter had *Anicilla* — see Thomas, 116). But it is not just the plaques which are to be interpreted as votive offerings by Christians. No.8 is a cup or bowl which reads *Innocentia et Viventia...runt*. Painter suggests that the lacuna should be filled in with something like *lib(entes) dederunt*. Here, too, 'the general sense of giving up ownership to Christ is clear' (p.14). (Note also Painter's discussion of the name Innocentia: at Rome a mid-III burial club had the name *Innocentii* for its members. One chamber in the tomb of this association carries the Christian graffito ΙΤΧΘΥΣ, combining the 'fish' anagram with the *tau*-cross: on the latter see *New Docs 1976*, **90**. Painter, 15 and n.14, gives references to discussion of this tomb at Rome.) This inscription is tooled with double-stroke lettering, another indication of workmanship from the Eastern Empire (Painter, 24). Also described as a cup or bowl is no.9, which carries the name *Publianus* on the exterior base, and around the rim a dactylic hexameter, A ⳩ ω *sanctum altare tuum D* A ⳩ ω *omine subnixus honoro*. Painter interprets the name on the base as the subject of the sentence on the rim, 'O Lord, I Publianus, relying on you, honour your holy sanctuary'. *Altare* is to be taken to mean 'almost certainly "sanctuary" rather than "altar"' (Salway, 719 ; cf. Thomas, 116, 149). The wording of this text is reminiscent of phrases in the Mass (see Painter 16, 23), and again indicates clearly that the vessel is a dedication.

Painter does not address himself to the question whether these votive offerings were wall plaques, and if so whether they presupposed the existence of a church building. Salway (719) recognizes more fully what is implied by them. Both no.9 above and the plaques, which — in view of the one or two small holes in most of them — must have been attached to some structure, show that 'the whole group represents fittings and furnishings, deliberately removed from a Christian shrine and carefully buried'. Not only is the Water Newton find important as the earliest Christian silver hoard from the whole Empire, but it was located originally in an actual shrine (ibid.). The presence of a Christian group in a town whose suburbs had sprawled so greatly (c. 250 acres) by IV is not at all unlikely. Salway notes (770) that we should not think of Durobrivae as a minor rural township. The existence here of a Christian community 'based on and perhaps originating from the semi-urban industrial workers of the potteries is more likely than in a "normal" Romano-British country town or among the agricultural peasantry'. While it may have been an exceptional British town it provided 'a reasonable setting for a third-century Christian community' — although the Water Newton collection does not prove this *per se* (Salway, ibid.). Thomas suggests (117, 118) that it is a set of church plate belonging to a well-off congregation.

Eusebius, *HE* 8.1.5, indicates that some church buildings existed before Constantine, but possibly after the return to toleration following the confiscation of church property during the Persecution of 303–04 believers wanted their meeting places to have a more permanent and solid form: see Eusebius, 10.4. (For the term καθολικὴ ἐκκλησία in two fourth-century inscriptions from Egypt, see *I.Pan* 27 [Bir Quattar, south of Mons Porphyrites, probably 340/1] and 28 [Mons Porphyrites, IV], with Bernand's discussion, pp.69–70, 72.) On this matter generally see R.M. Grant, *Early Christianity and Society* (London, 1978) 146ff., especially 149–51. A papyrus declaration (in triplicate) dated to the time of the Great Persecution, *P.Oxy.* 33 (1968) 2673 (3/2/304), is made by Aurelius Ammonios, ἀναγνωσ|τῆς τῆς ποτε ἐκ⟨κ⟩λησίας κώμης Χύσεως, 'reader of the former church of the village of Chysis' (*ll.*8–9). This man is a Copt, for he was unable to write Greek (*l.*35; on this phenomenon see briefly *New Docs 1976*, **80**). Ammonios reports that the church possesses 'neither gold, silver, money, clothing (ἐσθῆτα, 17; 'vestments'? — *ed.pr.*; garments for charitable distribution? — E.A. Judge), nor animals, slaves, lands, property either from grants or bequests, except bronze material' which has already been surrendered (*ll.*16–24). J.R. Rea originally published this text with the reading χαλκῆν πύλην, 'bronze door'. From this it has been inferred that we had very early documentary evidence of a public church building, prior to Constantine. Rea has subsequently revised the text at this point which now is to be read as χαλκῆν ὕλην (*ZPE* 35 [1979] 128; the correction is noted at *P.Oxy.* 48 [1981] p.xvii, where a further reference to ὕλη used of metal is supplied). Rea takes the phrase in *P.Oxy.* 2673 as a general allusion to a quantity of bronze-objects which may lack any sacramental significance. The removal of the 'door' from this papyrus means that *P.Oxy.* 2673 cannot be appealed to in support of the claim that public church buildings existed before Constantine. On this and other early papyrus documents evidencing early Christianity in Egypt see E.A. Judge/S.R. Pickering, *JbAC* 20 (1977) 47–71 (pp.59–60 for *P.Oxy.* 2673). Before leaving this question of the evidence for early church buildings, it should be noted that Lactantius, a contemporary of Diocletian, reports (*de mort. pers.* 12.2) that in Nikomedia at the outset of the persecution, *repente adhuc dubia luce ad ecclesiam praefectus cum ducibus... venit; et revulsis foribus simulacrum quaeritur, scripturae repertae incenditur.* Clearly there was a public church building in Diocletian's capital in Bithynia before the attack against the Christians began. Considerably less certain evidence is afforded by *AE* 184, an epitaph from Ferentinum in Italy, which has been most recently restored to say that the deceased rebuilt the 'basilica' destroyed by savage persecution: [*Illa quae basilicam saevis*]*sima persecutione deruta(m) de suis pr*[*opriis (sumptibus) refecit* (or *curavit*)...]. Previously it had been understood that the woman herself had been killed in the persecution (*deruta*); and this view may still be preferable. But if *basilicam* (or *ecclesiam*?) is accepted, the persecution referred to can only be Diocletian's; and the text may provide some documentary evidence for the existence of a church building before the onset of the persecution. Note also that Lact., *de mort. pers.* 15.7 — quoted above — attests implicitly the presence of meeting places used specifically by Christians in Britain before the persecution began.

Painter has also published a catalogue with excellent plates of the Mildenhall treasure, in which he offers a reinterpretation of how they may have come to Britain and through whose hands they passed. The text of Painter, *Mildenhall*, is very largely the same as his article in *BMQ* 37 (1973) 54–80, but the more recent publication has full plates. Found c. 1942 near Mildenhall in Suffolk, the hoard consists of 34 Roman silver objects of fourth-century date. The most important objects, the Great Dish (Painter, no.1) and the two platters decorated with Bacchic themes (nos.2, 3) may be earlier than mid-IV (Painter, *Mildenhall*, 12). While the ornamentation on these items as well as nos. 5–8 — four bowls with medallions of Alexander the Great, Olympias (?), a hunter fighting a bear, and a female head — is clearly pagan, there are eight spoons, five of which carry Christian inscriptions; from this it has been inferred that the owner of the group was a Christian. The preservation by such a person of high-quality plate with non-Christian motifs would be quite normal, either on aesthetic grounds or as family heirlooms.

Concerning the spoons, three (nos. 29–31) carry the ☧ monogram; this design on IV spoons is common (Painter, 15); and his quotation from an earlier writer is apposite, that 'the presence of the monogram on a spoon of this period, the fourth century, may be due merely to the prevailing fashion of placing religious emblems on common objects, by no means necessarily connected with worship' (p.20). The two spoons with Latin wording (nos.27 and 28) read *Papittedo vivas*, and *Pascentia vivas*, 'which may or may not have Christian overtones' (p.19; the same wording in *BMQ* (1973): 167). This comment is a little surprising. The name Pascentius occurs in six Christian inscriptions listed in Diehl *ICLV*, 1269 note, 1968C(b), 2117B, 3004A note, 3109A, 3442. No feminine forms are attested elsewhere to my knowledge; nor has the name been found in any non-Christian texts. Further *vivas* is a very common formula on Christian funerary inscriptions; numerous examples in Diehl. While the spoons ought not to be regarded as part of a funerary offering — the analogy is not exact, therefore — Painter's translations (*BMQ* (1973): 158, 159) 'long life to P.', appear to be trying to keep open the remote possibility of a non-Christian reference.

More far-reaching is Painter's argument that the graffito ευθηριου scratched on nos.2 and 3 may indicate that the owner was Eutherios, the Armenian eunuch who served a succession of emperors (Constantine, Constans, and Julian as the latter's chamberlain, *praepositus sacri cubiculi*). It is true that this name is rare: A.H.M. Jones et al., *The Prosopography of the Later Roman Empire* I (Cambridge, 1971) 314–15, lists only three others (all are IV²); from a later period one more is listed in *PLRE* II. Painter's hypothesis is that this collection (or at least the two Bacchic platters) may once have been in his possession (while he was in Gaul with Julian from 355–61) and were passed on by him before he returned to Rome, the new owner bringing the objects to Britain. Painter suggests that this new owner was the Christian general Lupicinus, who was sent by Julian to Britain with a large force to deal with Scots and Picts in 360. In Lupicinus' absence Julian was declared Augustus by his troops and openly avowed his paganism. Lupicinus was likely to be loyal to Constantius, and upon his return to Gaul Julian had him arrested. Friends or family still in Britain may have hidden the silver until matters became more settled. Thus, while Painter holds that the Mildenhall silverware is the unrecovered property of a Christian, this cannot be argued from the composition of the hoard but because Lupicinus the Christian may have been its last owner (p.23).

It must be said that Painter acknowledges the hypothetical character of his chain of suggestions. But the links are far too tenuous to provide a persuasive answer to the question of ownership. The graffito name on two items is insufficient to link the pieces with Julian's confidant; while to explain the hoard's presence in Britain from Lupicinus' expedition is unconvincing. Thomas largely accepts (103, 109–10) Painter's argument, but cf. Salway, 373.

The ☧ monogram is not an exclusively Christian symbol, for it can be an abbreviation in papyrus texts for ἑκατοναρχία (*PW*, s.v. *Siglae* [1923], col. 2301); χειρόγραφον (O. Montevecchi, *La Papirologia* [Turin, 1973] 477); χράω, χρῆσις, χρηστός and χρόνος (K. McNamee, *Abbreviations in Greek Literary Papyri and Ostraca* [*BASP* suppl.3; Chico, 1981] s.vv.). Cf. C.H. Roberts, *Manuscript, Society and Belief in Early Christian Egypt* (London, 1979) 83. But where it is Christian its presence is 'usually assumed to be an indication of a date later than AD 312' (Painter, *Water Newton Silver*, 11). This is to be closely associated with Constantine: K. Weitzmann, *Age of Spirituality. Late Antique and Early Christian Art, Third to Seventh Century* (New York, 1979) 63, notes that the symbol appears on his coins and medallions, alluding to the sign he saw in the sky before the battle of the Milvian Bridge 'and subsequently adopted as his primary insignia'. One of these medallions (Weitzmann no. 57, p.66; dated 313) shows it on Constantine's helmet. For other examples in that book see its index, s.v. 'Christogram' (p.726). Some other recently published early examples of this Christogram are:

1. *CIMAH* 1 (Sitten, Canton Wallis in Switzerland, 377).

> devotione.vigens.
> augustas Pontius aedis. A ☧ ω
> restituit.praetor.
> longe praestantius.illis.
> 5 quae.priscae.steterant.
> talis.respublica.quere
> d(omino) n(ostro) Gratiano Aug(usto).IIII.et Mer(obaude).co(n)s(ulibus).
> Pontius.Asclepiodotus.v(ir) p(erfectissimus).p(raeses) d(onum) d(edit)

Vigorous in zeal, Pontius the Praetor restored this august building (*cross*) far more outstandingly than the one which had stood there previously. Seek for men like that, Republic! In the consulships of our lord Gratian Augustus (his fourth) and of Merobaudes. Pontius Asclepiodotus, a man most excellent, governor, made the dedication.

Bibliography on this inscription extends back to the early 18th century (*CIMAH*, p.36): the text consists of three hexameters written in six lines, plus two non-metrical lines. For the dots between words see E.O. Wingo, *Latin Punctuation in the Classical Age* (The Hague, 1972). Only the Christogram flanked by A/ω at the end of *l.*2 suggests a Christian link for this text, for otherwise the wording offers no hint; and one's first reaction is that the symbol is a later addition, incised at the end of the shortest line on the stone. But Jörg believes (p.35) that it is to all appearance contemporary with the inscription. With this Christian (?) benefactor of what may have been a temple of Augustus, cf. **107**. *CIMAH*, p.36, notes that it used to be thought a pagan (or Christian) building, but is now generally supposed to have been an administrative building. Pls. 1.1 and 1.2 very clearly show that the Christogram has the 'open' style *rho*, as found several times on the Water Newton Silver: see Painter's comment, noted above, on the significance of this style. (*CIMAH* 19 is a tiny fragment of stone [St-Maurice, Canton Wallis, VI] which uses an open *rho* in its abbreviation of 'Christ' as XPE.) The alpha/omega combine a capital with minuscule: this is quite common, every example in the Water Newton hoard uses the minuscule-style omega (a couple are upside down, however: nos. 11, 12).

E.A. Judge has written me the following note: '*Respublica* is the common way in inscriptions of the western Roman empire of alluding to the local community however constituted, in this case the Civitas Vallensium; cf. *AE* (1979) 637, referring to J. Gascou, 'L'emploi du terme *respublica* dans l'épigraphie latine d'Afrique', *MEFR* 91 (1979) 383–398, and A. Mócsy, '*Ubique res publica.* Zu den Autonomiebestrebungen und Uniformierungstendenzen am Vorabend des Dominats', *AAntHung* 10 (1962) 367–384 (*non vidi*). Concurrently the term was being confined in literary usage almost exclusively to what we call the 'Roman Empire' itself, for which see W. Suerbaum, *Vom antiken zum frühmittelalterlichen Staatsbegriff* (Munster, 1977³), *passim.*'

2. P.J. Sijpesteijn/K.A. Worp, *ZPE* 32 (1978) 243–57, with addendum in ibid. 37 (1980) 268, publish an archive of eleven texts belonging to early IV (Hermopolite nome). Three of these texts (nos. 1, 3, 6) carry the monogram. The earliest, no. 1, *l.*6, appears in a certificate on the *recto* of *P. Vindob.* G. 13087 (pl. 6a), which is datable to 321/22, an extremely early papyrus example of the symbol as an indicator of Christianity, as they note.

102. χρηστιανή **in a Christian letter**
Oxyrhynchite nome   IV/V
ed.pr. — R. Pintaudi, *P.Laur.* 42 *recto*, pp.50–52 (pl.42 *bis*)

πάνυ ἐλυπήθην καὶ λοιπούμεθα πάνυ σφόδρα διότι [[τὸ κακὸν]]
ἐτόλμησας ποιήσῃς πρᾶγμα τοιοῦτο Ἀθῆατι χρηστιανὴ οὖσα, διότι
καὶ λαε[ι]κὴ οὖσα καὶ μηδέποτε εὑρέθη πράγματα τοῦ κόσμου.
     cm. 2
γνῶστι ὅτι σπεχουλάτωρα γέγονεν Θεόδωρος ὁ Τηείτης.
5 ἦλθεν μετὰ Θέωνος τοῦ ἀδελφοῦ μου.

Judging from its content the *verso* of this letter precedes the *recto*, and deals with someone's dismay at the behaviour of a sailor, who is described as a drunkard (μεθυσστοίς, *verso*, *l.*8). Note the paragraph break marked by the space on the *recto* — another occurs on the *verso*.

I was very pained and we are exceedingly pained that you dared to do such a thing to Atheas, since you are a Christian, because she also is a laywoman, and she has never been discovered (doing) worldly business. Know that
5 **Theodoros from Teis has become a *speculator*. |He came with Theon, my brother.**

The point of particular interest in this letter is the presence of the word χρησ-τιανή. A full discussion of its occurrence in documentary texts is reserved to the next volume of *New Docs*. However, note the following other attestations in papyri: *PSI* 14 (1957) 1412 (Oxyrhynchos, II/III; 'later III?' — Judge/Pickering [see below]), a letter in which it is mentioned that διεπ]εμψά|μην σοι δι⟨ὰ⟩ Σωτοῦ τοῦ χρησ⟨τ⟩ια[νοῦ] τάλαν|τα δυό, κτλ, 'I sent to you via Sotas the Christian two talents . . .' (9-11). *Ed.pr.* understood the word as a name, but J.R. Rea has suggested this restoration for the *PSI* text at *P.Oxy.* 36 (1970) 2785, n. to *l.*2. *P.Oxy.* 42 (1974) 3035 is a brief order to arrest, dated 28/2/256 in which the *prytanis* issues the instruction 'send up straightaway Petosorapis, son of Horos, Christian, or you yourselves come up', ἐξαυτῆς ἀνα|πέμψατε Πετοσορᾶπιν Ὥρου χρησι|ανόν, ἢ ὑμεῖς αὐτοὶ ἀνέλθατε. *Ed.pr.* understands this spelling as a variant of χρησ⟨τ⟩ιανόν. Close in time to this is *P.Oxy.* 43 (1975) 3119, a record of investigation concerning χρηστιανοί (259/60?). On the importance of these texts as the earliest papyrus attestations of the civil use of the term see E.A. Judge/S.R. Pickering, *JbAC* 20(1977) 47-71, especially 66-69. Together with evidence from elsewhere these examples can begin to help us plot the development of the process by which the word passed from a term invented by outsiders (Acts 11.26) to one which Christians were prepared to use of themselves.

Much later than these three and the *P.Laur.* example is *P.Lond.* 1 (1893) 77 (c. VIII), the will of Abraham, bishop of Hermouthis, in which he declares on oath that he 'owns no gold or silver in accordance with (?) the faith of the Christians' ἐν ὅρκῳ κατὰ τῆς | τῶν χρειστιανῶν πίστεως οὐδὲ χρύσιον οὐδὲ ἀργύριον οὐκ ἔχω (*ll.*71-72). What particularly complicates any conclusion about the presence of the word in early non-literary texts is the debate which has been proceeding for the last half-century over its occurrence in inscriptions from Phrygia, whether the presence of the word is an indicator of Montanism. From this it has been argued that the occurrence of χρηστιανός in inscriptions from elsewhere (Rome, Perinthos, etc.) indicates a Montanist presence. Some bibliography for this debate was given at *New Docs 1976*, **86**, to which one may add notices in *BE* (1952) 191; (1956) 24, 360; (1972) 282, and particularly W. Tabbernee, *The Opposition to Montanism from Church and State* (Diss. Melbourne, 1980). See in addition E.P. Gibson, *GRBS* 16(1976) 433-42, with the notice at *BE* (1977) 493. On the orthography of χρηστιανός see *New Docs 1976*, **76**.

Returning to *P.Laur.* 42, is λαε[ι]κή a synonym for χρηστιανή here? For the usage in Patristic texts see Lampe, s.v., 2. Its presence closely adjacent to χρηστιανή perhaps militates against it.

Finally, over a dozen papyrus attestations of the Latinism σπεκουλάτωρ — *ed.pr.* treats the form in our text as nominative — are listed in S. Daris, *Il Lessico latino nel Greco d' Egitto* (Barcelona, 1971), s.v.; ranging from II–V, the preponderance of examples belongs to IV. What meaning is to be applied to it at *P.Laur.* 42 is uncertain, perhaps 'courier'. Its sole NT occurrence (Mk. 6.27) requires the sense 'executioner'.

103. A cryptic Christian Letter?

Provenance unknown   III/IV
ed.pr. — P.J. Sijpesteijn, *P.Wiscon.* 74, pp.131–33 (pl.29)

Κυρίῳ μου ἀ[δ]ελφῶι Ἀφυγχίωι
Κύρας καὶ Ἀίας πλεῖστα χαίρειν.
πάντα ὑπερθέμενος ἐκσαυτῆς ἀπάντησων
πρὸς ὑμᾶς ἐπιδὴ ἡ μήτηρ ἡμῶν ἀπεγένετο
5 καὶ πάνοι χρίαν ἔχω{ ι}μεν΄ τῇ παρουσίᾳ σου. μὴ θε-
λήσῃς οὖν παραμῖναι παρά σοι τοῦ σαι ἀπαντῆ-
σαι πρὸς ὑμᾶς καὶ ἀπολέσωμεν τὴν
οἰκίαν ἡμῶν. οἶδας γὰρ καὶ σῶι ὅτι οὐδὲν δυνάμεθα ποιῆσαι [± 15 letters] τὴν παρουσίαν
10 [σ]ου. τούτου γὰρ χάριν καὶ τὸν ἀδελφῶν ἡμῶν
Μαρτύριον ἀπεστίλαμεν εἵνα σὺν αὐτῷ
ἐκσαυτῆς ἀπαντήσῃς πρὸς ὑμᾶς. χάρις
γὰρ αὐτῷ πλίστην ὅτι τῶν σκυλμῶν πεποίηκεν
πρός σαι ὑμῶν παρέχωντος αὐτοῦ τῶν μισ-
15 θῶν. ἀσπάζωμεν τὴν ἀδελφὴν ἡμῶν τὴν
Ἐλευθέρα σου καὶ τὰ ⟨ἀ⟩βάσκα⟨ν⟩τα αὐτῆς παιδία
καὶ τοὺς ὑμῶν πάντας κατ' ὄνομα. ἐρρῶσ-
θαί σε εὔχομαι πολλοῖς
χρόνοις, κύριε ἡμῶν ἀδελφαί.
20 μὴ θέλῃς ἀμαιλῆσαι καὶ ὕστερα μεταμελή⟨σ⟩ῃς.
ἐκσαυτῆς ἀπάντησων εἵνα πάντα τυπώσῃς.
ἀπ(όδος) τῷ κυρίῳ {μου} ἡμῶν   ἀδελφῷ Ἀφυγχίῳ
(*verso*)
π(αρὰ) Κύρα[ς] καὶ Ἀίας.

The papyrus was cut regularly on all four sides and folded four times vertically. The large handwriting suggests that the sender was not a frequent letter-writer (cf. *ed.pr.*, p.131). Note inconsistent use of the iota in the dative ending (1); read ἐξαυτῆς (3, 12, 21); ει/ι are interchanged as are ο/ω; ἡμᾶς (4, 7, 12; and probably 17); πάνυ (5); σε (6, 14); σύ (8); σε ἡμῶν παρεχόντων αὐτῷ (14).

> **To my lord brother Aphynchios, Kyras and Aias (send) very many greetings.**
> 5 **Set everything aside and come to us since our mother has died, | and we have particular need of your presence. So don't be prepared to remain at your place so as (not) to come to us and we ruin our family. For you know as well**
> 10 **that we can do nothing [without you. We await (?)] your coming. | For this is why we also sent our brother Martyrios, so that you might come to us immediately with him. We are greatly in his debt because he has taken the**
> 15 **trouble to come to you, we | provided payment for him. We greet our sister your Eleuthera and her children — may they be preserved from the evil eye — and all your (our?) family personally. I pray you may fare well for a long**
> 20 **time, our lord brother. | Don't be prepared to be neglectful and rue it later. Come straightaway so that you may organize everything. (*verso*) Give to our lord brother Aphynchios from Kyras and Aias.**

Although the possibility is not raised by *ed.pr.* a few features in this letter could well lead us to conclude that it emanated from a Christian milieu. On the face of it two sisters — *ed.pr.* takes their names to be Kyra and Aia, on the basis of *l*.23; but nominative forms are conventional for the senders' self-identification in the opening salutation (*l*.2), and given the orthographical variation in the letter as well as confusion in case and number (e.g., *l*.14) the writer may have regarded Κύρας and ᾿Αίας as nominative endings no less than genitives — write to a brother requesting his immediate presence to help them cope with their mother's death. The fact that they paid (14–15; μισθός does not usually mean travelling 'expenses', as *ed.pr.* translates it) 'our brother Martyrios' (10) to go and fetch Aphynchios suggests that Martyrios is probably not connected by blood. The wording of *ll*.10ff. is against a blood relationship also in view of the sisters' emphasis on their gratitude to Martyrios for taking the trouble of the journey. Is he then a fellow-believer? First, the names Martyrios/-ia appear to be confined to Christian usage: thought not frequent in the papyri (see *NB* and Foraboschi) they are attested from IV–VIII. If *P.Wiscon.* 74 is III/IV then we have here a very early example of the name. Diehl, *ILCV* III, index I, p.108 contains rather more attestations. *CIL* VI (Rome) has three examples (8306, 9920 and 37959) which can all be confidently posited as Christian either on internal grounds or from the location of the burial. Second, *ed.pr.* understands *ll*.15–16 to refer very possibly to brother/sister marriage: 'our sister who is at the same time your wife' (note ad loc., p.133). He does point out that τὴν ἀδελφήν may mean 'our beloved' as a term of affection rather than an expression of blood-ties. Eleuthera is probably Aphynchios' wife in view of σου (16), but she may be a Christian 'sister' of the writers (for ἀδελφός/-ή in Christian parlance see Naldini, 15–16); we should also note that they greet 'her (αὐτῆς) children' rather than 'your' children. For τὰ ἀβάσκαντα παιδία in Christian letters (dated III²–IV) see *New Docs 1976*, **24**, p.70. For another example of this formula in an indubitably Christian letter note *P. Wiscon.* 76 (provenance unknown, mid-IV), *ll*.25–28, ἀσπάζο|[μαι τὰ] ἀβάσκαντα οἰμῶν (= ὑμῶν) ταί|[κνα ἐ]ν θεῷ καὶ τοὺς ἄν|[δρας ὑμ]ῶν. One feature of this letter is its request to the addressees (the writer's ἀδελφαί) to provide hospitality for the person who brings the letter: κα]|[λῶς οὖν] ποιήσαται (= -σετε), ἀδε[λφαὶ Τα]|[αρπα]ῆσι καὶ Ταυσῖρ[ι, ἄπαν]τα | [ἑτοιμ]ά̣ζει⟨ν⟩ δοῦντι ὑμε⟨ῖ⟩ν τὴν | [ἐπιστο]λὴν ταύτην (*ll.* 7–11), 'you will do well, then, sisters Taarpaesis and Tausiris, to make everything ready for the one who gives you this letter'. That the courier is not named here or on the *verso* address indicates that the letter was written but could not be sent until a person was found who happened to be travelling to the destination.

For a similar request in a non-Christian letter note *P. Tebt. Tait* 51 (Tebtynis, II² or III), where one brother says to another: καλῶς ποιήσις | ἀποδεξάμε|νος τὸν κομί|ζοντά σοι τὸ | ἐπιστόλιον . . . ξένος γάρ ἐστιν, | καὶ οὐκ οἶδε | τοὺς τόπους (5–9, 13–15), 'Please receive the one who conveys the letter to you . . . for he is a stranger and does not know the area.'

To return to *P. Wiscon.* 74, one further though much less tangible aspect of the letter may hint at its Christian milieu. The opening and closing verses of 2 Jn. have not infrequently been understood as a covert allusion by the writer to one, or two, Christian groups: ὁ πρεσβύτερος ἐκλεκτῇ κυρίᾳ καὶ τοῖς τέκνοις αὐτοῖς, κτλ (*v.*1); ἀσπάζεταί σε τὰ τέκνα τῆς ἀδελφῆς σου τῆς ἐκλεκτῆς (*v.*13). Given the date of our letter — III/IV (on the basis of the handwriting), a more specific date being impossible to gauge — it would be intriguing if the allusions to the death of our mother (4) and the destruction of our family (7–8) were veiled references to persecution. Lampe attests μήτηρ of the Church from Irenaeus onwards (s.v., 2a(i)); while οἰκία is rare in the Fathers (used figuratively of Hades and Heaven), οἶκος is used of the Church (Lampe, s.v., 3, 4a). There is no way of *proving* a covert allusion here, of course, and the point is raised as no more than a fairly remote possibility. Would cryptic comments be felt necessary in a personally delivered letter? Quite possibly so, in case it fell into other hands than his for whom it was intended. 2 Jn. was no doubt personally delivered, yet note *v.*12 there: some of the matters the writer wants to raise cannot be put in writing.

A few philological items may be listed briefly: ὑπερτίθημι (3) in the sense found here occurs once — also middle — in ECL (see BAGD). ἀπαντάω πρός τινα (3, 6–7, 12), whereas ἀ. τινι at Mk. 14.13; but the absolute use at *l.*21 is paralleled at Lk. 17.12. 1 Pet. 2.24 is the only NT example of ἀπογίνομαι, 'die'; and this new papyrus example should be added to a revised MM entry. On παρουσία (5, 9) cf. *New Docs 1976*, **11**. For μὴ θέλω + aor. infin. cf. NT examples listed in BAGD, s.v., 1, 2. The absolute use of ἀμελέω (20) occurs at Mt. 22.5 (participle); there are a few NT attestations of μεταμέλομαι (20): Mt. 20.30, 32; 27.3; 2 Cor. 7.8; Heb. 7.21.

SEG 1238 reprints an epitaph for a certain Trophimos which may be from Bithynia or Pontus; because the *chi* in the final standard phrase, μνήμης χάριν, is in the shape of a cross, the text has been understood as crypto-Christian. Alternatively, to represent the letter in this way may be a mere stylistic fashion. See *SEG*, ad loc., for references on these possibilities.

104. The origin of the abbreviation ΧΜΓ: a Christian cryptogram?

Medinet Madi (Fayum)   IV
ed.pr. — D. Foraboschi, *O.Medinet Madi* 19, p.83 (pl.23)

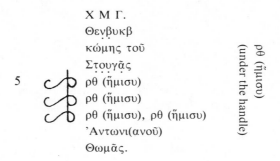

Χ Μ Γ.
Θενβυκβ
κώμης τοῦ
Στουγᾶς
5   ρθ (ἥμισυ)
    ρθ (ἥμισυ)
    ρθ (ἥμισυ), ρθ (ἥμισυ)
᾿Αντωνι(ανοῦ)
Θωμᾶς.

ρθ (ἥμισυ)
(under the handle)

Graffito on upper part of an amphora. The reason for the five-fold repetition of the amount is unclear.

5 Ch. M.G. To(?) Thenbukb of the village of Stougas, |109½, 109½, 109½, 109½, 109½ (kotylai) of Antonianan (wine?). (From?) Thomas.

'Is this the mysterious Christian symbol?' asks *ed.pr.* in her note on *l.*1. But is there any doubt about the abbreviation having a Christian association? More to the point, these three letters are an enigma which has still not been resolved. The abbreviation occurs on a wide range of texts from the late Roman period and the Byzantine world. What makes this example above noteworthy is that it is one of the earliest attestations of it, if the dating is correct. Other papyrus examples from this century include several from Karanis: *P.Mich.* 6 (1944) 378 (IV[1]; a duplicate copy of a list of payments in kind, forming part of an archive; *l.*1 reads † χμγ ϙθ); *P.Mich.* 8 (1951) 519; O.M. Pearl, *Aeg.* 33 (1953) 17–24, nos.16, 25, 31, 32(?) (IV; receipts for payments in kind; χμγ in *l.*1 of the first three, and possibly in the fourth); *P.New York* (1967) 8 (328/9 or 343/4; receipt for delivery of grain; *l.*1: χμγ). Note also *PSI* 13.2 (1953) 1342 (Hermopolite nome, 330–40; letter from a *sitologos* to an anchorite; *l.*1: χμγ ϙθ). On ϙθ in these texts see below. The fullest recent survey of the abbreviation χμγ is J.-O. Tjäder, *Eranos* 68 (1970) 148–90, which provides extensive bibliography. Since then note particularly A. Blanchard, *Proc. XIV Intern. Congress of Pap., Oxford 1974* (London, 1975) 19–24 (pl.11).

Earlier hypotheses, now generally discarded, to explain the original sense of the letters have included χειρός μου γραφή (see Tjäder, 156, 157–58), Χριστὸς Μιχαὴλ Γαβριήλ (see *DACL* IA (1907) cols 180–82, s.v. 'Abbréviations, IX' — yet at ibid, 'Amphores', cols. 1691ff. this explanation was rejected in favour of Χ(ριστὸν) Μ(αρία) γ(εννᾷ)), and a visual correspondence to Heb. אחד (= εἷς), by analogy with ΠΙΠΙ for יהוה. *P.Oxy.* 6 (1908) 940 n. to *l.*1 (on p.310) mentions this theory and notes that occasionally the order of the Greek letters varies, ΓΜΧ thus appearing somewhat closer to the Hebrew letter forms.

The letters occur usually at the head of all sorts of documents, chiefly Byzantine in date. Some are administrative texts (such as *P.Laur.* 45: see **77** in this volume), others have a magical element. A mutilated curse tablet from Beth-Shan/ Skythopolis in Palestine has the letters along with *nomina barbara* at the beginning of the text — see H.C. Youtie/C. Bonner, *TAPA* 68 (1937) 43–77, 128, no.2 (at pp.72–77). If their proposed date (III fin./IV) is correct, we have another very early example of the lettering. Although Jewish names occur in that text the curse tablet is to be seen as of Christian origin. More recently Youtie has published a brief papyrus order (Oxyrhynchos, IV/V) whose first and last lines read χμ‾, which he takes to signify χμγ: *ZPE* 37 (1980) 225–26. Among other 1977 publications note *P.Stras.* 654, a receipt (Hermopolis Magna, 425–50). *SB* 11230 (provenance unknown, V/VI) consists of 13 brief documents, all containing the abbreviation and Christogram, each containing one name; in some cases the person is specified as οἰκ(έτης?) ἄπα ᾿Ωτᾶ.

Tjäder and Blanchard make clear that the interpretation of these letters has been narrowed down to two options. They both prefer the view that the letters are an abbreviation for Χριστὸν Μαρία γεννᾷ, 'Mary gives birth to Christ'. *BE* (1953) 214 reports an inscription from the region of Heliopolis-Baalbek (447/8) which reads Χ(ριστὸ)ς Π(ατρὸ)ς Γ(ένν)α. This hitherto unattested formula is suggested to be a Monophysite counter to χμγ understood as a doctrinal slogan. If this is the case the new formula at least shows that χμγ was understood by some to refer to Mary. Note also several painted inscriptions from Athens in Lang, *Agora*: χμγ occurs at J2, 3, 5, 10–12, but ΧΘΓ (= θεοῦ?) at J7, and χγθε(οῦ) at J8. Are these latter two formulae also a doctrinal reaction to χμγ understood as a Marian slogan? Cf. also *SEG* 391 (Novidunum, IV), an inscription on the neck of an amphora reading Μ Θ Μα΄, which *ed.pr.* — I. Barnea, *Pontica* 10(1977) 281–82 no. 25 (*non vidi*) — interprets as Μ(ήτηρ) Θ(εοῦ), 41 (*sextarii*). There are, however, two arguments fatal to this understanding of the origin of χμγ. First, the full wording for which these letters are an alleged abbreviation has never been attested. It is true that there are two close approximations, as N. Lewis, *BASP* 13 (1976) 158–59, notes. *P.Grenf.* 2 (1897) 112a (c. VII) is a quotation from Ps. 1.3 on vellum preceded by a thrice-repeated formula: † Χ̅ς̅ Μαρία γεννᾷ καὶ † Μαρία Χ̅ς̅ γεννᾷ κ(αὶ) Χ̅ς̅ Μα|ρία γεννᾷ κ(αὶ), κτλ. The second text is an epitaph for a woman (G. Lefebvre, *Recueil des inscriptions grecques-chrétiennes d'Égypte* [Cairo, 1907; repr. Chicago, 1978] 663 [Nubia?, Byzantine date]), which at *ll.*20–22 reads ἀμ|ὴν Χριστοῦ Μαρία γ|εννᾷ ἀμ΄ ην, κτλ. Now if these are the closest approximations to the hypothesized Χριστὸν Μαρία γεννᾷ it is not satisfactory to explain the differences as scribal errors (nominative for accusative in the first, genitive for accusative in the second). The paucity of texts and the fact that appeal must be made to scribal error in both do not permit a confident association of these wordings with χμγ (*pace* Tjäder, 160–62). Even if it were to be sustained, the later dates of these texts might cause one to wonder if these wordings were not a subsequent interpretation of the letters. Second, while the all-pervading Christianization of the Roman world resulted in the addition of Christian markings (such as crosses) to Byzantine documents which were purely commercial or administrative in character, it is hard to imagine the acceptance of a consciously doctrinal slogan as a convention into such documents, which were not concerned with ecclesiastical matters at all.

Lefebvre 663 (quoted just above) leads us on to the second option. Because letters of the alphabet had a numerical equivalent, certain words could be represented symbolically by numbers. The combination Ϙθ (the first is the obsolete Greek letter, *koppa*) = 90 + 9, an isopsephism for ἀμήν (1 + 40 + 8 + 50). M. Drew-Bear, *CE* 54 (1979) 291–303, no.2 (Hermopolite nome, 12/10/504) is a lease of land whose first line reads χμγ Ϙθ. With the second group of letters pretty clearly being an isopsephism, one may be encouraged to think that the first is, too (though *ed.pr.* prudently disavows a dogmatic conclusion). Now the numerical equivalent for χμγ is 643, a number which can be reached also by a combination of the number value of the letters in θεὸς βοηθός. (Another isopsephic candidate, mentioned by O. Montevecchi, *La Papirologia* [Turin, 1973] 290, is ἡ ἁγία τριὰς θ(εός). But it is less satisfactory because of the need to abbreviate one element in the formula, and because it takes an overt doctrinal stand. For two other possibilities see Tjäder, 155–56.) This phrase is very widespread in its attestation (see **116** in this volume for some comments on it) and unlike the 'Marian' slogan is devoid of overt *parti pris*. This would make it very much more appropriate as a conventional addition in routine documents; the widespread use of the cross (in various styles) provides an obvious analogy to this.

While it is true that ephemeral documents on papyri are more likely to contain these abbreviations, they occur well outside Egypt. The XMΓ formula is very frequent in Syria from III–VII (see edd. n. to *P.Mich.* 6 [1944] 378, p.52): for concise discussion with numerous references see L. Robert, *Hellenica* 11–12 (1960) 309–11. W.K. Prentice, *CP* 9 (1914) 410–16, provides an excellent general survey of earlier interpretations while commenting particularly on the Syrian inscriptions. χμγ is known from Phrygia: C.H.E. Haspels, *The Highlands of Phrygia*, I (Princeton, 1971) pp.310–11, no.36, an epitaph for a husband and wife, at the end of which (*l.*6) stands χ̄μ̄γ̄. Haspels includes some earlier bibliography mostly not mentioned in this entry, and refers to three examples from Lykaonia with the formula at the beginning of the text (*MAMA* 8[1962] 74, 275, 279). For attestations from Nessana, Cyrenaica, and Crete, see Tjäder, 176 n.10. L. Vidman, *ZPE* 16 (1975) 215–16, notes that a Byzantine Christian graffito from the Athenian Parthenon has Ϙθ as its last two letters.

Tjäder holds that XMΓ first appeared in Syria in I² (p.168; 'at the earliest during the reign of Domitian', p.169), from where it spread elsewhere. It was a Christian 'secret "sign of recognition" (*symbolum*)' (ibid.). But this does not sit well with his other argument that the formula — he regards the abbreviation *VDN*, which he takes to stand for *virgine dominus natus*, as a Latin rendering of XMΓ, pp.164–70 — was 'a precise expression of doctrine, directed against some movement with different ideas' (168; at n.96 Docetism and the Ebionites are mentioned as possible targets), a succinct anticipation of what became part of the Creed (cf. p.165). Tjäder himself concedes, however, that he cannot account for why 'Mary gives birth to Christ' should have been adopted as a secret sign.

Thus, while no conclusive interpretation has yet been advanced for our understanding of the original significance of χμγ we have good reason to be cautious about favouring Χριστὸν Μαρία γεννᾷ along with the recent trend. However much the doctrinal force of the slogan may have been 'washed out' by its conventionalized application to a wide variety of documents, the irrelevance of doctrine for such texts makes it hard to accept that this was the agreed meaning of the abbreviation when it first began to be so used. This argument takes on greater force with the realization that the bulk of the early (IV) examples — from Egypt at least — are brief commercial records. The view (summarized well in

Pritchett, 411-12) that no one interpretation alone provides the answer may have applicability to later use of the formula, but clearly not to its origins. At least in the case of the Egyptian examples, one may wonder whether Wessely's suggestion of χειρός μου γραφή may be the least unsatisfactory view of the formula when it first began to occur. To raise this possibility afresh (Tjäder dismisses it very quickly) need not commit one to the view that it continued to be so understood by the Byzantine period; and certainly this interpretation is not without difficulties. But perhaps it deserves renewed consideration.

105. A *libellus* of the Decian persecution

Narmouthis   4/6/250
ed.pr. — J.R. Knipfing, *HTR* 16(1923) 345-390, no.37

Τοῖς ἐπὶ τῶν θυσιῶ[ν ἡρη-]
μένοις κώ(μης) Ναρμούθεως
παρὰ Αὐρηλίου Αὐνῆ Σιλβα-
νοῦ ἀπὸ κώμης Ναρμου(θέ-)

5   ως. ἀεὶ μὲν τοῖς θεοῖς θύων
δ[ι]ατετέλεκα καὶ νῦν δὲ
κατὰ τὰ κελευσθέντα ἐπὶ πα-
ρ[ο]ῦσιν ὑμῖν ἔθυσα [καὶ ἔ-]
σπ[ει]σα καὶ τῶν ἱερίων ἐγευ-

10   σάμην καὶ ἀξιῶ ὑμᾶς ὑπο-
σημιώσασθαι. διευτυχ(εῖτε).
Αὐνῆς ὡς (ἐτῶν) ια οὐλὴ
ἀγκῶνι δεξ(ιῷ).

     (m.2) Αὐρήλιος Σαραπόδω[ρος] σε-
15   ση(μείωμαι). (m.3) Αὐρήλιος Πατῶς [σεση(μείωμαι)]
     (m.4) Α[ὐ]ρήλ(ιος) [. . .] μων σεση(μείωμαι).
     (m.5) Α[ὐρήλ(ιος) . . .]πίων σεση(μείωμαι).
     (m.6) Α[ὐρήλ(ιος) . . .]ώνιος σεση(μείωμαι).
     (m.7) Α[ὐρήλιος] Ἰτῶνιν σεση(μείωμαι).
20   (m.1) (ἔτους) α΄ Αὐτοκράτορος Καίσαρος
     Γαίου Μεσσί[ο]υ Κυίντου
     Τραϊανοῦ Δ[ε]κίου [Εὐσεβοῦς]
     Εὐτυχοῦς Σεβαστοῦ
     Παῦνι ι.

Recto of a regularly cut-off light-brown papyrus. A margin all the way around indicates a complete document. The gap of 5cm. between *ll*.19 and 20 marks the break between the petition proper and its dating. Still visible on the papyrus is one vertical and one horizontal fold, and traces of illegible letters on the *verso*.

Bib. — *P.J. Sijpesteijn, *P.Wiscon.* 87, pp.191-92 (pl.37); P. Keresztes, *Latomus* 34 (1975) 761-781; O. Montevecchi, *La Papirologia* (Turin, 1973) discusses the Decian *libelli*, 288-291.

(*m.1*) **To the authorities in charge of the sacrifices in the village of Narmouthis, from Aurelius Aunes son of Silvanus of the village of**
5 **Narmouthis. | I have always been continuous in sacrificing to the gods and now have sacrificed in your presence according to the instructions, poured a**
10 **libation and tasted of the sacred meats, | and I request that you certify below. May you prosper. I, Aunes, aged about 11 with a scar on my right elbow.**
15 (*m.2*) **I, Aurelius Sarapodorus, | have certified.** (*m.3*) **I, Aurelius Patos, have certified.** (*m.4*) **I, Aurelius [....].mon, have certified.** (*m.5*) **I, Aurelius [Sera?]pion, have certified.** (*m.6*) **I, Aurelius [....]onius, have certified.**
20 (*m.7*) **I, Aurelius Itonin have certified | (*m.1*) Year 1 of Imperator Caesar Gaius Messius Quintus Traianus Decius Pius Felix Augustus. Pauni 10.**

This is one of forty-five surviving papyrus *libelli* from Egypt which were issued on the occasion of the Decian persecution (250-251). Forty-one of these *libelli*, including the one reproduced here, appeared in J.R. Knipfing, *HTR* 16 (1923) 345-390. Four further *libelli* have been discovered since, and have appeared in print (*PSI* 7[1925] 778; H. Grégoire et al., *Les persécutions dans l'empire romain* [Brussels, 1950] 114-15; J. Schwartz, *RevBib* 54 [1957] 365-369; *P.Oxy.* 41[1972] 2990). These documents provide the best independent evidence for the persecution of Decius, and as such stand together with the letters of Cyprian, his *de lapsis*, and the fragments of Dionysius of Alexandria to make this persecution extraordinarily well documented from a contemporary standpoint.

This *libellus* demonstrates the form of the document (cf. Knipfing, 346-347). Essentially, the libellus took the form of a petition, the bulk of which were written by public scribes. Five of Knipfing's 41 papyri, however, were written either by the petitioners themselves, or their friends or spouses (Knipfing, 348-349). The *libellus* is not a certificate of sacrifice, meaning a document issued by the state upon the completion of a prescribed act, but rather a request from the sacrificer asking for confirmation of an act publicly performed. The documents are addressed generally, although not unanimously, to the ἡρημένοι ἐπὶ τῶν θυσιῶν: evidently, commissions of a local nature were set up in connexion with the Decian edict in order to supervise its functioning. Sijpesteijn remarks on the number of signatories to the petition of Aunes. While the number is large (six), there is no other papyrus *libellus* from Narmouthis with which to compare it. It is possible that the larger number of signatories was required because Aunes was a minor, indeed, the only explicitly attested minor in the corpus of *libelli* who sacrifices without the remainder of his family. The only other minors who appear are the children of Aurelia Leulis, who perform the sacrifice with their mother, and have them confirmed in the ordinary way (Knipfing, no.30). It is, then, impossible to tell one way or the other as to why there were so many signatories to the *libellus*. The *libelli* do confirm, however, that minors were expected to sacrifice as well as adults.

One possibility which seems most reasonable is that the six signatories were the local commission to oversee the sacrifices. These local commissions are a problem. A signatory on another *libellus* (*P.Ryl.* 1 [1911]12 = Knipfing. no.25) states that

he is the current *prytanis* (presiding officer of the town βουλή). Knipfing argues
(351) on this basis that the town councils nominated the commission in an exercise
of power analogous to their attested responsibility of nominating municipal
pontifices. Whether it was analogous or not, it is evident that the βουλαί of the
towns were dealt out responsibility for various tasks from time to time by the
central government (A.K. Bowman, *The Town Councils of Roman Egypt*
[Toronto, 1981] 83). As such, it might be expected that the instructions
accompanying the edict did not specify the number of people expected to serve on
the local commission, leaving this decision to the local βουλαί since they were the
best judges of what local conditions required. A varying size of the commission
makes sense of the evidence which we possess. Of the thirty-four *libelli* from the
town of Theadelphia all are witnessed, where that part of the papyrus is extant, by
the same men, Aurelius Serenus and Aurelius Hermas. These two men may have
been either part or all of the commission for Theadelphia, not a large town, which
Montevecchi prefers to call 'un piccolo villagio' (*La Papirologia*, 288), and had
certainly all but died by the fourth century (cf. A.H.M. Jones, *Decline of the
Ancient World* [London, 1966] 308). Of the remainder of the *libelli*, two have only
one signatory, that from the village of Alexandrou Nesos (Knipfing, no.1) and that
from Arsinoe, a somewhat larger town, signed by the πρύτανις (Knipfing, no.25,
above). The only other *libellus* with an extant certification by the commission is that
of Aunes. Note the evidence for commissions in *Acta Pionii* and in Cyp. *Ep.*
43.3.1. It would seem from the varying number from town to town of those
certifying the *libelli*, and from the uniformity of the Theadelphian *libelli*, that the
local βουλαί interpreted their brief to supervise the sacrifices in a very individual
manner. This makes it quite plausible that those whose signatures were appended
to Aunes' *libellus* were the local commission, and it is unnecessary to look at the
number of signatories as 'unusual' since there is no frame of reference for what was
'usual' at Narmouthis.

On another question, the *libelli* shed a little light on the vexed question of the
nature of Decius' order to sacrifice. A *libellus* from Arsinoe (Knipfing, no.3, also
translated in J. Stevenson, *A New Eusebius* [London, 1960] 229) is the certificate
of sacrifice of one Aurelia Ammonous. This woman was a priestess of the god
Petesouchos and of the gods in the Moeris quarter of the town. Significantly, she
both wrote the petition herself and also embellished it, adding the words τὸν βίον
following the formulaic statement ἀεὶ μὲν θύουσα τοῖς θεοῖς διετέλεσα. Thus she
states rather ostentatiously that she has not merely performed the sacrifice for the
sake of the edict but has sacrificed as a matter of course all her life. She seems from
her statement a devout woman, perhaps a little indignant that she has been called
upon to prove her piety.

That it had been necessary for her to do so κατὰ τὰ κελευσθέντα indicates that
the edict was a general one. Not merely suspect Christians were obliged to sacrifice,
but indeed the citizenry of the Roman Empire, if not the entire population (cf.
G.W. Clarke, *Antichthon* 3 [1969] 68–73).

The Historical Content of the Document

The document is dated to Pauni 10 in the first year of Decius, that is, 4th June,
250. By 16th October, 249 he had taken office (*Cod. Just.* 10.16.3, although this
is discounted by S. Dušanić [*Chiron* 6(1976) 427–28] who prefers to see a period

of sole rule by Philip's young son and Caesar, Philip II), and the edict to sacrifice may have gone out as early as December (for the date, Cyprian, *Ep.* 37.2, although it is by no means self-evident from the epistle. The first attested martyrdom was that of Pope Fabian on 20th January, 250.). The edict required the entire population of the Empire to both sacrifice and have that sacrifice witnessed by local officials (Clarke, *art. cit.*, 69–70, on the extent of the edict; 69 n.39 on the prescribed rites). A. Alföldi has argued that there was not one edict but two, the first against the leaders of the Church, and the second with the wider application (*C.A.H.* XII, p.202 argues for a persecution in three stages; *Klio* 13[1938] 333 sets out the argument for the two edicts), but the evidence of the various martyrologies makes it clear that there was only one blanket edict (Clarke, *art. cit.*, n.38, see further id., *BICS* 20 (1973) 118–23).

The precise aim of the edict is uncertain. Either it was specifically intended as an anti-Christian measure, which is certainly what the Christians of the time felt, or it was intended as an act of solidarity within the Empire by which a state, bedevilled by political and social instability, could express itself in an act of piety (cf. J. Molthagen, *Der römische Staat und die Christen im zweiten und dritten Jahrhundert* [1970] 81–82). This view would have Decius an extraordinarily naive or ill-informed emperor on the matter of the Christians, given that Jews were excused from the act of sacrifice on the grounds of their religious sensibilities (Clarke, 69 n.49), and that Christians weren't.

Eusebius, however, certainly adduces a distinctly political motive for Decius' edict, claiming that it arose through hatred of his predecessor Philip whom Eusebius believes was probably a Christian (*HE* 6.39.1. On Philip's alleged Christianity, 6. 34.1). Philip's Christianity is unlikely, but this tradition is perhaps explicable by the bare fact that Rome's millennium occurred during his reign (in 247) and that the writers of history in the Christian Empire found it an historiographically neat point to have Rome's thousandth birthday celebrated by a Christian. This is certainly evident in the later account of Orosius (*contra Paganos* 7.21).

So, while these are two possible explanations for the persecution, the one that Decius did not mean to do so, but merely became involved incidentally, as it were (see most recently Charles Saumagne, *Saint Cyprien, évêque de Carthage, 'pape' d'Afrique (249–258). Contribution à l'étude des 'persecutions' de Dèce et de Valerien* [Paris, 1975]), the other that the persecution was a political backlash following the Christian, or at least sympathetic, Philippi, they are not ultimately persuasive. Far more compelling is the view of Joseph Vogt (*Zur Religiosität der Christenverfolger im römischen Reich* [Heidelberg, 1962], 21; id., *The Decline of Rome* [E.T. London, 1967] 70–71), both because of its internal coherence, and also because it is inconceivable to think that Decius would have been unaware of the Christian position on sacrifice. As early as late II/early III there is distinct evidence for Christian members of the *familia Caesaris* (G.W. Clarke, *HTR* 64 [1971] 121–22, in the court of the Severi; Commodus was also reputed to have had a Christian concubine; note also that Origen [*Contra Celsum* 8. 68, 69] makes it evident that Celsus was well aware of the tension between the Church's beliefs and whatever the state might require of it). There is no reason not to expect Christians in similar positions not to have apprised Decius of the implications of the edict. Such advice, if proffered, was ignored, so Decius' edict may be taken to imply hostility, or at the very least indifference.

What Vogt argues is that Decius was one of a number of emperors who had what might be termed an 'old-fashioned' view of religion and the gods inasmuch as they believed that fortune, both foul and fair, derived from them. On this model, the various disasters of the middle third century were only explicable from the notion that the gods were displeased, and for good order to be restored they had to be mollified. It was a common and indeed, if Tertullian is to be believed, a 'common man' viewpoint that the Christians were the source of divine displeasure and had to be dealt with (*Apologia* 40.2). This argument of Vogt's is supported by the fact that the Christians of mid-III were under no doubt at whom the order to sacrifice was directed. The spirit of the beginning of Cyprian's *de lapsis* is one of joy over a defeated enemy, Decius being dead and the persecution thus having finally ended. He speaks of *persecutio infesta* (5) and the death of Decius as *ultio divina* (1). More tellingly, Dionysius of Alexandria speaks of Decius' persecution (fragment of letter *contra Germanum* in Eus. *HE* 6.40); and his account of the events in Alexandria makes it plain that the issue was nothing other than Christianity itself, although the situation of the Christians in Alexandria was somewhat unusual (fragment of letter *ad Fabium* in Eus. *HE* 6.41).

The Decian persecution itself was a devastating experience for the settled mid-III Church. Cyprian speaks of great gaps in a once large Church (*de lapsis*, 4), the result of large numbers of people flocking to the capital of Carthage to sacrifice (8,9). So serious was it for him that he spoke of it in terms of a 'judgement' (6,7) upon a corrupt church. Eusebius, in an interesting historiographic note, adduces much the same reason for the outbreak of the 'Great Persecution' of Diocletian (Eus. *HE* 8.1; cf. G.W. Trompf, 'The Logic of Retribution in Eusebius of Caesarea, in B. Croke/A.M. Emmett (edd.), *History and Historians in Late Antiquity* [forthcoming, Sydney, 1983] 132–146). Those that did not sacrifice either fled to the country (Dionysius of Alexandria, fr. in Eus. *HE* 6.42), as we know of a number of bishops doing (Dion. *loc. cit.* speaks of Chaeremon, the bishop of Nicopolis, fleeing to the mountains of Arabia; Cyprian thought it judicious to go into hiding [*Ep.* 14.1.2]; Gregory Thaumaturgus, bishop of Neocaesarea, was obliged to hide among the mountains of Pontus [Gregory of Nyssa, *Vita Gregorii* 945D Migne]; Dionysius of Alexandria evaded capture for a while, but was ultimately secured [Eus. *loc. cit.*]), or procured forged *libelli* (Cyp. *Ep.* 20.2.2; 21. 3.2; 30.3.1; 55.14.1,5; 67.1.1; *de lapsis* 27–28), or simply waited to be denounced (Cyp. *Ep.* 24).

The persecution was the first empire-wide general attack on the Christians, and as such, through its involvement of all civil echelons of the imperial structure, from the emperor himself who was not only the initiator but seems to have heard cases (Cyp. *Ep.* 22.11; for discussions see F. Millar, *The Emperor in the Roman World* [London, 1977] 568; G.W. Clarke, *Antichthon* 3[1969] 63–68), down to the councils of towns like Theadelphia and Narmouthis. Early persecutions, even those sanctioned or sponsored by the emperor, had been either localized or limited in scope (cf. W.H.C. Frend, *Martyrdom and Persecution in the Early Church* [Oxford, 1965] 389–398). There is evidence, however, of martyrdoms, torture or apostasy from Spain, Rome, Smyrna, Neocaesarea, and right across North Africa. The situation in Alexandria was particularly violent as Dionysius' letters indicate. There, the local pagan population took the edict as a legal *carte-blanche* and justification for anti-Christian acts in which they had already been involved over the previous twelve months (Eus. *HE* 6.42). They broke into houses of Alexandrian

Christians and looted them, dragging out their inhabitants, torturing and murdering them. While the violence in Alexandria is atypical in terms of the passion of the pagan response, it does indicate the general atmosphere of hostility, passive or active, of the populace towards the Christians.

Despite the serious inroads which the persecution made on the Church, it ultimately failed. It seems to have flagged somewhat in the autumn of 250. Whether people were tiring of the endless round of prosecutions, or whether the bulk of the *libelli* had been issued within the first eight months or so, or whether enthusiasm for the project as a whole was waning, is uncertain. What is certain is that the prospect of any further persecution by Decius was removed by the death of that Emperor and his eldest son and Caesar in battle against the Goths in 251.

The effect of the Decian persecution, however, was to destabilize the Church seriously. Its threat had been so serious that even extreme Montanists had apostatized (Frend, 411; 435 n.144). The peace which followed the persecution was one in which many who had lapsed, either through sacrifice or through the purchase of *libelli*, sought to re-enter communion with those who had been *confessores* (i.e., they had been imprisoned or tortured) or *stantes* (those who had neither fled nor sacrificed, but had not been imprisoned); hence the many letters of Cyprian and his treatise *de lapsis* addressing this problem. While persecution was intermittent under Decius' successors, except for a more spirited revival by Valerian, peace of a sort was granted by Gallienus in what is called the 'Little Edict of Toleration' (text in Eus. *HE* 7.13). This peace lasted until the outbreak of the 'Great Persecution' under Diocletian on the 23rd of February 303 (for the date, Lactantius, *de mortibus persecutorum* 12.1).

The *Corpus Papyrorum Graecarum* project, announced in *Aeg.* 57 (1977) 276–77, includes a re-edition of the Decian *libelli* by G. Tibiletti as its planned vol.19.

(W.L. LEADBETTER)

106. The trial of bishop Phileas

The arraigning of bishop Phileas of Thmouis in Egypt under the Great Persecution and his subsequent martyrdom is known from our literary tradition (Eusebius, *H.E.* 8.9–10; cf. 8.13), from a very homogeneous series of eight Latin MSS dated IX–XIV, and from two lengthy papyrus documents one of which purports to resume the discussion at Phileas' fifth and final court appearance before the *hegemon* (Prefect) Culcianus. Phileas died between early 304 and winter 306/7, and the two papyrus texts were written within fifty years of his martyrdom, thus within the living memory of those who had known the bishop. Of these papyrus texts V. Martin published the first as *Papyrus Bodmer XX. L'Apologie de Philéas, évêque de Thmouis* (Cologny/Geneva, 1964). This document, consisting of thirteen surviving columns of text (some very mutilated) formed part of a codex which contained other Christian works; it has received considerable attention in the two decades since it appeared, both for its textual problems and its *Tendenz*. Martin's edition will shortly be superseded by the forthcoming publication of A. Pietersma, *The Acts of Phileas, Bishop of Thmuis. P. Chester Beatty XV* (*with a new edition of P. Bodmer XX and Halkin's Latin Acta*). Pietersma announced the discovery of this and other Greek and Coptic texts in the Chester Beatty Collection in *Bull. IOSCS* 7(1974) 10–18 (13–14 on *Phileas*; note also 15–16 on the discovery of papyrus fragments of a *Book of Jannes and Jambres*). In addition to the new papyrus version and the re-edition of *P. Bodmer* XX, the book includes a brief resumé by F. Halkin of the Latin MSS and their respective worths. Pietersma includes a bibliography, but one may note here two recent discussions of *P. Bodmer* XX, the latter of which having provided the occasion for the inclusion of this present entry in the volume covering 1977 publications: A.M. Emmett/ S.R. Pickering, *Prudentia* 7(1975) 95–103; G. Lanata, *MPL* 2(1977) 207–26 (pp. 207–13 had been printed earlier in the *acta* of the XIVth Papyrological Congress at Oxford [London, 1975] pp. 205–10). More wide-ranging is G. Lanata, *Gli atti dei martiri come documenti processuali* (Milan, 1973), whose book includes in its second part selections from fifteen Acts of Christian martyrs (Phileas, pp. 227–41). Pietersma's volume is expected to appear in 1983, and I am most grateful to him for allowing me to read and study its contents beforehand.

Naturally, neither *P. Chester Beatty* XV nor the new edition of *P. Bodmer* XX can be printed here — their length would in any case preclude it (the latter is over 200 lines long, the former has parts of over 230 lines). Pietersma translates *P. Chester Beatty* XV but not *P. Bodmer* XX, a version of which is already available in H. Musurillo, *The Acts of the Christian Martyrs* (Oxford, 1972) 328–44 (cf. his introduction, xlvi–viii). Musurillo was justifiably cautious about some of Martin's readings, and his translation is based on a text which incorporates some different wording from Martin's *ed.pr.* The translation below is a version of Pietersma's re-edition of *P. Bodmer* XX, which incorporates many readings suggested in reviews of Martin and elsewhere, as well as his own readings.

(*col.1*) **The defence made by Phileas, bishop of Thmouis, and** *archon* **of Alexandria, when he was brought into court for the fifth time and afterwards**
5 **met his end.** |**At his first defence after many abuses at the hands of the** *hegemon* **and much uproar and stretchings on the rack by the** *actionarii* **under**
10 **four piercings,** |**he was thrown into prison at Thmouis for two days. Then going about with bare feet and in chains he went on the long journey to**
15 **Alexandria and** |**was thrown into the prison and having been brought into court for the second time though again (***col.2***) insulted and receiving blows he was not deflected (from his stand). Likewise also at the third and fourth**
5 **arraignment after many insults and blows** |**Phileas was told, 'You have killed many people because you have not sacrificed. Pierios saved many when he submitted.' When he was summoned for the fifth time together with the group**
10 **of priests who were with him, twenty in number,** |**Phileas was questioned by the** *hegemon*, **'Can you finally be sensible?' Phileas said, 'I am constantly**
15 **sensible and I give myself training in sensibleness.'** |**The** *hegemon* **said, 'Sacrifice.' Phileas said, 'I do not sacrifice.' Culcianus said, ... [2** *pages missing***] ... (***col.5***) 'to sacrifice only [at] Jerusalem. Nowadays, too, the Jews transgress the law when they celebrate their rites in a foreign place.' Culcianus**
5 **said, 'What sort of** |**sacrifices, then, does God require?' Phileas said, 'A clean heart and a pure soul and reasonable perceptions which bring one to acts of**
10 **piety and justice, for the sake of which** |**each single person will receive**

recompense.' Culcianus said, 'Do we thereby show concern for the soul?'
15 Phileas said, 'For both soul and body.' Culcianus said, 'Why?' |Phileas said,
'I have said (i.e. that we do), so that you may receive the reward from above
if it does well.' Culcianus said, 'The (*col.6*) soul alone or also the body?'
Phileas said, 'The soul and the body.' Culcianus said, 'This body?' Phileas
5 said, 'Yes.' Culcianus said, 'This flesh |will rise again?' Astounded, once
more he said, 'This flesh will rise again?' Phileas said, 'This flesh will rise
10 again ... among sinners (?) ... everlasting punishment |or ... righteousness
... and everlasting life.' Culcianus said, 'Spare yourself and all your own
15 (people). Sacrifice!' Phileas said, 'I am sparing myself |and all who belong
to me. I do not sacrifice.' Culcianus said, 'Paul, did not he recant?' (*col.7*)
Phileas said, 'Certainly not!' Culcianus said, 'Who is the one who recanted?'
Phileas said, 'I refuse to say.' Culcianus said, 'I adjure you, was Paul the
5 recanter?' |Phileas said, 'Certainly not! The apostle of my Lord did not
recant!' Culcianus said, 'I have sworn; you swear too!' Phileas said, 'We are
10 not allowed to swear. |For the holy and divine scripture says, "Let your yes
be yes and your no, no."' Culcianus said, 'Have you never sworn an oath,
15 therefore?' Phileas said '(No), and if I have I sinned.' Culcianus |said, 'Well,
sin now.' Phileas said, 'There are differences between sins.' Culcianus said,
'Was Jesus God?' (*col.8*) Phileas said, 'Yes.' Culcianus said, 'Well how did
he not say about himself that he was God?' Phileas said, 'Because he did not
5 require this testimony, since he performed the works of God |with enabling
power.' Culcianus said, 'What did he do?' Phileas said, 'He cleansed lepers,
10 made blind people see, deaf people hear, |lame people walk, mute people
talk, half-withered people healthy. Demons he drove out from creatures with
15 a command. He made paralytics healthy, |raised the dead to life and did
many other signs and portents.' Culcianus said, 'And how is it that, being
God, he was crucified?' (*col.9*) Phileas said, 'He knew that ... that he would
5 be flogged and beaten and abused; and he wears a crown made of thorns |and
suffers with forbearance, providing also by this a pattern for our salvation;
and he consciously gave himself to this for our sake. For these things too the
10 scripture, |on which the Jews depend, thus hold; they prophesied his coming
15 down and ... |... [Culcianus said, 'Was Paul God?' Phileas said, 'No.'
Culcianus] (*col.10*) said, 'Well who was he?' Phileas said, 'He was the first
to herald justice to men. For the Spirit of God was in him, as were divine
5 powers. |For he did good with divine power and the Spirit.' 'Was he not an
untrained individual who conversed in Aramaic?' Phileas said, 'He was a Jew
10 and the first of heralds and he conversed in Greek, |being the first of Greeks.'
Culcianus said, 'Was he not an untrained individual? Surely he was not in the
category of Plato?' Phileas said, '... He surpassed Plato: not only was he
15 |more philosophical than Plato [but also than all philosophers. And he also
persuaded all men. But if you wish I will tell you] (*col.11*) his words.'
Culcianus said, 'Sacrifice now at last.' Phileas said, 'I do not sacrifice, may
I never do so!' Culcianus said, 'Is there a conscience?' Phileas said, 'Yes.'
5 |Again he said, 'Is there a conscience?' Phileas said, 'I said that there is.'
Culcianus said, 'Why do you not guard your conscience in relation to your
10 children and your wife and your brothers?' |Phileas said, 'Because my
conscience in relation to God is more important and takes priority over
everything. For the divine scripture says, "You shall love God who made

15 |you."' Culcianus said, '[Which God?]' Phileas, lifting up his hands to
heaven, said, 'The God who made (*col.12*) heaven and earth and the seas and
all that is in them, creator, invisible, inexpressible, infallible, immovable,
5 |incomprehensible, whom all creation serves and yields to and is subordinate
to, both things in the heavens and on the earth and below the earth ...
10 because he himself |is the sole ruler (α]ὐτο[κράτωρ]) of all things and there is
no other but he.' The lawyers said to Phileas while he was talking, 'Do not
15 stand against the *hegemon* in any more matters.' Phileas |said, 'I am replying
to what he asks me.' The orators said to him, 'Look at ...' [*2 pages missing*]
... (*col.15*) He said, 'Not unreasonably, but taking care for myself.'
Culcianus said, 'It's a favour to your brother that I'm doing; and you, do this
5 favour for me.' |Phileas said, 'I ask this last kindness. Use your severity and
10 do what is commanded you.' Culcianus said, 'If you were one |of the
uncultured who had surrendered themselves because of their neediness I
would not have put up with you. But since you possess sufficient abundance
15 to nurture and administer not only yourself |but also a whole city, for this
reason spare (*col.16*) yourself and sacrifice.' Phileas said, 'I do not sacrifice.'
The lawyers who were present said, 'He sacrificed in the council chamber.'
5 Phileas said, 'I did not |sacrifice. But if I did sacrifice let the *hegemon* say
(so).' And when he could not be altered or deflected, the lawyers and the
10 whole court together with the *logistes* asked |the *hegemon* that (time for)
consideration be given to him. Culcianus said, 'Do you want me to give you
(time) to consider?' Phileas said, 'I have considered frequently and this is
15 what I have chosen.' |And at this the lawyers and the court together with
(*col.17*) the *logistes* asked the blessed Phileas, trying to persuade him to yield
to what was commanded. And since he was not deflected they began abusing
5 |him, upsetting him so that he might consider it.
Peace to all the saints.

P. Chester Beatty XV consists of portions of a quire of 28 pages, the first half
of which contained the *Phileas* text, the second half Psalms of which 1.1–4.2
survive (cf. *P. Bodmer* XX which also had Psalms after the *Apology of Phileas*).
Pietersma thinks that the handwriting of each section may be identical. Surviving
fragments vary from 21 × 14.5 cm. down to 5 × 4 cm., and while no page survives
complete the number of lines per page can be reconstructed sufficiently to allow an
average of 23 to be posited. Orthography reflects fairly common deviations: ει⟩ι,
ι⟩η, ο⟩ω, etc. Note the false aspiration of οὐχ ὀλίγην at 10.3. Whereas *nomina sacra*
are — with a single exception — contracted in the Psalms portion, they are
unabbreviated everywhere in the *Phileas* (contrast the *Bodmer* version where
contraction occurs throughout); such non-shortening is rare in Christian literature
by IV. Two other features may be noted in this connection, the abbreviation of
εἶπεν to ει', and the all but consistent placing out in the margin of the name of the
hegemon. These three last-mentioned features — non-abbreviation of *nomina
sacra*, abbreviation of εἶπεν and *ekthesis* of the magistrate's name — lend support
to the suggestion that the *Chester Beatty* version of Phileas' trial reflects more
closely the actual court transcript (see further below).
As to philology a couple of items may be mentioned in passing. For the adverbial
λ[ο]ιπόν (2.4; restored at 5.9, 6.16) with an imperative cf. in the NT Mt. 26.45

(= Mk. 14.41; I take the verbs in these verses to be imperative, *pace* BAGD, s.v. λοιπός, 3a, α); note also λοιπόν at Acts 27.20; 1 Cor. 7.29; 2 Tim. 4.8 (is the force of λοιπόν in these last two passages necessarily inferential, as BAGD, s.v. λοιπός, 3b suggests may be possible?). Pietersma also notes that the phrase ἀπὸ μιᾶς in this text (11.8) lends weight against the view that the idiom at Lk. 14.18 is a Semitism; cf. BAGD, s.v. ἀπό, VI.

Biblical quotations and allusions appear at 1.1–4 (Ex. 22.20); 1.10–11 (Is. 1.11); 5.22–23 (cf. Deut. 6.5); 6.4–6 (cf. Acts 4.24; Ex. 20.11); 14.7ff. (cf. 1 Pet. 5.8, with Pietersma's note).

These linguistic features are really *parerga*, however. For the real importance of this *Chester Beatty* find is that it exhibits a 'striking affinity' (Pietersma) with the Latin recension. Not only do they agree with one another at the verbal level and disagree with *Bodmer*, but also *Beatty*/Latin are mostly at one where a longer or shorter text than *Bodmer* occurs in some places. Furthermore, *Beatty* agrees with Latin against *Bodmer* in the sequence of certain topics of discussion between judge and defendant. The writer of the *Bodmer* version has reworked the position of some sections to make them fit more smoothly into the whole. There are thus two versions of the Phileas hearing — *Bodmer*, and *Beatty*/Latin. The significance of this for the Latin MSS is that the Latin version can now be shown to have been transmitted for half a millenium and more with remarkable faithfulness. It must go back to the same half-century as the Greek versions on papyrus. While *Beatty* is not the direct ancestor of the Latin — they are not so close that the latter could be called a translation of *Beatty* — they are both closely related to the original court *acta* (cf. G.D. Kilpatrick, *TLZ* 21[1965] 219).

The view stated when *Bodmer* alone of the papyrus versions was known, that *Bodmer* had been altered for hagiographical reasons, now receives further endorsement from the contrast which *Beatty* provides. *Bodmer* has some stylistic pretensions (e.g., chiasmus at 10.8–10), laudatory epithets are included with the bishop's name, Phileas is made at least the equal of his judge. In particular, the *incipit* of *Bodmer*, ἀπολογία Φιλέου, indicates where lies the real interest of the writer of the document. 'The *acta Culciani* have been converted to the *acta Phileae*' (Pietersma). In view of the overall contrast which *Beatty* provides (its beginning is lost, however) ἀπολογία at the beginning of *Bodmer* cannot mean a 'defence at his trial', but Phileas' defence of the Faith, of Christian doctrine, as Martin had earlier suggested. In contrast to *Bodmer*, the language of *Beatty* is very much more spare. Phileas is not so prominent: This can be shown even at the level of speaker introduction formulae (see Pietersma's introduction). Very little extraneous comment appears in *Beatty* up until the end of the trial when Phileas exits to his death.

In these and other ways the new *Chester Beatty* papyrus reflects much more closely the court transcript made at the time of Phileas' trial. Yet *Beatty* is no bald transcript: that it too is a literary composition is clear from the presence of the concluding sermon. It is 'a martyrium which is directly based on the protocol and reflects the latter more closely than Bo(dmer) appears to do' (Pietersma). Certainly the first 1½ cols. of *Bodmer* are not the sort of passage which would conceivably have derived from court proceedings (so Kilpatrick, ad loc.): they summarize the situation up until the fifth and final hearing and emphasise the physical pressures brought to bear on Phileas.

It is the possibility now afforded by the soon-to-be published new *Beatty* papyrus that makes the textual tradition of the Phileas hearing unique for hagiographical sources. This group of closely related documents with their differences and similarities offers a good example to illustrate in microcosm some of the same issues which beset the Synoptic problem. *New Docs 1976*, **26** dealt with a group of closely related texts which could also be drawn on for the consideration of this question.

As an addendum to this new *Chester Beatty* material which reflects more closely the court proceedings against Phileas we may include mention here of *P.Mich.* 660 and 661 (Aphrodite, VI), two bilingual papyri (Latin speaker identifications, usually abbreviated; Greek text) written by the same hand and referring to the same events and people. These documents provide part of the transcript from the hearing concerning the murder of Victor, a presbyter, and a certain Heraklios. Details are somewhat obscure and there are numerous loose ends, but Sijpesteijn provides a reconstruction of the case (p.29), in which a soldier, Flavius Menas, charged with both murders, disclaims knowledge of Heraklios and argues that Victor died of natural causes: ἔ[μ]εινεν ἀηδιζόμενος ὁ αὐτὸς πρεσβύτερος ἐν τῇ ἐκκλησίᾳ, ἐγὼ ἐν τῇ Ἀνταίου, καὶ ἐξῆλθεν | [τὸ]ν τράχηλον αὐτοῦ [τοῦ] πρεσβυτέρου ἀπόστημα καὶ ἐξ αὐτοῦ ἀ[πέθνησκ]εν, κτλ (*ll.*7-8), 'the same presbyter remained in the church since he felt nauseous, while I was in Antaiu; and out of the throat of the presbyter himself came an abscess from which he died'. Victor's brother, and Maria, the wife of Heraklios, give accounts of the murder of each man (660.9-13; 13-19 + 661.1-2); and they and others attempt to show that a certain Theodoros is not guilty of the murders. The judge (*comes militum*) puts various questions during the hearing.

Some philological items which may be noted are:

ἀηδίζω — (660.7), the literal sense here makes this example worth adding to MM, s.v. ἀηδία, where one figurative attestation to the verb is provided. The verb does not occur in the NT, but at Lk. 23.12D the noun means 'enmity', while the adjective and adverb are found in ECL.

ἀπόστημα — (660.8), new in papyrus texts.

ἀρχοντικός — (660.5; 661.8), rare as a noun: here, 'government' (see *ed.pr.* n., p.33; once adjectivally in ECL (see BAGD, s.v.).

βοηθός — (660.1; also at 659.303), as a noun only at Heb. 13.6 (quoting Ps. 117.7; of God) in the NT.

γνωρίζω — (661.1), common in the NT, though not in the sense of recognizing someone.

ἔγκλημα — (660.6, 9), legal technical term; cf. Acts 23.29; 25.16.

μαγγανικός — (660.10), a new adjective, connected with μάγγανον, which here refers to a piece of wood taken from a pulley block which served as the murder weapon.

μειζότερος — (660.1-2; 661.20), at 3 Jn 4 in NT; two further examples to add to those given in MM, s.v. μείζων, ad.fin.

ὁ[λό]χειρ — (660.11), 'arm', a new noun, if *ed.pr.*, n. ad loc. is correct in his suggestion about the restoration.

πάλι — (660.17), instead of πάλιν, reflecting the weakness of final -ν; for other examples of the form see MM, s.v. πάλιν, ad.fin., who note that the shortened form is known in the W version of Jn. 1.35. See Gignac, I, 114.

σφραγίζω — (661.19), the phrase reads] διὰ τὸν [σῖ]τον [[σῖτον]] τὸν σφραγισ-θέντα εἰς τὴν συνωνὴ'ν', κτλ, 'because of the corn that has been sealed for the *coemptio*, etc.'. The *coemptio* was 'an obligatory sale of a certain number of products imposed on a group of persons, the prices being fixed by the government. Its purpose was to have enough supplies, primarily for the army . . .' (Sijpesteijn, p.39). Deissmann, *BS*, 238–39 (followed by MM, s.v.), saw a useful parallel in such phraseology to Rom. 15.28, καὶ σφραγισ-άμενος αὐτοῖς τὸν καρπὸν τοῦτον. This view has been questioned by H.-W. Bartsch, *ZNW* 63 (1972) 95–107 (followed by BAGD, s.v., 2d), but Deissmann's view is to be preferred because of the apposite choice of καρπός, analogous to a word like σῖτος in the phrase above. Between them, Deissmann and MM provide four examples to illustrate this usage in the papyri, none so late as this new *P.Mich.* text.

Another very fragmentary extract from a court proceeding, *P.Wiscon.* 48 (provenance unknown, II), concerns a person who has appealed several times to the prefect about mistreatment by some soldiers. Two brief philological observations are in order. At *l.*5, . . . καταγράψας ἀντίγραφον λιβέλλου τοῦ πεντάκις | [, appears to indicate that the complainant has submitted the *libellus* on five occasions (so *ed.pr.*). The numerical adverb πεντάκις is common enough, though found in the NT only at 2 Cor. 11.24. However, MM have no entry for the word, although they include four other πεντ- words. Secondly, at *l.*26 the papyrus reads ἰσῆλθον ἐν τῷ πραιτωρί[ῳ. On interchange of εἰς/ἐν see BDF §218. The phraseology parallels exactly three passages in the Johannine version of Jesus' trial: at 18.28 the Jews οὐκ εἰσῆλθον εἰς τὸ πραιτώριον; at 18.33, εἰσῆλθεν οὖν πάλιν εἰς τὸ π. ὁ Πιλᾶτος; and it is Pilate again who εἰσῆλθεν εἰς τὸ π. at 19.9. The governor's residence is referred to also at Mk. 15.16 = Mt. 27.27; and Paul is to be kept under guard at Herod's *praetorium* in Acts 23.25. The interpretation of Phil. 1.13, ἐν ὅλῳ τῷ πραιτωρίῳ, is not something that can be settled by philological criteria alone. MM's entry, s.v., provides a very succinct survey of the earlier debate over this passage.

On the type of document discussed in this entry see generally R.A. Coles, *Reports of Proceedings in Papyri (Papyrologica Bruxellensia,* 4; Brussels, 1966).

107. **Divine Constantine**

Pistia, Umbria   337(?)

ed.pr. — L. Gasperini, *Annali della Facoltà di Lettere e Filosofia dell' Università di Macerata* 9 (1976) 393–401 (pl.I,II)

> *Di*[*vo*]
> *Flavio*
> *Valerio*
> *Constan-*
> 5 *tino Aug*(*usto*)
> *ordo*
> *Ples*(*tinorum*)

A cippus recovered from below the pavement of the church of St. Mary, presumably once attached to a public building.

Bib. — *AE* 246

The council of Plestia to the deified Flavius Valerius Constantinus Augustus.

The handful of surviving dedications to the deified Constantine is now joined by this inscription. It pinpoints the fact that the establishment of Christendom had by no means done away with the imperial cult; rather had it clarified some of its ambiguities. The Caesars had mostly insisted on their own humanity, at the same time as they accepted or encouraged the cult as an expression of gratitude and loyalty. The reaction against Gaius and others who explicitly claimed divinity shows that most people could not take it literally. Similarly NT attitudes switch from seeing Caesar as God's servant for one's good (Rom. 13), to be honoured as such even if one is persecuted (1 Pet. 3.17,20), to denunciation of the beast whose blasphemous image one is compelled to worship on pain of death (Rev. 13).

The conversion of Constantine helped define the difference. He promoted his own family's temple and cult 'provided it is not polluted by the deceits of any contagious superstition', *ea observatione perscripta, ne aedis nostro nomini dedicata cuiusquam contagiose superstitionis fraudibus polluatur* (Dessau, *ILS* 705, *ll.*45–47); sacrifices were presumably stopped. But as one chosen by God he could both revive the traditional disclaimers of divinity and anticipate his own apotheosis in the form of a personal reception into heaven at death. For the differences his conversion made to the treatment of this motif, see S.G. MacCormack, *Art and Ceremony in Late Antiquity* (Berkeley, 1981) 121–132.

Paradoxically, the Christianization of the cult may actually have opened the way for people seriously to pray to their rulers for the first time. Their divine calling and sanctity ranked them with the saints in this respect, according to G.W. Bowersock, 'The imperial cult: perceptions and persistence', in B.E. Meyer and E.P. Sanders (edd.), *Jewish and Christian Self-Definition*, III (London, 1982) 171–182.

(E.A. JUDGE)

108. **Provision for widows in the Church**

Oxyrhynchos   27/1/480

ed.pr. — R. Rémondon, *Chr.d'Ég.* 47 (1972) 254–77 at p.266

⳨ Ἡ ἁγία ἐκκλ(ησία)   Πέτρῳ οἰ(κονόμῳ) Κοσμᾶ.
παράσχου Σοφίᾳ χήρᾳ ἀφ' (ὧν) ἔχεις ἱματίων εἰς καλὴν
χρείαν ἱμάτιον ἕν, γί(νεται) ἱμάτι(ον) α μό(νον). (*m.2*) † ἔρ(ρωσο).
(*m.1*) (ἔτους) ρνς ρκε Μεχεὶρ α γ̄ ἰνδικ(τίονος).

The papyrus (*verso* blank) has been cut from a larger sheet, and is presumably a blank section from a sheet which had already been used.

Bib. — E. Wipszycka, *Les ressources et les activités des églises en Égypte du IVe au VIIIe siècle* (*Pap. Brux.* 10; Brussels, 1972) 114 n.3; *P. *Wiscon.* 64, pp.95–96 (pl.21)

(*cross*) **The holy church to Peter, administrator (of the church) of (St.) Kosmas. Provide for Sophia, widow, from the coats you have one coat for good use, total: 1 coat only.** (*2nd hand*) (*cross*) **Fare well.** (*1st hand*) **In the year 156 = 125, Mecheir 1 of the third indiction.**

The above is a typical example of such documents. *P.Oxy.* 16 (1924) 1954–1956 are three very similar — same date and hand — brief orders to a wineseller to provide wine for widows of the Church. *P.Oxy.* 1954 (V) reads: Βίκτορι οἰνοπράτῃ. | δὸς ταῖς χήρ(αις) τοῦ Μιχαηλίου | οἴν(ου) δι(πλοῦν) α μ(όνον), κτλ (date). The edd. note that τοῦ Μιχαηλίου alludes to a charitable foundation. Sijpesteijn (p.95) refers to some other orders issued by the Church for the payment of money or provision of goods; his examples, *P.Oxy.* 6 (1908) 993 and 16 (1924) 1950, 1951, are orders to provide wine to certain individuals on the occasion of a festival. Wipszycka's monograph includes a very useful discussion (109–19) of the evidence for the Egyptian Church's charitable works. She mentions (p.114) two papyrus texts (dated VII) which refer to women responsible for widows (αἱ πρὸς χήραις).

109. Maria the *diakonos*
Archelaïs (Cappadocia)   VI
ed.pr. — G. Jacopi, *R. Ist. d'Arch. e Storia dell' Arte* (1937) 33–36, figs. 135–37 (*non vidi*)

<blockquote>

Ἐνθάδε κατα-
κῖτε ἡ τῆς εὐλαβοῦς κὲ
μακαρίας μνήμης διάκο-
νος Μαρία ἥτις κατὰ τὸ ῥητὸν
5 τοῦ ἀποστόλου ἐτεκνοτρό-
φεσεν, ἐξενοδόχησεν, ἁ-
γίων πόδας ἔνιψε, θλι-
βομένοις τὸ ἄρτον αὐτῆς
διένεμεν. μνήσθητι αὐτῆ(ς)
10 Κύ(ριε), ὅταν ἔρχη ἐν τῇ βασιλίᾳ σου.

</blockquote>

Stele of grey marble; a large cross decorated with ivy tendrils framed within an archway. The text is written beneath the horizontal arms of the cross, on either side of its vertical bar.

Bib. — *N. Thierry, *CRAI* (1977) 116, no. 2 (fig.16 on p.115); *SEG* 948a; *BE* (1939) 451, (1978) 498

> **Here lies Maria the deacon, of pious and blessed memory, who in accordance**
> 5 **with the statement | of the apostle reared children, practised hospitality,**
> **washed the feet of the saints, distributed her bread to the afflicted. Remember**
> 10 **her, | Lord, when you come in your kingdom.**

In view of the undoubted allusion to 1 Tim. 5.10 in this epitaph and the larger discussion of widows into which that verse fits, Maria is probably to be seen as a widow herself at the time of her death. That being so it is somewhat surprising that no members of her family are mentioned. Maria herself was not responsible for having the stele erected, given its third person style. Here we have, then, evidence for a widow who exercised the function of deacon in the Byzantine Church, memorialised by anonymous friends who were presumably fellow church-members.

Some philological points may be noted briefly. For τὸ ῥητόν = 'saying', see Lampe, s.v. ῥητός, 3. ὁ ἀπόστολος is used of Paul and the Pauline corpus in the Fathers (Lampe, s.v., G). 1 Tim. 5.10 includes a number of words which are either hapax or rare in the NT. The only documentary example of τεκνοτροφέω so far known is *IG* XII.5, 655.8 (Syros, II/III; noted in LSJ, BAGD), an honorific text for a woman. But women are not always the subject of the verb, although one might have expected it. MM's only citation, s.v., is literary (Epictetus 1.23.3), where the verb is used of dissuading τῷ σοφῷ τεκνοτροφεῖν. Neither *WB* nor *Spoglio* lists any papyrus examples. Again, the search for documentary attestation of ξενοδοχέω (for which the Atticists preferred ξενοδοκέω) draws a blank; but Lampe, s.v., provides several patristic references, both intransitive (as in 1 Tim. 5.10) and transitive. For θλίβω note several references in both *Spoglio* and *WB* Suppl. I (1940–66) I. Lief.; cf. also *BE* (1950) 241a for an epigraphical example. To this point in the epitaph 1 Tim. 5.10 has only been modified to the extent of omitting the conditional force of the clauses; but now the inscription departs from the NT wording rather more, filling out the clause beginning with θλιβομένοις — for δια-νέμω cf. Acts 4.17 (δ. εἰς) — and omitting the verse's final clause altogether.

*Ll.*9–10 quote, again with minor variation, the statement of the penitent thief, Lk. 23.42: Ἰησοῦ, μνήσθητί μου ὅταν ἔλθῃς εἰς τὴν βασιλείαν σου. Apart from the epitaph's alteration of μου to αὐτῆς to fit the context, the stone has ἔρχῃ (present) for NT ἔλθῃς (aorist). Both εἰς + acc. and ἐν + dat. occur as readings in different NT witnesses.

Another female deacon attested in an inscription may be noted here. Found in 1972 during excavations at Stobi in Yugoslavia, the brief text is printed in J. Wiseman, *Stobi. A Guide to the Excavations* (Belgrade, 1973) 59–60 (cf. J. Wiseman/D. Mano-Zissi, *AJA* 76 (1972) 407–24, the excavation report, which does not, however, print the text).

$$\text{ὑπὲρ εὐ[χῆς]}$$
$$\text{τῆς ματ[ρώνας]}$$
$$\text{ἡ εὐλαβ[εστά-]}$$
$$\text{τη διακ[όνισσα]}$$
$$\text{τὴν ἐξέ[δραν]}$$
$$\text{ἐψήφω[σεν.]}$$

Because of a vow of the matron the most pious deaconess paved the exedra with mosaic.

Wiseman dates this text IV or V. It is surprising that the woman's name is not given (unless it is Matrona, in which case we should capitalize the noun in *l*.2). The epithet εὐλαβής (frequently found as a superlative, as here, *ll*.3-4) is used particularly of women, according to Lampe, s.v. 1b. For its use with an ecclesiastical title see **97**. Examples which may be added from 1977 publications include S. Mitchell, *AS* 27(1977) 101, no.48 (= *SEG* 881); *P.Mich*. 13.669, *l*.1 (Aphrodite, 12-13/9/529, or 514); *I.Tyre* 1.21C (of a woman), 167 (of Jewish priests, ἱερέων: see *ed.pr*. pp.95, 153; for other Jewish texts from Tyre note nos.164, 166, 168 — a tomb reserved for Σαμαριτῶν ἐλευθέ|ρων), 203, 222B (both of males). At *l*.4 διάκ[ονος may be more likely if the number of letters per line was fairly similar. However, *BE* (1963) 152 reports a text in which ὑποδιακον may be an abbreviation for ὑποδιακόν(ισσα): see *New Docs 1976*, **79**. That entry reports on some other female deacons. The word is found several times of males in *I.Tyre* 1: nos.36, 50, 52A, 148 (abbreviated); 38, 51, 133, 203. The man in no.133 and two deacons (nos. 143, 201) also have a trade specified: tapestry-maker, carpenter, and goldsmith respectively. On these and other ecclesiastics with a trade see *ed.pr*. pp.108-109; cf. p.160. It occurs also at *MPR* 15 (Tomis, VI).

110. **Early Christian inscriptions from Romania**

Tomis (Constanţa)   III/IV

ed.pr. — A. Aricescu, *St.Cl*. 5 (1963) 323-27, fig. 5 (*non vidi*)

Ὑπόμνημα

Οὐδὲν ἐπ' ἀνθρώποις μύραις δ' ὑπὸ πάντα κυκλεῖται.
Καὶ γὰρ ἐγὼ σπεῦδον θρέψαι τέκνον καὶ εἰς ἐλπίδας ἄγεσθαι.
Ἀλλ' ἐμέο βουλὴν κρίσις ἔφθασεν οὕνεκα τύμβῳ.
5   Ὡς κρίσις ἐ[στὶ φίλοι μου ῥητὸ[ν] χρε[ὼν] ἀπέτισα,
πρίν [γε] μολεῖν μέτρον ἡλικίης καὶ εἰς ἄνδρας ἡκέσθαι.
Παῖς ὢν ἑξαετὴς τυτθὸς νεῖος Λίλλας ἐκαλούμην.
Ὦ τάφον οὐχ ὁσίως Βασσιανὸς γενέτης ἀνέγειρα
σὺν γαμετῇ Ἰανβαρίᾳ τῇ πολὺ δακρυτάτῃ,
10   μυρόμενοι παιδὸς τὴν ἀπαθῆ γένεσιν.
Χαίροις ὦ παροδεῖτα καὶ ὑγιένοις πάλιν ἄλλοις.

A bird is carved in the triangular pediment at the top of the stele; below it occurs the first word. Beneath this is a rectangular area containing three busts carved in relief, followed by the verse text, spread over 21 lines on the stone (the text above rationalizes these into metrical lines). Following the text is a figure, perhaps a fish or a leaf.
Bib. — *MPR* 1 (fig. 2)

Memorial. Nothing is in men's control, but everything is encompassed by
fate. For I was keen to rear a child and be led into hopes. But on account
5   of this tomb the decision (of fate) has anticipated my wish. |Since this is the

decision, my friends, I have paid the debt which was specified, before in fact
I reached the measure of age and arrived at manhood. I was a six-year-old
child, small and young, called Lillas. O grave, it was not right that I should
have built you, I, Bassianos the parent, with my wife Ianuaria who is very
10 tearful, |we who mourn the unfeeling existence of our child. Greetings,
wayfarer, and keep good health again for others.

Is this epitaph for Lillas Christian? Nothing in the epitaph hints at it, and words
like μύραις (= μοίραις, *l.*2) might be felt to weigh against a Christian attribution.
Certainly, the conventions of epitaphs with some literary pretensions are to be
found here: a metrical text, poetic language (e.g., ἐμέο, 4; μολεῖν, 6), different
speakers (including the deceased), address to the passer-by. Christian identification
in fact turns on the interpretation of the bird and the fish (leaf? — the photograph
in *MPR* is clear, but the design is almost impossible to see) above and following
the text respectively. Barnea, in *MPR*, himself queries whether the bird is to be
understood as a dove, and following the text he writes '(poisson ou plutôt feuille)'.
If these two problematical designs are the only ground for regarding this as the
earliest Christian inscription from Romania, a not unfair conclusion might be 'case
not proven'.

The same conclusion ought to apply to *MPR* 2 (Tomis, IV), a fragmentary
epitaph with a bird carved above the text, which Barnea takes to be a dove.
E. Pfuhl/H. Möbius, *Die ostgriechischen Grabreliefs* (2 vols + 2 vols of plates;
Mainz am Rhein, 1977, 1979), index, s.v. Vogel, Taube, include several examples
of doves on grave steles which on the ground of date alone are clearly not Christian
(e.g. nos. 382, 485, 569). Doves are also a symbol used by Jews: see index to *CIJ*
I, p.664. If the Christian status of *MPR* 1 is subject to some doubt, then the earliest
Christian epigraphical evidence for the area is IV at the earliest. By way of contrast
to *MPR* 1 note the much more explicit Christian wording of *MPR* 12 (Tomis, VI).

Ἔθηκεν τὸ τήτολον τοῦτο
Μάρκελλος, ὅπου κῖντε
ὁ μακάριος πατήρ μου Ὀρέ-
ντης κὲ μακαρία ἡ μήτηρ μο-
5   ῦ Μάρκελλα. Χέρε
παροδῖτα.

**Marcellinus set up this inscription (in the place) where lie my blessed father,
5   Orentes, and my blessed mother, |Marcella. Greetings, wayfarer.**

Note the first line here: τὸ τήτολον is a loan word from Latin *titulus;* cf. Jn 19.19,
ἔγραψεν … τίτλον … καὶ ἔθηκεν (cf. v.20). This epigraphic example of the word is
late but worth adding to the few references in MM, s.v.

Barnea's collection of material in *MPR* provides a very useful survey of the early
Christian remains for the area, predominantly Scythia Minor. The reception of
Christianity between III–VI came in no small part via the presence of soldiers in
the Roman army stationed there, who acted as unofficial missionaries (Barnea, 1).

Not only does this volume reprint with plates all inscriptions which Barnea regards as Christian (including those on gems, etc., a total of 96), but he provides a brief description of each of the 28 early basilicas (IV–VI) so far published; another three, yet to be published, push the total of these Christian edifices to 31, all but one of which are in Scythia Minor. Mosaics, sculpted capitals and paving are also dealt with. The final section of *MPR* presents a representative selection of minor Christian art (jewellery in the shape of a cross; a lamp in the shape of a fish with ☧ on one side, dated IV–V — fig. 88.6; bronze belt-buckles with cross, fish or dove design) and ceramics with Christian markings (mostly oil lamps).

A few other inscriptions from *MPR* may be noted here briefly. No.7, a broken Latin epitaph (Tomis, IV-VI), is the only inscription from Scythia Minor to mention a presbyter. This text includes the wording *ti|[t]ulum posui*, the Latin equivalent of the phrase discussed earlier in this entry. Inscribed on an irregular block of stone (no.29; Tomis IV–V) is ☧ below which occurs θυσ(ιαστήριον) χρηστι(αν)ῶν, Κύ(ριε), 'altar belonging to Christians, Lord'. The abbreviated forms of the first two words are not common, according to Barnea (ad loc.). From Callatis survives no.46 (IV–V) — an epitaph of 21 short lines set up by a husband and wife for themselves. Symplikios was a Syrian by birth and a legal advocate by profession (νομικὸς τὴν | ἐπιστήμην, 4–5). The last six lines provide the Christian identification for them, for after reaching an honoured old age, μεταξὺ δικαίων | ἐφ' ἐλπίδι ἀνα|στάσεως [ἐν]θάδ[ε] | ἥκαμεν, ζω|ῆς αἰωνίου ἀπολαύ|σε[ως], 'we have come here, among the just, with hope of resurrection (and) enjoyment of eternal life'. For the phraseology deriving from the NT note Acts 23.6, περὶ ἐλπίδος καὶ ἀναστάσεως νεκρῶν, where the hendiadys is an equivalent to the phrase in our inscription (cf. BAGD, s.v. ἐλπίς, 2a); ἐπ' ἐλπίδι ζωῆς αἰωνίου (Tit.1.2; cf. 3.7). ἀπό-λαυσις is not frequent in the NT: 1 Tim. 6.17; Heb. 11.25.

MPR 13 (Tomis, VI) is an epitaph for Herakleides, ἀναγνώς|της τῆς ἁγίας | καὶ καθολικῆς ἐκ|κλησίας. Barnea notes that the expression reflects the influence of the Niceno-Constantinopolitan creed (see his references, ad loc.). For a papyrus fragment of this creed see *New Docs 1976*, **60**. Most recently, R.J.H. Matthews, *Prudentia* 14 (1982) 23–37, provides a linguistic commentary on this creed.

111. Christian epitaph echoing Homer

Tyana (Cappadocia) end IV/V init.
ed.pr. — N. Thierry, *CRAI* (1977) 114-115, no.1 (fig. 15, p.115)

Γνώριζε τόδε
σῆμα, ὁδοίπο-
ρε. Ἐ(ν)θάδε κεῖτε
Εὐθυμία
5 ἀγαθέ, σωφροσύ-
νης ἀγαίτις·
Τοὔνεκά μιν ὑ-
ῶν πανυπέρτατος,

ἔξοχος ἄλλων,
10 Ἀθηνίων
τίμησε μητέρα
τὴν πινυτὴν τύμ-
βῳ τε στήλῃ τε.
Τὸ γὰρ γέρας ἐστὶ
15 θανόντων.

White marble stele; a cross and A/Ω stand in the pediment above the text.
Bib. — *SEG* 956; *BE* (1978) 498, (1979) 576

5 **Take notice of this grave, wayfarer. Here lies good Euthymia, |a leader in
self-control. Because of this the most distinguished of her sons who stands out
10 from the others, |Athenion, honoured his discreet mother 'with a tomb and
15 a gravestone. For this is the right of the |dead'.**

This text consists of five hexameters, the last being a quotation from Hom. *Il.*
16.457 = 675. Thierry points out that the only feature which distinguishes the
tombstone as Christian is the initial combination of the cross with A/Ω. The text
itself could otherwise be entirely appropriate for a pagan. The leaves incised
beneath the wording occur on both Christian and non-Christian epitaphs. The
revised text in *SEG* includes readings suggested by I. Ševčenko and reported in *BE*
(1979) 576.

Does a text like this reflect a Christian's knowledge of antiquity's most popular
author of Greek literature? Not necessarily: the line may have been one of the
standard conclusions that a mason might suggest to the client. In fact its presence
need not imply any conscious allusion to Homer at all.

Apart from Thierry no.2 (see **109**), she publishes seven other Christian epitaphs
(nos.3-9 = *SEG* 948b, 955, 950-54) and one new non-Christian epitaph (= *SEG*
949); none requires special mention here (although one might note her no.5 = *SEG*
950, the gravestone of Paul son of John δι|δασκάλου).

Another Christian epitaph has Homeric expressions in its five hexameters —
although no actual quotation — as is common for fourth-century epitaphs.
S. Mitchell, *AS* 27 (1977) 91–92, no.36, pl.13a (= *SEG* 847), publishes the
following inscription from Ankara.

†
'Αγαθῇ Τύχῃ.
'Ατραπιτὸν πρὸ π-
όληος ἀοίδιμος ἐν
ναετῇσιν, (*vac*)
5 δῖος 'Ιωάννης
τεῦξεν θρασυ-
κάρδιος ἄνηρ,
μήτιδι καὶ πραπί-
δεσσι κεκασμέ-
10 νος οὐ διὰ βουλᾶς,

"Ανκυρ' ἣ κλέος
εὗρε σὺν ἀντι-
θέοις πτολιή-
ταις ῥηιδίως
15 δ' ἐσάωσεν
ὁδοιπορέοντας
ἅπαντας.†
Αὖξι 'Ιωάννης,
ὁ εὐπάροχος
20 τῆς πατρίδος.

**(*cross*) For Good Fortune. The road in front of the city divine John has
5 constructed, he who is a subject of song among those who dwell (there). |He
10 was a man bold of heart, excelling in shrewdness and ingenuity |— (he did)**

not (act) through the council, by which Ankyra has found fame with her
15 **godlike citizens — and easily | he kept safe all wayfarers. (*cross*) Let John be**
20 **exalted, the provider of good for his | home town.**

This text can be regarded as Christian (so Mitchell) in view of the crosses at the head of the text and in *l*.17; the acclamation at the end would also be compatible with this. But in following the common contemporary practice of drawing upon epic for its phraseology the inscription illustrates clearly how 'unfelt' may have been the distinction between Christian and classical terminology. Here John is called 'divine' (5), his fellow citizens are 'godlike' (12–13; ἀντίθεος is a vague, conventional epithet in Homer); and the text begins with ἀγαθῇ τύχῃ. The issue raised by this epitaph thus complements that occurring in the soldier's epitaph discussed elsewhere in this volume (**17**).

Mitchell suggests that this John may well be identified with the person in two previously published inscriptions, a fragmentary dedication to an emperor, and a list of buildings which were provided for the city by the generosity of Ἰωάννου Εὐτυχικοῦ τὸ ἐπίκλην Ἀνατέλλοντος. The byname formula found here may be added to the discussion of double names in *New Docs 1976*, **55**.

I.Tyre 1 contains very few verse epitaphs, but two sarcophagi may be noticed here briefly. Nos.149A/B and 150 are to be dated III or IV; neither offers any positive indication that it is Christian. But the references to several classical mythological matters need not preclude the link, for the conventional nature of the wording of such epigrams is not incompatible with the outlook of a cultured Christian in this period. The somewhat fragmentary no.150 begins Λύδιος ἐς νεκύων χόρον ἔρχεται – – – – | Μουσάων θεράπων ἔξοχος ἠΐθεος (*ll*. 1–2), 'Lydios comes to the chorus of the dead – – – –, servant of the Muses, an outstanding youth'. The phrase Μουσάων θεράπων may mean something as bland as 'a devotee of culture'. This is the way D. Feissel interprets no.149A/B (two clearly related epigrams on the one sarcophagus), which he re-edits at *BCH* 102 (1978) 550–52 (cf. *SEG* 998):

A. πᾶσαν ὁμηλικίην παίδων ἀπεκαίνυτο Χρύσης
   ζωὸς ἐὼν Μούσαις ἠδὲ περιφροσύνῃ·
   νῦν δὲ πολύζηλον τοκέων ἄπο ἐλπίδ' ἀμέρας
   οἴκεται ἐκ βιότου δάκρυα πατρὶ λιπών.
B. οἴχεται εὐμαθίη, Χρύσης θάνεν, αἱ δέ νυ Μοῦσαι
   ἄχνυντε κραδίην οἷά τε φίλῳ ἐπὶ παιδί.

A. **Among children Chryses surpassed all his peers in age during his life by his culture and reflectiveness. But now, having deprived his parents of their much-admired hope, he has departed from life leaving tears for his father.**
B. **Readiness to learn has departed, Chryses has died, and the Muses grieve in their heart as for their own child.**

112. Death and Immortality

Tyre   late Imperial

ed.pr. — J.-P. Rey-Coquais, *I.Tyre* 1.204 (pl.48.1)

†

οὐκ αἴθα-

νες, Παυλῖ-

να (σ)εμνὴ κ-

αὶ ἄχρατος

5 παρθενίην ἐ-

κτελέσασα.

Broken marble plaque. Read ἔθανες (1-2), ἄχρα(ν)τος (4).

5 *(cross)* **You have not died, Paulina, since holy and undefiled |you have fulfilled your virginity.**

The initial wording of this verse epitaph, consisting of three trimeters, contrasts strongly with the cliché found commonly in the Tyre necropolis and elsewhere, οὐδεὶς ἀθάνατος (cf. **116**). Rey-Coquais refers to *IG* 14.1973 (Rome, III) which begins similarly, οὐκ ἔθανες, Πρῶτη. Cf. his comment, p.166. Several important common motifs are present in the remainder of the Tyre inscription — purity, chastity, perseverance to the end in this life. These are what assure the inscriber of Paulina's immortality. Rey-Coquais (p.153) suggests she may have been 'une vierge consacrée'. On ascetic renunciation among women in the late Roman world see most recently E.A. Clark, *Anglican Theol. Rev.* 63 (1981) 240-57; A.M. Emmett, *XVI. Intern. Byzantinistenkongress, 1981, Akten II.2* = *JÖB* 32.2 (1981) 507-15 (dealing with the terms ἀειπάρθενος and ἀποτακτικός).

113. The mysteries of death

Tyre   later Imperial?

ed.pr. — J.-P. Rey-Coquais, *I.Tyre* 1.29B (pl.4.3)

Θεὸς ἀθάνατος ἐκδικήσηι

μυστήρια καὶ εἴ(δ)η τὰ εἴκοσει

λίψανα τῶν ὀνομάτων τῶν

κλαπέντων τῶν ὄντων ὧδε,

5 ὅ τι οὐδεὶς οἶδεν ποιήσειν

εἰ μὴ μόνος Θεὸς καὶ (μ)ήτις.

τῶν λεκτικαρίων διὰ τὰ γενόμενα

δι' ὑμᾶς· ὦ δὲ ἐπιχηρήσῃ ἀνῦξαι

τόπον ἐμουτοῦ Ζήνωνος

The second of two inscriptions on a sarcophagus. At *l*.2 εἴ(δ)η = ἴδη.

Bib. — D. Feissel, *BCH* 102 (1978) 546–48; A. Ferrua, *Riv. di Ant. Crist.* 54 (1978) 136; *SEG* 996.

May immortal God avenge the mysteries and see the twenty corpses of the
5 **people who were here and have been stolen away, | a thing which nobody**
knows how to do except God alone. And let none of the gravediggers, because
what happened here was due to you, attempt to open the (burial) place
belonging to me, Zenon . . .

This enigmatic text — which is almost certainly Christian in view of the belief in the resurrection of the body implied in *ll*.2–4 — does not mean that twenty corpses were buried in Zenon's sarcophagus, but presumably near his (Feissel, 547). μυστήρια (2) is probably to be interpreted as a reference to death (so *ed.pr.*; though note Ferrua, 136, who understands it of the secret guilt of the gravediggers who have mingled the bones of the corpses). Cf. *CIJ* I.651 (Syracuse, V), Εἰρήνα νύμφη | ὧδε κεῖται. κατὰ τοῦ μυστηρί|ου οὖν τούτου μή|τις (following L. Robert, *Hellenica* 3 [1946] 98) ὧδε ἀνύξη (= ἀνοίξη), 'Here lies the bride Eirene. By this mystery may no-one open the tomb'. Rey-Coquais also mentions a further example of τὸ μ. τοῦτο = death (p.22 n.2). *I.Tyre* 1.108 (pl.47.1), of late Roman date, is worth reprinting in this context, too.

Ὄρκω τοὺς μέλλοντας κτᾶσ-
θε τὸν παράδισον τοῦτον
τὸν Κύριν τῶν μυστηρίων μετ-
ὰ θάνατον ἐμοῦ Γεμέλλου καὶ Κυρί-
5 λλας γαμετῆς μου μηδίνα θῖνε κατὰ
τῶν λιψάνων ἡμῶν· εἰ δέ τις καταθί-
ση, δώση εἰς ἐπισκευὴν τοῦ δημοσίο[υ]
ἀγωγοῦ καθ᾽ ἕκαστον λίψανον
χρυσοῦ /(ὀγκίας)/ (ἕξ)

I adjure those who are going to acquire this garden, by the Lord of the
5 **mysteries, after the death of myself Gemellus, and Kyrilla | my wife, not to**
place anyone on our remains. If anyone does so he is to give for the repair
of the public aqueduct, for each body, six ounces of gold.

This text is not clearly Christian, but it would be most intriguing if the Christian God, or Christ, were being alluded to here as ὁ κύριος τῶν μυστηρίων (cf. Rey-Coquais, p.166). There is no parallel to this phrase, or to the use of μυστήριον with this meaning in the NT; the noun is there more commonly followed by a dependent genitive rather than being in that grammatical position itself. For the opposite idea to the phrase note Mt. 22.32, οὐκ ἔστιν ὁ θεὸς νεκρῶν ἀλλὰ ζώντων. The usage of παράδεισος here is common enough, but is not the sense found in the NT. Rey-Coquais suggests (p.64) that the fine being stipulated by gold weight may reflect a lack of confidence in coinage which is being devalued. Respect for the dead, which the warnings against tomb violation presuppose, is common to both Christian and non-Christian burials.

Returning to the first text of this entry, *ed.pr.* thought (22) that the anonymity of the dead (*ll.*3–4) parallels in sentiment a formula frequent in Christian texts, οὖ ὁ θεὸς τὸ ὄνομα οἶδεν. In fact, however, ὄνομα has its occasional Koine (e.g. Acts 1.15 ὄχλος ὀνομάτων) and common Byzantine meaning of 'person' here, so the text is not employing the anonymity formula (Feissel, 547 and n.10). For a possible example of the formula in 1977 texts note the very brief αὐτὸς | οἶδεν (*SEG* 1181; Apollonia, Roman period (?); further references noted there). The formula is not confined to Christian texts: *New Docs 1976*, **69** included a mosaic inscription from a synagogue in Skythopolis in Palestine (VI?) which employs the phrase to refer to benefactors. But, as noted there, that text reflects Christian influence in its phraseology. What is the origin of this Christian anonymity formula? Deissmann, *LAE* 119, notes related phraseology in documentary texts and suggests that Phil. 4.3, ὧν τὰ ὀνόματα ἐν βυβλίῳ ζωῆς echoes the formula.

114. A Christian (?) wineseller

Tomis (Constanța)   VI
ed. — I. Barnea, *MPR* 9, pp.42–43 (fig. 5)

> . . . π]ιος
> [Σέππ]ονος
> οἰνέμπορ-
> ος Ἀλεξανδρίας (*palm*)
> (*pentagram*)

The stone is broken at the top, while the pentagram at the bottom is partly broken away.

N., son of Seppon (?), wineseller from Alexandria. (*palm*) (*pentagram*)

Barnea is to be followed against earlier views that this man came from Egypt rather than that he was a poor agent — because of the modest nature of the epitaph — of some Alexandrian businessman. However, his comment on the two symbols is curious: the five-pointed star (i.e. the pentagram) suggests that the seller is Jewish, but this is an 'interprétation à laquelle s'oppose la présence du symbole chrétien de la palme' (p.42). The palm is not used solely by Christians: numerous examples in *CIJ* I indicate that it was a popular Jewish symbol, and there are examples which are certainly neither Jewish nor Christian — see E. Pfuhl/ H. Möbius, *Die ostgriechischen Grabreliefs* (2 vols. + 2 vols. of plates; Mainz am Rhein, 1977, 1979) index, s.v. 'Palmwedel'. Perhaps we should consider that this wineseller who died so far from home was a Jew. No examples are attested in the index to *CIJ* I, however.

An analogous inscription may be mentioned. *SEG* 26 (1976/7) 817 reprints a text from Hadrianoupolis in Thrace, first published in Turkish in 1971 (*non vidi*) and re-edited by Z. Borkowski, *ZPE* 21 (1976) 75–76: Μιχαὴλ Ἐγυπτίου ὑδρομήκτου, '(work-place [or possibly grave?]) of Michael the Egyptian water-mixer'. The noun ὑδρομίκτης is very rare (not attested in LSJ); Borkowski suggests (75) that Michael was 'a street-seller of wine which was sold by the glass mixed with water'. He rightly discounts here the pejorative connotation which the word appears to have in two patristic passages (one a *v.1.*). No date is mentioned in *SEG* or Borkowski, but the name is indicative of a Jew unless we are in the period when Christians were taking over Jewish names. In either case we have an analogous inscription to the text above of/for a minor businessman from Egypt who plies his trade far from home.

P.Stras. 659 (Arsinoe, VI) is a fragmentary document concerning a debt owed to Θεοδώρῳ οἰνοπράτῃ υἱῷ τοῦ μ[α]καρίου Γεωργίου, κτλ (*l.2*).

115. The centrality of Jerusalem in an inscription concerning Christian Edessa

Ankara (?)   end IV–609
ed.pr. — B. van Elderen, *Calvin Theol. Jnl.* 7 (1972) 5–14 (ph.)

```
              ]ἰδίαν στολὴν καὶ . . . . ACEN![
                     ]ἔλαβεν ἀπόλαυ(σι)ν τὴν ἀτελεύτητο[ν
        εἰς τοὺς αἰῶ]νας· ὁμοίως δὲ καὶ ᾿Ιακὼβ σπουδάσας προσενένκε[
                ]Θῦ Χῦ πόλις καὶ παρ᾿ αὐτοῦ εὐλογίαν ἔλαβεν καὶ ἄρτον ἐξ οὐράγ[ου
5      ]ΗΝ σὺν τῶν ἁγίων ἀγγέλων εἰς τοὺς αἰῶνας· ὁμοίως δὲ καὶ Αὔγαρ[ος
        Αἰδέ]σσης διὰ ἐπιστολῆς λόγον ἔπενψεν εἰς τὴν ἁγίαν τοῦ Θεοῦ Χριστοῦ πόλιν[
                ]C περιετίχισεν τῇ πόλει Αἰδέσσης ὥστε ἀσάλευτον καὶ ἀνίκητον αὐ[τὴν
        τ]οῦ αἰῶνος τούτου· ὁμοίως δὲ καὶ οἱ Μάγοι σπουδάσαντες προσενέγκαι τὰ [δῶρα
   Θῦ Χριστ]οῦ πόλιν, ταῦτα αὐτῶν διαπραξαμένων οὕτως ἐπηγγείλατο αὐτοῖς ὅ[πως
10      μυρ]ιάδας σῶσαι ἐκ τοῦ ἔθνους ἐκείνου· καὶ ὀφείλομεν καὶ ἡμεῖς τὰ αὐτὰ δι(α)πρά[ττεσθαι
        ]ιν οἱ γονῖς ἐκ τῆς αἰωνίας κρίσεως καὶ ἡμεῖς σωτηρίας τυχώμεν[
        κατ]αλυπάνοτες τὴν ἁγίαν τοῦ Θῦ Χριστοῦ πόλη· οἱ γὰρ ταῦτα πράτοντες[
        πι]κρὰ δάκρυα κατενέγκωσιν κράζοντες· Κύριε, κύριε ἄνυξον ἡμῖν[
        ]σιν ἀκοῦσαι παρὰ τοῦ δικαίου κριτῇ· Οὐκ ὖδα ὑμᾶς τῆνες ἐστέ· πορεῦθαι
15                                                    [ἀ]π᾿ ἐμοῦ.
```

No single line is complete, the stone being broken on all sides. While we may have the ending of the text, its beginning is lost for an unknown number of lines. Mitchell (see bib. below) suggests c. 10–12 letters may be lost on the left hand side, c. 6–7 on the right.
Bib. — *S. Mitchell, *AS* 27 (1977) 92–96, no.37 (pl.12); *SEG* 848; *BE* (1978) 495

...his own garment and ... he received everlasting enjoyment ... forever. And similarly James was eager to offer ... city of (the) God Christ and 5 received from him a blessing and bread from heaven ... |... with the holy angels forever. And similarly Abgar ... of Edessa by means of a letter sent word to the holy city of the God Christ ... he built a wall around the city

of Edessa so as to (make it) unmoveable and unconquerable ... of this age.
And similarly the Magoi were eager to offer [gifts] (to?) the city of the God
Christ, and when they had accomplished these things thus he offered to them
10 that ... | ... to save multitudes from that nation. And we ought also to
accomplish the same things [in order that?] our parents [may escape?] from
everlasting judgment and we may meet with salvation ... [not?] abandoning
the holy city of the God Christ. For those who do this ... will weep (*lit.*, bring
down) bitter tears, crying out, 'Lord, Lord, open up to us' ... to hear from
15 the just judge, 'I do not know who you are. Go | from me'.

The circumstances of the evangelization of Edessa in Syria — which in fact
occurred end I/II init., but was generally associated with the later Abgar VIII, 'the
Great' (177–212); on the date of Christianity's introduction see H.J.W. Drijvers,
Cults and Beliefs at Edessa (*EPRO* 82; Leiden, 1980) 193 — is recounted at some
length in Eusebius, *HE* 1.13, though dated there to a period soon after Christ's
ascension. Eusebius associates it with the reign of Abgar Ukkama (4BC–50AD),
who was suffering from an incurable disease and having heard of Jesus' miraculous
healings wrote a letter to him in Jerusalem, inviting him to come and settle in
Edessa. Jesus replied by letter that it was not possible for him to come, but that
after his ascension one of his disciples would do so. This disciple proved to be
Thaddaeus (in Eusebius' account; some other versions of this story call him Addai),
who introduced Abgar and his people to the Way. On Abgar the Great see Drijvers,
13–14.

The pious fraud which devised this connection between Abgar and Jesus may
well have been stimulated by Mt. 4.24, καὶ ἀπῆλθεν ἡ ἀκοὴ αὐτοῦ εἰς ὅλην τὴν Συρίαν,
κτλ, a verse unmistakably alluded to in Eusebius' account (so van Elderen, 7).
Certainly, the legend of the correspondence between the two gained wide currency
in the fifth century, not merely in Syria or the Greek East, but in Egypt, northern
Anatolia and Macedonia (van Elderen, 7–8; Mitchell, 94–95). Eusebius emphasizes
the authenticity of the letters by quoting extracts (translated from Syriac) from
written documents he had found in the archives at Edessa: ἀνάγραπτον τὴν
μαρτυρίαν ἐκ τῶν κατὰ Ἔδεσσαν ... γραμματοφυλακείων ληφθεῖσαν. As well as the
letters of Abgar (1.13.6–9) and Jesus' reply (1.13.10) we are given a further
extensive extract from the archives (1.13.11–22), which narrates Thaddaeus'
evangelistic efforts in Edessa and concludes with a date equivalent to 30AD. So
popular was this traditon that the letters acquired a 'talismanic significance'
(Mitchell, 95) and were inscribed on city walls and near city gates where they had
an apotropaic function, to keep enemies at bay. *P. Got.* (1929) 21 (provenance
unknown, VI–VII) is one version of Jesus' letter to Abgar, re-edited by H.C.
Youtie, *HTR* 23 (1930) 299–302 (= *Scriptiunculae* I [Amsterdam, 1973] 455–59).
Jesus is represented as having written the letter personally: ἐγὼ Ῑς χειρεὶ τῇ ἐμῇ
ἔγραψα (5). Youtie includes observations on the relationship of this text to other
surviving versions of the letter, and agrees with the suggestion that the papyrus may
have been used as an amulet. On such genuine religious pseudepigraphy see
W. Speyer, *Die literarische Fälschung im heidnischen und christlichen Altertum.
Ein Versuch ihrer Deutung* (Munich, 1971); id., *Entretiens Fondation Hardt* 18
(1972) 333–66.

Returning to the inscription, in content we are given a series of edifying examples which draw upon biblical and non-canonical Christian literature and urge 'us' to act in like manner. While the allusion in the very fragmentary *ll*.1–2 has not been identified, van Elderen has shown that Ἰακώβ (*l*.3). refers to James 'the Just' to whom the risen Lord appeared: *tulit panem et benedixit et fregit et dedit Iacobo Iusto ...* (Jerome, *de vir. ill.* 2 which draws on *Gosp.Heb.*; for text of the former see C.A. Bernoulli, *Hieronymus und Gennadius, de viris inlustribus* [Freiburg, 1895; repr. Frankfurt, 1968]). With this quotation cf. *l*.4 of this inscription. Further, the mention of the angels (*l*.4) may be an allusion to James' subsequent life in heaven after his martyrdom (Mitchell, 94; note σύν + genitive in this phrase).

The second of the three ὁμοίως δὲ καί sentences, which help to give the text some form, deals with the Abgar-Jesus correspondence (*ll*.5–8). The suggestion that the city would be impregnable to attack finds a parallel in the early V Syriac text, *Doctrine of Addai* (van Elderen, 11). In *ll.* 8–10 the Magi are in view: they were traditionally believed to have visited Edessa on their way home from their visit to Palestine. In Matthew's account of them (2.1–12) note especially v.11, προσήνεγκαν αὐτῷ δῶρα in relation to *l*.8 of the new text.

Following these three examples, which implicitly share the common link of Jerusalem (James, its first bishop; Abgar directed his letter there; the Magi went there and were re-directed on to Bethlehem), *ll*.10–15 provide an injunction not to abandon the holy city (note the inconsistent abbreviation of *nomina sacra* in *l*.12). Those who do so are warned of their fate via an allusion to the parable in Lk. 14.22–30 (especially vv. 25, 27), or the wording of the parable in Mt. 25.11–12.

Some philological points: for ἀπόλαυσις (2) in the NT note 1 Tim. 6.17; Heb. 11.25. The ὁμοίως δὲ καί formula occurs in several places in the NT, but not in a series of closely connected statements as here. σπουδάζω + infin. (8) is common in the NT. For κατ]αλυπάνοτες (= καταλιμπάνοντες, *l*.12) note Gen. 39.16 and cf. ὑπολιμπάνω at 1 Pet. 2.21 (𝔓[72] attests ἀπολιμπάνω as a variant in that verse).

The inscription — not discussed in Drijvers — remains an enigma. Is it a liturgical text (van Elderen, 14)? It sounds more like a homily or sermon extract, but why would that be inscribed on stone? (A tiny fragment of Chrysostom, also on stone, was noted in *New Docs 1976*, **65**.) The original site of the text is uncertain, but Mitchell thinks Ankara or its environs may be more likely than Edessa itself. May it nevertheless reflect in some way, obscure to us now, the outlook of one party engaged in the doctrinal disputes which affected Edessa and the Eastern Church generally in the fifth century?

The likely allusion to the parable of the wise and foolish virgins (Mt. 25.1–13) at the end of this inscription makes mention of another Ankara text relevant here. Mitchell, ibid. 101, no.49 (= *SEG* 882) prints a brief epitaph first discussed in an unpublished thesis by I.W. Macpherson.

† ἐνθάδε καθεύ-
δη ἡ μιὰ τῶν ε′ λαμ-
παδιφόρων παρ-
θένων, ἡ θεοφι-
5   λεστάτη τοῦ Χρισ-
τοῦ Στεφανία ἡ-
γουμένη.

(*cross*) **Here sleeps one of the five maiden 'torchbearers', the most God-**
5 |**beloved daughter of Christ, Stephania the abbess.**

Mitchell discusses the term *lampadephoroi* and associates it with a Byzantine
church custom described by Gregory of Nyssa, *ep.* 6.10 (text quoted in Mitchell).
BE (1978) 497 is surely right to see in the term an allusion to the parable in Mt.
25, especially vv. 1–3, δέκα παρθένοις, αἴτινες λαβοῦσαι τὰς λαμπάδας ἑαυτῶν …
πέντε φρόνιμοι. Lampe, s.v. θεοφιλής, d, i, is aware of the superlative used as a title
for ecclesiastics and emperors, but gives no indication that it is used of female office
holders in the Church. For ἡγουμένη of a monastic superior see Lampe, s.v.

116. Pilgrim graffiti in the Sinai
(cf. *New Docs 1976*, 93)

Some 267 inscriptions (a few illegible) in Greek and Nabataean from Wadi
Haggag have been published by A. Negev, *The Inscriptions of Wadi Haggag, Sinai*
(*Qedem* 6; Jerusalem, 1977). The overall date range of these short texts is II/
III–IV, although a small number are V or later. The great majority are Christian
graffiti in Greek, though there are some which can be shown to have been written
by Jews. There is evidence for Christian monasticism in the Sinai from IV[1], but the
number of pilgrims to the area increased considerably after St. Catherine's
Monastery was built. Negev suggests (79) that the small number of certainly Jewish
texts from this location may indicate that 'the few Jewish pilgrims who found their
way there did so under the influence of the Christian movement'. To travel to holy
places in the Sinai via Wadi Haggag was not the most common route; pilgrims
made famous by surviving accounts of their journeys usually entered the Sinai from
Egypt, the route being both shorter and safer. The most recent examination of
pilgrimages made by people like Egeria (381–84) and Jerome (385) is E.D. Hunt,
Holy Land Pilgrimage in the Later Roman Empire, A.D. 312–460 (Oxford, 1982),
which includes a map indicating pilgrim routes. Note also I. Finkelstein, *IEJ* 31
(1981) 81–91, who publishes details of some recently discovered prayer niches of
Byzantine date at a number of places within the vicinity of St. Catherine's
monastery in Southern Sinai. Generally facing east, their location indicates the
route 'used by pilgrims and monks, and each prayer niche marked a spot that was
sanctified by tradition as being connected to events associated with the giving of the
law to Moses. At each niche the pilgrims would stop to pray before continuing on
their way. The climax of the path was the peak of Jebel Musa, believed by the
pilgrims to be Mt. Sinai' (Finkelstein, 86).

Certain features of the texts from Wadi Haggag may be noted briefly. No. 117
reads: † Κ(ύρι)ε δός μοι | ἄφεσιν | ἁμρατιῶν (= ἁμαρτιῶν). | Κυριακός. Ἀμήν. The
common name Kyriakos appears also at nos. 104 ('K. the deacon'), 138, 163, 170.
Does its use in this way imply 'I am the Lord's person'? — it was 'apparently used
only by Christians' (S. Mitchell, *AS* 27[1977] 78). Other examples from 1977
publications are *I. Tyre* 1.179; *P. Mich.* 664, *ll*.11, 47 (Aphrodite, 585 or 600).
H. Solin, *Die griechischen Personennamen in Rom. Ein Namenbuch* (Berlin, 1982)
I, 410–14 lists occurrences of the name in Rome, grouped by date: the prevalence

rises steeply by III/IV. *I. Wadi Haggag* No.110 is a text by which the authors are fulfilling a vow (εὐχή; for vows by Christians see *New Docs 1976*, **4**); in 110 Κυρια[κὸς] | Χριστός makes clear the adjectival force of the word. The same form of words appears at no.5, † ᾿Αβραάμις. Κυρ(ια)κὸς Χρ(ιστό)ς. The NT uses κυριακός adjectivally but not as an epithet of proper names: 1 Cor. 11.20 (κ. δεῖπνον); Rev. 1.10 (ἐν τῆκ. ἡμέρα). S.R. Pickering has drawn my attention to *P.Oxy.* 48 (1981) 3407 (mid–IV), the earliest papyrus reference to Sunday. A landlady issues orders in connection with the moving of some rocks. She says in a matter-of-fact way, 'They have agreed to take them [i.e., the rocks] away on Sunday, that is, tomorrow, the 11th.' For Sunday she uses the word κυριακή. See ed. n. to *ll.*15–16 concerning working on Sunday and the identification of Sunday with the Sabbath. For earlier discussion of the term see Deissmann, *Bible Studies*, 217–19 (cf. *LAE* 357–59).

No. 32 consists of the abbreviation ΚΥΑΚΩΙΣ, which Negev fills out as Κύ(ριος) ῎Α(λφα) κ(αὶ) ῎Ω(μεγα) ᾿Ι(ησοῦ)ς. Another very abbreviated inscription (71) reads † Κ(ύρι)ε ᾿Ι(ησο)ῦ Χ(ριστ)ὲ Μ(έγισ)τ(ε). (Negev's transcription of the last word is a printing error, as both the photograph and his comment make clear; the text was previously published by him in *Eretz-Israel* 10 [1971] 185, no.40.) Negev mentions the rarity of the epithet μέγιστος in Christian inscriptions. For μέγας (μ.μ., μέγιστος) as epithets of gods see *New Docs 1976*, **68**. Also uncommon is the formula χάρις, found on no.247; χάρις. μνη|σθῇ Θεόδοτος | ὁ ἔπαρχος Κλ|αυδίου. Negev knows of only one other example, an unpublished epitaph (probably pre-Christian, but uncertain whether pagan or Jewish). No. 247 itself does not indicate the religious affiliation of Theodotos. The same is true of *I. Tyre* 1.85, χάρις Θεωδώτου ὑγία, where the name is written as a monogram (see pl.56.2 in that volume). However, Negev notes that a number of Syrian inscriptions have the phrase Θεοῦ χάρις (based on 1 Cor. 15.10): *IGL Syr.* 1 (1929) 147 (θεοῦ χα); 2 (1939) 294 (doubtful); 4 (1955) 1250 (restored), 1570, 1600, 1703, 1726 (χάρ⟨ιτι τοῦ⟩ θ⟨ε⟩οῦ), 1785, 1959, 1985; 5 (1959) 2538 (cf. the non-Christian 2483B, Μεγάλαι χάριτες τοῦ θεοῦ [sc. ῾Ηλίου]). From Tomis note *MPR* 8, θ(εο)ῦ χάρις.

Another formula rare to Palestine and somewhat so in Syria but very common in Christian inscriptions from Egypt is εἷς θεὸς ὠ (= ὁ) βοηθῶν which occurs in no. 86 (= *Eretz-Israel* 10 [1971] 185, no. 37), as well as nos. 198, 242, 246 (the last two are Jewish), 251. On the formula see *New Docs 1976*, **5** (on no.242 = *Eretz-Israel* 12 [1975] 136, no.9 = *SEG* 26 [1976/7] 1697), **68**, **69**. Negev's discussion of no. 242 is by far the longest in his book (pp.62–67). He refers to eight other examples of the formula known from Palestine some of which are clearly pagan. F. Manns, *SBF* 27 (1977) 234–36(ph.) = *SEG* 1018 (cf. *BE* [1978] 533) is a clear-cut example, although its Jerusalem provenance is not certain. This bronze amulet (dated not before IIAD) reads Εἷς Ζεὺς | Σάραπις, | Μέγας ὁ | ἐπήκοος | Σάραπις. Since the majority of these texts are not to be dated before the time of Julian, the formula may be associated with his attempt to head off the dominance of the Christian movement. In fact, one pagan example from Ascalon (dated 362/3) and two from Gerasa are dedicated to Julian (Negev, 62–63; cf. G.W. Bowersock, *Julian the Apostate* [London, 1978] 93). After surveying some of the conclusions made by E. Peterson, *ΕΙΣ ΘΕΟΣ* (Göttingen, 1926), Negev suggests (64) that 'the εἷς θεός formula was created in the later part of the third century, possibly by Jews. It was soon picked up by the adherents of Julian Apostata, and very soon also by Christians and again by Jews in Syria, Palestine and Egypt. However the Egyptian

Christians used it most'. To the side of the text of no. 242 is written Υ ᛁ Θ with a seven-branched menorah below it. Negev interprets the letters as needing to be read right to left to elicit θεὸς 'ι ὕψιστος, the central sign being taken as the Hebrew letter *dalet*, an unparalleled abbreviation for אחד , 'One'. 'This single letter should have contained the whole essence of the man's belief . . . as did the two Greek ones' (Negev, 66). The text is to be dated after 300. (Relevant also to the mention of Julian above and his promotion of competitors to Christianity to revivify the pagan tradition is a series of bronze Roman coins with a silver surface dated end 362/mid–363, inventoried as *Apis*, III, 112–49. These coins, called Maiorinae, have a wide geographical spread including Lugdunum, Aquileia Thessalonike, Herakleia in Thrace, Syrian Antioch, Nikomedeia, Kyzikos, and Constantinopolis. The obverse portrays a head or bust of Julian; the reverse has the Apis bull with one or two stars above its head. The bull on no.145 [Kyzikos] has been interpreted as a Christian symbol; see ed. n. to that item. On Julian and Apis see Ammianus Marcellinus 22.14.6–7.) Though no examples occur in *I. Wadi Haggag* of the phrase εἷς καὶ μόνος note the recent discussion of J.-P. Ponsing, *RHPhR* 60 (1980) 29–34, who suggests that it is of Egyptian origin, and was adopted by Jews and Christians became of their commitment to monotheism. The εἷς θεός formula occurs in other 1977 publications, including P.J. Sijpesteijn/K.A. Worp, *ZPE* 27 (1977) 158–59, no. 6 (= *SEG* 1123), a brief undated Christian epitaph from Upper Egypt: εἷς θεὸς ὁ βοήθεος Μουσῆς. This formula is combined with χάρις κυρίου on a Christian amulet, I. Barnea/V. Culica, *Epigraphica. Travaux dediés au VIIe Congrès d'Épigraphie grecque et latine, Constanza, Sept. 1977* (Bucharest, 1977) 249–54 (*non vidi*; cf. *SEG* 420): εἷς θεὸς ὁ βοηθῶν σοι νε[ικάσαντι]. | ἡ χάρις κυρίου ἐ[στί] σοι | Θεοπέμπ[τῳ]. This lead tablet (IV/V, Sucidava, in Dacia) is in the shape of a T (a *tau*-cross? — cf. *New Docs 1976*, **90**); as well as the text it carries 'a relief, representing a winged person who holds with his hand a circular medallion against his breast' (*SEG*, ad loc.). *I.Pan* 14(W) is a Christian graffito from Wadi Bir El-Aïn: εἷς θεὸς (ὁ) βοηθῶν. Θεόφιλος. A very striking non-Christian example to illustrate the βοηθός formula used commonly by Christians is F. Manns, *SBF* 27 (1977) 236–38 (ph.) = *SEG* 1016 (Jerusalem?, n.d., *ed.pr.*), θεὸς | βοη|θὸς | Ποσι|δῶν | βοήθει. Cf. *BE* (1978) 533. Again, Hajjar, *Triade* I, 29 (pp.47–49), an inscription from Baalbek in Syria, begins with Ζεῦ βοήθι in its request that 'those of the third *dekania* be remembered'. Note also *I.Tyre* 1.41, εἷς θεὸς ὁ μόνος ἀθάνατος (cf. *ed.pr.* p.166). Contrast with this last the cliché found on both Christian and non-Christian graves, οὐδεὶς ἀθάνατος: from *I.Tyre* 1 note nos.27, 38, 48, cf. 62 (Christian); 20A, B, C, 23, 55, 74, 101, 114, 140, 177 (no indication that they are Christian); cf. *ed.pr.* pp.164–65. On the formula see M. Simon, *Rev.Hist. Rel.* 113(1936) 188–206. At no. 27 *l*.3 D. Feissel, *BCH* 102 (1978) 545 n.6, suggests ᾿Ις θεούς (= εἷς θεός) for the lettering which *ed.pr.* had interpreted as ᾿Ι(ησοῦ)ς ὁ [θ]εοῦ (υ)(ἰὸ)ς. Well worth mention too in connection with the βοηθός formula is *I.Tyre* 1.160 *bis* (late imperial): θεὸς βοη|θός· βάσ|κανε φεῦγε. | καλῶς ἶπες, 'God (is our) helper; flee, envious one. You have spoken well'. Rey–Coquais interprets this stone, which closes off a grave loculus, as a sort of dialogue between the deceased and the passer-by. βάσκανος refers to the evil eye here (so *BE*[1978] 522, p.199; *pace ed.pr.*), which is attested frequently in Christian contexts. The text thus illustrates the blending of superstition and orthodox faith (so *ed.pr.*).

Returning to *I. Wadi Haggag*, a biblical reminiscence is contained in no.97 with the formula κ(ύρι)ε φύλαξον ὑπὸ τὴν | σκέπην σου τὸν δοῦλον, κτλ; cf. Ps. 17.7. The phrase occurs in two other inscriptions, both from N. Syria, one of which is rather closer to the wording of the Psalm (Negev, 31). A clear allusion to Jn. 1.1 appears in no.106: † Κ(ύρι)ε ᾽Ι(ησο)ῦ Χ(ριστ)έ. Χ(ριστ)ὲ καὶ λώγε | τοῦ Θ(εο)ῦ. ὁ Θ(εὸ)ς συν-όδευ|σεν σὺ(ν) τοῦ δούλου | σου Σερηβ. ᾽Αμήν. Note the genitive/dative confusion in *l*.3. For the verb συνοδεύω cf. Acts 9.7. The inscription uses it in a semi-figurative manner; more thoroughly figurative is *Ep. Barn.* 1.4 (cited by, BAGD, s.v.), ἐμοὶ συνώδευσεν (sc. ὁ Κύριος) ἐν ὁδῷ δικαιοσύνης. The related noun occurs with its literal sense of 'caravan' in no.100, a plea that the Lord will keep safe Θεόφιλον κ(αὶ) τ(ὴ)ν συνοδίαν αὐτοῦ. For this meaning in the NT note Lk. 2.44. Negev thinks the Theophilos mentioned here could be either the bishop of Alexandria from 385 who was 'active in church life of the whole East, and builder of churches', or, more plausibly, the professor of law from Constantinople who was in Justinian's service from 530–c.548, during which time St. Catherine's monastry was built in the Sinai. Another possible link with St. Catherine's may be found in no. 101, an invocation to bless a number of people including Nonna and Stephen. 'In this group of pilgrims one is tempted to identify Nonna as the daughter of Stephen, the builder of the monastery of St. Catherine in the time of Justinian, mentioned in a dedicating inscription engraved on a wooden beam, preserved at St. Catherine' (Negev, 32–33). The formula Κύριε ἐλέησον (abbreviated in various ways) occurs on nos. 111, 113, 188. It should be noted that this phrase is not confined to Christian liturgical usage: BAGD, s.v. ἐλεέω, provides references to passages in non-Christian literature where other gods, such as Isis, are requested to show mercy. See comment on the epithet ἐλεήμων at **14**.

Negev, *IEJ* 31 (1981) 66–71, publishes 16 further inscriptions found on an ancient camel route a few km. from Wadi Haggag. All are very brief: Nabataean (1–3, 6–9, 11, 13–15), Greek (4 — Christian; 12), bilingual Greek/Nabataean (10), Thamudic (16); no.5 has crosses only.

117. Ezana again (cf. New Docs 1976, 94 *bis*)

Discovery at Axum in 1969 of a new inscription (*SEG* 26 [1976/77] 1813 = *New Docs 1976*, **94 bis**) of an Axumite king named 'Ezana', to which may now be added the chance unearthing of a new stele with inscriptions of 'Ezana' in Ge'ez, Ethiopian and Greek (E. Bernand, *ZPE* 45 [1982] 105–14), has revived an old controversy about the origins of Christianity in Ethiopia. A good deal of confusion has arisen, however, because neither Anfray, Caquot and Nautin nor Altheim and Stiehl, whose work was reviewed in *New Docs 1976*, **94 bis**, discuss adequately the arguments of Y. Kobishchanov, *Axum* (rev. edn; ET: Philadelphia, 1979). Further commentary is therefore required.

The original excavations at Axum at the turn of the century brought to light several 'Ezana' inscriptions, in particular *Deutsche Aksum-Expedition* IV (Berlin, 1913) nos. 4 (Greek), 6 (ps.-Sabaean), 7 (non-vocalized Ge'ez), 10 (Ethiopian) and 11 (Ethiopian). All these inscriptions together with the most recent one (*ZPE* 45 [1982] 106–7: *ll*.3/4, 27, 31, 36–37), clearly refer to Ezana as 'son of the unconquered god Mahrem' (*walda mahrem za' aytemawā'e*/υἱὸς θεοῦ ἀνικήτου Ἄρεως), and are thereby distinctly pagan. This poses a problem: on the assumption that all these inscriptions refer to the same Ezana then he must be the mid–IV Ezana; so the conversion of Ethiopia implied in the letter of 357 from Constantius II to the Axumite royal brothers Ezana and Seazana (Athanasius, *Apol. ad Const.*, 31 [Migne *PG* 25, pp. 636–37]) was accomplished by this king. Hence these inscriptions must all belong to the pre-Christian phase of Ezana, except for the vaguely monotheistic *DAE* no.11 which would appear to represent a transition stage from pagan polytheism to Christianity.

Although a single Ezana was indeed the original assumption, as research progressed it became clearer that these inscriptions covered the reigns of two separate kings: Ezana I (mid-IV) and Ezana II (mid/late V), the latter being indicated on his inscriptions as 'son of Elle Amida' (*walda' alē 'amidā*/υἱὸς τοῦ Ἐλλεαμιδα) — details in Kobishchanov, 64–73, 80–90; F. Altheim/R. Stiehl, *Klio* 39 (1961) 234–48; id., *Die Araber in der Alten Welt*, IV (Berlin, 1967) 503ff. and V.2 (1969) 539ff.; id., *Christentum am Roten Meer*, I (Berlin, 1971) 402ff. and 467ff. The new Greek inscription, *SEG* 26 (1976/77) 1813, discovered along with others of king Elle Asbeha, or Kaleb (VIAD), and his son, is unique in that it is an unequivocally Christian inscription of 'Ezana son of Elle Amida', that is, Ezana II (mid-late V). When considered in conjunction with a closely related inscription (*DAE* 11) it appears that Ezana II, once pagan (*DAE* 11), became the first Christian monarch of Ethiopia (*New Docs 1976*, **94 bis**; cf. Kobishchanov 82–84; 252 n.169).

Since *SEG* 26 (1976/77) 1813 belongs to the later fifth century Altheim and Stiehl (*Klio* 58 (1976) 471–79) are likely to be correct in suggesting that the theological terminology of the inscription is exclusively Monophysite. This is only to be expected, since the bishops of Axum from the time of Frumentius (Rufinus, *HE* 1.9 [Migne *PL* 21, p.479]) to well into VI (John Malalas 434.6–18 [Dindorf]) were appointed by the patriarch of Alexandria, and the patriarchs were Monophysite from mid-V. What this inscription still does not explain is the conversion of Ezana II. Yet it does reinforce the conviction that, contrary to common belief, Ezana I was never a Christian. The sources traditionally taken to support such a view (Ath., *Apol. ad Const.*, 29–31 and Rufinus *HE* 1.9 utilized in Socrates, *HE* 1.19, Sozomen, *HE* 2.24 and Theodoret *HE* 1.23) show only that there were Christians in Axum in mid-IV and that Frumentius spent some time at the Axumite court. Both Athanasius, who knew Frumentius, and Rufinus, who acquired his information from Frumentius' brother, are very reliable sources for the work of Frumentius in Axum (cf. Kobishchanov, 67–71). Their conspicuous failure to actually mention a conversion to Christianity by Ezana I is telling. Nor does the fact that Constantius II addressed a letter to Ezana and his brother necessarily imply that the king himself was a Christian, especially since it proposes the banishment of Ezana's former tutor Frumentius (Ath., *Apol. ad Const.*, 31). Further, there is no need for the assumption that Frumentius was a missionary to India rather than Ethiopia since the Romans normally referred to the Axumites as 'Indians' both in Latin (Ruf., *HE* 1.9) and Greek (Jo.Mal. 457.3ff. [Dindorf]). It was Ezana II, already inclined to a monotheistic religion (*DAE* no. 11), who was converted (perhaps by the then Monophysite bishop of Axum) to what was by this time the faith of possibly the majority of his subjects, although it was not until the reign of Elle Asbeha (517) that Christianity actually became the state religion of Axum (Jo.Mal. 434.12–18 [Dindorf]).

INDEXES

1. Biblical Passages

OT

Book	Passage	Page
Gen.	1.7	11
	.27	14
	10.12-13	87
	19.11-13,17-19	87
	36.14-15,23-24	87
	39.16	115
Ex.	2.5-10	1
	5.14-17	87
	6.22-25	87
	7.15-17	87
	15.20-21	100
	20.11	106
	21.17	54
	.37	23
	22.1	23
	.20	106
	24.11	1
	30.12	95
	34.18-20	87
	.35-35.8	87
	40.21	26
Num.	31.49	1
Deut.	6.4	4
	.5	4,106
	.13,16	4
	18.15	4
Josh.	23.14	1
1 Sam.	28.2	2
1 Kings	18.26-33	87
	.41-19.2	87
	20.11-14,22-26	87
	22.6-10	87
	30.19	1
Est.	8.10-12	87
Judith	2.19	87
	10.13	1
Ps.	17.7	116
	22.1-2	88
	26.1	88
	31.9-10	87
	36.4-8,18-23	87
	39.3-6	87
	46.6	93
	51.4-7	87
	52.2-5	87
	68.23	7
	77.48-52,60-66	87
	90	88
	110.4	2
	117	87
	117.7	106
	122	87
	131.15-16	88
	143.7-13	87
	145.8-146.6	87
Ode	1.1-2,8-15	87
	2.32-39	87
	12.3-5	87
Prov.	3.11	82
	4.26-5.8	87
	6.8-16	87
	10.19	97
	23.26-27,31-32	87
Cant.	2.1-6	87
	.17-3.2	87
	5.8-13	87
	5.13-6.4	87
Job.	16.19	97
	31.32-34	99
	.39-32.1	99
Wisd.	10.19-11.11	87
Hos.	14.10	97
Micah	7.18	94
Is.	1.11	106
	7.14	95
	31.9	97
	45.18	11
Jer.	2.2-3.25	87
	25.10-12	87
	41.3,10-11	87
	42.9-10,16-17	87
Dan.		89
	6.27	90
	7.7	8

NT

Book	Passage	Page
Mt.	1.23	95
	3.3	97
	4.7,10	4
	.20	97
	.24	115
	5.7	14
	.41	28
	6.2-4	55
	7.3-5	24
	8.6	97
	9.16	73
	10.17-33	91
	.42	97
	13.13-14	58
	14.14D	82
	15.4	54
	.16	21
	20.1,7	61
	.28	58
	.30,32	103
	22.5	103
	.32	113
	.37	4
	24.45,49	15
	25.1-13	115
	.21,23	15
	.36,38	35
	.40	97
	.43,44	35
	26.9	20
	.29	34
	.45	106
	.63	13
	27.3	103
	.23	28
	.27	109
	.28	3
	.64	69
	28.19-20	100
Mk.	1.11	97
	2.4	2
	.21	73
	5.26-27,31	91
	6.27	102
	.55	2
	7.10	54
	9.10	34
	.12	44
	.39	54
	.41	97
	10.45	58
	12.26	56
	.29,30	4
	13.9	91
	.30	1
	.34	53
	14.13	103
	.14	18
	.41	106
	15.16	106
	.17,20	3
	.21	28
Lk.	1.2	51
	.28	97
	.32	4
	.33	6
	.36	9
	.46-47	97
	.68	4
	.70	2
	2.14	93,97
	.44	116
	4.8,12	4
	6.41-42	24
	.44	56
	7.20-21,34-35	91
	8.23	76
	.29	36
	9.37	77
	.43	51
	.47	21
	.51	76
	10.19-22	91
	.27	4
	11.28	97
	12.11	45
	.18	34
	14.18	106
	.22-30	115
	16.19	3
	17.12	103
	19.1,8	23
	.12,13	18
	.23	7
	20.19-25,30-39	91
	.35	4

2. Words

This index does not register all occurrences of words in texts printed in this Review, but simply those words which receive some notice in an entry. Item numbers in bold type indicate more than a passing reference. An asterisk (*) indicates that comment is offered on the MM or BAGD entry. New words are marked with a dagger (†).

A. Greek

B. Latin (selected)

3. Subjects

4. ECL, Patristic and Jewish Writers

5. Texts Discussed

Listed below are all texts new or old appearing in 1977 corpora and conspectus volumes and referred to in this work. Of other texts only those referred to in a more than passing manner are listed. Bold type indicates substantial discussion of a text at the item number given, or that a non-1977 text has been reprinted here. It is not the normal practice of this Review to suggest new readings or dates, but where they are offered an asterisk (*) beside the text in this index will indicate it.

DATE DUE

GAYLORD			PRINTED IN U.S.A.

Despite the scattered and fragmentary sources we possess, it is apparent that throughout late antiquity the neighbouring regions of Nubia and Ethiopia were in constant turmoil, with the Blemmyes and Nobadae at war with the Romans (see the 'Blemmyomachia' in E. Livrea, *Anonymi fortasse Olympiodori Thebani Blemyomachia (P. Berol. 5003)* [*Beitr. zur. kl. Phil.* 101; Meisenheim am Glan, 1978]), with the Axumites and with each other (see the letter from one king to another in J. Rea, *ZPE* 34 [1979] 147–62); while the Axumites tangled with the Himyarites and the Romans. The known inscriptions of Ezana I, including the most recent one (*ZPE* 45 [1982] 106, *l*.6), refer to a campaign against the Blemmyes (Βουγαεῖται; cf. V. Christides, *Listy Filologické* 103 [1980] 129–30). The new inscription of Ezana II in fact refers to a mid/late V campaign against the Nobadae (ΝΩΒΑ, *ll*.23, 26) who had been oppressing neighbouring tribes. This is clearly the same campaign, or at least part of the same series of campaigns, referred to in *DAE* no.11 (Kobishchanov, 83–5). Consequently, in the light of the above discussion a positive date for *SEG* 26 (1976/77) 1813 would be 467 or 472 or 478, perhaps even as early as 461.

(B. CROKE)

E. VARIA

118. The following Christian texts were encountered in 1977 publications (and those from 1976 reviewed in this volume) but have not been treated at all in this Review. ('Christian' here is used very broadly to refer to a text which may be distinguished by its content, or merely by the presence of certain signs, e.g., a cross on an official document.) Nearly all of these are late Roman or Byzantine in date.

AE: 96,104(?),145,175,185,204-13,228,282,718,765,766,790,795, 830;

BE: 203,289,292,304,307,308,322,345(= *New Docs 1976*,**65**),374, 425,475,484,541,581,582; cf. **119** below;

BCH Suppl. IV: pp.453-65 (cf. *SEG* 140);

Budischovsky, *Cultes isiaques*: pp.157-59 nos.lc-3c,5c; pp.221-22 nos.65-68;

Buresch, *Aus Lydien*: 49,51;

CIMAH: 3-8,10-15,19,21,22,26-28,31,33,34(?),36,41-46,49-56,58,59;

I.Pan: 1b,12-14,29,30;

I.Tyre: 9,11-13*bis*,15,16,19,21c,22,30,33a-b,34,39c,58-61,70,73,81, 82,84,86,88,91a,97,98,104,109-13,121,127-29,135a,136,138, 146,147,151*bis*,152,153,155,156,158,161a,162,164,169,171, 173,175,181,183-86,200,202,212a,212c,216,218,222a-b,224, 225;

I.Wadi Haggag: 1,2a-b,6,8,9,23-26,28-31,33-40,41 (probably), 42,45,46,50, 51,54,56-58,60,61,65,66,72-77,79-81,83-85,87-91,94-96,99, 102-04,107-09,114-16,122-26,128,131-32,135,138-53,156,158, 159 (probably),161,162,164,168,170,171,174-76,178,184,185, 187,189,190,193,194,198,201,202,204,239,249;

Lang, *Agora*: F322-24,Ha46,Hc22,He39,I43,J1,4,6,9;

MPL: pp.43-48;

MPR: 4-6, 9-12, 14, 16-20, 22-27, 30, 31, 35, 36-39, 41 (= *New Docs 1976*, **90**), 42 (= *New Docs 1976*, **60**), 43-45, 47-50, 51 (cf. (*New Docs 1976*, **59**),52-71,73-80,81 (cf. *New Docs* 1976,**90**), 82 (cf. *New Docs 1976*, **90**), 83 (cf.*New Docs 1976*, **4**),84-96;

O.Brüss.Berl.[2]: 50,54,0.17;

P.Laur.: 26,29,31,34,46-48;

P.Mich.: 665,666,672,673;

PSI Corr.: 835(?);

P.Stras.: 656,658,660;

P.Vindob. Salomons: 9,10,15,19,20,23;

P.Wiscon.: 45,67;

SB: 11014, 11076, 11079, 11084, 11137-41, 11163, 11179, 11225, 11231,11240;

SEG: 140,218,259,304,(= *BE* 284),358-64,390,409,570,686-700, 830,872,945,950-55,978,993,1003,1006,1007,1011,1013,1015, 1019,1020,1124,1140,1148,1174(?),1175-79.

119. *BE* 24, 28 are two useful cross-reference entries, the former listing references to Jewish texts in Greek treated in *BE* for 1977, the latter listing Christian texts (cf. 25-27 for further Christian material).

120. Miscellanea epigraphica

A series of essays on various aspects of classical Greek epigraphy is collected together in Pfohl, *Studium*. Most are written especially for the volume (the one exception is M.N. Tod's essay on 'Epigraphy and Philosophy', *JHS* 77 [1957] 132–41). Other subjects treated include 'The epigraphical tradition of the Greeks' (Pfohl), W. Peek on epigraphical *praxis*, A.E. Raubitschek on letter forms of fifth-century BC inscriptions, A.G. Woodhead, 'Epigraphy and History', and three discussions of aspects of epigraphy and archaeology (F. Lorber, Raubitschek, W. Thompson). The pieces by Woodhead, Thompson and Tod are all translated into German.

IGLS is the basis of W. Liebeschuetz' survey of 'Epigraphic evidence on the Christianisation of Syria', *Limes: Akten des XI. internationalen Limeskongresses, 1976* (Budapest, 1977) 485–508. His study shows how epigraphy helps to define the differing paces of religious transformation in various parts of Syria under the Empire.

121. Corrigenda to *New Docs 1976*

The following corrigenda to *New Docs 1976* which affect clarity have been noticed:

p.5,   beginning of entry **1**: for '*P.Coll.Youtie* 51-5' read '*P.Coll.Youtie* 51–52'.
p.36, first new paragraph, *l.*2: for 'used' read 'use'.
p.44, middle of last paragraph: for 'Clement 1.3, 14.1' read 'Clement 1.3, 41.1'.
p.54, beginning of entry **15**: add date in right hand margin, 'I'.
p.75, end of B: for 'ambiguous' read 'unambiguous'.
p.82, first line of entry **33**: for '2243' read '2343'.
p.147, third column: for '2 Cor. 2.5' read '2 Cor. 6.7'.
        for '2 Cor. 3.10, 13' read 'Gal.3.10, 13'.
p.149, first column, s.v. θεός, εἰς θ.: add '5'.
p.150, subject index, s.v. bilingual inscriptions: delete 'Greek-Coptic — 58.'
p.152, *nomina sacra*, on amulet: delete '22'.
p.155, second column: for '*SEG* 1688' read '*SEG* 1668'.
p.155, second column, delete *SEG* '1716 — 58.'